PATRONAGE AND POLITICS
IN NINETEENTH-CENTURY
BRAZIL

Patronage and Politics
in Nineteenth-Century
Brazil

RICHARD GRAHAM

STANFORD UNIVERSITY PRESS
Stanford, California
1990

Stanford University Press
Stanford, California
© 1990 by the Board of Trustees of the
Leland Stanford Junior University
Printed in the United States of America

CIP data appear at the end of the book

SOURCES OF ILLUSTRATIONS

The photograph of Lacerda Werneck is from
the private collection of Eduardo Silva
through his courtesy. All the others are from
S. A. Sisson, *Galeria dos representantes da
nação* (*1861*) (Rio de Janeiro, 1862). Both of
the cartoons are from *Semana Illustrada*:
"Violent Elections," Aug. 25, 1872;
"Francisco Belisário Soares de Souza and His
Book," Feb. 8, 1873.

For Sandra

Preface

MY INTEREST IN the role of patronage in political life may be said to have begun as an undergraduate with Robert Walcott, my teacher at the College of Wooster, who introduced me to the works of Lewis Namier and the subject of clientage in eighteenth-century England. Years later, while studying the role of the British in Brazil, I began to take up issues relating to slavery, and my attempt to explain its abolition forced me to consider the nature of politics there, the stance of slaveowners, and the relationship between the state and society. In searching through the official and personal correspondence of political leaders—most of which had never been consulted by historians—I became aware that patronage was their major and abiding concern. Hence the present book.

In studying the nature of nineteenth-century Brazilian politics, I have received grants from the John Simon Guggenheim Foundation and the National Endowment for the Humanities, as well as enjoying a stint as Senior Fullbright-Hayes Research Fellow. The University of Texas at Austin, through its University Research Institute, Institute of Latin American Studies, and Department of History, also helped fund the necessary travel to Brazilian archives. William Glade, as director of the Institute of Latin American Studies, and Standish Meacham, as chairman of the Department of History, proved particularly supportive through the various phases of this research.

In Brazil I benefited, as have so many others, from the devoted work of archivists and librarians. The archives I consulted are listed in the Sources Cited, and I extend my thanks to the staffs of all of them. I particularly received assistance from the personnel of the Arquivo Nacional do Rio de Janeiro and the Instituto Histórico e Geográfico Brasileiro.

Leslie Bethell, Warren Dean, Joan Meznar, and Fernando Novais read all or portions of earlier versions of this book and made suggestions for its improvement. I did not always take their advice, but I always found it worth considering. Most of all I enjoyed the sense of shared enterprise resulting from the intellectual stimulus, provocative criticism, insightful suggestions, and generously focused engagement of Sandra Lauderdale Graham.

R. G.

Contents

Tables

Illustrations

PATRONAGE AND POLITICS
IN NINETEENTH-CENTURY
BRAZIL

Introduction

PATRONAGE FORMED THE connecting web of politics in nineteenth-century Brazil and sustained virtually every political act. Electoral victory especially depended on its skillful use. It is my aim here to explore the specific way in which granting protection, official positions, and other favors in exchange for political and personal loyalty worked to benefit especially the interests of the well-to-do. Detailing the nature and mechanisms of patron-client ties can serve not only to expand our understanding of Brazilian political history, but also to clarify the link between social elites and the exercise of power. I suspect it will also help unravel puzzles regarding relationships of authority throughout Latin America and, perhaps, in the Mediterranean world in general. Certainly the techniques through which those who were to be controlled came seemingly to acquiesce in and perhaps sometimes even to approve of the system of their own control are relevant to other periods and other places. More particularly, the meaning and nature of managed elections constitute issues of moment to every Latin Americanist, as do parties that form and reform with seemingly fuzzy programs, the constant search for places and sinecures, and the transactional quality of personal relations within an ostensibly impersonal polity. But since it is only through the actual practice of patronage within particular political institutions that its workings and significance can be truly grasped, I have chosen to focus on Brazil from 1840 to 1889, that is, during the reign of Emperor Pedro II.

Men of property dominated the Brazilian state in the nineteenth century. Contemporaries understood that well, and those who wrote about such matters did not, on the whole, consider it a bad thing. Perhaps because some Marxist historians subsequently pointed it out, others have struggled to deny that dominance, either alleging a democratic quality to nineteenth-century Brazil or finding most power to reside in groups other than the landed oligarchy. My intent is not to fill an ideological pigeonhole, but rather to understand how politics seemed to those who practiced it, what those men purposed, and how their anxieties and fears were translated into political action. Preventing social conflicts from erupting into disorder and destroying a way of life that benefited the propertied was a predominant consideration in building the Brazilian political system, as has probably been and still is true elsewhere. In this sense my task is not to make a new point but to explore the details of an old one, tracing how patronage connected to social and economic structures.

Patronage meant both the act of filling government positions and the protection of humble clients, even landless agricultural workers. In this book I show how in nineteenth-century Brazil these two kinds of patronage were entwined through elections. The two levels of patronage—the local and the national—have usually been studied separately, typically by anthropologists on the one hand and political scientists on the other. Historians have generally ignored elections in the villages and towns of nineteenth-century Brazil, dismissing them as unimportant, given that the makeup of Parliament did not depend on them. But if they were unimportant, why did people throughout Brazil, even in its remotest corners, get so excited about them, to the point of risking their lives for the sake of victory at the polls?

I argue that elections tested and displayed the local patron's leadership. Through a two-tiered system of indirect elections, voters chose the locally prominent to form the Electoral Colleges that would, in turn, choose Deputies to Parliament.* The family and the household formed the bedrock of a socially articulated structure of power, and the local leader and his following worked to extend that grid of dependence. In a predominantly rural society, a large landowner expected to receive the loyalty of his free workers, of nearby

---

* Until Chapter Seven, where the law of 1881 establishing direct elections is discussed, I reserve the word "elector" for a member of the Electoral Colleges.

small farmers, and of village merchants, demonstrated through their support in many ways, not least at the polls. Moreover, a much broader swath of Brazilians participated in elections than has heretofore been acknowledged, thus broadening the number of participants in electoral acts that publicly demonstrated the "natural" superiority of some over others. A challenger to the leadership of a local potentate had to build a following of his own; displaying its size could easily mean using outright force to unseat the formerly dominant chief. So elections and violence went together.

At the national level the result of elections could be foretold almost absolutely, but locally for certain men everything hinged on their outcome. Appointment to official positions helped expand the leader's circle, and this fact impelled him to solicit such appointments from provincial authorities, members of the national Parliament, Cabinet ministers, and even the Prime Minister. To demonstrate his worthiness for such appointment, he had to win elections, so that, in a circular yet real way, he was leader because he won elections and he won because he was leader. The local patron found himself thus enmeshed in a system that made him client to someone else who depended on still others in a series of links reaching all the way to the national capital. For their part Cabinets exercised their authority not against local leaders but through them, and these landed bosses, in turn, sought not to oppose the government but to participate in it. Thus emerges a crucial point in understanding politics in nineteenth-century Brazil that greatly lessens the significance of any hypothetical opposition between private and public power.

This book focuses on the internal politics of Brazil. In this it contrasts with those works, including my own, that have paid primary attention to Brazil's export economy. Although I share Fernando Henrique Cardoso's view that political and class relations within Brazil intimately meshed with the demands of the international economy, I center my attention on politics, not on economics, that is, on the network of patronage rather than on the network of production and exchange. Instead of stressing international dependence, I emphasize how class relations within Brazil created the personal dependence of clients on patrons and thus shaped the nation's domestic politics.[1]

For a long time and to some extent even now, the political history of nineteenth-century Brazil has been treated as the story of Cabinets and Kings, or of parliamentary divisions. Even its best practitioners, beginning with Joaquim Nabuco in 1897 and including Sérgio Buarque de Holanda in 1972, made little effort to understand the internal mechanisms of political action or to relate such action to society.[2] Most twentieth-century historians, moreover, have looked back on the period nostalgically, using their descriptions of the Empire to criticize—sometimes subtly, sometimes not—Brazil's subsequent republican or dictatorial regimes. In doing so they placed undue emphasis on the figure of Pedro II or, at best, on some of his advisers. In the present book I pay little attention to the particular actions of the Emperor, since he played only a limited part in the day-to-day political practices whose meanings for contemporaries I seek to understand. And many of the qualities of subsequent Brazilian political life that Brazilian and foreign observers have decried characterized the Empire as much as any other period.

Historians have been divided over whether the nineteenth-century Brazilian state served primarily the interests of a ruling class of wealthy land- and slaveowners or whether it possessed a life and purpose entirely its own. The controversy has implications not only for Brazil's present condition but also for the theory of the state. In the 1930s Caio Prado Júnior maintained, as have many historians who followed him, that the only real question in Brazilian history was to determine whether landowners or merchants formed the dominant class; the government would inevitably reflect its wishes. In his book *Evolução política do Brasil*, which originally bore the subtitle *Interpretação dialética da história brasileira*, he argued that Brazil's break with Portugal in 1822 sprang from the desire of the Brazilian landed class to free itself from a colonial metropolis dominated by merchants. Landowners then built a political system they could control, and only when a new, progressive Brazilian bourgeoisie of merchants and bankers challenged their landed power did the system weaken, finally collapsing in 1889, with the overthrow of the Empire.[3]

I too see the wealthy as using the structures of a government that they themselves created to advance their interests. But I do not see those interests as leading so directly to adopting this or that policy, tax law, tariff regulation, or labor act, but rather as exerting an influence on concepts of the good and the true, of properly deferential behavior within a hierarchical social structure, of loyalty to one's patrons and care toward one's clients. In short, although there were some issues around which classes coalesced or diverged, I understand interests more often to have been mediated through ideology, an ideology demonstrated and strengthened through political action. Nor do I believe merchants and landowners, as such, clashed with each other, for I find that many were either one and the same person or closely related, and that men divided from each other along other lines. Finally, I do not see the end of the Empire as having been impelled by the rise of a new class with a distinct ideology. Both early- and late-nineteenth-century landowners felt the pull of the capitalistic world economy, and both developed similar seigneurial relationships with their workers and dependents. That is why the search for places of local authority continued to characterize the Republic as it had the Empire.

An alternative historiographical current has stressed cultural factors and the search for status as the determinant of Brazil's political character. Nestor Duarte asserted in 1939, for instance, that power in Brazil always remained within the private sphere of the family, an institution that nurtured a deep hostility toward the state. Even while acknowledging that by family he meant the family of the "big house," that is, the planter family, he refused to focus on economic interests or the way in which government responded to them. For him, "the big house . . . is the best indication of an extra-state social organization that ignores the state, that does without it, and that will struggle against it."[4] Oliveira Vianna advanced a similar argument, though seen from the other side, in a series of studies that began in the 1920s but had their clearest formulation in 1949. He recognized, as do I, the power of the large landowners over their dependents, and knew that each landowner was allied with others through family ties. But he understood them to be determinedly opposed by a state that sought to restrict their influence, dominate them, discipline them. The introduction of elections and the semblance of democracy, he said, had greatly complicated and retarded this constructive effort, since landowners controlled the votes within their fiefdom.[5] Readers will find much evidence in the present book of controlled elections and family influence, but I reject the implied divorce between the state, even the central state, and the landed bosses. And I certainly do not suggest, as he does, that the increased power of an authoritarian state, to be exercised over an otherwise anarchically predestined people, was a goal ardently to be desired. Culture, moreover, is formed and shaped; it is itself a process, not just a given, and in that shaping the interests of some are favored while those of others are eclipsed. In nineteenth-century Brazil culture and tradition bolstered the place of the few, of the propertied. Class and status intertwined.

A more recent and highly influential work by Raymundo Faoro, significantly titled *Os donos do poder* (The Power Holders), argues with much verve and literary power that all Luso-Brazilian history since 1385 can be understood as an effort by a "bureaucratic estate" to gain ascendancy over the rest of society: under Emperor Pedro II, its struggle seemed victorious, since the Conservative Party usually triumphed over the Liberals, who (he said) represented the landowners; the establishment of the Republic in 1889 momentarily reversed the tables and placed the planters in control.[6] I differ with Faoro on almost every point, but especially regarding the state. I do not see it as autonomous and free from its social and economic context, nor do I believe Brazilian politicians, judges, or other officials represented only the interests of a reified state once they stepped through the portals of a governmental office. Holders of positions at different levels of government often clashed with each other, so that central authorities did indeed sometimes struggle against local power holders, but, at both extremes and throughout the political system, officials responded with special sensitivity to the landed interest, if they were not themselves landowners.

All these approaches impose present-day categories on historical actors that those actors did not necessarily recognize, and yet historians deduce from those categories what the actors intended and give them roles they may not have chosen. In contrast I wish to focus on the meanings they gave to their own actions, considering individuals, whether in or out of government, as whole persons with multiple engagements, sometimes conflicting, sometimes in doubt. What did they understand themselves to be about? Did politicians, for instance, preoccupy themselves primarily with advancing the particular economic interests of landowners and merchants, or did they principally focus on strengthening the sinews of central power? My conclusion is that they did neither. As revealed through their correspondence, they devoted the great bulk of their energy to building networks of patronage, widening their following, or finding a powerful protector for their political fortunes. Political men in nineteenth-century Brazil were predominantly (albeit not exclusively) concerned with patronage, whether dispensing it or seeking it—often both. In that preoccupation and through the actions that demonstrated it, they in fact legitimized the existing social structure in which men of property stood at the top. Politics indeed worked to that end, but not solely or even principally through the pursuit of particular governmental policies. Rather, that goal was reached through an entire style of life and practice.

Finally, while the ideology of patronage served the interests of the economic elite, it also provided a plumb line against which the behavior of that dominant class could be measured and checked. Its members, therefore, violated the code only gingerly. For that reason this pattern of political behavior could be accepted by more people than one might expect. It was rooted in an ancient social system and ultimately in familial and interpersonal relationships built up over a long time. I do not see it as a stage to be superseded by the inevitable triumph of an impersonal and universalistic "rational" bureaucracy, nor do I examine a pathological condition. Patronage worked for some if not for others, and preserved a structure that only a Revolution could have destroyed.

PART ONE

THE STRUCTURES OF
POLITICS

ONE

Families, Clients, and
Social Control

WHEN PORTUGAL'S PRINCE-REGENT, soon to be crowned
João VI, arrived in Brazil in 1808, driven out of Europe by Napoleon's army, he did not merely set up a court-in-exile but installed
the complete apparatus of his government. He evidently liked Brazil, and even the defeat of Napoleon did not persuade him to return
to Portugal. He reluctantly did so only in 1820, when the newly
created Portuguese Parliament so demanded and threatened his
throne if he remained overseas. Brazil then moved inexorably toward independence, formally declared in 1822 by his own son, who
crowned himself Emperor Pedro I. Brazilians thus began to elaborate the formal institutions of their new government, a process that
took another twenty years. That process may be considered complete by the first years of Pedro II's long reign (1840-89), and the
next chapter will examine those institutions, which remained more
or less unchanged for almost half a century. Other, less formal institutions were inherited from colonial times, and no one thought
either to make them or alter them: they just were. All sections of
the country were profoundly shaped by a steady focus on family
and household, a latent tension between poor and rich, a keen sense
of social hierarchy, and the constant practice of exchanging benefits
for obedience. These social patterns exerted a deep effect on politics and gave the structures of government a particular, Brazilian
meaning.

Regions

Before turning to those enduring realities that made it possible for all Brazilians to understand each other, we need to acknowledge another, more divisive one: the force of regionalism. Brazilians felt powerfully bound to place, perhaps precisely because of family ties and the links of patronage, but also, for some, because of their property in land. Agricultural and pastoral activities, especially for export, defined distinct zones of political connection, and recognizing regional ties is the first step toward an interpretation of Brazil's political life. Historians of nineteenth-century Brazil have sharply delimited its regional economies, each focused on a single product. Coffee, sugar, and cotton led the list of exports, and cattle raising also proved profitable; each product marked off distinct regions. Their rivalries often proved problematic for the political system, even helping to undermine the Empire—which a Republic replaced in 1889—so this study must begin by attending to those regional divisions in that vast land, even though elements of unity ultimately prevailed.

The area of earliest settlement had long concentrated on producing slave-grown sugar for an overseas market. A narrow strip fifty to one hundred miles deep, characterized by abundant rainfall and a rich soil, ran along the coast from the tip of the Atlantic-ward bulge in Rio Grande do Norte southward just beyond the city of Salvador (see map). Almost all the sugar Brazil exported came from that Northeastern zone and from a small center of sugar cultivation around Campos, in the province of Rio de Janeiro. Brazil had long lost the near-monopoly of world production it had enjoyed in the seventeenth century, but its sugar planters continued to prosper until the 1870s, and even after that they could rely on a gradually expanding domestic market.[1] Nevertheless, from 1840 onwards Northeastern leaders acutely sensed the loss of their economic and political predominance within Brazil as the coffee planters in the South took the lead.

Politically as well as economically, the coffee region formed the other pole of Brazilian activity. By the 1840s coffee accounted for nearly half of all Brazilian exports, and earnings from it fueled an unprecedented growth in Brazil's national wealth and governmental

Map of Brazil

revenues. Soil types, altitude, and climate favored the coffee bush in southeastern Brazil, and from the 1820s coffee cultivation spread rapidly up the hilly valley of the Paraíba do Sul River along the stretch where it runs parallel to the coast some 50 miles inland. By 1850 coffee also became the predominant crop west of the city of São Paulo, although this new area did not challenge the older region until the 1880s.[2]

Numerous planters built substantial fortunes from coffee. Although Francisco Peixoto de Lacerda Werneck (1795-1861)—who received the title of barão do Paty do Alferes in 1852*—exceeded most in his success, his extensive surviving correspondence and local political prominence make him worthy of special attention as a member of the planter class. His father, an immigrant from the Azores Islands, had married into a family of some wealth, accumulated from eighteenth-century trade to the then-prosperous gold mining region (which lay about 300 miles to the northwest of Rio de Janeiro). To a royal land grant already held by Francisco's mother, his father had added another in the Paraíba do Sul Valley. As only child, Francisco inherited them both and turned to planting coffee. His own marriage into an important family of coffee factors aided him still further, and he eventually came to own seven plantations with over 1,000 slaves. His most important holdings lay in the county of Vassouras, but he owned rural and urban property elsewhere, including a house in the capital, from which he rode in a splendid coach to attend gala occasions at the Emperor's court. He took a lively interest in the affairs of the entire coffee economy. In 1847 when his son, recently returned from studies in Europe, inherited a plantation through his own wife, Francisco penned a famous *Memoria*, often reprinted, on how to set up a plantation, care for the coffee bushes, organize production, and manage slaves.[3] Like many of his contemporaries, he must be understood as a progressive and dynamic landed entrepreneur, equally interested in profit and in dominion. I will have more to say of his political role and that of his family.

No other agricultural product so clearly demarcated a region as to command political loyalty in the way sugar and coffee did. To begin with, none accounted for more than a tenth of Brazil's exports by the 1840s. Most of the production of long-staple cotton—native to Brazil—centered in the less humid, slightly higher regions of the Northeast, back from the coast thirty to a hundred miles. Small farmers predominated in that area, although some men held large estates. Cotton remained an item of little importance to Brazilian planters, despite a brief flurry of interest in cotton produc-

---

* The spelling of words in Portuguese has varied greatly over the last 100 years. In this book I use modern spelling for place names but, to avoid anachronisms, I have kept nineteenth-century spellings for all personal names.

Francisco Peixoto de Lacerda Werneck, barão
do Paty do Alferes (1824-61), ca. 1855

tion in the province of São Paulo provoked by the U.S. Civil War.[4]
Tobacco predominated in the region around the town of Cachoeira,
in the province of Bahia across the bay from Salvador. It too tended
to be produced on small properties, and their owners had little political clout. The Amazon River region produced cacao and rubber,
gathered from trees that grew wild in the forest, but only late in the
Empire did that region's wealth provide a basis from which to challenge (even then, only slightly) the political dominance of sugar and
coffee growers. Indeed many leaders in the Amazon dreamed of establishing sugar plantations there, deploring the contrary tendency
of workers to wander into the forest to gather rubber.[5]

Cattle raising did set off particular regions of some political importance. Foreign observers described three distinct cattle economies, each with its own culture. In the arid parts of the Northeast, away from the sugar-producing coastal strip and westward even of the transitional cotton areas, cattle ranching had been a major occupation since the sixteenth century. Occasional droughts devastated this scrubby region, but cattle and cattlemen always returned at the first rains. To the south the inhabitants of Minas Gerais centered their economy on beef production, with steadier results. From this area of rolling grassy plains and scattered gnarled trees, herders drove their cattle to Rio de Janeiro, where the demand for fresh meat steadily increased as the city grew in size and wealth with the rising exports of coffee. Of all the ranchers of nineteenth-century Brazil, however, those of Rio Grande do Sul emerged as the most prosperous and powerful. The region's gently undulating grasslands and rich plains especially favored spreading cattle herds, and by 1863 the province exported nearly seven-tenths of Brazil's hides. It also produced salted or jerked beef for consumption by slaves on coffee and sugar plantations to the north. In this southernmost province a distinctive culture and intense regional loyalty repeatedly challenged the centralizing tendencies of politicians in Rio de Janeiro.[6]

Commonalities

Brazilians remained predominantly rural. Apart from Rio de Janeiro—206,000 people in 1849, 229,000 in 1872—cities tended to be small. If one considers Brazil's seven largest cities in 1872, the list includes one with only 11,730 inhabitants, and the seven together accounted for only 617,428 people in a population of some 10,000,000, or 6 percent of the total. To be sure cities grew rapidly; by 1890 Rio de Janeiro had a population of 430,000, and 11 percent of Brazilians lived in cities of more than 10,000.[7] The top political leaders always lived in the cities, at least while Parliament was in session, and this fact lent an urban patina to political action, but a predominantly rural society meant that the true basis of political life lay in the country, on plantations and ranches.

In addition to the low level of urbanization, several other characteristics of Brazilian society spanned all regions. First, whether in the cities or on plantations, black slaves did much of the physical labor. Although practically every kind of agricultural activity (as well as stock raising) counted on slaves, they were concentrated in the sugar- and coffee-producing regions of the Northeast and Southeast, respectively. Slaves also worked as artisans and domestic servants, not only on plantations but in the towns and cities. The 2,500,000 slaves in Brazil accounted for between a quarter and a third of the population at the middle of the nineteenth century. Many were held singly or in groups of two or three, the widespread ownership of slaves thus ensuring broad commitment among the free to the survival of the institution. Some planters, however, owned hundreds and occasionally even thousands, making Brazil a place where wealth was measured largely in human beings. Parliament did not abolish slavery until 1888, and slaves continued to work the land until that date, although the effective end of the slave trade in 1850 and the passage in 1871 of a law freeing all children subsequently born to slave women had signaled that slavery would eventually, if tardily, come to an end. An internal slave trade from the Northeast to the Southeast after 1850 had gradually set apart some regions from others even on this issue, at least to a degree.[8]

Even less altered by regional differences than slavery, understandings of household and family deeply affected the nature of Brazilian politics. The importance of these institutions as the basic units of the polity requires that they be discussed here at some length, all the more so since these cultural elements proved particularly resistant to change. Although families and households appeared in many forms, the universally shared ideal took for granted that they would be headed by a man. The father exercised legal authority over the entire household, and the law delegated to him the right to punish its members, whether wife, child, servant, or slave. A father could, legally at least, imprison his sons no matter their age if they lived with him and if he did it to "punish or correct bad habits or behavior." The law regarded the property of sons-at-home, again regardless of age, as their fathers'.[9] When the Constitution forbade a son from voting if he lived with his father and thus attempted to ensure that each family cast only one ballot, it recognized the father's authority; for, as one legal commentator explained regarding sons-at-home, "their will is still dependent on their parents." Lawmakers, said a journalist, wished to make sure a voter would "not be in very close personal dependence on another, as were sons-at-home, married women, household servants, and those who live from alms." And certainly, he added, "the weakness of sex does not allow one to presume an independence of will among women, even if single and of age or widowed." [10] The term *pai de família*, * that is, paterfamilias, implied not only care but authority. A nineteenth-century dictionary defined the phrase as meaning "head of the couple" and "chief of the family." [11]

The state especially protected the family. The law forbade a person from willing most of his or her property to anyone outside the testator's family and thus shielded it from the vagaries of individual interest. Yet some exceptions to this rule are suggestive: a son could be disinherited for publicly insulting his father, or a daughter for marrying without her father's consent—unless by so doing she had raised her social position. [12] Public employees took seriously their responsibility toward private families. Foreign service officers and the police thought it their duty to inform a baker that his married daughter had left her husband for another man; her failure to obey her husband became her father's responsibility and a matter of official interest. Government correspondence frequently appeared on black-bordered paper, indicating the death of a correspondent's relative and symbolizing the centrality of family ties. Thus in adopting such paper for all correspondence for a full year after the passing of his "cousin and brother-in-law," the Minister of War drew attention to the relationship, stressing its importance and relevance to public action. [13]

Families represented an important source of political capital. They naturally focused, as elsewhere, on enlarging their property, and over several generations successful families accumulated significant resources. The connections that led men to official positions and local dominion formed an important part of those resources and, through politics, families struggled to secure them, often against other families. Not by accident did a newspaper, in praising a deceased coffee planter, juxtapose the two qualities: "head of an important family, having exercised the highest county positions." In pursuing their political interests, families usually voted together: "One of my brothers-in-law who is an elector also voted [for the

---

* I have kept the use of Portuguese words in the text to a minimum and those I use with any frequency are listed in the Index by their first occurrence.

candidate], and all my sons-in-law and my son who were in the [Electoral] College worked dedicatedly for [him]," wrote a politician in Bahia. From a rural parish in Rio Grande do Sul, a campaign worker listed "the Conservatives here upon whom we may rely, beyond the members of my family." The Liberal Prime Minister in 1885 bitterly complained that a Liberal candidate "received no help from the Leão family," which he expected to act as a unit.[14]

Families did not always stand together, but their failure to do so merited comment. In Pará, for instance, "there is here a group of men who hate each other to the death, and they are not constrained even by the close family relationship of some of them." In Bahia in 1856 Manuel Pinto de Sousa Dantas, a young candidate for Parliament, wished his two uncles would support him, but recognized

Manuel Pinto de Sousa Dantas (1831-94), 1861

that one of them would back his own son instead. "My [other] Uncle José Dantas, no matter how much he would like to help me, will not enter into a war with Uncle João" and, anyway, added Manuel, it would not be proper to "plant intrigue between them." Manuel later reported, however, that his cousin, not so squeamish, had taken "steps that may be described as imprudent, since they will tend toward the destruction of an [important] principle, that is, of the unity of families." Members of a family sometimes fought each other, but the practice elicited surprise, condemnation, or apprehension.[15]

The boundaries of a family extended well beyond father, mother, and children. The protection in exchange for loyalty that family ties entailed stretched, first of all, to a broad range of blood relationships and, next, to a similarly large number of connections through marriage. Although somewhat more tenuous, the ties of ritual kinship could also be important. To be a *padrinho* (godfather), *afilhado* (godson), or *compadre* or *comadre* (ritual co-parent) in Brazil, as in other Iberian cultures, brought with it important religious obligations and property commitments, and thus influence, even authority. All these family connections implied mutual obligations to aid one another in elections or in securing positions within government, so much so that, by extension, Brazilians often referred figuratively to a protégé as an *afilhado* and to his protector as a *padrinho*.

Any distinction between family and household remained vague in the perceptions of contemporaries. They often used the word "family" to include many persons not related by blood, marriage, or ritual co-parenthood. In the case of a plantation, the term could suggest slaves, hired hands, tenants, *compadres, afilhados*, relatives far and near, in short, all those who lived on or from the property. A householder thus expanded the circle of those who, as dependents, acknowledged his authority.[16] Often the documents described a free person as *agregado à minha família* (attached to my family) or as a *morador nas minhas terras* (one who lives on my land), shortened in practice to *agregado* and *morador*.

An *agregado* or *morador* depended on someone else, especially for housing or at least a space in which to live and, more important, for social place. He or she might actually be a family member, even a respected parent, sister, or brother who lacked an independent source of income;[17] more often the *agregado* was a poverty-stricken agricultural worker, free but likely black or mulatto, to whom a landowner granted the right to raise subsistence crops on some out-lying patch of the large estate. In exchange the *agregados* proffered allegiance at times of armed struggle against neighboring land-owners and loyalty in electoral disputes.[18] As one engineer described the situation in 1879, on coffee plantations much land was not used by the planter or his slaves; on the "large remaining area, . . . one notes a great number of people who settle there with the permission of the landowner or planter and who are called *agregados*. These *agregados*, far outnumbering the slaves, are poor citizens. . . . By their dependence on the owners these *agregados* constitute an en-slaved class, which, although not subject to any tribute in money or labor, . . . are so, nevertheless, by the electoral tax [i.e., their vote], which they pay at the right moment at the ballot box, or else risk eviction."[19] In the Northeast, in the cotton- and food-raising area between sugar-producing coast and cattle-raising interior, the land-lords—owning smaller and less prosperous tracts than on the coast—frequently did not possess any slaves and peopled their es-tates almost entirely with *moradores*.[20] There, as in every corner of the country, the patron's care on the one hand and the *agregado*'s loyalty or service on the other dominated the relationship as the elite conceived it; the *agregados* probably had other ideas, but with rare exceptions, they kept these to themselves.

Some householders led a still-larger group made up of those, of-ten other householders, who owed them favors or to whom they could represent a threat. "Small landowners [*sitiantes*]," said a con-temporary, "lived in the shadow of the great" land- or slaveowning families.[21] They knew that the wisest course lay in seeking the pro-tection of the more powerful. Small-town merchants and owners of country stores also depended on these great families, for even when their members owed money to a tradesman, eventual collection de-pended on the goodwill of the debtor, unless the storekeeper found a still more powerful magnate to defend his interests.

From family, household members, *agregados*, and other depen-dents, a planter or rancher built his following, or *clientela*. Clients depended on their leader and offered him loyalty in return. In this regard it made no difference whether the specific case fell within the political or the economic sphere: a patron offered employment just as he shielded dependents from any claims of authority put forth by others.[22] The word *patrão*, literally patron, principally meant employer. Such employment need not always be licit. One provincial administrator in Bahia complained that "the bosses [*chefes mandões*] furnish meat and manioc-meal to those idlers and evildoers who choose as their way of life to serve as bodyguards—or, as they are called here, 'broad chests'—and defend them when Justice seeks to punish them for their criminal conduct." Even runaway slaves could receive such protection from a slaveowner.[23] In return the chief bore responsibility for the actions of those whom he led. When a country storekeeper complained of a planter bent on protecting "a dark mulatto, thin, wearing blue pants, a white jacket, and a straw hat, armed with a machete and a gun," who had "fired some lead pellets" at the complainant's store, the police, rather than apprehending the delinquent, required the planter to sign a pledge of good behavior (*termo de bem viver*), thus asserting his responsibility for the behavior of those whom he sheltered.[24] If the head of a household successfully maintained his authority over its members, he could expect other institutions of the state to yield to his jurisdiction; he therefore typically required strict obedience within the walls of his dominion.

The size of his *clientela* was the measure of a man. Claims to vast lands—and, when appropriate, the ownership of slaves—displayed success and powerfully aided the work of increasing one's following, but the crucial resource remained the loyalty of others. With the backing of this large retinue, a rural boss could exert enough influence over judges and police officials (or secure such appointments for himself) to offer protection and grant favors to respectable people, and thus increase the number of his *amigos*, or friends, binding the loyalty of his growing clientele through gratitude if not through force. For this reason every man sought a patron from whom he derived protection, and every man strove to build himself a following.

Whereas clients received real benefits and actively sought out patrons, it was the propertied who shaped the society to make that necessary.[25] The system of land tenure, for instance, powerfully encouraged the practice of patronage. Overlapping royal land grants and the traditional rights of squatters combined with a virtual absence of systematic surveys or land registries to create a chaotic system of potentially conflicting claims that victimized the weak and placed a premium on strength, whether measured in wealth, armed men, or political influence.[26] As the son of the barão do Paty do Alferes explained, since a grant typically safeguarded the claims of possible earlier recipients and could only be legally valid if the property were improved within a few years, a counter-claimant could, long afterwards, challenge the legitimacy of the holding on either ground. It would then be difficult to find an impartial judge to evaluate conflicting depositions. When selling land, the seller indicated that he sold it "as he possessed it," taking no responsibility for the validity of the title. Few surveyed their land, each landowner seeing in the vagueness of his property's borders an opportunity for later aggrandizement. To be sure, once a region had long been settled and certain lands had become clearly associated with particular families, such conflicts may have lessened; the fairness of judicial judgments would then only vouchsafe the legitimacy of the political leadership exercised by established families. But when circumstances provoked novel uses of agricultural resources in new economic frontiers, greatly heightening their value, conflicts could sunder the customary relationships, and only a following assured landownership. On the other hand, *agregados* could be attracted only by those who held land. The young Lacerda Werneck noticed that this reality put a greater premium on holding land than on using it, so that "like the dog in La Fontaine's fable, they profit not, but will not allow others to profit." Certainly all evidence is that the few held most of the land, while most rural workers remained landless. From this fact above all derived the political force of the rural chief. Clients sought him out because of his landed wealth, and he was able to maintain and extend his holdings because he commanded them in a numerous entourage.[27]

Social Control

The social purpose of political action, of elections, and of appointment to office logically derived from the guiding principles of Brazilian social organization, two in particular. First, practice and preachments constantly ingrained the notion that all social relations consisted in an exchange of protection for loyalty, benefits for obedience; recalcitrance merited punishment. Second, virtually every institution served to stress the social hierarchy, insisting that for every individual there was a very particular place, even if the most important distinction lay between the propertied and the poor. Measures of social control were all the more necessary because of obstacles to its imposition in Brazil, particularly the geographical mobility of the landless free. Even more important loomed the universal problem that those to be controlled had a will of their own. Politics contributed to and drew meaning from these larger social concerns.

The family paradigm oriented social relationships between leader and led, and within it force and benevolence intertwined.[28] Obedience and loyalty purchased favors. Obedience and loyalty allowed the follower to escape the patron's application of force. Obedience and loyalty ensured protective care and thus constructed an important defense against force applied by other would-be leaders. As inevitable corollary, failure to obey or be loyal subjected one to punishment by the patron and left one openly vulnerable to exploitation by others. No dichotomy existed between force and benevolence: each drew its meaning from the other. They simply represented two aspects of the same technique for controlling others. The family suggested both. Just as a father could write, "hug and bless my children for me. . . . They should remember me by doing as they are told so as to deserve my friendship," so an ex-slaveowner could declare, "I have always said that the planter should treat the freedman as he treats his children: with kindness and energy, that is, with love."[29] The threat of punishment and the promise of benevolence shaped the lives of wives and children, slaves, *agregados*, small landowners, village tradesmen, and other followers of the patron, catching them all in a powerful web of obligations owed and gifts expected. These realities also colored all other relationships of power, particularly the overtly political. Everyone was taken up in a constant process of mutual, if unequal, exchange. In short the elite maintained social order through a generally shared understanding that obedience merited protection.[30]

As a technique of domination that permeated all society and politics, the unspoken bargain needs to be examined in more detail. Senator José Thomaz Nabuco de Araújo noted it in referring to the

moradores in Northeastern sugar mills, "who from time immemo-
rial have considered the planters their supporters and protectors,
who have always had toward them a just and reverential respect—for they let them have lands to cultivate and game to eat,
without paying the slightest monetary contribution, rendering the
smallest personal service, making the least payment in kind, or carrying out any improvements on the land of the plantation." They
were, he said, "united with the millowners by force of habit, by the
influence of ancient custom, by ties of gratitude." When these *moradores*, however, voted against the candidates of the planters, allegedly persuaded to do so by the use of force, "the just relationship
that existed between the sugar millowners and their *moradores* was
destroyed, customs were altered, and it only produced evil results
because such men cannot remain on plantations that they somehow
betrayed." In the coffee region, too, Lacerda Werneck's oldest son
noted that the *agregado*'s claim on security remained tenuous, and
he could be evicted at the pleasure of the proprietor.[31] As in a family,
the patron's offer of safeguards and benevolence implied the right
to mete out punishment as well.

Generosity toward the poor received constant praise because the
propertied in general recognized that such acts validated the implied exchange and preserved the proper structure of society. A
priest at a funeral took care to mention that the deceased maintained "his pocket always open to venerable old men." Another
funeral orator in 1860 stressed the "aid of alms" that the dead man
had granted generously: "his house, his regard, his money, were the
treasures of the poor." Whether the rich actually dispensed such
generosity is not so important as the insistence on it as a principal
virtue. We have here a celebration of patronal values. And to some
degree these values did become internalized by members of upper-
class families: the barão do Paty do Alferes wrote in a personal
letter that "to help a family in misfortune, to be a guardian angel
and lend a hand to the unfortunate, . . . is something for great souls,
is right in short for men of independent circumstances."[32]

These techniques of control—rewarding obedience with benevolence and using force to punish disobedience—found specific elaboration with regard to slaves. More than anyone, but like all those
in superior positions, the slaveowner confronted the central problem of how to make others act according to his will rather than

their own. To this end masters combined harsh discipline for the recalcitrant with favors for the docile and compliant. The owner's kindness, it bears repeating, gained purpose only as it accompanied his right to exert maximum force. Many planters or their overseers did not hesitate to use the whip, the stocks, or other punishments to get sixteen or even eighteen hours of work a day out of those they drove. Other slaveowners, however, such as the barão do Paty do Alferes, perceived that fullest control required care as well: "Extreme oppression dries up their hearts, hardens them, and inclines them toward evil. The master must be severe, just, and humane." House slaves and artisans may have enjoyed better food, better clothes, and especially a greater chance of being freed for exceptionally loyal service than field hands, but they could be reduced to agricultural labor with equal ease. Such relationships between masters and slaves simply exaggerated the controls fathers exercised over their families and households, so the family provided the language of slavery. The son of the barão do Paty do Alferes declared, "Paternal solicitude for the fate of the slaves accompanies good discipline and an [orderly] regimen." In exchange for such solicitude, the master expected loyalty. A deceased planter was eulogized at his death for successfully eliciting correct behavior: "He was always a humane master, and for this very reason was loved by his slaves. . . . Like the biblical patriarchs of old, he always lived among his servants and family members surrounded by respect and affection." [33] The relationship of masters and slaves thus mirrored the family, albeit in a distorted fashion. And as a means of control it did not always work: slaves resisted in a variety of ways, from working "lazily" to running away, from sabotage to revolt, from infanticide to suicide, and it is not my purpose to suggest otherwise. [34] But clearly to exert authority was the masters' essential goal.

The manumission of slaves, for example, encouraged good behavior, for it demonstrated that loyalty and obedience would be rewarded. The frequency with which Brazilian slaveowners granted freedom to individual slaves surprised foreign visitors in the nineteenth century, and society bestowed approbation on slaveowners who did so. The proportion of free blacks and mulattos in Brazil reached 74 percent by 1872, and they accounted for 44 percent of the total population. [35] The freeing of slaves depended on signs that they accepted the values of those who emancipated them. Although unusual in its particular expression, the following example illustrates that more general rule: when a group of Masons buried one of theirs at a ceremony attended by "many of the most elevated social position," they "freed a black slave woman who appeared at the door of the building hailing Masonic sentiments in memory of our deceased brother." One may be sure few who challenged the values of hierarchy and deference would have been rewarded with manumission, and masters reasonably counted on continued loyalty even after bestowing freedom. Sometimes owners manumitted a slave on the specific condition of continued faithful service for a fixed number of years or until the death of the master, and the law even provided that manumission could be revoked for such acts of ingratitude as hurling insults at the former master.[36] Since freedom was a gift from superior to inferior, not resulting from an agreement between equals, it exemplified the uneven exchange or bargain that characterized most relationships whether social or, as I will show in subsequent chapters, political.

To deal with the free poor, the elite similarly relied on the threat of punishment. Conscription served the purpose well. Impressment seemed an appropriate response to crimes considered minor. As the chief of police of Rio de Janeiro reported about one young man, "being convinced he had stolen two bolts of silk from a Frenchwoman on Ourives Street, . . . I decided to recruit him because there was not sufficient proof of his crime for me to begin judicial proceedings." Others found themselves "jailed for disorderly conduct" and then drafted "to make them correct their vices." José Muniz, taken prisoner for deflowering a seven-year-old, "never works, is irregular in his behavior, and lives with his mother who supports him," reported a police official in Bahia; "I think it would be good for you to send him to the Army or Navy, since the mother of the girl absolutely refuses to have him marry her daughter." A county judge in Bahia sent in three recruits. One of them, a mulatto, had "tried several times, according to public knowledge, to kill his father-in-law, cutting him a few times with a knife, and set fire to some thatched houses as well as the cane field of a *compadre*, whom he did not succeed in killing." The second, a black, "used to go around with a gun and on any pretext threatened shots, and on several occasions hid the slaves of others in the house where he lived, also according to public knowledge." As for the third, a mulatto "without a trade, very daring, when I surrounded his house, he loaded a gun and declared from within that he would resist." One police official judged several men "appropriate for recruitment for being recognized *capoeiras* and *capangas*," that is, members of fighting gangs of blacks and hired thugs. For such crimes were men sent off to the Army without trial.[37]

As some of these examples demonstrate, forcing men to work frequently surfaced as a purpose of military recruitment. Justification for impressment could be found in the fact that "he never works" or is "without a trade." As one Northeasterner reported, "many rural proprietors . . . take advantage" of the draft, "harboring and protecting those who are to be recruited in order to use their labor without charge except for food and clothing." Later, when Parliament tried substituting a lottery for forced recruitment, a member of the sugar planters' association noted that "before the lottery recruitment law, those who did not work and had no means of livelihood were sent to the Army. That means of correcting those who do not work having been extinguished, a law to make work obligatory will [now] be essential." The lottery, however, proved a dead letter, and forced recruitment continued—doubtless to the same purpose. Obedience and loyalty meant work first of all, and those who defied the rules ended up in a levy.[38]

Observers often described the enlisted men as black or mulatto, and hence, one can conclude, they were poor. Since besides appealing to a patron for protection, a draftee could legally buy his exemption from service, as a father did for his son in 1859, the better-off escaped. The author of a newspaper editorial spoke out in behalf of "those whose extreme poverty prevented them from paying fifteen milreis to exempt their sons from recruitment, or those whose luck it was to be a dependent farmer [*morador*] of a patron who did not belong to the governing party."[39] An English traveler may have mistakenly assumed racial solidarity, but he accurately identified the class background of those conscripted when he argued that "should a general rising of slaves occur, the result might prove disastrous, as the greater part of the privates in the army are negroes or mulattoes, and the majority of the freed blacks, at least in Rio, notoriously form the dregs and scum of the population."[40]

The fate of the draftee was a sorry one. Conditions in the Army or Navy remained so deplorable that the Minister of War had to tell a provincial president in 1856 that recruits should march to Rio, "with all security but not in irons." As one commentator described the situation, the

authorities can legally and at their wish order any non-exempt citizen grabbed; stick him in a dungeon; make him walk to the provincial capital with the necessary care to make sure he does not run away; install him as a soldier in the Army; place him on a steamship; send him from there to the very end of this vast country; keep him in military service for a long and indeterminate time; [and] make him die far from the land of his birth.

And he concluded: "If [forced] recruitment were addressed to the well-off classes," if repression were "to fall on the well placed," the military draft would "fly out the window."[41] But impressment remained for the poor and served as a tool through which they could be controlled by their betters, even, as we shall see, to being compelled to vote as ordered.

Shielding some of the poor from the threat of being drafted surfaced so frequently as a theme in the documents of the epoch that one cannot but believe the real purpose of the draft lay in forcing everyone to seek identification with a household that could offer this aid. Obedience merited such protection, and the poor worked desperately to secure a patron's help in escaping transfer from the National Guard (a local militia) to the Army or, more likely, direct impressment into it. Rival leaders demonstrated their patronal influence by protecting their own. A National Guard commandant complained in 1842 that some of his men, "who should be assigned [to Army duty], are under the protection of proprietors and planters, either as hired hands or as *agregados*. The planters use their influence on their behalf or counsel them to hide." Even during the war with Paraguay (1865-70), a Guard commandant reported he could not send troops to the front because they were "protected by the very ones who should counsel them to take part in a cause that is so much ours." In the capital as well, a police official admitted in 1873 that quite a few escaped his recruiting net, "befriended [*apadrinhados*] by respectable families of this place." It was to Lacerda Werneck that a young man appealed for aid when he had gone to town and been seized as a draftee; the planter wrote the provincial authorities to get him released on the grounds the young man, as an only son, supported his widowed mother, adding, in a paternalistic appeal, that he, Lacerda Werneck, could not bear "to see the tears of a helpless woman."[42] Protecting the poor from recruitment also meant building a clientele.

The acceptance of a multilayered social hierarchy—by focusing tensions all along its extent rather than between two groups—further aided the propertied in exerting control. Here lay another means of assuring social order: allow almost everyone to feel superior to someone else. There is no equivalent word in current English usage for the Brazilian concept of *condição* (literally, condition), a term used to indicate precise social place. The nuanced distinctions of social ranking restrained the threat that freedmen might otherwise pose, and this partially explains why the manumission of slaves could be encouraged: freed blacks would easily fit into one of many possible social niches. Attention to variations of skin color further contributed to locating people along a continuum of status, some being either darker or lighter than others. Brazilians took for granted that people could generally be distinguished, as one of the Lacerda Wernecks put it, "according to the order, scale, or category into which [they were] placed within society." This view meant that no one thought himself equal to anyone else; all met within a hierarchy and found themselves either above or below all others. One judge, on coming to interior Bahia and finding imprisoned a "graduate of the University of Paris, a property holder," saw it as "extremely scandalous and abusive that an honest man, a *pai de família*, a Brazilian honored with an academic diploma, should be confined in a filthy jail like the one in this village." Apparently the jail was good enough, however, for the ordinary sort. Not even children in a single family, albeit similarly tied to their father, could be considered equal to each other. Still less could equality be said to apply to other members of the household, even those of some standing. Although a coffee planter generously paid for the schooling of a friend's orphaned son, he displayed sharp irritation when the lad's sizable bills arrived at his desk: "I must say this boy's expenses are not in harmony with his position, nor will I agree to have him there like a *lord* and incurring more expenses than his circumstances permit." If even those within the "big house" so decidedly affirmed their rank with regard to each other, how much more likely were they to assert their superiority over small landowners, *agregados*, and salaried workers. As one author perceived in 1890, on hearing talk of democratic reform, the "plutocrats, attached to marked social inequalities, are not likely to regard even the small planter or *agregado*, much less their employees, as having equal rights."[43] Householders thus carefully ranged themselves with reference to each other.

The National Guard imitated society in its gradations. Created as a militia in 1831 by landowners anxious to counter the unsettling influence of an unruly Army,[44] its ranks clearly distinguished social classes. All male citizens between the ages of eighteen and sixty and possessing an income above a certain minimum could be legally called on to serve. Whether elected—as they were before 1850—or appointed, officers came from the "affluent classes." Legitimate birth provided only one of several grounds for appointment, and typically officers held land and owned slaves.[45] A provincial president in Bahia described his choice for a National Guard colonel as "the richest and most illustrious citizen of the district," while a president in Sergipe admitted he faced problems in finding suitable men to recommend as officers, especially in the capital, "where wealth is rare." He considered one appointment but rejected it on learning that the candidate was "the son of a poor man and owns nothing aside from his salary." The president did recommend another, however, because "besides the wealth of his father, who is one of the most affluent real estate owners in the province, he possesses his own fortune." The president also urged the appointment of still a third candidate, noting that although he was not wealthy himself, he was "the nephew of a rich man without children who, I am told, spends on him some of his income. This old man . . . is one of the richest and best reputed in the province." In Rio de Janeiro a commentator at the Ministry of Justice added a marginal note: "This old man, . . . whose nephew is proposed, . . . is perhaps the richest man in Sergipe. . . . The appointment will be a sign of esteem for the uncle from whom he will inherit." In turn a commission served as a statement of social position: if arrested, National Guard officers did not enter ordinary jail cells, but remained in an "open room."[46]

In contrast to the officers, the rank and file were "artisans, workers, and breakers of the sod," "slavedrivers on coffee plantations, muleteers," petty squatters, or "men of color." Governmental instructions specifically excluded tavern keepers, artisans, storekeepers, and fishermen from the officer corps. The existence, fur-

thermore, of two categories among the men—active and reserve—
ensured that respectable people never served unless as officers.
Many occupations or positions, such as judges, lawyers, notaries,
and doctors, specifically entitled one to be classified in the reserves.
Even those on the active list could be exempted from service if they
were students, employees of hospitals and charitable institutions,
county councilmen, post-office workers, or owners and supervisors
of private establishments with more than twenty employees or, in
the case of ranch managers, if they ran enough cattle to produce
more than fifty calves a year. If a man could not meet any of these
conditions, political influence on the registration board could still
secure exemption. In any case, even to establish one's legal right to
be classified in the reserves and thus exempt from irksome service
required several documents, difficult for a working man to obtain.[47]
No wonder that, in this domain as in others, those in the poorer
class, for whom service in the Guard could be truly onerous in taking them from their small plots, often at harvest time, hoped to find
a patron who could protect them from the recruitment board. Thus
one landowner approached Lacerda Werneck, the future barão do
Paty do Alferes, then a colonel in the National Guard, on behalf of
his *comadre*'s son. An erroneous summons had been issued, he said,
since the young man did not have the minimum income to serve in
the Guard; "and if you see that through this means there is no way
[to exempt him], tell me if you want a certificate of poor health, but
I do not think you will need it."[48]

A clear-cut social hierarchy did not deny the possibility of social
mobility, but on the contrary, drew strength from it. The very fact
that some did move a step or two upward or downward both legitimated the ladder of rank and made it all the more necessary to insist
on its existence. Changing social locations required each individual
constantly to define and redefine his or her own position vis-à-vis
others. A few mulattos even served in the Chamber of Deputies and
at least one in a Cabinet, but that did not keep Brazilians from
unhesitatingly applying categories of race and color, indeed demanding it. One politician declared, "We enjoy full democracy in
Brazil. . . . We live with everyone; we sit the freedman at our table
and rely more on the trustworthy freedman than on many Brazilian
citizens":[49] tolerance did not mean the end of social ranks, but demonstrated them. The simultaneous existence of myriad layers and

limited but real fluidity has led historians to picture nineteenth-century Brazil either as a society of immutable estates or as an example of a fully liberal democracy.[50] It is precisely because it fit neither model that Brazilians then focused so much attention on social gradations and used politics and patronage as a means of asserting the propriety of ranks. In short the very movement of nineteenth-century Brazilians, both geographical and social, required the predominance of an ideology of hierarchy.

Still, we must not be so blinded by the complexity of social hierarchy that we fail to notice that at its extremes, not counting the slaves, lay the many propertyless and the few propertied. Contemporaries viewed this polarity as orienting social life, and it is, therefore, the most appropriate distinction for the historian to make. For all their notions of social gradations, nineteenth-century Brazilians did not dwell nearly so much on differences of occupation or particular sources of wealth, whether lawyer or doctor, merchant or planter, as on that major division between haves and have-nots. At one end stood the "influential citizens by virtue of their possessions and social role." At the other were the "workers giving off a vile miasma of *cachaça* [cane brandy] and cigarette smoke." A National Guard officer in Rio Grande do Sul saw the main division of society as being between the "class . . . of well-off citizens" and the "class of those less favored by fortune."[51] In decreeing that canes could be carried only by the old, the ill, or "respectable persons [*pessoas decentes*]," municipal lawmakers assumed that everyone automatically recognized such people. Tradesmen and craftsmen, no matter if they owned something, were lumped with manual workers and summarily dismissed from consideration. When a provincial president in Bahia forwarded complaints received about a local electoral board's behavior during an election, the board chairman replied, "It is sad that . . . men who call themselves artisans, that is mechanics, along with complainants who on the whole are a watchmaker, a goldsmith, a tailor, a bookbinder, etc.—except for one old man who is a court attorney—should make so bold as to write you, . . . staining outrageously the honor of the parish board, whose unusual enlightenment can be seen in its public acts." Similarly a parish priest recounted how some members of a lay brotherhood "who were ironsmiths, tailors, cobblers, etc. tried to argue with me on canon law, but I rebuffed them, saying they were not entitled to discuss it with me."[52] They too must be made to display deference and subservience or receive sharp rebuke.

One middling social group seemed to escape authority and for this reason loomed as potentially dangerous: the muleteers. In reality upwardly mobile small businessmen who sometimes even became planters themselves,[53] muleteers appeared to the elite as simply undisciplined vagabonds who roamed Brazil without legitimate reason. This was so even though coffee planters, for instance, relied on them in shipping their products from the Paraíba Valley to small coastal ports along the South Atlantic or into Rio de Janeiro itself. Most interior towns counted on muleteers to link them commercially to each other. Such men provided an overland connection even from coffee-rich São Paulo and Rio de Janeiro to sugar-producing Bahia and Pernambuco and well beyond, to Piauí, Maranhão, and Pará, cutting through the cactus breaks of the Northeast and ferrying their animals across the numerous rivers in the South.[54] For this very reason—the range of their movement—muleteers could not be identified with any household. A sugar millowner complained that "the muleteers, living like nomads, without the precious habit of work, without an attachment to the soil, . . . besides being so many work hands robbed from agriculture, constitute a seminary from which have come almost all the famous assassins and horsethieves. . . . Whoever has traveled in the interior of our provinces must have met with these innumerable bands of muleteers who clog the roads."[55]

The muleteers, however, only exemplified a more general problem, for the lower classes, despite the draft or because of it, enjoyed considerable geographical mobility. The availability of unused land that could not be permanently or securely claimed, and for that very reason never merited permanent improvement, fostered much wandering from place to place. *Agregados* were legally free to leave their protector, and did so if they could find another. Landowners sometimes complained of how *agregados* would abandon their patrons "without the least apology."[56] To deal with the shifting and allegedly shiftless free poor required constant attention from patrons and the careful exercise of time-worn instruments of authority. In every location the prominent and propertied required that the recently arrived be provided with constant reminders of their social place, for the predominance of a local *senhor* must be clearly and unquestionably stated, lest geographical movement tend to weaken deference or allow some to escape his sway. Much political action had no other purpose.[57]

How much movement was there? It is difficult to verify geographical mobility because most of it occurred within a province and so does not show up in the printed census figures (the only ones we have). I have examined the place of birth of the free in a few selected parishes that lay along provincial boundaries and found that a significant proportion had been born across the border, as shown in Table 1. Considering that the figures represent immigration from only one direction or, at most, two, one can assume that the proportion of those born outside most parishes was considerably higher. The large geographical size of some nineteenth-century parishes, furthermore, means a person could move a significant distance and still remain in the same parish. Finally, since these figures cannot be broken down by age, they include all children in a very young population. The table thus does not fully reflect the mobility of adults; but clearly it was extensive and posed a challenge to established leaders.

Despite all the tools used to enforce social control, the very demand for respect acknowledged that the poor could hold an alternative view of the proper order of society. One police official felt he had to jail an "insolent" troublemaker for speaking to him insultingly at a hearing. "I took this just measure for the affront because, although he has practiced [other] acts that deserve punishment, he had not yet received any." A judge bitterly complained of the lack of "respect toward the authorities" that he encountered at a village in Bahia. Having come there to preside at a trial, he recounted how some forty persons, "improperly dressed [*em trajes caseiros*]," carried out "a demonstration in the streets . . . without the least respect for my person." In the courtroom some ten or twelve of them walked out "brusquely and dragging their feet, interrupting the silence of the tribunal." All in all, he concluded, his task could not be carried out because of "the state of disrespect and insubordination." Among these troublemakers at least one poor man was scornfully described as having left "his clearing [*roça*] to insult . . . and make noisy uproar." In another instance a beleaguered priest endured "a lot of insults and jibes [*ditos jocosos*]" when it became known that he had been unsuccessful in securing a transfer to an-

TABLE I

Geographical Mobility of the Free Born, Selected Parishes, 1872

		Born out of province		
Province, electoral district, and parish	Total free population	Birth-place	Number	Percent of total
PIAUÍ:				
Parnahyba:				
N.S. da Graça da Parnahyba	4,726	MA	1,234	26.1%
		CE	1,925	40.7
N.S. dos Remedios do Burity do Lopes	3,880	MA	1,210	31.2
		CE	1,073	27.7
Piraruruca:				
N.S. do Carmo de Piraruruca	2,945	CE	148	5.0
N.S. da Conceição de Pedro II	4,123	MA	356	8.6
		CE	154	3.7
Independencia:				
N.S. do Bomfim do Prin. Imperial	8,581	MA	2,645	30.8
		CE	2,344	27.3
Parnaguá:				
N.S. do Livramento de Parnaguá	5,187	BA	238	4.6
		MA	230	4.4
S. Raymundo Nonato:				
S. Raymundo Nonato	5,702	BA	629	11.0
PERNAMBUCO:				
Boa Vista:				
S. Maria da Boa Vista	2,241	BA	119	5.3
Barreiros:				
S. Miguel de Barreiros	8,724	AL	1,244	14.3
MINAS GERAIS:				
Muriahe:				
S. Paulo de Muriahe	2,887	RJ	282	9.8
Leopoldina:				
S. Sebastião de Leopoldina	4,835	RJ	449	9.9
N.S. da Conceição do Laranjal	3,247	RJ	457	14.1
Santanna de Pirapetinga	3,275	RJ	300	9.2
N.S. da Piedade	3,523	RJ	288	8.2
N.S. da Conceição da Boa Vista	3,019	RJ	360	11.9
Bom Jesus do Rio Pardo	1,687	RJ	421	25.0

(continued)

TABLE 1—*continued*

Province, electoral district, and parish	Total free population	Born out of province		
		Birth-place	Number	Percent of total
SÃO PAULO:				
Bananal:				
Bom Jesus do Livramento do Bananal	7,325	RJ	63	0.9
		MG	743	10.1
Mogy-Mirim:				
S. José do Mogy-Mirim	8,520	MG	396	4.7
N.S. da Conceição do Mogy-Mirim	3,492	MG	324	9.3
Casa Branca:				
S. Rita do Passa Quatro	2,064	MG	143	6.9

SOURCES: Candido Mendes de Almeida, *Atlas do Imperio do Brasil comprehendendo as respectivas divisões administrativas, ecclesiasticas, eleitoraes e judiciarias* (Rio de Janeiro, 1868), especially p. 10 and mappa IIB; Brazil, Directoria Geral de Estatistica, *Recenseamento da população do Imperio do Brazil a que se procedeu no dia 1° de agosto de 1872* (Rio de Janeiro, 1873–76).

NOTE: Parishes were selected arbitrarily among those along a provincial boundary. AL = Alagoas, BA = Bahia, CE = Ceará, MA = Maranhão, MG = Minas Gerais, RJ = Rio de Janeiro.

other parish. "I declared that I would not say mass there unless public authorities guaranteed good order in the church, making due silence reign." Among those who challenged his authority he pointed particularly to "a youth recently returned from Paraguay, where he had gone drafted [i.e. not as an officer], who thinks that he should continue to make war even inside church." That young man led "a group of disorderly blacks, slaves, and young men without breeding, armed with knives, clubs, and spears," who had surrounded his house on New Year's eve, "throwing . . . bottles at the front of my home," provoking "a great racket [and] agitating the whole village."[58] If the propertied and the proper sought deference from the poor, they did not always succeed in getting it.

Protest was especially likely if the understood bounds of correct behavior had been transgressed by those above. The colored poor, for instance, did not hesitate to resort to arms when they thought themselves threatened with enslavement. In various parts of the Northeast in 1851, "free mulattos, blacks, and half-breeds [*pardos, pretos, e cabras*]," the "majority of those less well off," "the lesser people [*povo mais miudo*]," formed groups of 400, 200, and 80, "all armed," to resist a law on a civil registry and census, for fear that it really intended to reduce free men of color to slavery.[59] *Agregados* on coffee plantations in Rio de Janeiro also forcefully defended their interests at one point. Falsely believing the law entitled them to claim any lands they had worked for as long as ten years, a number of them "made common cause," wrote the provincial president, to demand the titles they thought to be theirs. When some were jailed, others took up arms to secure the release of their companions. Nothing came of it, except the imprisonment of the "mutineers," but the incident reveals a sense of common exploitation and a firm willingness to use force to secure a shared goal.[60] The most significant protest of the free poor occurred in the mid-1870s in the Northeast just west of the sugar zone, when a new tax imposed on the foodstuffs that peasants sold on market day, their still present fear that a national census was designed to enslave free men of color, and the use by merchants of the newly adopted metric system to cheat them of their due sparked a major revolt that lasted several months.[61]

Faced with such potential resistance from the poor, the propertied were forced to feel out the extent of their authority very carefully; one defiant gesture could even undermine their view of themselves. They worked diligently, therefore, to overcome their self-doubt, maintaining their distance-with-proximity through measures that would stress the social hierarchy and their own superiority within it. The accoutrements of status also proved effective devices for maintaining the proper relationship among those of diverse social place: through the defense of honor and rank—sometimes requiring lavish expenditure or displays of open-handed generosity, sometimes impelling contempt for the poor—the wealthy sought to validate what deference they did receive from others. At the inauguration of his plantation chapel, the barão do Paty do Alferes explained, "I could not but organize a public demonstration," and there "was no other way" than to order sweets from the city of Rio, but "only dry ones because the ones in syrup can be made here."[62] A splendid occasion could reinforce the claim to authority and garner additional clients. It not only enhanced the position of the individual but strengthened an entire system. Politics served the same purpose.

Government

Political institutions had as one principal purpose the maintenance of order, and that concern derived from the imperatives of
class rule. Contemporaries acknowledged unself-consciously that
the preservation of political order interlocked with the needs of the
propertied. A political tract recognized that planters, "notable by
the fortune you have acquired," would be "men of order, proprietors interested in preserving it."[63] The desire for obedient behavior
in the body politic blended with the requirements of employers for
docile laborers, making it difficult to know which principle supported the other. Keeping the bulk of the free population at work,
said a newspaper, would not only channel their energies toward
production but "accustom them to obedience." An industrialist
agreed, arguing that "factories are in miniature a representation of
the state. The workers are subject to a rigorous discipline that in-
fuses their spirit with the notion of order, the habit of obedience,
and respect for their superiors [so that] in their life as citizens they
respect constituted authority.... Citizens educated to respect and
obey their superiors will not think of disturbing public order."[64]
Whichever came first, proprietors saw firm governmental authority
as being in their interest.

The focus on discipline resulted from the conviction among the
propertied that the lower classes could easily be led astray. An official in the province of Ceará, lamenting the misbehavior of "the
most qualified and prestigious man" of a certain town, asked,
"What can we then expect from the ignorant masses he directs?"
Another one in Bahia similarly railed against the "most dangerous
intrigues" in which the opposition participated "to excite the passions of the inexpert multitude." Such ignorant masses and inexpert
multitudes posed a constant danger to society, for they were, as a
parliamentary commission saw it, "receptive to the voice of malevo-
lent, ambitious men who upset public order." Even when the poor
threatened rebellion, it was understood as the result of agitation by
their betters, traitors to their class.[65]

It was not only or even principally the lower classes, therefore,
who threatened social peace, for they merely responded to the
irresponsible blandishments of others. Order must be imposed

also on many of the propertied for the sake of their own class. All must learn the practice of deference. Thus, when one Cabinet asked for the dissolution of Parliament, it couched its request in the language of subjection, denouncing those tactics of the opposition that "tended to weaken the principle of authority." The Emperor as well, when considering some politicians' attacks on a particular Cabinet, proposed the creation of an official newspaper to "defend the immutable principle of authority."[66]

As members of the upper class displayed the qualities of stern but caring fathers toward their slaves, dependents, extended family members, and other clients in exchange for deferential loyalty and obedience, they saw the Emperor as fulfilling the same role for them. An endless number of their petitions ended with the suggestively humble phrase, still current today, "hoping to receive grace [*esperando receber mercê*]." The ruler played the part of a father to the entire country. One petitioner referred to the Emperor as "our common father" and asked for "paternal munificence." A provincial administrator reported the measures he had taken to aid the victims of yellow fever "so the Imperial Government will always appear as the Father of the People [*Pai dos Povos*]." And when some objected to the ancient court ceremony of kissing the king's hand, an apologist for established institutions insisted "this act of deference is not a tribute of vassalage but a sign of exceptional regard. . . . The monarch is chief, he is the father of the nation; do children degrade themselves when they kiss the hands of their parents?"[67] Senators, judges, police, and other officials each in turn willingly put on the cloak of paternal authority. The structure of family, household, and *clientela* gained legitimacy by being mirrored in that of state and universe, with authority flowing downward from God to King to household head to slave, and gratitude and obedience being offered in return. An imagined set of bonds worked to benefit, if not God, at least those humans toward the upper end of the social scale. So it was the propertied who, not surprisingly, most frequently invoked the metaphor of family that permeated political discourse. If, like the Emperor, they were successful in securing the deference that befit the head of a family, they would not require the costly open use of force to defend their class interests and maintain order.[68]

Underlying their insistence on the principle of authority lay a deep pessimism about Brazil and Brazilians. Since they saw themselves as backward, ungovernable, slothful, and anarchic, they concluded that only strong government would do. God gave Brazilians "understanding" and "liberty," said the injured members of a local electoral board, but "either through a weakness inherent in our species or through degeneration and perversity, the elements of truth are [here] transformed into lies, of justice into iniquity, of reason into error, and of virtue into vice." The Council of State, in turning down a proposed change in company law, claimed that although the proposal was "in keeping with the conditions of the English people, with their *self-government*, with the sober character of the British citizen, the cautious, pensive man who respects his own dignity and knows how to maintain his political liberty without corruption and therefore will not abuse this freedom, . . . it is our sad duty to note the truly deplorable condition of Brazil." The population, it said, consisted of adventurers, without traditions, "without the independence that characterizes Englishmen." So the Council decided to postpone any changes until "better times." No Councillor specified, however, how such times should be brought about. A petitioner for a government position in a Conservative government acknowledged that in his youth he had joined a political revolt in Pernambuco but had now "abandoned the idea of a democratic government for Brazil" because "our people have not been brought up for this."[69]

Others then and since have claimed that Brazilians lacked the education and training necessary for democracy. By implication, defects in the Brazilian's nature would have made such efforts either ineffective or impossible. Even those who desired change often despaired of success because of the alleged flaws in the Brazilian character. Just after the abolition of slavery for which Joaquim Nabuco had so long campaigned, he declared that a meanness of spirit in his countrymen subverted every effort at improvement: "There is no healthy idea in Brazil that does not lead immediately to dishonest exploitation." Two qualities, he later wrote, most prominently characterized Brazilians: "slackness [and] indolence." They wanted only "leisure, the 'freedom' to stretch out and sleep"; the political corruption of Brazil stemmed from the "national problem as a whole, that of race, of [large] territory, of climate." A government in the hands of moral men must exert a necessary discipline over such an unruly citizenry.[70]

The argument that Brazilians lacked the capacity for liberty in order laid the ground for a defense of authoritarian government. If forced to choose between liberty and order, the propertied preferred order. The state, like the family, stressed obedience and deference in exchange for benevolent protection. In the first instance this emphasis bolstered the institutions of the state; but ultimately it reinforced the entire network of patronage and the position of all patrons. Like any other measure of social control in Brazil, government action worked to strengthen a hierarchical society and to further the interests of the few. Many legal provisions defended the rights of the individual, but in practice everything depended on gaining the goodwill of an effective protector.

Regardless of regional interests, the propertied united in their concern for the maintenance of order and social peace. A widely shared view of society as a ranked order formed an essential base from which to work toward such a goal, all the more necessary since everywhere the steady and unsettling movement of people threatened notions of fixed place. The military draft, by forcing every man to seek a patron, worked toward ingraining a deferential stance among the poor. And the exchange of loyal obedience for the succor of a patron applied in every connection, including that between fathers and children. Even when the state sternly disciplined the propertied, it was understood to serve their interest paternally by reinforcing the principle of authority they held so dear.

The propertied also united in their recognition that government most ably fulfilled its purpose when it dispensed patronage in exchange for loyalty, displaying in its own structure the proper relationships of all social actors. Patronage, therefore, formed the prize over which they competed, even when they defined their economic interests in terms of exports and desired political prominence for their own region. For as long as positions of legal authority proved forthcoming, they could be confident of their ability to build a clientele and thus assure the security of their class.

Locating Power

THOSE WHO OWNED PROPERTY in early-nineteenth-century Brazil held ambivalent views about central government. If it offered them an effective tool for keeping the propertyless subordinate, it could also threaten their own authority locally. To solve this dilemma men of substance eventually made sure that they or their friends occupied the positions of power at every level of the state apparatus. Despite hesitations and reversals, by the 1840s they had unambiguously decided to throw in their lot with central power. It was a wise choice for them, since indeed the various institutions of governance they created proved a mighty bulwark against disorder. These two matters—the emergence of their belief in the efficacy of central government and the political institutions they then created—require our careful attention, for appointments to office within that governmental structure enabled the well-off to strengthen their class position and expand their individual clienteles. They made the central government theirs and then relied on its patronage to maintain their dominance locally.

Building New Institutions

From earliest colonial times the oligarchs of Brazil had been accustomed to exercise considerable power through the County Council (Senado da Camara Municipal) and to withstand the efforts of faraway governments to interfere in what they considered their affairs alone.* The first such council, chosen from among the

* I do not translate the word *município* as municipality, because that term referred not just to an urban center, but also to the surrounding area, which was

homens bons, "the respectable—and respected" to use Charles Boxer's phrase, took up its duties in São Vicente at the very moment of the colony's foundation in 1532. Its more famous counterpart in Salvador, created in 1549, almost immediately adopted an adversarial stance toward administrators sent from Portugal and, on the whole, enjoyed considerable latitude in making decisions, not least because of its influence in Lisbon itself. County Councils in more remote areas found it even easier to go their own way. From the 1740s, however, councilmen (*vereadores*) everywhere suffered a gradual erosion of their authority over matters of local interest. As leaders in Portugal, like "enlightened despots" elsewhere, sought to revitalize the imperial economy and secure more revenues, they interfered ever more frequently in county business. Even though the Brazilian-born often occupied positions of major responsibility in the imperial bureaucracy, serving also in Asia and in the mother country, and although Portugal continued to govern through the colonial elite and not really against it, energetic administration nevertheless tended to lessen the former neglect and thus diminish the room for decision left to the locally prominent. So much so that occasionally, as in 1789 in Minas Gerais, men of property schemed toward an independent republic, albeit ineffectually.[1]

By the end of the eighteenth century, property holders in Brazil also sensed some menace to their position coming from below. Even if the threat of a generalized slave revolt sprang mostly from their imagination, stories of the bloody slave uprisings in Haiti and their own knowledge of runaway communities in the interior of Brazil heightened their apprehensions. They readily acquiesced in the harsh punishment of those mulatto artisans in Salvador who in 1798 plotted to establish a republic with fraternity, equality, and liberty for all, including slaves, some of whom had even joined the movement. Most Brazilian leaders could not countenance any challenge to rule from Portugal if that would provoke social disorder, no matter how they chafed at the increasing control exercised over their lives and affairs by Portuguese administrators.[2]

Although the transfer of the court from Lisbon to Rio de Janeiro

---

sometimes of vast extent; I have chosen to use county, since a *município* roughly corresponded to the U.S. unit. The jurisdiction of a County Council included both urban and rural portions.

in 1808 at first resolved the dilemma, it eventually made things worse. The arrival of the King and the entire state machinery meant that the center of government now rested within Brazilian territory, and the mercantilist restrictions on trade with other nations ended; it also meant the immediate presence of the King's men. Minas Gerais and São Paulo, to which difficulties of transport had always provided a special barrier from bureaucratic meddling, now felt most intensely the proximity of government. On the other hand, leaders in Maranhão and Pará, who had once been able to take advantage of favorable cross-Atlantic winds for quick communication with Lisbon, discovered that travel time to the capital had actually increased. If, in one instance, local elites resented proximity, in others they felt burdened by distance. In truth an emerging sense of local interest versus central control found excuse for expression in any change. But, at the same time, the fear of slaves and the constant need to keep the poor in check remained very much alive.[3]

The split direction of oligarchic sentiment surfaced clearly in the events of the early 1820s and the immediately succeeding years. In late 1820 a liberal revolt broke out in Portugal aimed at replacing the absolutist monarchy with a constitutional one. The merchant community of Lisbon took the lead in elaborating that movement's goals, and these included, along with the creation of a parliamentary system, the reinstitution of colonial restrictions over Brazil. Even so, several prominent Brazilians supported the constitutionalist cause as a way to curtail the King's authority and at the same time prevent a radical move in Brazil toward the creation of a republic—which they saw as undermining social order. João VI acquiesced before this alliance of Portuguese and Brazilians, accepting the principle of constitutional government in late February 1821.

But the coalition of Portuguese and Brazilians soon divided over the issue of the attempts to recolonize Brazil. Once the Cortes, or Parliament, met in Lisbon, it demanded the return of João VI to Portugal. He reluctantly complied, over the objections of the Brazilian faction, leaving his son Pedro as Prince-Regent in Brazil. When the Cortes also decreed the dismantling of all the separate institutions of governance created in Brazil since 1808 and their centralization in Lisbon, the appointment of military governors in each province, and the return of Pedro to Portugal as well, the Brazilians closed ranks firmly in opposition. Among these Brazilians should be counted many Portuguese-born immigrants who had set roots in Brazil, invested there, and hoped to remain; some had been there well before the King's arrival in 1808. This "Brazilian" group consisted in the main of conservative landowners and merchants but also included a number of more liberal and even radical leaders, principally professionals and artisans, and even some mulattos and free blacks. Their alliance could not long survive.

In January 1822 the impetuous Pedro declared that he would not obey the Cortes, preferring to remain in Brazil. He appointed José Bonifácio de Andrada e Silva to head a Brazilian Cabinet. The son of a wealthy family in Santos (São Paulo), José Bonifácio had lived and worked for many years in Europe as an engineer and mineralogist. Whether from his knowledge of the French Revolution or the class interests of his family, he ably worked to find a middle way, opposing Portuguese authority while giving no ground to the more radically democratic Brazilians, whom he termed "anarchists and demagogues."[4] The Portuguese armed forces in Rio de Janeiro, outnumbered and cowed by the pretensions of the Prince, left for Salvador in March 1822. Pedro soon took further steps to untie Brazil from Portugal. He formally declared the nation independent in September, and in December he had himself crowned Pedro I, Emperor of Brazil. By July 1823 forces loyal to him had dislodged the Portuguese Army from Salvador, and soon the last Portuguese garrisons in Maranhão and Pará also surrendered. Pedro now ruled in all Brazil, although many of his backers in the provinces retained some doubts about any government centered on Rio de Janeiro, rather than in their own region.

A Constituent Assembly for Brazil, summoned in June 1822, met in May of the following year. At first the structure of government loomed as the most important issue. The assembly's members almost immediately expressed their suspicion of a highly centralized system, and Pedro fell to quarreling with them when they drafted a Constitution severely limiting the power of the sovereign. Before they had finished he acrimoniously dissolved the Constituent Assembly, promulgating instead a Constitution drafted by his own Council of State (March 1824). In fact it incorporated most of the features of the earlier draft, including a bicameral Parliament with a Senate and Chamber of Deputies, an independent judiciary, and a cabinet-style government.[5] Especially important among its changes, however, it granted the Emperor a "Moderative Power," that is, the right, among others, to dismiss Parliaments, appoint Cabinets, and choose lifetime Senators from the three candidates who garnered the most votes.

Once again succeeding events revealed that the tension between crown and country overlay another one between master and slave, between the well-to-do and the poor. When Pedro submitted his Constitution to the County Councils for ratification, Pernambucan leaders would have none of it, revolting instead and calling for a republican government with provincial autonomy. But the sugar millowners who at first led this opposition movement soon trembled at the suggestion of their urban allies—professionals and artisans—that slavery should be abolished. Equally significant, most Councils in the rest of Brazil already seemed to prefer the new Constitution, with its firm royal and central authority, to the uncertainties of a possibly decentralized republic. The revolt in Pernambuco sputtered out in six months.

Though strong central government seemed triumphant, regionalist leaders soon found other ways to oppose Pedro's authoritarianism. Indeed the Constitution itself provided legitimate means through which to express opposition, and Pedro lacked the temperament for prolonged political infighting. Dissatisfaction with his rule mounted. A particularly sore point was that in appointing Portuguese-born Ministers, he slighted Brazilians eager for power, not least in order to enlarge their control of patronage. In April 1831 Brazilian political leaders, aided by mobs in the streets of Rio de Janeiro, persuaded him to abdicate in favor of his five-year-old son, also named Pedro (1825-91), and leave for Portugal. A regency of three chosen by Parliament and hopefully more responsive to regional interests would rule during the young Pedro's minority. Central government had suffered a severe blow.

In the event, the victors in this struggle with the Emperor proved to be a moderate faction of Brazilian liberals. Although drawing principal strength from an important segment of the landed class, they also enjoyed the support and creative abilities of lawyers and other professionals. Backed by a network of Masonic-like secret societies (Sociedades Defensoras da Liberdade e Independencia Nacional), and especially strong in the provinces of Rio de Janeiro, Minas Gerais, and São Paulo, these men proceeded to institute a series of reform measures. Even before the abdication of Pedro I, they had succeeded in creating elected justices of the peace, most often drawn from the landed gentry, to whom they granted broad powers so as to weaken the crown judges. With Pedro I out of the way in 1831, they moved more boldly. They elaborated and promulgated a Code of Criminal (Trial) Procedure that instituted the jury system and asserted the right of habeas corpus. The code also allowed the elected justices of the peace to gain even more authority by combining police and judicial functions, permitting them, for instance, to arrest as well as try. The liberal leaders then reduced the size of the Army and created, to counter it, the National Guard, formed of local citizens with elected officers. Finally, they enacted a law by which County Councils would prepare lists of locally acceptable candidates to be appointed as county judges, thus regaining some of the Councils' lost authority.

By 1834 the movement on behalf of local autonomy had run its course, and an amendment to the Constitution, called the Additional Act, suggested some cautious pulling back from the earlier liberalism.[6] True, the two houses of Parliament, meeting jointly as a constituent assembly, did abolish the Council of State, a nonelected body to advise the Emperor on the exercise of the Moderative Power that many saw as the bastion of authoritarianism. And the Additional Act called for the election of Provincial Assemblies with important responsibilities, including the election of provincial vice-presidents (with presidents still centrally appointed). The powers of these legislatures, however, came principally at the expense of the County Councils, whose every measure the Assemblies could now veto.[7] Thanks to its ambiguous wording, the Additional Act could also be interpreted as giving the Provincial Assemblies the right to appoint county executives, a major innovation. Even the Councils of capital cities lost the last bit of their ancient authority, and the Council of Rio de Janeiro—not within any province but now set apart as "neutral"—fell to steady but impotent bickering with the Minister of Empire. Although the Additional Act has generally been seen as a decentralizing measure, on the whole it tended toward curtailing truly local autonomy, though not yet toward centralization in Rio de Janeiro. The propertied, in other words, now saw provincial government as the fitting place to exert their power.[8]

They soon began to discern the advantages of strong central government as well. One reason for the cautious approach even of the Additional Act had been that those leaders who had condemned centralization when it had been exercised by the arbitrary Pedro I quickly felt its appeal once they held power themselves. Furthermore, the earlier liberal reforms, in returning some decision making to the localities, had had the effect of encouraging unseemly local factionalism (especially over the election of justices of the peace), wrangles that, in sometimes getting out of hand, encouraged disrespect for the "better sort." And the principles of individual liberty could all too easily encourage social unrest.[9]

Finally and most important, a series of regional revolts, besides undermining the unity of the Empire, tended to weaken property owners' authority over the lower classes, raising the specter of social disorder. The fear of revolution quickly tempered the desire for local autonomy. Many of these regional uprisings had only vaguely defined goals and drew life principally from parochial rivalries among elites, but they easily escaped the control of those who began them. Thus in September 1831 mobs in Recife attacked Portuguese shopkeepers who seemed to monopolize retail trade at the expense of consumers. Slaves joined in, believing their freedom at hand. Although the uprising was quickly quashed, the image of social disorder left a deep mark on political consciousness. Six months later a more serious movement south of Recife, despite its conservative tenor, had the same disturbing effect. With support from Portuguese merchants in the city, its leaders called for the restoration of Pedro I, while participants fervently declared their opposition to what they saw as the godless tendency of the reformers in Rio de Janeiro. Made up of small landowners, *agregados*, and slaves, these guerrillas fought until 1835, and their principal leader continued the struggle with a small group of followers until 1850. Sugar millowners found the entire venture alarming. In 1835 a revolution broke out in Belém, where men of considerable means initiated a movement toward limited independence; but blacks and Indians became more prominent within it the longer the fighting dragged on. Their rage against whites and the rich expressed itself in widespread looting, murder, and mayhem. The government clearly understood the social import of the movement and, when it bloodily overcame the rebels in 1840, ordered the formation of a "worker corps" for all males over ten years of age who had no property or acceptable occupation. The total death toll reached 30,000, perhaps a fifth of the provincial population.

A revolt of African slaves and freedmen in Salvador in 1835 proved even more threatening. Other slave uprisings had preceded it, but none so organized or so pregnant with overtones of a racial war. Planned to coincide with a major religious festival, but discovered and thus precipitated a day early, the uprising involved hundreds of blacks, led by Muslim Africans. It was put down within hours, but the questioning of prisoners revealed unsuspected cohesion among Africans and extensive networks of communication into the countryside, greatly frightening not only whites but also free mulattos, whom the Africans had avowed to kill. The prosecutor clearly linked racial fear and class interest to political needs when he charged that the rebels had "designed in their hideouts the most horrendous plans, which, if carried out, would have resulted in the extinction of those of white and mulatto color, the destruction of government and the Constitution, [and] the loss of our properties." As a result public order appeared precarious not only in Bahia but elsewhere. In Rio de Janeiro a few months later, the Minister of Justice alerted the chief of police to rumors of similar plots there and urged "the greatest vigilance so that pernicious doctrines that can endanger the public peace shall not spread among the slaves or, much worse, be put into effect, as has happened in some provinces, principally in Bahia." [10]

The outcomes of two contrasting autonomist movements starkly display the social dynamics at work in Brazil at this time. Only in Rio Grande do Sul did the propertied remain firmly in charge of an insurgent movement. Led from the beginning in 1835 by the major cattle owners of the region, who were dissatisfied with the central government's tariff policies on jerked beef, it generally aimed, despite divisions among its leaders, to create an independent republic, perhaps in confederation with Uruguay and Argentina.[11] By 1837 that effort promised to succeed. The opposite occurred in Bahia. There a group of merchants, professionals, and Army men in the city of Salvador rebelled in 1837, demanding a federal form of government, perhaps a republic. The organization of a battalion of freed slaves, however, caused sharp dissension among the other ranks and provoked the immediate opposition of the sugar mill-owners of the surrounding region. Within weeks the movement had collapsed. Success required social cohesion and the unchallenged dominance of the well-heeled.

As the erstwhile reformers looked about, they saw discord where they had dreamt of peace, violence instead of rational discourse, dismemberment where they had hoped for confederated unity. Throughout Brazil local elites increasingly began to fear disorder more than central power. Many of their spokesmen at the capital now became conservative, all of them tempered their rhetoric, and the initiative passed to the restorers of "order."

During this very period, moreover, coffee production leapt ahead astonishingly. Coffee exports had tripled from 1822 to 1831, and increased another two and a half times by 1840, outstripping sugar as Brazil's leading product.[12] Since the province of Rio de Janeiro produced almost all this coffee, its political weight within the government increased accordingly, and many Rio planters now became adamantly committed to the goal of strong central authority emanating from their capital. Concurrently, growing revenues augmented the government's ability to assert its power. The combination of expanded resources, a renewed devotion to central power within the province of Rio de Janeiro, and a general apprehension elsewhere about social unrest or even slave rebellion provoked a brusque shift toward conservatism, a retreat Brazilians soon labeled a return, or *regresso*.

The swing toward conservatism implied a change in leadership. The Additional Act, besides restricting county authority, had called for the nationwide election of a single Regent rather than the choice of a triumvirate by Parliament. A sharp division between the Parliament and the Regent resulted from their differing electoral bases. Diogo Antonio Feijó, the first winner, although a firm champion of liberalism, proved personally authoritarian. His disillusionment in dealing with a recalcitrant Parliament while the country seemed to fall apart soon prompted him to resign. He was succeeded in September 1837 by the conservative Pedro de Araújo Lima, later marquês de Olinda. A sugar millowner from Pernambuco, Araújo Lima had consistently opposed liberal reform.

The political history of Brazil from that point until 1850 is characterized by the successful elaboration of those institutions that would ensure social order under the firm control of men of property. Araújo Lima immediately appointed a centralizing Cabinet

headed by Bernardo Pereira de Vasconcellos. Vasconcellos, once a
leading liberal, now advocated conservative measures as the only
course by which the Empire could be saved from dismemberment
and anarchy. He had come to believe that government must be
backed by those propertied classes that "in sudden changes have
everything to lose and nothing to gain."[13] Vasconcellos thus mirrored the general shift in elite opinion. In his Cabinet he placed a
landowner from Rio de Janeiro, Joaquim José Rodrigues Torres, the
future visconde de Itaborahy, and later added one of Rodrigues
Torres's close relatives, Paulino José Soares de Sousa, the future visconde de Uruguay, a judge trained in the legal traditions of the Portuguese Empire at Coimbra University. Both only in their thirties at
the time, these two men would eventually emerge as the core of the
Conservative Party, exercising their influence for several decades.
People liked to call it the Saquarema Party, after a village close to
the leaders' properties where electoral violence had secured their
triumph.[14]

First efforts toward the *regresso* encountered some difficulties.
With the help of Paulino de Sousa, Vasconcellos began drafting legislation that would undo the liberal reforms of the past ten years.
In May 1840 Parliament passed a Reinterpretation of the Additional Act. With specious justifications, it reduced the powers of the
Provincial Assemblies, especially regarding the appointment and removal of public employees. A minority in Parliament saw this measure as the end of provincial autonomy and particularly feared the
loss of patronage for regional leaders. They appealed to the fifteen-
year-old Emperor and in July 1840 organized demonstrations in
Rio de Janeiro to demand his immediate crowning, three years before the constitutionally mandated age. Since Pedro agreed, the
Conservatives found it difficult to object. The regency thus ended,
and the young boy received the crown as Pedro II. In gratitude he
appointed a Cabinet from the opposition, or Liberal Party, ranks.
It soon fell to bickering, however, and could not agree on how to
deal with the rebels in Rio Grande do Sul, for whom some desired
a general amnesty. Pedro's personal advisers then persuaded him to
dismiss the Liberal Cabinet in March 1841 and appoint a Conservative one instead. The new Cabinet once again included Paulino
de Sousa, to be joined two years later by Rodrigues Torres and another Conservative, Honório Hermeto Carneiro Leão, the future

marquês de Paraná, also a planter from Rio de Janeiro. The coffee-planting interests thus held half the portfolios.

Now it was Paulino de Sousa who counted on the help of Vasconcellos in the Senate to push through a series of conservative laws. In late 1841 he secured from a compliant Parliament passage of the most important of them: the Reform of the Code of Criminal (Trial) Procedure. This bill gave additional powers to district judges; called for the Minister of Justice to appoint county judges, who must now also be legally trained; and stripped the elected justices of the peace of most of their authority, turning the bulk of their powers over to appointed *delegados de polícia* (police commissioners) and their deputies, or *subdelegados*. These police officials were empowered not only to arrest suspected miscreants, but to issue search warrants, hear witnesses, and prepare the written case against accused criminals—the sole basis for judgments—as well as actually to judge certain minor cases. The new law also authorized the police, rather than the elected justices of the peace, to appoint the inspectors in every ward or quarter (the *inspetores de quarteirão*), thus carrying the authority of the central government, at least in theory, to every nook and cranny of the Empire.[15] Other measures included the reinstitution of the life-tenured Council of State; the doubling of the property qualification for jurors; an increase in the size of the Army; and passing to the central government the right to name each province's vice-presidents.

The final straw came with a new electoral law issued in May 1842, placing the centrally appointed police delegados on the local electoral boards to supervise the voting. The Conservatives, said an early chronicler, thus tried to "establish their electoral dominion." The opposition, sensing that through such a measure they would forever lose their chance of regaining power, felt they had no recourse but to take up arms. A revolt broke out in São Paulo, soon echoed in Minas Gerais. But the rebellion failed after a few weeks, despite the prestige lent to it in São Paulo by the support of Diogo Antonio Feijó, once Regent of the Empire, and the boundless energy of the young Teófilo Ottoni in Minas Gerais. Rio de Janeiro's coffee planters, with only a few exceptions, like the wealthy Joaquim José de Souza Breves, supported the government. Once again fear of a slave revolt dampened the enthusiasm of potential leaders.[16] Meanwhile the revolution in Rio Grande do Sul began to enter its declining phase, and the government enjoyed several successes in that long struggle. Central authority thus began to set down roots.

Even many leaders who had remained nominally Liberal now began to see the advantages of central power. In 1844 intraministerial discord led the advisers of the young Pedro II to recommend a change of Cabinets once again, and he appointed a moderately liberal one. Rather than moving to reverse the conservative measures of their predecessors, the new Ministers kept the basic laws in place. They granted an amnesty to all those involved in past regional revolts and thus brought to a close the civil war in Rio Grande do Sul. They passed a new electoral law removing delegados from the electoral boards. Otherwise, however, they made few changes in the political system (as was true also on the later occasions of Liberal dominance), much to the disgust of the more radical members of their party, such as Teófilo Ottoni.

In 1848 Pedro II once more exchanged the Liberals for the Conservatives. The election that they then supervised proved a triumph—only one Liberal got elected to Parliament—and paved the way for strengthening still further the conservative tenor of the Cabinet. Headed by the former Regent Araújo Lima, now visconde and later marquês de Olinda, it soon included (again) Paulino de Sousa and his wife's brother-in-law Rodrigues Torres. Through family and friends another member, Euzebio de Queiroz Coutinho Mattoso da Camara, was also closely tied to coffee planters. The firm leadership it exercised enabled this Cabinet to pass and enforce a number of measures, not necessarily conservative ones, that had once been too controversial to succeed. It finally suppressed the African slave trade in order to end British pressure on Brazil and simultaneously free planters from their debt to illegal slave traders; it passed a public lands law (in the event unenforced) to prevent the free acquisition of land by squatters; it pushed through a long-debated commercial code desired by the merchant community; and it undertook measures designed to attract foreign capital for railroad building in the export-oriented districts. In 1850 it ended the election of officers in the National Guard, making such posts appointive. This government thus completed the task of creating the institutions of tight central authority, institutions that remained virtually unchanged until the end of the Empire in 1889. Joaquim Nabuco, the first major historian of the period, still enthralled by the

Empire's mystique, expressed the approval of many when he said in 1898 that that Cabinet "gave birth to order in all the nation, previously anarchic."[17]

It is important to remember, however, that those at the center, as in colonial times, imposed that order through the locally prominent. Most of the time local men still occupied the official positions, even if their appointments issued from Rio de Janeiro. They had few complaints against the central government, for (as a scholar once put it regarding a later period) "centralization damaged only their opponents."[18] In this way politicians in the capital simultaneously yielded to the small-town interests of the propertied nationwide and ensured that local elites transmitted their views even to the Prime Minister.

The Apparatus of Government

Brazilian political institutions, as firmly implanted from 1850, resulted from the perceived need among men of substance for a system in which they could resolve their differences without undermining order. They consciously decided to construct a stable, centralized political system. It was not imposed on them by an abstract political elite.[19] As an upshot of the apparatus they created, power holders in Rio de Janeiro legally appointed a vast array of officers throughout Brazil. And it was through the skillful use of patronage that the capital truly emerged as center.

In considering those institutions and those places to be filled, the actions of the Emperor loom visibly large. Pedro II, tutored by men chosen by Parliament, had learned to be more alert than his father to the complex interplay of economic and political might within Brazil, while at the same time adopting the legitimizing language of the Enlightenment to describe the relationships between state and citizen. From 1850, as he came to assert his own style, he used the prerogatives vested in him by the Constitution with care not to offend the economically powerful; indeed, he worked toward their predominance. To be sure he constantly advocated moderate reforms, but Cabinet members heeded his advice only as it fit the interests of their class; he was never able—and rarely wished—to impose changes that would endanger the property that sustained authority. He took pains never to discredit his office by actions of personal immorality or moments of levity. A sober, often somber man, Pedro II directed a stream of instructions to Prime Ministers on the smallest matters, even copy-editing their instructions to subordinates. By attending to the minutiae of government, however, he demonstrated not that he wielded vast power, but that he exercised so little over any fundamental issue. In the end, when some of the propertied came to desire his removal, he slid from his throne without a blow.[20]

Yet the Emperor did play a crucial role in the political system. When the nation returned representatives to Parliament, a majority of them invariably supported the Cabinet. Only the Emperor, then, by dismissing one Prime Minister and summoning a rival, could bring in another party to control the machinery of government and thus produce an electoral victory for what had been the opposition. Nor did his choice fall automatically on a shadow Cabinet: when, in 1874, Liberal politicians then out of office met to plan their strategy, and some proposed to name a head of the party so he would become Prime Minister once Pedro II ousted the Conservatives, a wiser member of the group admonished, "We must not forget that we are in Brazil and not in England. . . . Here the head of the Cabinet will be whomever the Emperor chooses." The Emperor's role as a supreme arbiter whose decisions could be accepted without loss of face or status is consistent with a hierarchical view of society: however much one person might struggle for superiority over another, both contenders acknowledged that above them another held still higher rank. Although a politician might occasionally insist that the Emperor acted merely as the nation's "functionary and delegate, not its guide and tutor," most political leaders, at least until the late 1860s, preferred precisely that paternal image. His place had a purpose. A writer noted in 1882 that even the Emperor's so-called "personal power," that is, his allegedly capricious choice among the parties, remained "indispensable to the preservation of public peace." Furthermore, since the political parties relied on virtually the same social and economic constituency—and in some cases alternating support from identical voters—Pedro II did not threaten any social group or economic interest when he switched the party in power. Rather, he responded to the rhythms impelling or restraining modest changes in direction among political and bureaucratic leaders closely in touch with regional and local concerns and, by peacefully arbitrating among them, maintained—perhaps unwittingly—the secure political dominance of the economically entrenched. As one preacher put it, just as God sustained the harmony of the spheres through "a marvelous order that results from opposing forces [without which] the stars would fall in on each other," so the constitutional King, "placed above all passions, regulates all interests [and] maintains public order." [21]

The Emperor appointed the Council of State, consisting of twelve experienced politicians who served for life. In choosing them he relied, by custom, on nominations from the Prime Minister. Pedro II turned to the Council, in turn, for guidance on the exercise of his Moderative Power, especially his right to appoint and dismiss the Cabinet. Further, since each Cabinet either had to hold the confidence of Parliament or had to ask the Emperor for new elections, the Council of State opined on whether to grant the request. Other attributes of the Moderative Power on which the Council advised included the selection of life-tenured Senators from the three candidates who received the most votes in each province. Since any decree or law required the Emperor's sanction, and he normally consulted the Council before granting it, the Council of State (through its committees) also became an adviser to the Cabinet on many legislative matters. Sometimes the law specifically charged the Council with extra duties, for instance, approving the creation of new companies with limited liability. Finally, the Council of State acted as a court to consider cases involving disputes between branches of government and suits brought against the government, thus exercising a judicial review over the constitutionality of laws and decrees. To be appointed to the Council of State was the crowning achievement of a political career. [22]

The Prime Minister (Presidente do Conselho) selected his Cabinet members with a careful eye to balancing competing political ambitions, regional strengths, and parliamentary skills and contacts. The Cabinet then guided the policies of the government. It drew up the budget for submission to Congress. It proposed legislation for debate. It drafted the annual Speech from the Throne to be delivered by the Emperor on the opening day of Parliament. [23] Most important, the Cabinet directly or indirectly named all administrative officers, including police officials nationwide; chose all officers in the National Guard; appointed, subject to some restrictions, all judges and bishops; and authorized most military promotions. As I have already indicated, however, it would be a mistake to see it as imposing its commands on unwilling county chiefs, for Ministers had themselves risen politically by careful cultivation of these men who shared their goals. Brazilian men of wealth took an active role in politics at both the local and the national level, and one scholar, relying primarily on information available in biographical dictionaries, has been able to show that from 1840 to 1889 at least 57 percent of Cabinet members had links to land, either directly or through family.[24] The Cabinet thus remained in alliance with the local oligarchs, even as its members headed a vast system of patronage.

Its appointment of provincial presidents stands out as most decisive, for the law appropriately called them "the first authority" of the provinces. A president represented the Emperor himself and was ceremoniously received in that role when he arrived at the provincial capital: if he came by ship, it flew the Emperor's flag, and an honor guard welcomed him as he disembarked amidst fireworks and music. The law required provincial presidents to carry out directives issued by the Cabinet and ensure compliance with the laws of the Empire. Charged with enforcing the law and defending the Constitution, presidents intervened in a great variety of matters, large and small, vetoing or (later) suspending the application of provincial laws, annulling the work of a surveying crew that had established a squatter's claim to land, or specifying which public lands should be given to veterans. Presidents issued passports for travel from one province to another and answered petitions from humble fishermen for the return of their licenses.[25] Their chief function, however, was to produce electoral returns favorable to the Cabinet, and they used patronage as the principal tool in accomplishing that task. To the same end the Cabinet relied heavily on the presidents for political information and sound judgment in the appointment of loyal supporters.

Because they soon accomplished their principal task, or to keep them aloof from particular provincial factions, presidents could expect a very short time in office. They served at the pleasure of the Prime Minister and, in his constant reshuffling of the national bureaucracy, he moved them from province to province, brought them to Rio de Janeiro to fill key positions, promoted them to Cabinet posts, or shoved them into minor sinecures when he found them lacking. A significant number of presidents simultaneously held seats in Parliament and departed their provincial capitals for Rio de Janeiro at the beginning of each session, leaving the day-to-day administration of the province in the hands of vice-presidents. Six of these in each province, usually provincial party stalwarts, succeeded to the president in their numbered order.[26]

The provincial presidents' principal agents both in enforcing the law and in gathering political intelligence were the chiefs of police— one to a province—and their delegados (commissioners) in each county and subdelegados (deputy commissioners) in each parish. Each delegado and subdelegado could count on six (later three) substitutes.[27] Aside from the chief of police, these officials received no salaries but derived their personal income from their usual, private activities. They customarily lived in the locality, and preference in appointment to the post went to the "affluent."[28] In the countryside most held land and sought such official positions in order to exert added authority and extend favors, exemptions, and protection to their clients. In the cities presidents preferred to appoint lawyers or judges but occasionally found it advantageous to name military officers to these positions; they could all be expected to side with the forces of order and the interests of the propertied. By not relying on professional bureaucrats to carry out its instructions, the Cabinet kept open the lines of communication and recognized the power and importance of local bosses.

These leaders, in turn, relied on such appointments to expand their clienteles. The passage of the controversial law of 1841 that gave judicial responsibilities to delegados made them the focus of decision making for ordinary citizens. It bears repeating that delegados not only pressed charges, but also assembled evidence, heard witnesses, and presented the county judge with a written record of the inquiry on which the judge based his verdict. Besides issuing warrants and granting bail, they judged minor cases, such as the violation of municipal ordinances. Delegados could rely on powerful legal instruments to carry out their will—for instance, the right of preventive arrest for almost any crime and the right to require sworn pledges of good behavior (*termos de bem viver*) that could then, if violated, lead to arrest and almost automatic conviction.[29] Delegados could temper the severity of the law with paternalist mercy, especially for the politically compliant; but no doubt remained in anyone's mind that such benevolence could as easily turn to punishment. Their first duty was to maintain the peace: "My jurisdiction has not undergone the slightest alteration. I have imprisoned several people in order to punish them and have made those who do not properly comport themselves sign sworn pledges of good behavior," wrote one of them. A subdelegado proudly reported that he and his men placed themselves at the Largo da Saúde, a principal square in the city of Salvador, "during the busiest hours of the novenas of Our Lady of the Boa Morte in order to caution and disperse the groups of black urchins [moleques] who, I am told, gather there yelling, shouting, and mocking passersby." [30]

In imposing law and order the subdelegado relied on inspectors for each quarter or, as I call them, ward inspectors. They held authority over a minimum of twenty-five hearths each and reported to the subdelegado. They could interfere in every aspect of a person's life, although the system was only as tight as the inspectors chose to make it. They issued passes to those who wished to go to another district, and at least one of them seized a youth for impressment into the Army for having arrived in town "without the required passport." [31] The ordinary citizen secured from ward inspectors an affidavit attesting to his occupation and good behavior in order to get a license to carry a hunting gun. Ward inspectors could be expected to know who in their district had smallpox. They made nightly rounds to see that the uniformed city policemen did their job. [32] Their principal task, like that of the delegados, was to ensure public order. One chief of police stressed that ward inspectors should focus, first of all, on the "vagrants, beggars, habitual drunkards, prostitutes who disturb the public peace, and rowdies who . . . offend the morals [bons costumes] and peace of families." He also charged the inspectors with "dispersing illicit gatherings" and making sure that in "taverns and in any business house . . . there be no disorders, music, dances, shouting, gatherings of slaves, or forbidden gaming." Ward inspectors should be especially alert to knots of slaves on streets or roads and prevent slaves from "using clubs or any instruments with which they can work evil, or going about shouting, or using dishonest words and actions." Ward inspectors should, furthermore, make sure that all citizens lived peacefully, avoiding "riots, turbulence, or jeers." When order seemed threatened, a delegado might instruct the ward inspectors to "notify the greatest number possible of police in your quarter to present themselves on the 6th of September next at the barracks (the jail) armed for police service." Both men and officers had to be told what building had been designated as headquarters, since all held other, ordinary occupations.[33] That condition also meant that a particular definition of order could prevail: some people accused inspectors of using their power to secure private advantage. At least one inspector allied himself with those wishing to stymie an investigation by a county judge.[34]

The greatest local power of delegados and subdelegados derived from their right of impressment. If, as I noted in the previous chapter, the draft was the instrument of social control par excellence, it was wielded by these local police officials, typically men of property. Ward inspectors drew up the initial list of the draftable, and subdelegados, justices of the peace, and parish priests sat on the boards that completed the task, exercising their discretion on exemptions.[35] Sometimes recruitment appeared to be the principal task of police officers. In the last two months of 1859 (a period I chose arbitrarily), the president of Bahia sent thirty-five letters to subdelegados; of this number, sixteen dealt with the recruitment of draftees or the capture of deserters, five with slaves, and the remaining fourteen with a wide variety of crimes. One subdelegado in the city of Rio de Janeiro supplied his share of draftees by posting himself outside the church on Christmas Day. "When Christmas mass ended I recruited the individuals who were suitable for service in the Army or Navy, as well as those who did not present legal documents." Doubtless, like the justices of the peace who held this responsibility before them, delegados drafted men "sometimes through caprice and enmity." In any case, through this means those appointed to these official positions came to hold complete authority over the poorer sort, and such an appointment could be a powerful tool in building a clientele.[36] At the same time delegados, subdelegados, and ward inspectors, by their number, made it probable that potential leaders of local disaffection could be drawn into the framework of authority, and the system of patronage made that possible.

Unlike delegados, subdelegados, and ward inspectors who, as civilians, held purely legal authority over the citizenry, others, armed with weapons and organized into officered regiments, exerted physical force on the recalcitrant. The intimate connection between governmental centralization and social control ultimately turned on these forces, whether the provincial police, the National Guard, or the Army. Funded by provincial taxes and directly responsible to the provincial presidents, the provincial police corps served full time. Bearing various names in various provinces and over time—Pedestres, Ligeiros, Corpo Policial, Caçadores de Montanha, and Urbanos, to mention a few—they were all absorbed into the Army during the Paraguayan War (1865-70), to be recreated afterward, usually with the name of Polícia Militar, indicating their military organization, uniforms, weapons, and full-time status.[37] These corps never counted on many troops. In 1862 the corps for the entire province of Bahia had only 336 men, led by thirteen officers; almost all the men were posted in the interior rather than at the capital. Even the police chief of Rio de Janeiro province complained that his forces were stretched thin: "The Police Corps has very few soldiers. . . . The force of Pedestres is so divided up . . . that the parishes [of the capital] have only one each, and some not even this much." Nevertheless, they played a crucial role. Instructions specified that when delegados and subdelegados "need armed force to maintain order . . . they will as a rule ask for it through the chief of police," but if that proved impractical, "they will make such requisitions directly from the commanders of armed forces located in that place, going first to the Police Corps and, if it is lacking, . . . to the National Guard." For as one Prime Minister put it, "next to religion, . . . the police are the most important factor in the tranquility of nations."[38]

More numerous by far than the Police Corps was the National Guard, theoretically made up of ordinary citizens from every walk of life. Organized into companies of 60 to 140 men, the Guard was divided into a cavalry and an infantry. Administratively the Guard fell under the jurisdiction of the Ministry of Justice, although in times of war its units could be assigned to regular military duty and would thus take orders from the Minister of War. Its officers, typically affluent landowners, as we have seen, received their commissions (after 1850) either from the provincial president or the Minister of Justice, depending on their rank. The highest rank was that of colonel, later renamed Superior Commandant, one for each county. The Guard's formal purpose was "to maintain or reestablish order and public tranquility." It daily provided men for such duties as capturing criminals, conducting prisoners to trial, transporting valuables, patrolling the towns and cities, guarding the jail, and not least dispersing communities of runaway slaves.[39] An elder statesman noted at the time that the weakness of other forces meant that "in many places the greater part of police duties fall on the National Guard." Complaints regarding the arbitrary use of its powers eventually led to an 1873 law removing its policing functions.[40]

The regular Army—called troops of the first line—also provided physical force to be used against the recalcitrant. Until 1865, however, it remained relatively weak. With no real war of independence in which to establish its claim to patriotism, and indeed burdened with the memory of the Portuguese Army's role in fighting against the planter-led militia in Bahia, the Army began with a bad reputation, which was hardly improved by the mutinies of disorderly troops in the cities of Rio de Janeiro and Salvador in the 1830s. Liberal leaders in 1831 reduced the Army's size to a token force of some 6,000 men; although the Conservatives tripled that number later in the decade, its power remained limited.[41] In 1850 the president of Paraíba complained that he could call on very few soldiers for help in resisting the free colored "rebels" coming from Pernambuco, and the president of Rio Grande do Norte added, "The troops of the line are very slack and do not deserve any confidence. They are divided across the province in small detachments at the command of a few bosses [*mandões*], and many soldiers are married and burdened with children. The Police Corps is even worse and goes for months without receiving pay." The Paraguayan War led to a sharp increase in the size of the Army. As the war dragged on, moreover, the proportion of troops drawn from the National Guard fell from 74 percent to 44 percent, and the number of men recruited directly into the Army increased correspondingly, as did the number of their officers.[42] After the war the Army continued to be summoned to maintain public order, especially once the National Guard had been relieved of this duty; one politician in the 1880s even described it privately as "more apt, by its organization, background, and education, for police service than for the duties of war."[43]

The Church also depended on the government's patronage, while joining other institutions in maintaining order. There were twelve bishoprics. Following colonial precedent, the government proposed its choices for these sees to the Vatican, and Rome consecrated them. Provincial presidents similarly nominated (to the bishops) priests for a parish, so the clergy depended at least partially on political favoritism for their promotion or transfer. The Church did not collect the tithe, and churchmen received only modest salaries paid by the government, often depending on baptismal, burial, and marriage fees for their survival—unless they owned land and slaves, as many did. (Other ordained clergymen sought employment as chaplains on plantations or in the wealthy lay brotherhoods of the cities.) National leaders frankly recognized that the Church served a particular social purpose: without it, said a Cabinet member, the people, "entirely loosed from the salutary yoke of Religion would plunge down the road of vice, to their detriment and that of Society." Whereas in earlier times priests actively engaged in rebellions, by midcentury they preached order and obedience to constituted authority. As a parliamentary committee saw it, "Social conflicts are always born from the lack of subordination of man to God, of rights to duty, of reason to faith." True, in the 1870s some bishops did question whether that authority resided in the Emperor or the Pope; but the parish priest could have had little doubt that he owed his appointment to the men in Rio de Janeiro.[44]

Another pyramid of centralized control connected judicial offices. In contrast to the delegados and National Guard commanders and more like churchmen and Army officers, judges hoped for advancement within a professional hierarchy. Although they might own land, slaves, or businesses and desire assignment to locales of their family strength, they received a salary from the government and endured frequent transfers from place to place. At the top of the judicial hierarchy (aside from the Supreme Court, which heard a very limited number of cases) towered the four Regional High Courts or Relações (increased to eleven in 1873). The members of these courts (desembargadores) served for life, although measures to force their resignations were not unknown. Their replacements came from lists of the fifteen district judges (juizes de direito, literally, law judges) with the greatest seniority in that region.[45]

Most judges sat in either a district or a county court.* A district judge could count on remaining in one place for his first four years; at the end of that period he was either reassigned for a term of three years or promoted to a district court of higher rank (there were three gradations), though the promotion did not always take him to a more attractive place. Thereafter he faced the likelihood of a move once again. At any time a district judge could lose his position by being named provincial chief of police; after serving in such a position even for a short time, he would be returned to the bench, though not necessarily at his old location. He could also be retained without a seat, receiving his salary while awaiting a vacancy. District courts acted as courts of first instance for many cases, but in others they heard appeals from the county judges (*juizes municipais*). In most places a county judge also held the profitable posts of probate judge and commercial judge, but in larger centers the government named special judges to these courts. County judges held office for four years, after which they could be promoted, continued in the same rank, or let go. They could not be moved during those four years.[46] Anyway, even lifetime judges knew that the government "grants promotions and distributes graces, honors, and pecuniary rewards"; the judiciary, one writer acknowledged, could not be a truly separate power "so long as magistrates depend on a government that names them, moves them, and retires them whenever it so pleases, to satisfy the presidents."[47]

Substitute county judges (six in each county; three after 1871) were not required to have a legal education and did not enjoy tenure, receive a salary, or look for advancement within the judicial system. The law specified they should be "citizens of the place notable for their fortune, intelligence, and good conduct." They played an important role. Sometimes a county judgeship would remain vacant for months and even years, while the substitutes (according to their numbered order) carried on. Or a substitute might exercise jurisdiction in one part of the county while the county judge sat elsewhere. Since a county judge automatically substituted for a district judge in the latter's absence, a local squire could end

---

* I here translate *comarca* as district, but this judicial unit should not be confused with the electoral district (*distrito eleitoral*), on which I will have more to say below.

up, at least temporarily, occupying that post as well. Almost by definition, substitute judges entwined with local interests in the same way as did delegados and National Guard officers. In one case in a remote area of Paraíba, a third substitute county judge held court because the county judge and his first substitute were absent and the second substitute had fallen ill. He was no sooner seated than he freed an indicted assassin and threw out a case against a horse thief; the district judge appealed in alarm to the president of the province to appoint a "legally trained judge [*juiz letrado*]" and meanwhile ordered the sick substitute judge to take over judicial duties even if he had to hear the cases in his home. The district judge thus implied that a professional judge would be more loyal to the larger legal framework than were these substitutes, so likely motivated were they by their particular interests.[48]

The judicial system added substantially to the central government's power of patronage. By 1865 Brazil was divided into 208 judicial districts, eight of which then lay vacant; twenty-one additional district judges served as chiefs of police—one in every province—and another thirty-four awaited assignment. By 1889 the number of districts had increased to 461 and the judicial personnel included 521 county and probate judges, 91 High Court and seventeen Supreme Court judges, as well as 438 county prosecutors (*promotores*). In most counties the Cabinet or its delegates could appoint not only the delegado with his substitutes, from two to four subdelegados also with their substitutes, and ten to twenty or more ward inspectors, but also one county judge and his substitutes, one public prosecutor, and usually one district judge, as well as numerous scribes, bailiffs, jailers, and doormen. If those in the center still failed to hold absolute sway, they at least enjoyed a flow of information from some of their appointees regarding the deeds and misdeeds of the others, and a clear avenue for contact with the smallest hamlet.[49]

District and county judges, necessarily drawn from the legal profession, shared a common education in one or the other of Brazil's two law schools, located in São Paulo and Recife. The resulting esprit, sense of intellectual superiority, and shared forensic culture proved crucial to their role in perpetuating a favorable attitude toward hierarchy and paternalistic control. In solidifying national unity, the Empire relied especially on these law graduates, or *bacha-*

réis, with their similar backgrounds, education, and experience.* Not all went on to become judges or even lawyers, for law school provided the only equivalent to a liberal education in Brazil; many graduates entered journalism or pursued other professions. The law schools supplied the political cadres of the entire country, and most politicians held law degrees.[50]

A correct social background typically characterized these graduates, a fact of great importance in understanding who held power in nineteenth-century Brazil. Admission to law school depended as much on knowing the right people as on entrance examinations. For that matter, so did passing one's courses: as one worried father explained in 1860 to a leading planter in the province of Rio de Janeiro, "my son in São Paulo did not receive the letters that I asked of you on his behalf, as well as some I sent him. . . . He wrote to say that for the lack of them he failed Rhetoric."[51] Many middle-class youths from the cities, even a few mulattos, managed to find a patron and gain entrance, but probably the majority of successful applicants counted on well-to-do relatives. Moving the law school from the then small town of São Paulo to Rio de Janeiro, it was frankly argued, would "open the way for the lower classes to pursue their studies and place higher education and judicial employment within their reach, with grave future risk to the institutions of this country."[52] Law school certainly put students in contact with members of the economic and political elite. As Francisco Peixoto de Lacerda Werneck, the barão do Paty do Alferes, wrote his son Manoel, attending law school in 1854:

I was glad to learn that you are becoming a companion of the son of Euzebio [de Queiroz Coutinho Mattoso da Camara], whose friendship can always be advantageous. But you must also set him a good example, as studious, prudent, and well behaved, for he is an awesome eyewitness for your future. His father will always be one of our best men of state and can help you a lot later, but you must not let on that this is your motive because then people will say you favored him out of some ulterior motive, and all that you do for him will lose its merit."[53]

We do not have available the letters Euzebio de Queiroz wrote to his son, but other evidence suggests a father in politics would surely

* The term *bacharel* (pl. *bacharéis*) applied to anyone who had completed higher education, including the graduates of the engineering school and the two medical schools; but the two law schools attracted by far the most students.

advise a son to curry favor with a classmate so closely related to a man of Lacerda Werneck's wealth and social prestige. Through these contacts and later ones, even judges from modest backgrounds could establish alliances with the wealthy or find brides among the best families and thus pole-vault into the elite.

Such connections could prove crucial to a judge's later professional success as well, since his usefulness to the central government depended largely on them. For, paradoxically, although the loyalty of judges to the central government was crucial, what mattered equally was their close contact with local leaders in virtually every county seat. These connections enabled them accurately to relay the views of village potentates to the capital. Simultaneously, the locally powerful relied on judges as much as did national leaders and for the same purpose. Judges principally served, in the words of the historian Thomas Flory, as a "sliding fulcrum" through which leveraged influence could be applied in both directions. Judges built up contacts that could last a lifetime. As one politician put it, in thinking about a certain locality, "I was . . . once a judge there and have a few friends." And, of course, although judges had to decide cases in ways that countered the interests of individual property holders, they rarely if ever challenged property ownership itself; in this they reflected the shared purpose of political and economic leaders. Not only did their legal education in Roman law stress the principle of authority, but the place of property holders in society at large meant even those from less affluent backgrounds pursued legal careers precisely to join that elite, not to subvert it. That is why it is a mistake to imagine a dichotomy between the state and those who dominated society.[54]

Just as the social structure was characterized by a multilayered hierarchy, so political institutions were marked by a clearly ranked order, with the occupant of each position holding a very particular status that always placed him above or below others. I do not refer only to the elaborate ceremonies that characterized life at the court where, one of Brazil's most eminent jurists noted, the Emperor "should be surrounded by all respect, tradition, and splendor [for] the national consciousness must believe [that] he is over the social cupola, watching over the destiny of the nation."[55] To a lesser degree every public servant played a like role. The law specified in detail the uniform that could be worn as a sign of one's official position. Thus someone who sat on the Council of State could be visually distinguished from a Cabinet member. Such clothes were not reserved for rare special occasions; Ministers of State, for instance, dressed in them for their weekly meeting with the Emperor, and Deputies wore them at least for the annual sessions where they debated a response to the Speech from the Throne. A provincial president must have attracted immediate attention in his dark green coat and white pants with gold stripes down the outside of the legs, especially if he also wore his sword. Not surprisingly, those who confronted such finery in greeting a president on his arrival in a province took pains to display their own "medals and honors [*comendas e galões*]." Regulations minutely described the uniform of many bureaucrats, as well as the appropriate forms of address for their rank. The elaborate rituals of the Emperor's court and the complex rules of protocol that determined precedence and behavior among titled nobility, courtiers, judges, Senators, and Councillors of State demonstrated to the whole country that particular place formed the core of one's social identity.[56]

Centralization, rather than being imposed from the capital city, grew out of the propertied's active participation in politics at all levels, even the highest. Men of substance learned that struggles on behalf of regional autonomy often threatened to unsettle their position of superiority over others. They eventually resolved that dilemma by throwing their weight behind the institutions of central authority, while carefully maintaining their control over them. In search of order they established firm ties across regional boundaries, despite sectional loyalties. To be sure their common focus on exports may have encouraged their effort to build a state through which they could connect to foreign markets, as some who emphasize Brazil's international dependence have maintained.[57] But that interest does not suffice to explain their support for centralized government; rather, as this chapter has made clear, they chose this course because the Empire, by granting firm legal authority to men of property and legitimizing that authority with the weight of a traditional monarchy, served them better than they could expect from fragmented republics.

Ward inspectors, subdelegados, delegados, and National Guard officers worked in harmony with Cabinet members in enforcing public order on slaves and the poor. A common devotion to the crown expressed this unity symbolically, but its essence lay in national networks devoted to maintaining the principles of hierarchy, deference, and obligation. That alliance between the central government and the locally powerful explains the longevity of the system. After 1840 or 1850 any presumed division between the state and men of wealth in the various provinces must be doubted; by that time most of the rural potentates throughout Brazil had come to recognize the value of central authority, not least because it bolstered their own.

Patronage forged the essential links. Local leaders needed appointment to positions of authority to extend their clientele and advance their position within the scale of power and status. At the same time the Prime Minister in Rio de Janeiro counted on the influence of those men, even in the most remote village of the backlands, to bolster the power of the central government. For that reason a county judge's skill in connecting local bigwigs with the directors of the imperial political system could prove crucial to his own promotion to a district judgeship or eventual admission to a Regional High Court. Similarly, chiefs of police and provincial presidents, while looking to the Cabinet for their future, made sure they kept in close touch with the locally prominent. The Cabinet carefully weighed advantage in making appointments and ordering promotions, transferring some, dismissing others, always attentive to the interest of the propertied. Filling these positions with their clients, their friends, and their relatives formed the very essence of national politics. In all this, Parliament played a key role, for Cabinets had to gain its support even if appointed by the Emperor. To this end, Cabinets had to win elections.

THREE

Elections and Patronage

Throughout the half-century reign of Pedro II, Brazil enjoyed all the appearances of a functioning representative democracy. Foreign observers were virtually unanimous in praising a political system that seemed so like the bourgeois regimes of Europe. The main focus of their enthusiasm lay in the regularity of elections and in the alternation of parties in power. The government scrupulously observed the Constitution, individual rights seemed protected, and no military leader or other dictator overthrew the elected government. A Senate of some 50 members, chosen for life, and a Chamber with approximately 120 Deputies formed the legislature. Parliamentary government meant that, in practice, Cabinets had to receive the approval of the legislature in order to govern, even if the Emperor could dismiss one Cabinet and summon another; when a Cabinet failed to gain the confidence of the Chamber of Deputies, it asked the Emperor to dissolve it and call new elections. Until 1881 these were indirect, carried out in two stages: voters chose electors who met in Electoral Colleges, one to a district; electors voted for Deputies, and when a Senator died they chose three names from which the Emperor could select a replacement. Liberal Cabinets succeeded Conservative ones (when they did not join in a coalition, as they did from 1853 to 1856), and a Progressive Party, combining Liberal and Conservative elements, had some success in the 1860s. Even a Republican Party, organized in 1870, succeeded in gaining a small parliamentary representation in 1884.

Getting behind these appearances to discover the meaning of elections for the participants requires attention to several interrelated dimensions of Brazilian politics at both the local and the central level. That is my purpose in this and the next several chapters. Successfully building a following, whether locally or nationally, obviously meant securing the loyalty of others; such a loyal following could be demonstrated most effectively by winning elections. Therefore, the government—that is, the Cabinet in office—used the power of patronage to secure the election of a Chamber of Deputies it desired. And the local boss used his victory at the polls to demonstrate that he deserved to be given official positions, either for himself or his friends, while his rivals did what they could to challenge that electoral dominance. At the same time, because the maintenance of order required a generalized belief that everyone enjoyed liberty, and that opponents could reasonably hope to win elections, participants in the system emphasized the fairness of the electoral process. Efforts to ensure open and free elections, alongside a no less real concern for winning them, naturally created much angst for those in charge of the voting.

Contradictory Impulses

Nineteenth-century Brazilian political leaders in fact struggled with three conflicting impulses. First, they knew that the legitimacy of the political system rested on mechanisms that would allow all members of the elite to exercise some authority or reasonably hope to do so if they wished. Fair elections could secure that end. Second, they sensed the precarious base of the social edifice and sought to solidify it by imposing public tranquility and orderly behavior. Elections, therefore, must not lead to widespread violence, for such divisions might uncap a volcano. Third, leadership in a hierarchical society depended on public demonstrations of loyalty. Elections could not be lost. In short, elections must be fair and orderly but the ruling party must always win. In the end the Brazilian political elite resolved its problem through the skillful use of patronage to exert firm electoral control, and the principal concern of this chapter is to explore the specific techniques employed. First, however, let us be clear on one point: the country's leaders genuinely desired and believed it possible to arrange elections in such a way that the opposition could be satisfied, reckoning they had at least some voice. Holding elections at all signified that Brazilian elites cared about this matter, for otherwise, if victory for the government were assured, why hold them? Besides the other purposes to which they could be put, elections derived importance by legitimizing the structure of power. Constant efforts to legislate fair elections demonstrate a concern to open up politics to men of diverse opinion, so they would not turn against the regime.

We might think this preoccupation with elections surprising. Representative government was not a heritage from colonial times but an exotic imported ideology; and democratic principles did not fit the stratified Brazilian society, which is why the contrary belief in the necessity of imposing order surfaced so pertinaciously alongside—or above—the belief in electoral freedom. But Brazilians did persist in holding elections, and their belief in the eventual perfectability of the process remained genuine, despite all evidence to the contrary. Two considerations underlay that insistence on elections. First, like many other peoples at the time, Brazilians felt the overwhelming impact of the "Age of Revolution" and the European and North American belief in freedom. Every educated person, not just intellectuals, sensed the pull of a system of ideas emanating from the world centers of political and economic power. Precisely because of the energy of capitalism, its liberal ideology held an appeal even in areas like Brazil not central to its birth and development. A further encouragement toward liberalism perhaps lay in the fact that Brazil was so much engaged in an export economy and thus closely tied to that capitalist world. Certainly members of the upper class envisioned themselves as part of a European civilization, and it now enshrined freedom and the will of the people. There were some rare dissenters, to be sure, like the member of Parliament, who insisted that "one thing does us a lot of harm: that is the example of practices abroad. Our governments, on the whole, legislate for this land like . . . Locke for Carolina."[1] But most political leaders believed the principles of John Locke perfectly applicable to their land, if not at present, then eventually. They concluded, at least halfheartedly, that individual freedoms must be defended, the press must be open to all opinions, and elections must not only be held but be free, allowing significant rights to the minority.[2] By holding elections they defined themselves as part of the European and civilized world.

There was a second and more pragmatic consideration: with free elections came the legitimacy that could vouchsafe order. It was widely recognized that peaceful behavior could not be permanently compelled solely from above. Since some who deemed themselves entitled to power would inevitably not hold it, their protest must be accommodated if it were not to threaten stability. A means had to be devised to reassure them that their turn would come. Pedro II noted that "for the government itself to maintain order with all due authority, it must avoid unjust exclusions."[3] Public harmony required at least the belief in liberalism, if not its practice. To maintain the regime's legitimacy, the conditions of political life must assure opponents the right to voice their opinion, organize their party, and nurture the hope of victory. That hope depended, in turn, on a perception of fairness in elections. Not only did free elections, along with individual rights, encourage the politicized opposition to accept the existing system but, in a larger sense, liberalism legitimated the control of the whole society by the very few and deflected the hostility of the propertyless, where it existed. Even more important, the apparent liberalism of the regime may have assuaged the unspoken guilt of the very classes who monopolized power. Although an imported doctrine, it served a purpose and fit a need.

So it was important to assure opponents that they could sometimes win. Since it was impossible to take care of every potential adversary's ambitions, it was necessary constantly to seek new or improved legal mechanisms that would at least present the appearance of fairness in elections. Every electoral law attempted new measures to protect the right of the opposition, limit the government's control over elections, and increase minority—that is, the losers'—representation. Such an effort bespoke the social need to believe in electoral honesty. That the laws often had the opposite effect of that intended does not minimize the seriousness of purpose among those who drafted them. The rights of the minority to participate freely in elections, to have a voice, even to win here and there, formed an essential part of lawmakers' priorities.

The electoral law of 1846, which remained the basic one for thirty-five years, deliberately laid out a series of provisions designed, as one contemporary put it, to "free the voting public, preventing police agents from officially interfering in elections." Critics maintained, however, that because candidates ran province-wide, the system still prevented the minority from getting any parliamentary seats. In May 1853 José Thomaz Nabuco de Araújo, a prestigious and brilliant statesman, then a Conservative, didactically pointed out to a Parliament entirely made up of his fellow party members that any ruling party could gain from the presence of some representatives from the opposition. He urged the Cabinet in the future to support the election of "broad-minded and moderate opponents," since "this would truly place the country into the representative system, a system that cannot fail to die and be invalidated by unanimity."[4] In September of that year Pedro II appointed a Cabinet that declared it would reconcile moderate Liberals and Conservatives by making space in the system for both groups. The Conservative Honório Hermeto Carneiro Leão, visconde and later marquês de Paraná, presided over a Cabinet that included, for instance, the distinguished former leader of the 1842 Liberal revolt, Antonio Paulino Limpo de Abreu, visconde de Abaeté, alongside Luiz Alves de Lima e Silva, marquês and later duque de Caxias, who had made his name in large part by military exploits in quelling such rebellions. It also included Nabuco de Araújo as Minister of Justice. With the backing of these men, Paraná pushed through a measure in 1855—first proposed by the Liberals in 1847—calling for the division of each province into several electoral districts, each of which would choose only one Deputy.[5] Several Liberals did gain seats in the next election, and the Liberal jurist José Antonio Pimenta Bueno believed, at least in 1857, that the law's purpose had been achieved, and that it had strengthened the freedoms of the minority.[6]

Others soon noted that the measure actually gave the governing party even more power than before, because party leaders could now concentrate all their effort on a few doubtful districts. Indeed, one aspiring politician in Bahia wrote to a Cabinet member that, thanks to this law, "only the Deputies the government wants will be elected (at least in this province). . . . Therefore, if you protect me, I will be elected." In a province-wide election, he went on, he would not have feared to compete with some of the lesser candidates, "but most unfortunately it is by districts and thus the influence of the government is the *only* effective one." If, he concluded, the Prime Minister could not support him in his home district, "then assign me to another one (in the backlands), and there the *action* of the government will be even more infallible."[7] One commentator observed that the 1855 law yielded a few Deputies to the opposition "when the government commands or allows them to be elected."[8] So in 1860, just five years after that first reform, Parliament responded to such complaints by greatly enlarging the districts to form units from which three Deputies would be elected, except in the smallest provinces, where the elections would once again be province-wide.[9]

The principle of allowing some representation from the opposition endured. In 1868, with the Conservatives once again newly installed, a politician in Bahia wrote to João Mauricio Wanderley, barão de Cotegipe, who was in the Cabinet, saying, "I know how strongly you feel that we should make a just concession, [or] at least [enough] so our adversaries will not cry out that we have completely closed the ballot boxes to them." A few days earlier this politician had himself noted that it would be advisable to allow at least one of Bahia's fourteen seats to be won by a Liberal "in order to show that the election was a free one." The next year the Liberal Party proposed that the problem be solved by modifying the law so that each elector would vote for only two-thirds of the number of Deputies to be chosen in his district, thus allowing the minority some chance of winning delegates. In 1875 a Conservative Parliament accepted that proposal and also returned once again to province-wide elections. Yet the law, dubbed the *lei do terço* (the one-third law), soon provoked further criticism from the outs. One Liberal politician, ignoring his own party's role in originating this plan, even found it "ignominious for the opposition that, as a great favor, there is conceded to it a one-third representation." And, of course, a little careful planning among electors responsive to the ruling party could still make sure that all its candidates won.[10] In 1881 a Liberal government repealed the one-third provision, creating once again single-member districts in still another, futile attempt to safeguard the interests of the minority, that is, of the opponents of the Cabinet then in power.[11] The search for the kind of fairness that could command broad acceptance of the Empire's political system, and so preserve the peace, thus continued.

It was precisely toward elections that the members of the Brazilian elite most clearly displayed the contradictions that permeated their stance on liberty and order. Freedom formed an important part of their rhetoric and surfaced constantly as a theme in political discourse. Yet order remained the predominant concern; only order could truly secure liberty, since "anarchy and despotism" went together, indeed were virtually synonymous.[12] Elections exposed the authoritarianism that marbled their view of freedom, and tested the possibility for coexistence among these principles. On the one hand, of all freedoms, free elections were most vital. Yet on the other, contested elections sparked disorder that could threaten the dissolution of society. Note how the official use of force in elections could be justified: the president of Ceará, in electoral instructions sent to delegados and subdelegados, insisted that "under no circumstance" should force be used "as an instrument of coercion and terror, unless against the provokers of disturbances and of disagreeable scenes." The telling exception allowed coercion or terror against those who undermined decorum. A local electoral board captured the proper tone in reporting that the election had been "calm, moderate, and just," and force had been used only to "maintain public order," since many of those who now protested against the board's conduct "threatened to win by means of disorder."[13] If government officials, representing the party in power, believed elections could be both tranquil and fair, then, logically, disorder must come only from those opposed to the ruling party, "the side interested in disorder."[14] And they were right: only the opposition to the party in power would benefit from challenging authority. To that degree, freedom was for one's supporters.

Steps to prevent anarchy and maintain discipline at the local level could also be so easily used to ensure the governing party's victory that if an election did occur peacefully, many Brazilians assumed that it had been manipulated and their freedom compromised: the winners must have completely subdued the losers through fear. If, on the other hand, the opposition dared demand its rights, it often encountered force, to which only force could be an adequate reply; then anarchy reigned. So if elections were fair, they were disorderly, and if orderly, they were unfair. A provincial president was pleased to report that nothing need be feared in one district famous for its electoral "turbulence" because one party would simply not participate in the election. But lamentably, he added, in another district the Regional High Court had granted the appeal of over 800 persons to be included in the list of registered voters and had thus encouraged the opposition to believe they had a chance of winning; this they would now strive to do "by any means." [15]

Be that as it may, the official emphasis on liberty, on free elections and other freedoms, did succeed in establishing the legitimacy of the political system for a long time. Enough liberty existed, or was thought to exist, to purchase compliance. Losers in elections did not fail to protest, but they did not revolt on any large scale, at least not between 1848 and 1889. In 1876 Manuel Pinto de Souza Dantas complained that "never was the electoral farce in this poor Brazil any greater or more indecent," going on to say that "the people suffer, political and civil guarantees are taken away, [and] the country is a prisoner of an intolerant and reactionary party." Yet Dantas never supported any plot involving the violent overthrow of the government or Cabinet. Indeed, when in power he managed elections as well as anyone. As one sardonic writer explained, when Conservatives held power, Liberal leaders "tell those below, 'Shut up,' for soon we will rise, and then we will bite in our turn." [16]

A final impulse further complicated political practice. Those in power could not afford to lose elections because the measure of a man depended on the extent of his following, and a lost election would visibly reduce that retinue. To be dismissed by one's superior in government could be tolerated, for that was as it should be; but to be rejected by one's own followers indicated a failure of leadership, of strength, of character, and ultimately of clientage itself. Precisely because the local elite frequently shifted and renewed itself, the strongest individual within it constantly needed to assert his authority by electoral victory. At the Cabinet level the voters' rejection undermined the very hierarchy elections should uphold, whereas to be dismissed by the Emperor reinforced it. A loss at the polls implied that those below could, by their own effort, come to the top; such an example would be much too dangerous when witnessed by the propertyless. It never happened. Neither the Cabinet nor a local boss could tolerate any doubt about the power to command. As one contemporary noted, the majority on the electoral board would necessarily ask, "What do they expect? The board is ours; we must certainly win the election, or lose our moral authority [*sob pena de desmoralizar-nos*]."[17] For dominance must be visibly maintained and victory assured even in apparently free elections. The government usually swept the field and always won a majority in Parliament. As Prime Minister in 1886, the barão de Cotegipe shrugged off those critics who found the Conservative victory that year suspiciously uniform: "As for the attacks of the opposition, they cry out because they hurt."[18]

Finding a way to satisfy these conflicting demands demonstrated the genius of Brazil's political operators. They worked in two ways. First, the legality of all elections could be reconciled with the need to win elections if those in charge of each formal step of the electoral process owed their allegiance to the Cabinet and always tilted toward the ruling party's interest. That dependence maintained an election's legal basis, and challengers encountered overwhelming obstacles in attempting to discredit its results. Second, the use of patronage could also be used to deflect potential opposition by placing its would-be leaders in positions of authority within the government. Doing so allowed elections to be carried out with all legality while delivering Deputies to Rio de Janeiro who would support the Cabinet. Patronage made it possible to reconcile victory with order and apparent fairness.

The Strategy of Patronage

The great effort at exercising patronage began, in a sense, with the Emperor himself. He took a place atop the "great pyramid," as one jurist called it, by appointing the Cabinet. The Moderative Power (which he exercised in consultation with the Council of State) included the right to "freely name and dismiss the Ministers of State" and dissolve the Chamber of Deputies and call for new elections. From 1840 to 1889 Pedro II, always with the advice of the Council of State, dismissed Parliament eleven times; and seven Parliaments served their full four-year terms. A total of eighteen national elections thus took place during his reign. Since the Cabinet that supervised elections could, by its use of patronage, get the Chamber of Deputies it wanted, it followed that, as one politician ironically commented at the time, "the best and most valued prerogative of the Moderative Power" consisted of "the right to elect representatives of the nation." In 1868 Senator Nabuco de Araújo,

José Thomaz Nabuco de Araújo (1813-78), 1861

now a Liberal, succinctly condemned the "fatal syllogism" by
which "the Moderative Power can call whoever it wishes to organize the Cabinet; the Prime Minister makes the election; that election produces a majority. Here is the representative system in our
country!"[19]

The Prime Minister captained the electoral effort, for his political
life depended on it. He chose his Cabinet with elections in mind,
and no one doubted the results. As Paulino José Soares de Sousa
(later visconde do Uruguay) wrote privately to a friend in 1852:
"The opposition struggled furiously in the election here, with lots
of means. We defeated them completely because we're in the government; if they were in the government they would have won completely. . . . That is the system." In 1866, when the "pure" Liberals

struggled against the Progressive Party, a politician noted that "if the Cabinet is *pure*, the election will take on that color . . . and if it is progressive, those elected will be progressive." When a Prime Minister noticed the ability of a young aide, he said to him one day: "We need to make you, at least, a Deputy." And he did. Another politician promised a friend seeking health in the spas of Europe: "If our friends rise to power, you needn't hasten your return in order to secure your election. Carry out your second cure at Carlsbad and return well." One critic of the regime summed it up: "The representatives of the nation merely represent the Cabinet." [20]

The Cabinet always secured favorable electoral results because it held the power to make all other appointments. Three sorts of positions required its attention. First, certain posts directly controlled particular aspects of the electoral process. Second, those who filled some places—often the same ones—could use their authority to affect the behavior of voters, influencing and even forcing their vote. Finally, voters or, rather, their patrons and electors could be won over by the grant of desirable public offices for themselves or their clients.

The Cabinet appointed or controlled the appointment of a great number of people who legally played a public role in elections. Even before the dissolution of a Parliament, the Cabinet took pains, "by naming presidents and chiefs of police that it trusts, moving district judges, . . . firing some [public] employees and rehiring other ones, . . . to proceed to all the preparatory acts necessary for the good outcome of the election." One vociferous critic, Aureliano Candido Tavares Bastos, decried the system whereby "a judiciary dependent on the executive, [and] political, administrative, and police centralization assure the obedience of the nation, and are enough—along with the help of military and religious corporations—to consolidate the supremacy of the executive, that is, the domination of the crown." [21] Of course, the system did not always work with the certainty ascribed to it by either critics or supporters, and in particular places and at particular times the government could lose an election. After all, a very large number of people shaped the outcome, and arrangements sometimes went awry. Local rivalries also had to be taken into account. Effective control of Parliament, however, never faltered as long as party members there remained united.

To secure a cooperative Parliament, the Cabinet relied most of all on the energy of provincial presidents. A contemporary observed that "the most unknown citizen, once named president of the province, becomes immediately and by this simple fact the only electoral power in the province." Pedro II noted that "the presidents serve principally to win elections," and he expected them to be fully informed and involved in electoral organization, although he claimed that "those I know to have interfered in elections will never again be presidents if my opinion prevails."[22] His opinion apparently never prevailed. Sometimes berated for ordering the presidents about for electoral purpose, Cabinet members faced equal condemnation from their supporters if they did not: "Our friends lost the election because the province did not have a president [and because of] the indescribable ineptitude of the vice-president." Depending on one's political preference, a person looked forward to the arrival of a new president with fear or hope: "We are trying to put the finishing touches on our ticket for provincial assemblymen; much depends on the president who is about to arrive. We very much hope it is Tiberio, or another good friend. But whoever it is, stress to him the need for serious cooperation toward the victory of our ticket."[23]

Good presidents already knew their task. In 1871 the president of Rio Grande do Sul wrote to the Prime Minister to report on the deep divisions in the Conservative Party there and the lack of any leader capable of bringing the factions together. He confidently added, however, that "since I, as the political delegate of the Cabinet over which you preside, have supreme control of the party, I easily substitute in the absence of another chief." Therefore, he concluded, all the local factionalism would not be "an obstacle to the realization of the political thought of the Cabinet . . . when it has to present itself in the electoral arena." Not all presidents liked doing what they had to do, and one, writing from Pará, wished he could "free myself totally from party concerns and the consideration I must render to the *friends* of the government." Another president, this one in Minas Gerais, in forwarding to the Cabinet "a summary of the information that I have collected on the candidates who present themselves in each electoral district," added that he hoped to "be discharged as soon as the electoral campaign for

Deputies is over," contending that for urgent personal reasons he had to leave office.[24]

Once the president had taken up his post, he would initiate electoral action at all levels. Energetically exercising his legal right to watch over the proper execution of the laws, and always appealing to their letter if not their spirit, he could dismiss a justice of the peace who would normally chair the meeting of the Electoral College on the grounds that he did not reside in the parish. Or a president could remove the chairman of a local electoral board because he simultaneously held another public position that had been declared incompatible with such authority or even on the grounds that a person indicted for a crime, although he could vote, could not preside over the board.[25] Sometimes all the necessary changes could not be made in time. In such cases a president had the surprising authority to postpone an election, rescheduling it for a more opportune time, although legally not beyond three months. He could also rule on the legality of elections for justices of the peace and for county councilmen—and thus on who would serve as chairmen of the parish electoral boards and who would tally the votes of the Electoral Colleges. Such authority could prove crucial at election time. A president's decision could be overruled by the Minister of Empire, as well as by the courts, but in the meantime his was a power to be feared.[26]

The appointment of judges provided Cabinets with a still more powerful lever within the electoral machinery. Regional High Courts heard appeals from the registration procedure and ruled on cases involving charges of illegal behavior at elections. Endless arguments centered on the presence of allegedly false voters or *phosphoros*, and High Courts made the final decision. A political leader in Bahia wrote to the Prime Minister suggesting the appointment of certain judges to one High Court because "we are now in a minority and fear injustice on appeals from the registration process." A Conservative president reported from Minas Gerais that, "because the Liberals count on all the justices of the High Court (except Dr. Belém), their arrogance steadily grows worse."[27] By deciding on the legitimacy of registration procedures, a court could "include in the registration an increasing number of *phosphoros!* Just from the parish of Sant'Anna [a High Court judge] has admitted, in this last revision, nearly 200!" Regional High Courts also ruled on the validity of an election and could declare it null and void. "I was bowled over," wrote an experienced politician, "by the news of what the High Court had done and the small number of electors to which the province of Rio de Janeiro was reduced. What will be, in view of this, the result of the election in that province? Is there no limit to partisan passion? And then, later, they complain." [28]

District and county judges also exerted a powerful force on electoral results. District judges could be installed in difficult jurisdictions to bring about an electoral compromise, but more often they appear to have unabashedly sided with one faction or the other. The president of Rio de Janeiro province wrote to one of his district judges in 1860, alerting him to some planned shenanigans in his district and instructing him to go to the troubled parish, because "it is better to prevent than to punish such abuses." In Bahia in 1856, when a group of electors who had been refused their voice in the Electoral College came to lodge their complaints with the district judge, he told them that he had orders from the government to "receive no protests," and allegedly ordered the notary public to issue false statements against their plea. Presidents reported with particular care on the political preference of each county judge. In Rio Grande do Sul a newly appointed Conservative president began work immediately by carefully going through the list of existing judges and their substitutes. Then he canvassed local party leaders for their suggestions for substitute county judges, delegados, and subdelegados. The answers proved predictable: "these three," said one respondent, should not be kept on "because those two are extreme Liberals and this one is doubtful"; another made a list of potential replacements, saying "the quality of any of these citizens is good and all are Conservatives." [29]

The law, as I have shown, attempted to circumscribe the government's right to move judges and severely limited the power to dismiss them. Still, it left enormous room for maneuver. Even a judicial promotion could be used to harm one's enemies: "The much touted appointment of Dr. Affonso de Carvalho to a faraway High Court was made, it is said, so he cannot preside over the process of counting the votes." One Deputy alleged that some remote judicial districts of the far interior had been purposely raised to the highest rank to make such transfers of district judges legal—places "whither to later exile those judges, now in excellent districts but of second rank, who incur the displeasure of the government."[30] Occasionally the government resorted to more forceful means: in 1862 João Lins Vieira Cansansão de Sinimbú, a Liberal Minister of Justice in a compromise Cabinet, imposed forced retirements, with pay but without office, on many tenured judges. With electoral purpose in mind, the Liberal Cabinet in 1844 transferred 52 out of 116 district judges; in 1848 the Conservatives transferred 70.[31] County judges—who were untenured—were naturally even more vulnerable than district judges. As one letter writer put it in 1878: "All the [county] judgeships in Piauí are filled by judges who have finished their four-year term." Now, with the "rise of the Liberal Party," these places could be filled with "friends of our party." The candidates knew very well that the replacement of county judges offered the key to their election. Hoping to become a Deputy, Manuel Pinto de Souza Dantas suggested that his brother be named county judge in the town of Pombal (which means dovecote): "without a stick or a stone he will call the *doves* to our banner."[32]

In all these ways the Prime Minister, acting either directly or through others, could almost determine the results of elections, and do so entirely within the law. He appointed the provincial presidents, and they could undo the election of justices of the peace (who presided over the electoral boards and Electoral Colleges) and of county councilmen (who controlled the appeal from the registration process and—in the cities that headed voting districts—tallied the results from the Electoral Colleges). With advice from the presidents, the Minister of Justice could move and remove county and district judges, as well as those who sat on Regional High Courts, and thus obtain favorable rulings on the legality of any electoral procedure.

The Power to Coerce

An even more direct way in which the party in power could shape electoral results was by controlling offices that, although not involved in the electoral process, had influence over voters. In the absence of a secret ballot—ballots consisted of lists of names deposited in the ballot box in full view of all spectators—government pressure could be highly effective. Although "the simplest rustic knows how to palm one ballot in order to deposit another one previously received,"[33] such an action constituted disloyalty and involved serious risk. Most voters would not have had sufficient independence to keep the contents of their ballots secret. One member of Parliament described how "the *phosporos* and the 'police-voters' purify the electors: ... The police take charge of this through weak or dependent voters who can be intimidated or threatened, or through those who should [really] deserve the government's ill-will, the potentates of hamlets and parishes." In these words the speaker also suggested how local and central interests intertwined. On the other hand clashes between local leaders, combined with the huge extent of national territory, meant that appointees might not always act as instructed. One politician noted that in elections for provincial assemblymen, for instance, "local interests enter in a lot, and the pressure of the government on the electorate is not so strong or so systematic as it is for the election of a Senator in the entire province." Moreover, elections in the cities proved hard to manipulate. Conservatives acknowledged that the city of Rio de Janeiro formed the "stronghold of dissidence." Over all, however, the Cabinet could count on favorable responses through careful appointments to office.[34]

Practically every public office had, by definition, power to exert sanctions or grant rewards. Whether occupants routinely used these powers to win elections is more difficult to prove, but the bits and pieces of information that have surfaced suggest that contemporaries saw every appointive office in terms of possible electoral gain. Some even prevailed on their subordinates in the public service. An inspector of the customshouse, for instance, organized his workers into shifts and then, along with Conservative chiefs of other bureaus, used "twelve guards and nightwatchmen of the customshouse to take [them and] many other employees of the Treasury, Navy, and Telegraph, under constant guard, to the ballot box. . . . Our adversaries thus intimidate Liberal voters."[35]

Even faculty members in the law and medical schools could have a significant influence on voters. The president of São Paulo reported in 1861 that one district judge fell under the sway of the law school faculty because of his hope for the academic success "of his two sons, one of whom is in the first year and the other in the third, and of a son-in-law in the fifth year." He added that six professors "presented themselves as candidates in the last general elections, winning principally by relying on their power to pass or fail students at their discretion." Faculty at the medical school in Bahia exercised similar powers, and one Conservative worriedly noted that the school was "becoming a nest of Liberals." Manuel Vitorino Pereira, the Liberal political leader there, whom a Conservative accused of being absolutely "possessed" and ready to "openly persecute and fight everything that is Conservative," relied on his brother, the vice-director of the medical school and Vitorino's "blind instrument," to "politick even in the distribution of examining teams!"[36]

With these realities in mind and driven by the constant concern for reducing the charges of illegitimacy, Parliament declared a number of positions off-limits to candidates for elected office, forbidding the holders of certain posts from running for office in the districts over which they held authority. By an 1855 law these "incompatibilities" applied not only to the presidents of provinces and the heads of provincial secretariats, but also to commanding officers of the National Guard, Army generals, Treasury inspectors, chiefs of police, delegados, subdelegados, and district and county judges. Those who wished to run had to resign a specified number of months before an election.[37] In response at least one candidate felt it advisable to ask for "an assignment that can lend me some prominence . . . since the new law of incompatibilities . . . somewhat hampers the ambitions of judges."[38]

Some notion of how public positions seemed susceptible to political purpose can be inferred from the steadily expanding list of incompatibilities. In 1860 legislators added probate judges, as well as the substitutes of all the above officials; in 1875 they expanded the list, no doubt in response to complaints about influence over voters, to include bishops, vicars, custom inspectors, Regional High Court judges, public prosecutors, and even inspectors and directors of public education; and in 1881 they added the general director of the national Treasury, the chiefs of the national bureaucracies within each ministry, the heads of all tax offices, the administrators of the Post Office, teachers in the law and medical schools and all other institutions of higher education, and the judges of the ecclesiastical courts.[39] Many commentators, however, questioned the effectiveness of these laws. As Joaquim Nabuco put it, the law forbidding provincial presidents to run for Parliament in their own provinces led to the formula of "mutual election: elect me and I will elect you." In any case, given the Cabinet's power to squash protests from the opposition, political actors often ignored the law or, as one observer explained, "the incompatibilities were left only for adversaries." A Deputy noted in 1875 that no one had ever been refused a seat in Congress because of these laws.[40]

Failing all else, those in office could use outright force to coerce voters. The use of violent methods, it is true, had the disadvantage of undermining the claim to legitimacy and thus threatening the larger social interests elections served. Sometimes, however, the risk seemed worth the gain and, in any case, one could always rely on the pretext that force had been needed to maintain order.

The government sought to influence voters through the appointment of those capable of using force against them: first of all the chiefs of police, delegados, subdelegados, and ward inspectors. As a member of the Council of State acknowledged in 1868, with a Conservative Cabinet named to replace the Progressive one, he "could not imagine the possibility of there being an election . . . without a general turnover in administrative agents from the ward inspector to the highest police official." Contemporaries generally agreed that if a new party took over the Cabinet, "it cannot fail to change the immense phalanx of police authorities or be condemned to commit suicide." The presidents bore principal responsibility for making these police appointments. In preparation for elections in Ceará, a president dismissed "3 public prosecutors, 5 delegados, 3 assistant public prosecutors, 10 or 12 subdelegados, 2 jailers, and one administrator of the public jail in this capital."[41] Aside from providing information to the registration and electoral boards, none of these officers had an official role in the election process. Their importance derived rather from their legal right to marshal force and thus primarily from their ability to threaten or "pressure the voter." A delegado in São Paulo province got ward inspectors to "intimidate the voters to receive, at the right time, the ballots from the delegado, threatening them with 15 days in jail and a 30 milreis fine [U.S. $15.60] if they failed to do so." So it became the common view, as one critic reported, that these police officials set out to "intimidate" the people at election time: "voters who do not yield to their demands are invited to go pass a bad night under guard." Another observer said these functions gave the police the power to "make elections."[42]

The delegados threw themselves happily into the electoral fray. It bears repeating that delegados, although centrally appointed, usually came from the local squirearchy and each headed a local clientele. To be given legal authority to screen out voters or disarm adversaries greatly aided their attempts to build a following, even if they always acted in the name of order. In 1863 a subdelegado in a far western corner of Bahia reported that although "spirits are somewhat overexcited, . . . I intend to make sure the election takes place placidly." He later recounted his method: when the chairman of the electoral board summoned him to "maintain tranquility and the security of the ballot box at the parish church" (the normal voting place throughout Brazil), he had posted three of the six men from the provincial Police Corps who had been assigned to his district "at the main doors of the church . . . to search all those who came in and forbid any armed person from entering," and set the other three to guarding "the weapons [seized] at a spot outside the church." The president of Ceará authorized delegados and their deputies to extend their surveillance beyond the church doors, that they might "gather up" any "drunk" near the church and search all persons suspected of bearing "forbidden weapons." It was up to the delegados to decide whom to search.[43]

In the National Guard the government found another important means of influencing elections. "The easiest way for you to count the elections as won here is for you to name Captain ——, who has a large following and much honor, . . . to the position of superior commandant and myself as chief of staff, removing Lieutenant Colonel João ——. If you cannot make this appointment before September, give me orders and the necessary men and . . . I'll change things around here even by force of arms," wrote an ambitious local leader.[44] A principal electoral responsibility of provincial presidents, therefore, consisted of weighing appointments to the officer corps of the National Guard. João José de Oliveira Junqueira, when running for Deputy from Bahia, insisted that for his party to be successful, "the superior commandants of the National Guard, the commandants of the [Police] Corps, and the [civilian] police personnel should be changed, the sooner the better." Later, when he was himself in the Cabinet, Junqueira boasted that he was making a number of appointments to the Guard in preparation for upcoming elections.[45]

The regular armed services provided a final instrument of force to be used by the government at election time. As a first step, Army officers could affect the votes of their subordinate officers (the rank-and-file did not vote). As reported by the Conservative president of Rio Grande do Sul in 1871, a veteran general of the Paraguayan War—Manuel Luis Osório, the marquês do Herval—pushed the Liberal cause among his officers in the province, while another one used his position as inspector of troops to "exercise a very decisive influence" on them. So political purpose quickly surfaced in military appointments. When the marquês do Herval became Minister of War in 1878, he unabashedly shuffled military personnel around, down to second lieutenants, based on their political preferences. In 1882 his successor, also a Liberal, received a letter from a fellow party member in Pernambuco asking that a certain Army major be named director of the War Arsenal in Recife. The letter writer added, "We should prepare ourselves for being placed in the opposition by creating elements of force and support. . . . Major ———, when he was adjutant at the War Arsenal during the time of the Conservatives, neutralized political persecutions against our fellow party members."[46]

Only a thin line at best separated the purpose of ensuring order from that of winning an election, and the military played its part. In 1860 opposition candidates waged an animated campaign in the city of Rio de Janeiro. Teófilo Ottoni, a leader of the 1842 Liberal rebellion in Minas Gerais, had twice been passed over for Senator, even though he had received more votes than either of the other two candidates on the "triple list" presented to the Emperor. He had become a symbol of dissidence, and in 1860, then fifty-three years old, he captained the campaign in the urban districts of Rio de Janeiro. Using a white handkerchief as his symbol, he successfully mobilized the urban populace. He found an ally in Francisco Octaviano de Almeida Rosa, thirty-four, the mulatto son of a physician, who had risen in the Liberal Party thanks to his keen mind and legal skills, but even more because of his biting commentaries as editor of a party newspaper. The candidacy of these two men loomed as a direct challenge to the Conservative government; as tempers flared threats to order seemed a greater danger than the loss of a seat or two in Parliament. The Minister of Justice informed the city's chief of police that he had asked the Minister of War "to send some help from first-line troops to the Police Corps . . . for patrols that should make the rounds on the 7th, 8th, and 9th of this month," that is, on election days. Furthermore, the police chief could call on other troops at the barracks "for any extraordinary occurrence." He added that "the firmness and energy of the [civilian] authorities are better than the employment of force," thus admitting that an appeal to the armed services confessed failure. At a Cabinet meeting members laid out exactly which units were to be ready for action in the city, parish by parish. For example, in the turbulent, lower-class district of Sant'Anna there would be "2 patrols of cavalry and 3 of infantry within earshot of a whistle, and 30 men . . . posted at the barracks in the Campo [de Sant'Anna]." The doodle marks of the Minister of Justice ("*Phosphoros* / Petition / Firemen") can still be found to suggest that the appearance of allegedly false voters would require measures to restrain the angry crowds. His notes continued: "At the central police station—30 men of the Police Corps for any special mission and 20 plainclothesmen on call by the chief of police to be used in the various parishes." The election proved turbulent nevertheless, and Ottoni and Octaviano emerged victorious.⁴⁷

The election of 1860 also proved challenging to Conservatives elsewhere in the country, and leaders repeatedly turned to the regular armed services to "maintain order." The president of the province of Rio de Janeiro asked the Minister of the Navy to "order a warship to anchor near the parish of Ribeira and the Saco de Jerumerim and [to instruct] its commander to come to an understanding with the respective authorities [there] in order to lend them any help that may be necessary toward maintaining peace and quiet, should it be disturbed." The president of Espírito Santo was more cautious, insisting that the armed forces he sent to Itapemirim act only when local civilian authorities asked for help "in writing" and not be used to favor one "local party" against another. In Ceará, as in Rio de Janeiro, the provincial president resorted to dispatching troops of the first line to various points. And in Pará an irate district judge reported that the delegado had come to the parish church accompanied by four soldiers, "all second corporals as indicated by the bright wide stripes they wore on their sleeves," thus to intimidate the voters.[48]

Complaints inevitably surfaced against the military role in elections. One electoral board included in its minutes the protest of its minority members that on January 10, 1858, "there was placed at the doors of the parish church a force of the line composed of fourteen soldiers with bayonets in place, commanded by Lieutenant Figueiredo, on orders from the delegado, . . . and they closely searched all the electors and substitutes who arrived there to form the electoral board; . . . thus terror spread and the people suffered coercion." Thirty years later the chairman of an electoral board reported that when he arrived at the place designated for the election, he found it closed and surrounded by the "public forces presently assigned to this city and composed of soldiers of the line and police, all of them armed with carbines and bayonets, the surrounding area being filled with armed *capangas* [electoral thugs]." The soldiers told him they stood there "on orders from above," and the building remained closed all day.[49] The recognition that armed forces were used not merely to maintain order but also to impose the will of one group over others is reflected in the frequently repeated provisions of the law that forbade the "movement of troops" or any "show of military force" within a radius of one league or six kilometers of the voting place. Nevertheless, as one contemporary observed, "at the whim of the provincial president, detachments of first-line troops, of the National Guard, or of the police create the most docile and regimented voters."[50]

For being so feared, recruitment into the National Guard or regular armed services early became the preferred threat with which to win electoral support. Such a specialized use of this general means of coercion merits specific attention here. One statesman maintained that the authority to call up men for service in the National Guard could prove a "terrible electoral instrument," which "those who have much power locally" and are usually "chiefs in the National Guard use to their own advantage." Such allegations are backed up by many specific examples in the contemporary records. One National Guard captain allegedly tried to force "a Conservative voter to accept a ballot of the Liberal Party, threatening him with imprisonment and Guard duty because this voter belonged to his company."[51] In 1846 lawmakers found it necessary to specify that for the two months before any election and for one month afterwards there should be no impressment into the Army or Navy. Local officials, however, often ignored or evaded the law. One district judge reported from São Paulo in 1860 that the delegado used "recruitment . . . to terrify the people . . . in order to oblige them to vote, like him, in the Liberal Party." When the judge admonished him that according to law no draft should take place at election time, the delegado replied that "only at election time can it be carried out, since that is when the individuals who are on the roll of recruitable ones turn up." [52] The Paraguayan War, by increasing the demand for soldiers, heightened opportunities for electoral pressure. "The inefficiency of such a recruitment system as a way of filling the ranks of the Army has been proved over and over again," concluded one observer; "but as an electoral tool its efficiency is beyond doubt." [53]

Force had its major use in the opportunity it opened up for the exercise of benevolent restraint. If used too frequently as a coercive measure, force lost its effectiveness; but if held in reserve, it could evoke gratitude. Reportedly one delegado ordered a sweeping recruitment effort whenever elections drew near. "Do you think," asked a commentator, "that the ranks of the Army were filled with such a levy? Not so. The fathers, mothers, brothers, and other relatives of the recruits rushed to throw themselves at the feet of the delegado, and the good man, touched, always ended up satisfying them 'for this time,' and received the blessings and sincere thanks of all those people. They were definitely people on whom . . . he could count in the next electoral campaign." One provincial president explained that officers routinely excused their men from service in the Guard if they "had helped them in the elections." [54] As with every power of compulsion, its true use lay in exempting those who proved loyal and obedient.

Rewarding with Positions

In some ways the conventional use of patronage, the granting of positions as prizes and rewards for electoral support, proved even more effective than the gift of positions that directly controlled the voting process or held the possibility of pressuring voters. For this kind of benefit addressed the interests of local patrons and thus appealed more immediately to those who would always exert systemic authority over voters, as over others. The most desired positions extended the authority of the appointee and thus attracted clients to him by the very act of being granted. The patron's search for appointive offices and for electoral victories formed the two sides of his struggle for clientage: securing appointments would produce loyal followers, who demonstrated their fidelity by voting as they were told; electoral victory demonstrated local authority and helped secure appointments to office.

Political leaders regularly used appointments as rewards for the party faithful and their relatives after an election. Commissions in the National Guard were especially sought after. Sometimes candidates offered positions in advance to those who would help them in elections; one commandant alleged that the Liberals had once "promised the same post to 10 or 20 individuals." The collections of laws, wrote one muckraker, brimmed with edicts "creating, dividing, and incessantly subdividing the commands, . . . so more officers can be appointed to broaden and perfect electoral influence." It was not easy to counter the appeal of such commissions. The marquês do Herval tried to win over some electors who had received commissions in the National Guard from the Conservatives saying, with heavy-handed flattery, "I am sure you do not place more importance on the fictitious official position the government has given you than on the affection of your old friends, comrades, and party co-workers, since you do not need an official position to have genuine social importance and be well considered."[55] Affonso Celso de Assis Figueiredo, later visconde de Ouro Preto, maintained that even after the National Guard lost its police functions in 1873, positions as officers remained "highly honorific distinctions with which the parties guerdon their best ward heelers." Indeed, appointments as National Guard officers so consistently went to the electorally prominent that the very word *coronel* came to be synonymous with political boss.[56]

Many other miscellaneous positions could be used as rewards or promised rewards as well: "With a little place on the Supreme Court and a few small touch-ups at the tax office, the happiness of the Conservative candidates in this capital would be *complete*." A commercial concession, said one candidate, "will bring me three votes [in the Electoral College]: everything now is elections." And often the filling of one job brought with it the right to fill others. Thus one letter writer, in recommending someone to a post, noted that the position, "in addition to being lucrative, is of major political importance for the south of the province, [since through it we can] accommodate many fellow party members and friends." Relatives shared in the bounty. A successful candidate in interior Bahia sought a position for the brother of a man "to whom I am much obliged because he was entirely ours."[57]

So the Cabinet ultimately came to control local elections through its benevolence to local bosses. Having received a position, they were bound to those who had granted it to them. A certain "nomination . . . did not fail to help him understand that kisses are not answered except with hugs," wrote one politician. About another case he allowed that disloyalty would not be tolerated: "I'll take care of him if by any chance he forgets the benefits received." A measure of the Cabinet's task can be found when it was not fulfilled. A Conservative politician drew a new Prime Minister's attention to the need to restore a certain Conservative boss to the position he had earlier held in Lençois, in the far interior of Bahia, a position from which the man had been removed by the Liberals. If the incumbent "continues to fill that position, despite being a great Liberal and an agent of Sr. Zama, then it is the same as if the government had made a public statement that it will help this caudillo of disorder, our born and irreconcilable enemy." Four days later he stridently returned to the subject, claiming that the office seeker had been "iniquitously cheated [out of his former position] by our adversaries; the delay is of great moral reach."[58]

The power to appoint brought with it the power to dismiss, rewards implied punishments, and wayward clients sometimes needed to be taught a lesson. The Minister of War noted in 1872 that from Bahia "they have written me that the inspector of the Arsenal behaved badly during the election and aided the Liberals. His replacement by —— has been decided on." Both Liberals and Conservatives would probably have approved the inclusion, in a list of Police Corps officers to be dismissed "for the sake of morality and discipline," one who "furthermore is a Republican." Punishment could also be wreaked on the local patron of a member of Parliament who did not behave: "Did you read in the *Jornal do Commercio* today the article by Deputy ——? I must say frankly that, if I were governing alone, I would answer him by proposing tomorrow the dismissal of whoever made him Deputy." [59]

Not all political leaders approved these techniques. As Prime Minister in 1885, the formidable barão de Cotegipe, having forgotten his own forceful actions in earlier times and somehow excusing those he still practiced, exclaimed, "Enough dismissals! The system of terror is a bad system." He responded to criticisms of his refusal to dismiss Liberals en masse by saying, "The voracity with which people throw themselves at positions, the [illegible] that they want to carry out against *all Liberals*, besides being unjust, is in many cases impolitic, since it furiously casts into the opposing camp men who would not be hostile, some through loyalty, some through fear." Others also knew that the practice could have dire consequences. In 1855 a Bahian politician wrote Cotegipe: "I am sorry about what happened to my friend Manuel Dantas, and I believe there was some haste in dismissing him. . . . I suppose he is very irritated and perhaps his family [too]. I fear that rancor will make them undertake commitments with certain people that will be harmful to us." He was right to fear the worst. Not then, but later, Dantas emerged as a major Liberal challenger to the Conservatives' national power. [60]

Yet the use of patronage for electoral gain did not seem wholly inappropriate. Pedro II himself, usually so ready to wring his hands in despair at the misuses of patronage, allowed that for positions "of trust" the qualifications of appointees could be overlooked. [61] A reform party program even more specifically acknowledged that a Prime Minister should be free to make appointments to those positions "of trust necessary to the manifestation and execution of his political thought." One Prime Minister specifically denied that competence—rather than party affiliation—should be the only criterion for public employment, since such posts, created to serve the state, could be given only to those who fully adhered to the plans of its directors: "The public functionary who, forgetting the duties of his position, links up with the adversaries of the Cabinet and machinates against it, makes his continuing service impossible." The same would be true at the provincial level. How could a president, asked one politician, be expected not to dismiss those who "warred against him openly . . . holding hands with those who most extraordinarily attacked him. That would be an anomaly in matters of administration."[62] Not to play the patronage game would indeed indicate political weakness. When a Liberal government appointed some Conservatives as judges, a politician in Pernambuco exclaimed, "The Liberal Party is always doing one of these asinine things." The Liberals, however, were not really that naïve. As one Conservative reported from Bahia, "They have just won over this man by giving him, as a deal, the nomination of —— as district judge."[63]

The right to make appointments to office provided the tools through which Cabinets secured majorities in Parliament. Whether as prizes and punishments or by selecting those who could favorably affect the behavior of voters or directly impinge on the electoral process, the Cabinet sought to ensure its victory at the polls. To lose an election meant rejection by one's followers, implied a failure of leadership, and might even undermine the entire system of clientage. Elections must be won. The effectiveness of patronage is reflected in the parliamentary support every Cabinet enjoyed after an election it supervised. At the same time the scrupulous observation of the legal provisions on elections, at least most of the time, ensured that opponents remained content to await their turn.

It was no mystery that government interference in elections damaged established institutions all the way to the center by lessening their legitimacy. Since the Cabinet could always get the electoral results it wanted, only the Emperor could alter the parties in power, and when he did that he invited the hostility of those who were turned out. As José Antonio Saraiva so clearly put it soon after the Emperor had dismissed a Liberal government in a controversial act in 1868, "This excessive power is fatal to the monarchy." Extinguishing the Moderative Power of the Emperor would be unnecessary, he added, if "a freely elected Chamber lays out the rule" that to the Emperor's "right to dissolve it will correspond the right of the country to reelect the same Chamber, so as to say, 'You erred.'"[64] Because this never happened, politicians from both extremes simply criticized the Emperor when they were out of office, and made no attempt to change electoral practices once they got back in.

Political leaders in nineteenth-century Brazil found themselves tugged in diverse directions. The survival of the political system depended on maintaining its legitimacy, both before those groups permanently excluded from effective participation and for those within the political elite but temporarily out of power. Such a goal required a widespread belief in the proposition that Brazilians enjoyed individual freedom and participated in fair and impartially conducted elections. These same leaders nevertheless feared that the smallest sign of disorder could open the way for wider disturbances, threatening the very survival of society itself. Elections had to take place in peace, and the opposition could not be allowed to shatter that tranquility. Finally, however, elections had to be won by the government. Otherwise, basic principles of hierarchy could be undone. These contradictory ambitions posed serious and continuing challenges to the country's political leadership.

PART TWO

THE CONDUCT OF
POLITICS

FOUR

The Theater of Elections

AT THE LOCAL LEVEL the electoral process in nineteenth-century Brazil presented a dramatically layered social system and instructed the people on its appropriateness, propriety, and value. In this way elections worked to ends entirely congruent with the needs and desires of the propertied and imperceptibly meshed with society's structure. It was partly their unremitting concern with social ranking that made elections so important to most of the participants, whether patrons or clients. Satisfying an almost unconscious need, elections worked to solidify among a mobile population the clearly ranked hierarchical order. This is one of the least recognized uses of elections, and yet it is the one most deeply rooted in Brazil's social structure. A broad suffrage made it possible.

Law

Nationwide elections began in Brazil in 1821 after the liberal revolutionaries in Portugal called for an elected Cortes to draft a constitution. Just as Portugal had provisionally adopted the Spanish Constitution of 1812, so it drew from Spain the instructions for this first electoral act. These instructions, with additional comments or amendments inserted where applicable to Brazil, instituted a three-tiered indirect election that took place in the various provinces of Brazil between May and September, resulting in the choice of representatives who went off to Lisbon. Once Pedro decided, in 1822, to cease obeying the Cortes, he determined to summon a meeting of delegates to draft laws just for Brazil. His chief adviser, José Bonifácio de Andrada e Silva, wished to limit participation by simply summoning representatives from the existing County Councils of the capital cities of each province; but these men had no sooner arrived in Rio de Janeiro than more radical leaders, impelled by notions of representative government new to Brazil, succeeded in obtaining from Pedro I a Constituent Convention with popularly elected delegates instead. But José Bonifácio at least managed to avoid direct elections; copying some features of the Portuguese instructions, he determined that voters in each parish would choose electors, who would in turn designate their representatives or, as they were called, Deputies. The instructions further specified that an elector must not only be a "virtuous and reputable person of understanding and of unquestionable loyalty to the Brazilian cause," but also be "of means appropriate to his position."[1]

Not surprisingly, those elected indirectly to a Constituent Convention called for indirect elections in the Constitution they drafted. They also specified property qualifications for voters, with still higher ones for electors. The Constitution Pedro I actually issued by fiat in 1824 kept these provisions, though with some modifications of detail. Executive decrees then set out specific rules for the conduct of elections. From 1824 to 1842 elected county councilmen acted as chairmen of electoral assemblies in the various parishes of their counties. The parish priest drew up the list of certified voters and assisted the councilman in the work of the election. The other members of the electoral boards were chosen by acclamation, a procedure that soon resulted in violently disorderly scenes. Ostensibly to counter this tendency, the Conservative Cabinet in 1842 decided that the centrally appointed delegados should preside over elections, along with one elected justice of the peace and the parish priest.[2]

All electoral rules up to this point resulted from instructions or decrees issued by the Cabinet, and not from a law debated by the Deputies. In 1845, however, once the Liberals again controlled the Parliament, they set out to draw up a comprehensive and minutely specific electoral law that attempted to provide for every contingency. The resulting law of 1846 remained the basic one until 1881, although some details were altered.[3] It was within the terms of this law that elections took on their full meaning and purpose within a precisely ranked society and a polity articulated through patronage.

Elections could well occupy the attention of local communities almost all the time. They occurred frequently, for one post or another, and the process of drawing up the list of registered voters, often a long-drawn-out business in itself, ushered in each New Year. Voters directly elected justices of the peace and county councilmen every four years. At least that often, and more frequently if Parliament were dissolved, they chose the electors who would, a month later, name the Deputies to the national chamber. In the same way every two years voters selected provincial assemblymen. After 1860 voters also (still indirectly) elected Deputies whenever one died, resigned, chose to represent another district where he had also been elected, became a lifetime Senator, or accepted a Cabinet position. Every election could be disputed, and annulled elections meant conducting new ones. Elections, repeated so often, became a constant preoccupation in local life, and few could remain aloof from the process.[4]

Historians, like contemporaries, confront a tangle of ambiguity in determining who could legally vote. The 1824 Constitution had extended the vote to "the mass of active citizens,"[5] and by its terms certainly took in far more people than the electorate for county councilmen in colonial times—even going beyond the practice of most contemporary European countries. To be sure, in a taken-for-granted way it excluded slaves and women without even mentioning them, although it opened the polls to freedmen and illiterates and voiced no distinctions based on race. As I have noted, the law did exclude sons who lived with their fathers. Exceptions to that rule allowed public employees to vote even if they still lived at home, presumably because that employment signaled a countervailing allegiance. Although the normal voting age was twenty-five, a man could vote as early as age twenty-one if he had married, taken holy orders, or accepted a commission as a military officer.

The law's provisions on age and residence were clear-cut and little argued. Debate focused interminably, however, on the constitutional requirement that every voter must have at least 100 milreis in annual "net income," raised to 200 milreis in 1846 (roughly U.S. $100).[6] After the middle of the century, commentators agreed that the amount specified was so low that almost anyone could earn that much except "beggars" and "vagabonds."[7] One political essayist remarked that the law excluded only "women, children, and the village idiot." A Conservative member of Parliament said with some distaste, "We have . . . universal suffrage; everyone can register"; and though a Liberal counterpart did not go so far, he acknowledged that "he who has [only] 200 milreis in income is a poor man in Brazil."[8] Indeed, at the rate of at least two milreis a day reported by a foreign observer in the 1880s, free workers on coffee plantations could earn the required amount in just 100 days. Even domestic servants, had they not been excluded by other provisions of the law, could have earned enough to have qualified, or at least this would have been true for those in special demand, such as cooks and wet nurses.[9]

But whether just any income could be considered "net" income was an important sticking point. In the case of income from real property or from commerce, the significance of the constitutional phrase could be easily fathomed, but when the law used the same phrase to refer to income from employment, doubts arose. One advocate of restricting suffrage argued that it should be extended only to those whose annual salary if invested at 5 percent would return 200 milreis. An opposing view held that "the simple wage-worker . . . employs the capital of his physical effort"; thus all his salary should be considered net earnings on his investment.[10] The question was never legally resolved.

A further complication emerged from the provision that *criados de servir*, or servants, would be excluded. Who were they? The Constitution specifically stated who was not to be considered a servant: bookkeepers and "head cashiers of commercial establishments, administrators of plantations and factories," and servants in the imperial household above a certain rank. All other employees, these provisions implied, could be considered servants. Yet the first electoral law drawn up specifically for Brazil and antedating the Constitution had excluded not *criados de servir* as such, but "all those who receive salaries or wages [*salarios ou soldadas*] in any way whatever." The projected—but never promulgated—Constitution of 1823 had also excluded "day laborers [*jornaleiros*]." Jurists reasonably argued that the obvious omission of such language from the Constitution meant that the exclusion of servants did not extend to most employees. Their interpretation might at first sight seem certain in light of the constitutional provision that the required annual income must derive from "real property, industry, commerce, or *employment*."[11] In nineteenth-century usage, however, employment customarily referred only to public employment; since such positions were thought of as a form of property from which income derived as from an investment, the inclusion of employment there made sense.[12]

A moderate reformer acknowledged that the true spirit of the law had been to exclude anyone who depended on another for his "daily bread," thus losing his "independence," and a legal glossarist explained that servants "are totally dependent people, even more so than sons-at-home"; to grant them the vote would be to give it to the masters "whom they serve." But whether those who received salaries or wages had surrendered their independent civil identity remained an open question. One critic blamed the alleged vulgarity of the voters on registration boards, the bulk of which were inclined to place primary emphasis on income without considering its source, so that the majority of voters "have no property and live from their wages [*soldada*] on the land of others." Another observer insisted that "in our elections the vagabond without a skill or means of livelihood, the obvious indigent, even servants transformed into 'companions' [*camaradas*], have the vote." A petitioner protesting the exclusion of some would-be voters argued that of course they all had sufficient net annual income, "since some are businessmen, and others husbandmen, farmers, or day laborers [*hums são negociantes, outros criadores, outros agricultores, e outros jornaleiros*]." He took it for granted that wages would meet the requirement.[13]

It is important to note that in any case Brazilians did not consider an *agregado* a servant or employee. Though some considered the *agregados'* right to vote a flaw in the system, few questioned their legal prerogative to do so. Indeed in the extended household of the political chiefs, the *agregados* were crucial to electoral success. As the son of Lacerda Werneck put it, "The large landowners consent to have *agregados* because our electoral system demands it." A rancher in Ceará with holdings measuring sixteen square leagues had "settled on his land 360 *moradores* who pay no rent, but he says that when he needs workers they tend to lend a hand for free, only being given food, and that occasionally he gathers 200 or 300 men. At election time he delivers a load of 400 voters to [the town of] Icó." One coffee planter in the province of Rio de Janeiro assured a friend that he had "come to an understanding with the visconde de Baependy [another planter] to send ten voters that I have on my lands to go there for the struggle. . . . So you can rest easy, for every effort will be made for you not to be defeated." Participants in the Agricultural Congress of 1878, representing principally the interests of coffee planters, discussed the electoral role of *agregados* at some length. If proposed new voting rules became law, claimed two delegates, "planters will cease to maintain and feed on their lands innumerable *agregados* who do not bother to work, counting on the plantations' granaries in exchange for their votes"; some planters had effectively turned their plantations into "chicken coops of voters." Still another planter stated that "on the great properties . . . the free population consists almost entirely of what are called *agregados* or, better, electoral bullies for hire." In speaking of what they knew firsthand, these men vented their understandable frustration at finding themselves dependent on their own clients. Clearly, the law did not exclude the *agregado* per se from the polls, although the amount or source of his annual income could be raised as an objection to his admission to them.[14]

Another and very different question is, who did vote? Or more precisely, who actually appeared on the list of registered voters? Theorists could argue at length about the true meaning of constitutional provisions, the right of employees to vote, or the advisability of changing the law to exclude *agregados*, but the actual practice of registration depended on the dominant local faction. The justice of the peace who had won a plurality of votes in the last election presided over the five-member board (*junta de qualificação*), thus becoming "the key to the election." The electors in the parish, that is, the winners of the last general election, chose the other four board members, although the law sought to assure minority representation through procedures that varied over time.[15] Usually at least two of them would be friends or allies of the chairman, even his relatives. As one coffee planter confidently wrote:

I wish to form the registration board before mass on the 17th, and so I will go early, inviting you and your brother to be at the main church before ten o'clock in the morning. . . . If you would care to give us the pleasure of coming here to dinner on Saturday the 16th, we would much appreciate it, and please say the same to your brother. It is my daughter Rosa's birthday, but we are not inviting many people who are not of the family.[16]

The planter and chairman thus purchased loyalty with an irresistible display of intimacy. In short a narrow coterie of the locally powerful decided who could vote.

In compiling the list of voters, the registration board either worked from new lists supplied by the justices of the peace in each district, victors in the last election, or used the previous list, simply deleting or adding names. Since the law did not specify what documents would prove whether a voter had sufficient income, was or was not a servant, or had the other requisite qualifications, in case of dispute the board relied on sworn statements from witnesses. Because some would swear yea and others nay, the registration board remained legally free to decide, and did so according to its own political preference. In the end, then, the official qualifications for voting—income, occupation, residence, and even age—had very little to do with who voted.[17] As one politician perceived, "In the present system, who is a voter? He is a man who, registered today, is tomorrow unregistered by a contrary board."[18]

It is impossible to determine exactly what proportion of adult free males actually made it onto the list of registered voters. In 1870 the Ministry of Empire published a list of all the country's parishes that indicates the number registered in each. Two years later Brazil began a census of the national population summarized by parish; I say began because in 1876, when the results were sent to press, not all returns were in. In the intervening years some parishes had doubtless been expanded, others split, and still others done away with altogether. The census names several parishes that do not appear in the 1870 list, and vice versa. The population in the meanwhile had grown and shifted. Finally, since the census itself had a decided effect on the number of electors allowed each parish (although practically none on the number of Deputies from each province), a possible political purpose makes its figures suspect. For all these reasons, not to mention electoral fraud, one finds several gross anomalies when comparing the two sources, and many parishes had more registered voters than free adult males.[19]

Still, by calculating the median participation rate for all the 1,157 parishes found in both lists, the historian can establish some general notion of the expectations that characterized the registration process. For Brazil as a whole, 50.6 percent of all free males twenty-one years of age or older, regardless of race or literacy, appeared on the rolls of registered voters.* Half of all parishes allowed between a third and three-quarters of their adult males to register. There are no figures for the number of registered voters who actually voted, but the boards drew up the lists specifically so the registrants could be called on to support their chiefs. Parish leaders in nineteenth-century Brazil, who could exclude as easily as include, evidently wanted a large number of the men to participate in the electoral process.[20] Still, as can be seen from Table 2, there were significant regional variations. Parish bosses in the East, São Paulo, and provinces further south either held a large sector of the free population in lower regard or had less confidence in their own ability to control voting behavior than did their counterparts elsewhere: at least they registered a smaller proportion, although still a large one.

This inclusiveness contrasts markedly with the situation at later times. Until 1881, when a changed electoral law drastically reduced the number of voters, the property qualification had relatively little impact. Age and sex alone disqualified the bulk of the free, not the property requirement.[21] Historians, by failing to calculate contemporary earning power, have unduly elevated the significance of that restriction; one even claims that it limited political participation to the "dominant class."[22] An examination of electoral records would be enough to dispel such a notion, for the polls, although closed against those who supported the wrong candidate or depended on the wrong patron, were open in another sense to almost all free adult males, regardless of class or race.[23]

A broad suffrage did not signify a democratic polity, but it did make possible one important purpose of elections: they served as

---

*For those 25 and older, the proportion registered would be even higher, but since some voters aged 21 could legally vote, and since the census data permit calculations only for the 26-and-older group, and since I wish to allow myself the smallest possible ground on which to argue for widespread electoral participation, I have decided to use the lower age.

TABLE 2

Percentage of 21-Year-Old Free Males Registered to Vote
by Region and Province, Early 1870s
(Median of all parishes)

Region and province	Registrants	Region and province	Registrants
North	66.0%	East	38.2%
Amazonas	41.5%	Espírito Santo	54.0%
Pará	62.7	Rio de Janeiro	52.6
Maranhão	82.5	Minas Gerais	32.7
Piauí	57.7	São Paulo and South	39.0
Northeast	64.1	São Paulo	35.5
Ceará	49.5	Paraná	40.0
Rio Grande		Santa Catarina	—a
do Norte	47.5	Rio Grande	
Paraíba	73.5	do Sul	43.0
Pernambuco	64.5	West	60.4
Alagoas	86.5	Goiás	61.5
Sergipe	46.0	Mato Grosso	56.0
Bahia	68.5	All Brazil	50.6%

SOURCES: Brazil, Ministerio do Imperio, *Relatorio*, 1870, Anexo C; Brazil, Directoria Geral de Estatistica, *Recenseamento da população do imperio do Brazil a que se procedeu no dia 1º de agosto de 1872* (Rio de Janeiro, 1873–76).

NOTE: The total number of registered voters was 1,039,659, or 44.1% of all free men 21 years of age or older.

a The report of the Ministry of Empire allows one to calculate that 48.6% were registered in the province of Santa Catarina as a whole; but the report does not break the figures down by parish, so it is impossible to calculate the parish median. Accordingly, the regional and national totals do not include this province.

dramas in which participants used the language of social rank to distinguish among voters rather than to exclude them. And the gentry defined that ranking. The geographical mobility of so many Brazilians required that the "lesser" learn their place below the "greater." And because rival patrons rose and fell, they needed a stage from which to declare their present place.

Theater

There could be no doubt of his authority when the justice of the peace strode into the church of a remote village on the morning of election day and boldly took his place "at the head of the table," with two members of the board on each side and "me, the scribe, immediately to his left." Because as planter, rancher, or man of other property he had additional sources of authority, the chairman's position at the table displayed and affirmed the proper arrangement of society, and other actors thus received instruction on the patronizing or deferential stances appropriate to their respective places. As witnessed and acted, the hierarchical nature of society here played itself out again and again.[24]

For such a drama to succeed, not only must there be many participants, but all electoral operations must be insistently public. "In those times an election meant ... a lot of people, a lot of excitement," a judge later reminisced. They began on Sundays, a day when most people could attend. They took place in the parish churches, central and well known to all. A reference to an election taking place "with doors wide open" dates from the earliest voting in independent Brazil, and the law of 1846 specifically required open doors. The law also insisted that elections be announced by "proclamations [editais] posted at public places and published in the newspapers where there is one." The list of registered voters had to be affixed "in the main church in an appropriate spot and within sight of all." And voters did receive word, for they traveled from afar, as in Bahia, "covering themselves with dust." Nothing was to be done at night; elections were a daytime affair. Proceedings began at 9:00 A.M. and concluded "at sunset." Sometimes an electoral board, like one in São Paulo, rushed to finish, "the sun being almost set." Another, in Minas Gerais, considered but discarded the alternative of working at night: "And it being 2 in the afternoon, the work of the parish assembly was interrupted at the request of the board members so they could go eat dinner and, returning to the church, it was 5 o'clock and the sun had set, and it being discussed whether at least one roll call [of voters] could be made, they decided that it could not." The fact that the minutes of electoral boards could be falsified and written even in utter privacy does not lessen society's expectation that elections would be emphatically public. For the important task of sorting social roles, only a highly visible public performance would do.[25]

The campaigns themselves focused public attention. Although candidates solicited votes from electors primarily by letters addressed to them or to the other parish notables, each local patron demonstrated his importance by encouraging the voters, his clients, to participate in noisy demonstrations. Rival groups simultaneously proclaimed shared beliefs and competing allegiances when they

"[ran] through the streets of this town at night with music and fireworks, [shouting] *vivas* for His Majesty the Emperor, the legislative
assembly, religion, or particular persons, according to the predilection of each group." Such goings-on sometimes became generalized
merrymaking or degenerated into armed confrontations, and in
1860 the president of Ceará province had to issue orders forbidding
"parades of groups through the streets that only serve to provoke a
greater excitation of feelings," adding that "popular gatherings of
any kind with drumming and spirits and especially those commonly
known by the name *samba*" should particularly not be permitted.[26]
On election day itself patrons treated their voters to "fine delica-
cies." When the political chieftains gathered their *agregados* and
dependents in town, they would sometimes try to isolate them as if
in a corral to prevent them from being tempted to accept a ballot
from an opponent's camp in exchange for cash or other reward.
Or, as one delegado explained, to display their strength such groups
might "enter the streets of this city regimented in close-ordered col-
umns to the sound of thunderous *vivas* and, after a splendid and
encouraging victory lunch, go deposit their ballots in the box, pro-
ceeding in close order to the church with their chiefs in the lead."[27]

   With the attention of the public fully focused on it, the electoral
process provided an excellent opportunity to elaborate the detail
of social rankings. Although in the end most clients of the powerful would vote, the vocabulary of the registration procedure had
already emphasized the importance of social place. For the registration board to screen out servants but not bookkeepers and head
cashiers of business houses or managers of plantations and factories, it had to publicly discuss occupation, residence, age, income—in short, status.[28] Among those between the ages of twenty-
one and twenty-five, the board took special note of military officers,
law graduates, and "clerics of holy orders," who could vote despite
their youth. Among churchmen, however, the board distinguished
between the secular clergy and the religious "who live in cloistered
communities" and took a formal vow of obedience; the latter, because not independent, could not vote. For each case a public examination of social place might occur. Did the prospective voter live
in his father's household, and, if so, was he married? How old was
he? What was his income and where did it come from? All these
questions set some apart from others, highlighting subtle distinc-

tions. Even when argument ensued and a prospective voter, confident of his patron's power and backing, rebuffed a challenge, the fact of rank remained central to the discussion. After 1875 the registration board also identified the voter by specifying whether or not he knew how to read and the names of both his parents, thus forcing some not only to admit their ignorance but to confess their illegitimate birth.[29]

On election day the chairman read out the names of the voters from the list drawn up by the registration board. As he recited each name the voter would step forward, presenting himself to public view, ballot in hand. But wait: was this the same person whose name appeared on the list? According to the law, confirming the voter's identity was the first duty of the electoral board. The identification of voters further played to the need to make class distinctions. One writer noted that in the "better" neighborhoods of Rio de Janeiro, where "all the voters are well known—he is the international merchant or wholesaler, . . . the capitalist, the banker, the [urban] property owner, the doctor, the lawyer, . . . —as each name is called an individual known by all responds." In contrast stood the poor, the newly arrived, "the nomadic factory worker who works at one place today and another tomorrow. . . . Outside a narrow circle of those near where he lives, no one in the parish knows him." In case of doubt or challenge, the board called witnesses. Suitable ones included the justice of the peace himself, the parish priest, or any citizen whom the board deemed a "trustworthy [*abonadas*]" witness; since the board had to agree on and therefore discuss who would make an acceptable witness, it thus made distinctions even among those who would testify. Now excitement peaked. Here challenges appeared, the mask of deference might slip, and orderly procedure slide toward violent outburst. Would the authority of the electoral board and, above all, of its chairman hold? Or would a rival patron succeed in weakening that authority, perhaps momentarily loosing pent-up resentments among voters, only to reimpose respect for rank and place at the next election?[30]

As each man voted the chairman scratched off his name from the list of voters. When all the names had been called once, the names of those who had not been present were called a second time. By then the proceedings might have already spilled over into a second or third day; but a minimal interval of one night always intervened before the chairman called out the names of the absentees a third and final time, in order to "guarantee the voter's exercise of his rights." Sometimes a voter had to wait several days before his name was called. Each voter deposited, as a ballot, a list of names in the box. He did so publicly because, as one commentator explained, one only does things secretly that one is ashamed to do in public. When the third reading of voters' names had been completed, the board opened the ballot box and counted the lists to make sure they matched the number of voters.[31]

As the board opened the ballots, more discussion of qualifications—and hence of social rank—ensued. Did the candidate for elector have twice as much income as that required of the ordinary voter, as the Constitution specified? Could he by any chance be excluded as a freedman who could vote but not be chosen as elector? Voters were supposed to indicate the occupations of the candidates on their ballots; although intended as a way of firmly identifying the persons they chose, the provision suggested that all electors had to have known occupations, recognized by everyone.[32] As the board recorded this information, one can imagine the opportunity for impertinent questions or snickers from the crowd if some voter had identified a failing planter, for instance, as a *sitiante*, or farmer. Although ready to accept the notion of hierarchy, those present may nevertheless have played with its specificity, standing outside an imposed ideology.

Elaborate instructions guided the tallying of the votes. As one member of the electoral board read off the names on each ballot, the other members, assuming responsibility for certain letters of the alphabet, wrote the names down. When a name was called a second time, the board member wrote a number "two" next to the one on his list, and so forth; the last number written down would then be the number of votes the candidate had received. When all the ballots had been read, each member of the board announced the names on his list with the total number of votes the person had received, and the scribe recorded these names and placed them in descending order of their vote count. To break a tie, a little boy (no older than seven) drew lots from the ballot box. All the candidates receiving votes, no matter how few, would be listed. The chairman of the board then read out this roll for all to hear, and the scribe copied it into the special book he kept for the purpose and posted another list on the church door. The parish's quota of electors was filled by the men at the top of the list, and the immediately following runners-up were their substitutes.[33]

Thirty days after their selection, the electors met at the town designated as head of the district for the third and final act of the election. The Electoral College's proceedings, like those for registration and balloting, remained open to the public, but at this point no bit players took part, and the audience thinned out. Here other purposes of elections became paramount, but the formal steps deserve brief mention here. Only at this point did the names of candidates for Deputy appear, and electors voted for as many of them as the province would send to Rio de Janeiro. Their task had not ended, however, for they continued to be electors until the next voting took place and thus played a substantial part in organizing subsequent parish registration boards. They could also be summoned to choose a Senator or perform other electoral acts in the interval.[34] The provincial capital's County Council tallied the results from each Electoral College and issued the credentials of each Deputy. (From 1855 to 1875, when provinces included several districts, the County Council that headed each district performed this function.) The Council recorded the results received from each College, listed in order—from the most votes to the least—the persons receiving votes, and issued copies of its minutes to each Deputy. These he took with him to Rio de Janeiro to be presented in Parliament.[35] For the full social import of elections, however, we must look not to Rio de Janeiro but to the villages and towns.

Voting—and the registration process—took place in the parish church, redolent with symbols of unquestioned authority and graded degrees of authority. Churches even displayed, by their internal layout, the differing status of various saints. And some rooms had a higher symbolic impact than others: election officials gathered around a table "placed in the nave of the parish church," and rival groups disputed control of that sacred ground; one faction had to settle in the end for a side chapel. If the annual registration and the voting coincided, a decision had to be made on where each activity was to take place. In one case the voting took place in the nave, and the registration board was removed to a "hallway" of the church—necessarily, as the board explained, because it could not use the sacristy, where the blessed host was lodged for the worship of all. The event also gained importance from the particular church building: a few electoral boards impressively met in a cathedral, but in rural places workers sometimes rushed to finish building a church or at least one wall where the proclamation summoning voters could be posted.[36]

Locating elections in churches linked the social order to a holy one reaching to God himself, and the repeated performance of church rituals further heightened the sacredness of the civil drama. Once the chairman of the electoral board had opened the ceremony, but before the voting began, "the Most Reverend parish priest preached a sermon relating [*analoga*] to the [electoral] act, after which he celebrated mass." Some priests received fees for celebrating election masses; others charged nothing. Once the voting and counting were completed, the chairman of the board "summoned the newly chosen electors to the church, where a solemn Te Deum was sung." The Electoral Colleges similarly performed their tasks only after hearing mass and, as soon as the County Council had tallied the results, it proceeded—along with the elected Deputies, any electors present, and "the People"—to the provincial capital's "principal church" for a Te Deum.[37] The perceived importance of the religious ceremony and the precise observance of the law led challengers to question whether elections were valid if the religious ceremony had to be omitted because of the "illness of the vicar." They were.[38] Customarily, however, incense, bells, and the solemnity of sacred ritual accompanied the no-less-theatrical performance of the election.

In the civil as in the sacred acts, emphasis fell on the real difference between each social level. The justice of the peace and members of the electoral board clearly occupied a position apart from the great mass of the people. The law specified that during the process of organizing the board there should be a railing or other suitable division between the board's table and the assembled voters, so that the citizens might "inspect and verify" its work while leaving it free to go about its business. Once the board had been properly constituted, however, the separation between it and the voters was to be removed, allowing those present to "circle the board and examine its acts." Thus, the distinction having been sharply drawn, witnesses could legitimize it by their presence.[39]

In a predominantly illiterate society—only 21 percent of the free

could read and write—the written word and the books of minutes
took on a power of their own. A forensic culture determined that
acts gained validity only by being recorded. Hence those who could
manipulate that esoteric reality enjoyed an impressive advantage.
Attention centered always on the written record. "During a small
tumult" in a small Northeastern village, "the book of the [board's]
minutes was snatched away by force." The law made elaborate provision for the security of "the book," its safekeeping in the archives
of the County Council, the careful recording of the minutes in
it, the signatures of all board members at the end of each section,
and the initials of the chairman on each page. The minutes constituted the only account with legal standing, so an 1881 law set a
harsh penalty for "tearing or destroying books and papers relative
to the process of election": one to three years of hard labor and a
fine of 1,000 to 3,000 milreis (U.S. $440-$1,320). And this was
above and beyond any punishment for other crimes to which such
an act contributed. Designed to prevent fraud, such provisions
heightened the importance of the book and further raised the social
standing of the literate.[40]

Voting was not restricted to those who could read and write, but
literacy clearly separated the few who conducted elections from the
many who merely voted. The very fact that illiterates did vote made
them simultaneously actors and audience in a drama that set them
below their betters. In other contexts contemporaries recognized a
clear division between those who could read and those who could
not.[41] And the functions involved in carrying out the election process could only have been performed by men who read and wrote
easily. The chairman of the electoral board, for example, opened
the performance by reading out loud and "in an intelligible" fashion the first two chapters of the election law, some six printed pages
in all. Although the scribe who kept the minutes may have had to
nudge and prompt the other members of the board, they too must
have been literate, since as they opened the ballots, "[one member]
read while the others wrote the names that appeared on these ballots." In contrast, when the ordinary voter complained of the electoral board's actions, he would likely have had to ask someone else
to sign for him. Those chosen as electors must also have been literate—though the law did not specifically require it—since in place
of a scribe the Electoral College elected two of its members to serve

as secretaries, and all the members signed their ballots.[42] The literacy of election officials is attested, finally, by the reaction to the occasional exception. The Minister of Empire found it necessary to write to a provincial president that a county councilman "who admits not knowing how to read or write except to sign his name with difficulty" must nevertheless be considered eligible, since "the law does not exclude" him from the post. The occurrence seems to have been rare enough and significant enough to require a special inquiry.[43] Granting the vote to illiterates ensured their presence as minor actors in a drama in which the literate found their social superiority visibly reinforced.

Certainly a great deal of scratching of pens went on during election days. The process began with the filling out of ballots, that is, a list of names put forward for the Electoral College, and their distribution among the voters. As one planter instructed a friend, "Have the ballots made with only 7 names, leaving the 8th place for us to fill in with Mattheus or another on Saturday as we deem fit." Another landowner paid for the expense of hiring this copying done, but one delegado found himself dismissed for having filled them out "in his own hand," thus displaying a lack of impartiality.[44] Before the election ended the importance of the official scribe became doubly evident. He copied his draft minutes into the official book and made a separate list of the winners for posting on the church door. Next he transcribed the minutes over and over again, one copy for the County Council, another for the provincial president, and one copy for every elector chosen. No wonder the law required County Councils before each election to "prepare table, chairs, paper, ink, . . . and whatever else may be necessary to effect this solemn act with all dignity." Even so, one justice of the peace complained that, although he had received the registration list, he had not received "the lined paper" for the board members.[45] Elections were truly the apotheosis of writing in an illiterate society.

As in all carefully designed and presented performances, costume revealed role. Actors displayed their status and authority, the superiority of some and the inferiority of others, through their clothes. The justice of the peace, although the lowest figure in the judicial pyramid, often appeared as the only representative of that ranked system in the parish, proudly decked out in his sash of office, "one hand wide," consisting of a yellow stripe between two green ones and worn "from right shoulder down to the left side." One justice of the peace, a major coffee planter in Valença, had to remind his successor that the sash "is not the property of the judge but of the office." The parish priest or vicar, robed especially for raising the host at mass, could scarcely be mistaken for an ordinary voter, or even for a simple member of the electoral board when he participated in its work (although at least one priest, "having said high mass," went "home to change vestments and eat something" before returning to his task on the board). A costume for each role heightened the scene's dramatic impact.[46]

Most colorful of all, the officers of the National Guard—drawn as we have seen from the landed and slaveowning class—maintained order at elections wearing "rich uniforms," which they themselves provided. The uniform of a cavalry officer, for instance, included dark green pants with a double red stripe running vertically along the outside of the leg, and a red, close-fitting jacket with short tails and a stiff high yellow collar. Heavy gold braid epaulets, yellow trim down the front and at the cuffs, and brass buttons decorated the jacket. Across his chest, diagonally from his right shoulder to his waist, he wore a wide white leather strap bearing a medallion with the imperial insignia; and around his waist he wore a scarlet sash with a golden tassle, surmounted by a white belt fitted with a scabbard for his gold-hilted sword. Completing his finery were white gloves, shiny black boots, and a gold-trimmed black helmet topped by a red plume. In full panoply like this, officers of the National Guard were imposing figures, elegant, stiff, and unapproachable, players of a particular part, signaling unquestionable superiority as well as authority. As they summoned and dispatched their men or met each other on election day, saluting and clicking their heels, they gave sharp expression to the hierarchical relationships that suffused everyday connections.[47]

The ordinary voter also dressed for the occasion: he wore shoes. And shoes spoke volumes. There was a small riot in one parish in 1860 when a coachman, known to be a slave, arrived at a polling place wearing shoes, because everyone assumed that, being shod, he had been brought in to vote for his master's faction. Patrons so often supplied new "shoes and clothes" to voters that these benefits came to be seen as a right. One ex-judge later compared the voters to foot soldiers, who "held the right to rations, which were furnished generously, and . . . equally the right to a uniform or at least to a certain part of one; for since there was then in fact universal suffrage and not all could present themselves in a sufficiently decent way, it became necessary for the paymaster to bear the cost of a more or less presentable set of clothes and, even more critically, of a good pair of shoes." By their dress voters claimed a station above those not allowed to vote.[48]

Even those who did not vote played a part in the drama as stage-hands, so to speak. Women and slaves had hand-sewn and pressed the uniforms and vestments. They doubtless demonstrated these and other skills with pride. They cooked large quantities for the assembled voters lounging about the square or concocted choicer fare for the board members, who might return home to "eat something" before resuming their duties or stop work to take their "dinner" at two o'clock.[49] Even cleaning the church and its ornaments for the grand occasion provided an opportunity to show attentive care. Here no doubt some could handle the vestments while others could only sweep. Women and slaves took up a role that revealed their social standing while witnessing and thus acknowledging the assertive parts played by others, more highly located in the social system.

A summary display of these rankings took place at sunset on each day of the election. In a ritual centered on the ballot box, participants demonstrated the entire array of social positions and heightened the attention focused on the problematic nature of electoral results. These boxes were sometimes "small chests of red morocco" with three locks and a "slot" through which voters slipped the ballots. At night the presiding justice of the peace closed the slot with wax, impressing it with his seal. He then placed the ballot box "inside a strongbox with three keys, one of which was kept by the chairman, one with board member——, and the other with me, the secretary, the strongbox [also] being sealed, and tied by a white ribbon." The electoral board then carried this box to the most public and visible part of the parish church, which remained open throughout the night. National Guardsmen took turns guarding it, the changing of the guard carried out formally and ceremoniously, presumably by the flickering light of torches, candles, or whale-oil lamps. Such a ritual attracted support. When a county judge once suggested that a ballot box should be turned over for safekeeping to the parish sacristan, others insisted that, on the contrary, it should be guarded by the "National Guard and other citizens who took it on themselves to care for it where it stayed in the same visible place of the parish church." The next morning spectators saw them carefully untie the ribbon, publicly turn the three keys, and remove the ballot box from the chest; all could inspect the seal as it was solemnly broken. By such elaborate displays actors not only asserted the honesty of the procedure, but performed distinct roles according to their position.[50]

Two final acts pointed to the locus of power and stressed the importance of electoral procedures. As the electoral board concluded its tasks, it prepared a list of the voters who had not appeared. Voting was compulsory for those on the registration list, but the board normally excused all voters and forgave them their fines for not appearing, thus adding one more gesture of magnanimous paternalism to distinguish those who had power from those who did not.[51] Then, to draw this lengthy ceremony to a fittingly celebratory and public end, the board took the ballots themselves to the front steps of the church and burned them in a small bonfire, doubtless attracting the lively attention not only of participants in the process, but of women, children, slaves, and others shut out from the main event.[52]

Extending the vote to a broad segment of the population served a particular purpose. In each ritual every individual asserted his place and played out a preassigned role. The National Guard officer, the justice of the peace, the priest, the voter, each performed a distinct part. Individuals did not always occupy the same place in the social pyramid—a man with shoes might jump from slave to voter—but elections repeatedly affirmed the gradations of society. Insofar as a measure of fluidity and mobility in society existed, it ranged up and down a fixed ladder, clearly recognized and emphasized by electoral procedures. The rites repeated at each election asserted and reinforced the ordering of society and the desirability of that ordering. They defined and preserved the various and particular gradations that comprised the whole and instructed actors and audience alike on the nature and propriety of that order.

Elections were, first of all, elaborate dramatic performances that insistently reiterated the conviction that the only proper basis of social organization lay in a clear recognition of everyone's social superiority or inferiority. Many more participated in these electoral events than is usually acknowledged—indeed more than in most countries of Europe at that time—yet that participation served not to manifest an egalitarian ideology, but to ensure that some would be called on to play bit parts while others of higher standing stood in the spotlight. Because elections were indirect, this system of broad participation did not endanger the imperial structure or governmental control of the end results. Rather, in assigning roles, whether working out the list of registered voters and verifying their identity or establishing the qualifications of the elected, electoral procedures repeatedly imprinted the appropriateness of inequality on the public consciousness. The stage for this drama, as well as its costumes, chorus, and crew, all served to advance that unspoken end.

FIVE

Leadership, Fraud, and Force

A COUNTY LEADER STRUGGLED for electoral victory not to oppose the government, but to be the government. If he could garner the most votes for himself or his protégés, that would prove his leadership. He could then count on being appointed to important local positions. Besides his commission in the National Guard, he would be named delegado or substitute county judge, with the authority to appoint his clients as subdelegados, ward inspectors, notaries, and jailers. If he did not choose the county judge, as was quite likely, he would certainly make sure that the man named agreed not to oppose him. A hold on such positions would, in turn, enlarge the chief's clientele and ensure his influence on the voting process, making his next electoral victory all the more certain.

To challenge that leadership, therefore, required building an alternative following. Displaying the size of that following meant either successfully bringing charges of electoral fraud to public attention or, more immediately effective, using outright force to unseat the incumbent. For this reason elections and violence went together. To counter the power of a ruling boss, a challenger had to use force or the threat of force. As he won some measure of power, he could accuse the county chief of illegal acts in elections. That is, electoral boards and local officials only committed the charges of fraud to paper when a challenger had already gained enough influence to insist on inserting into the record the views of the faction he led. Just as both the locally governing group and its challengers always based their cases on the claim of "order" against "anarchy," so also with honesty against fraud: when the charge of fraud appeared, it signified an opposing force had already achieved sufficient strength to demand some voice in the crucial documents. To get that far, to secure a space in which to makes one's charge of malfeasance, required first the command of force, extralegal by definition. Then, as a rising chief increasingly made his presence felt, he could be pacified by being given a few positions of authority too, for himself and his clients. He knew that if he made his power known, he could not long be ignored by the central government. If success did not come now, with the party currently in power, then it would surely come later with the other. When a new leader finally controlled all the positions of legal authority, no more charges of fraud emerged. In the meantime, to be seen as leader of the strongest faction sometimes required unscrupulous means and decisive action. Violence—from one side or the other, real or only threatened—did not run counter to the electoral process but formed an essential part of it.

As a necessary corollary to the ambition of local chiefs, national leaders ruled through one faction or another. A Minister of Justice put it bluntly, in discussing his policy on appointing National Guard officers: in those places "where there is only one battalion, we should prefer the strongest faction, the most legitimate, and the one that offers more guarantees of loyalty, dedication, and aptitude."[1] So a two-way manipulation resulted, not just from the "top" down, but from the local to the central government, securing appointments for the predetermined village powerful. From the point of view of those at the national capital, the secret of good governance lay in knowing when to grant at least some positions of legal authority to a challenger. It meant keeping in constant touch with the flow of power at the village level and deliberately ignoring the forceful clashes involved in gaining it. The roots of what later came to be called *coronelismo*—the tendency to give local bosses free rein as long as elections returned congressmen supportive of the goals of national and regional leaders—were firmly planted in the nineteenth century.[2]

It is the purpose of this chapter to explore the local base of electoral behavior, for it is at that level that these important meanings of political struggle are clearly revealed. And only when that dimension is understood does the nature of patronage as a two-way flow of influence become clear. Before examining how leaders of local factions used electoral fraud and violence to assert their power, however, we must first inquire what sort of men they were, how they related to the central government, and what they purposed in local elections.

Leaders

Typically the men who ruled locally derived their ability to attract a clientele in the first instance from their control of property, even if not all the propertied had an equal hand in district politics. As planter-delegates to a congress of agriculturalists perceptively put it in 1878, it was "necessary to respect the social and economic fact, which we witness in this country, that a great part of the rural population—the preponderant part of the population of the Empire—in one form or another is subject to the big landowners who possess the more productive enterprises."[3] No one was ashamed of that reality then: that was how it was and how it should be.

Certainly in areas of great export riches, planters inevitably emerged in the vanguard of local politics. Among the coffee-planting families in the county of Vassouras (in the Paraíba Valley), these six towered in wealth: Ribeiro de Avellar, Souza Werneck, Lacerda Werneck, Santos Werneck, Correia de Castro, and Paes Leme. Two others, the Miranda Jordão and Teixeira Leite families, owned local businesses, especially lending money to planters and serving as factors or commission agents for them, although they also held some land.[4] These eight families together controlled county politics. In 1842, when parish electoral boards were organized by a triumvirate of priest, delegado or subdelegado, and justice of the peace, Paulo Gomes Ribeiro de Avellar, as justice of the peace, and José Pinheiro de Souza Werneck, as subdelegado, joined the priest on the board in one parish. Among the other three board members were Francisco Peixoto de Lacerda Werneck, the future barão do Paty do Alferes, who that very year, as commandant in the National Guard, had led his forces in fighting the liberal rebellion in São Paulo and Minas Gerais. When the voting took place, eight of the ten victorious electors bore familiar names:

> Joaquim Ribeiro de Avellar
> Claudio Gomes Ribeiro de Avellar
> Manoel Gomes Ribeiro de Avellar

Paulo Gomes Ribeiro de Avellar
José Gomes Ribeiro de Avellar
José Pinheiro de Souza Werneck
Francisco das Chagas Werneck
Francisco Peixoto de Lacerda Werneck[5]

Thirteen years later, in 1855, these families still monopolized county and parish offices: among the county councilmen and their substitutes, we find the names Teixeira Leite, Souza Werneck, Paes Leme, and Miranda Jordão. In the central parish of the county, Pedro Correia de Castro (barão de Tinguá) served as justice of the peace, along with three Teixeira Leites. In the parish of Paty do Alferes, the subdelegado belonged to the Ribeiro de Avellar family; his substitute was Augusto Soares de Miranda Jordão—a wealthy planter and banker—who simultaneously held the position of county councilman. Three of the four justices of the peace in this parish bore the family name Ribeiro de Avellar, including the family head Joaquim Ribeiro de Avellar, barão de Capivary.[6]

Another example of a wealthy landowner who wielded much local power was Joaquim José de Sousa Breves (1804-89). As early as 1822 the estate of Breves's father—who was just then beginning his coffee plantation in the county of Piraí in the Paraíba Valley— seemed an appropriate place for Pedro I to spend the night while on his way to São Paulo, where he would declare Brazil independent. In 1831 the younger Breves married the daughter of a neighbor, José Gonçalves de Morais, later barão de Pirahy, a match that made him one of the largest landowners in the region (eventually he possessed some twenty coffee plantations). His brother, José Joaquim, married another Morais daughter. Besides the rich coffee lands draining into the Paraíba do Sul River, Breves owned properties stretching down the escarpment to the coast and an estate on the spit of Marambaia beyond Sepetiba Bay across from the small port town of Mangaratiba.[7] His wealth rapidly increased, and by 1861 the two brothers (and their children) shipped nearly 3.4 million pounds of coffee a year, not including that produced on the lands of their father-in-law. The production of that one family accounted for at least a third of all the coffee shipped from two counties in the Paraíba Valley, and perhaps 1.5 percent of the country's total exports.[8]

More than a landowner, Breves was a slaveowner. In rapidly expanding his coffee groves, Breves sought an abundant source of labor and early turned to protecting slave traders. Perhaps the energy he devoted to the cause of local autonomy—he emerged in the 1830s and 1840s as the local champion of Liberal programs—derived from his need for compliant officers of the law to overlook his excesses in this respect. At least we know he used the port of Mangaratiba to import large numbers of Africans illegally. As late as 1851 the British Foreign Minister bitterly complained to the Brazilian minister in London that "Joaquim Breves, the well-known slave importer of Marambaia whom the competent tribunal had justly found guilty of importing slaves into Brazil, has been acquitted on appeal to the Superior [High] Court at Rio de Janeiro." Breves is said to have owned more than 4,000 slaves. In the fields they sang biting ditties about his clashes with his father-in-law over the boundaries of their estates and about his sexual relations with slave women.[9]

Breves displayed his wealth with flamboyance. He kept two small steamboats of his own to ship his coffee from Mangaratiba to Rio de Janeiro, but often sailed on them himself when he wished to appear at court ceremonies. In 1855 he paid a substantial sum to the Church to allow masses to be said in his plantation chapel, and ten years later he built on his estate a splendid mansion, designed by his son-in-law, the Italian minister to Brazil. His contacts in Rio de Janeiro proved useful when, after his daughter died, he worked to prevent the Italian diplomat from taking their Brazilian-born child back to Italy. When entreaties failed, Breves ordered his own grandchild kidnapped; faced with a fait accompli, the father finally agreed to leave her with Breves, although not before the matter created a diplomatic brouhaha embroiling even the Council of State.[10]

As a local political leader Breves wielded a heavy hand. In 1840, with the Liberals temporarily in the ascendant at the capital, his clients as justices of the peace succeeded in keeping his opponents permanently under indictment. When his own supporters later landed in jail, he organized a jail break that resulted in the death of one man and the wounding of several others. In late 1841 the Conservatives took over in Rio de Janeiro and appointed the coffee planter Honório Hermeto Carneiro Leão, later visconde de Paraná, as provincial president; he ordered the district judge to embark on a "rigorous conscription of the ne'er-do-wells who infest the area," a roundup designed to thin the ranks of Breves's followers. With the Liberals once again in power in 1844, Breves's manipulation of a local election proved so blatant as to provoke a denunciation from the parish priest. In 1849 he was still at it, for we find his actions as head of a faction in the Electoral College again stirring protests. As he confided at that time to Senator José Thomaz Nabuco de Araújo, he had so many enemies that he feared assassination and traveled only on "back roads," letting no one know his route. As late as 1860 the president of the province of Rio de Janeiro still had to admit to the Minister of Empire that "I too am afraid of the malicious intervention of Joaquim José de Souza Breves in the elections." Indeed Breves apparently headed the band of some 200 men who descended the escarpment to Mangaratiba that year and broke up the work of an electoral board insufficiently attentive to his wishes, an action that provoked the dispatch of a gunboat from Rio de Janeiro. In 1871 he was accused of entertaining the county judge on his plantation and rendering him "significant favors" in return for favorable judgments.[11]

Similarly in the sugar-rich county of Escada in Pernambuco, planters monopolized the positions of local authority. The planter and seigneur Henrique Marques Lins had a son-in-law as delegado and a brother-in-law as subdelegado. As commandant of the National Guard battalion, Lins himself issued orders through fifteen company commanders, eight of whom possessed, among them, sixteen sugarmills. The County Council there included three members who together owned thirteen plantations. Out of seventeen justices of the peace in the various parishes, twelve owned nineteen sugarmills.[12] Nabuco de Araújo, while still a Conservative leader in 1841, found it proper that such wealthy men should rule. Speaking of the Cavalcanti family in Pernambuco, he said:

These Cavalcantis before our independence already appeared as captains-general, lieutenant-colonels, colonels, and officers of the civil guard and militia, and in all the governing positions; the sugarmills that most of them own were acquired by inheritance and not secured after the Revolution; list the sugarmills of the province, and I guarantee you that one-third of them belong to Cavalcantis. . . . Such an ancient, rich, and most numerous family, made up of members who always occupied the best social positions, . . . will only cease to have [political] influence when society is over-turned, when all those elements of regular and legitimate influence are obliterated by the predominance of violence, by the confusion of anarchy, by the upending of society.[13]

Elsewhere in Brazil as well, in areas not so wealthy, the proper-tied generally occupied the positions of local power or determined who would do so, as is perhaps true universally. Thus Francisco Fernandes Vieira, visconde de Icó, a cattleman in the interior of Ceará, whose first son was a Senator, could also take pride in the fact that another one was a delegado and a third a subdelegado, while his son-in-law was district judge, his cousin was the county judge, and a nephew was the public prosecuting attorney. I have already given examples of many other such local bosses, men of substance, whom the national government appointed as delegados, substitute county judges, and officers in the National Guard. Al-most all of them headed electoral factions in their districts built on loyal followers.[14]

A successful local leader made sure to maintain strong links to provincial legislators, members of Parliament, Cabinet figures, and even the Prime Minister. The relationships between court and vil-lage remained intimate, direct, and frequent, despite several formal levels of authority. For this reason it is a mistake to differentiate too markedly between the central government and local factions. One National Guard colonel in Bahia "has friends in the Liberal ma-jority of the [Provincial] Assembly, some of whom owe him their election, one who, besides this, is his son-in-law, and all of whom well understand his services [to the party]." Others could appeal to members of the national Parliament: in reporting on the actions of one landowner in the far backlands of central Bahia (Pilão Arcado and Sento Sé) who refused to accept the interference of any other authority in the elections, the provincial president reported that his immunity resulted "principally from the protection [he receives] from those he supports for Deputies, who here [in Salvador] and in Rio de Janeiro use whatever means their ambition may suggest to defend him." Through such connections a local boss could reach the Cabinet itself. When a district judge in the county of Bananal (São Paulo) admonished a delegado for electoral misbehavior, the unabashed official replied that he had acted under the direct au-thority of a Minister. The provincial president who related the incident not only defended the delegado, but added that the delegado's partner in all this, his first substitute, "was recommended to me by very important people in Rio de Janeiro and is an intimate of some of your colleagues [in the government]." In this way, as one politician put it, "the predominance of an oligarchy is firmed up, with one or two chiefs uniting to make Deputies of their sons, nephews, relatives, godsons, *compadres*; . . . or the government draws these influential chiefs to it, promising them the world, with the result that it can obtain everything." [15]

José Dantas (1816-67), a large landowner in northeastern Bahia, held the rank of captain in the National Guard and the post of substitute county judge. Yet he protected cattle rustlers and horse thieves or, if they displeased him, shot them dead in church during mass. "Because of his electoral influence [he] is extraordinarily protected in Bahia, [and] his evil influence extends even into Sergipe." No "police authority . . . dares place one foot within his fief." In 1856, five years after that report was filed, José Dantas backed the electoral ambitions of his nephew and godson, Manuel Pinto de Souza Dantas, who won election to Parliament and quickly emerged as a major politician, eventually becoming Prime Minister. So if provincial presidents sometimes sought to extend control over local bosses, they soon learned that the very system that had earned them their position also ensured constant connections between their superiors in the Cabinet and those selfsame bosses. [16]

This is not to say that members of the central government could yield unquestioningly to the pressure of the strongest local party for too long, since they would then give up some maneuverability in extending their own clientele. The newly installed president of Rio Grande do Norte, for instance, bewailed the fact that in that province

all the members of the Provincial Assembly, the County Councils, the military [officers], the National Guard officers, the magistrates, the provincial employees, the justices of the peace, the electors, the delegados, in short, all power belongs to a party that has held dominion for eighteen years, except for brief intervals. The tendency of this party is to guarantee its places and diminish central authority. Pretty soon the government will have nothing more to do in this province, except to name a president every six months to be an automaton, good only for signing letters and approving provincial laws. . . . To a man with his hands tied you cannot say, "Be forceful!" [17]

And no matter how much a regional chieftain gained, it never satisfied him. He then attempted to apply more pressure in Rio de Janeiro, to the disgruntlement of national leaders, who no doubt resented having their own freedom of action circumscribed. A landed boss from Alagoas had arrived at the national capital "haughty and excitable, believing we want to penetrate *his domain* because we won't dismiss the [provincial] president without a plausible motive, and full of complaints that we have done nothing—although he is the district judge where his sugarmill is located, and he has [a friend and relative] as judge in the Regional High Court and [another] as a Senator, a brother as a Deputy, a friend a baron, etc., etc." So at some point those politicians who made it to the center had to say "no" to a specific local boss. But just as a district judge might rule against an individual landed potentate but not against them generally, so the provincial presidents and thus even the Prime Minister often had to offend some village strongmen, but never dared counter them all at once. "To do a a general cleanup," explained one president, "would raise the opposition of the friends of the government." [18]

Clashes between presidents and local bosses became particularly likely when Cabinets changed hands. Such conflicts did not reveal competing visions of the locus of power—public or private—but simply worked out the ties between capital and village. A landowner like José Antonio Saraiva, nicknamed the "messiah from Pojuca" (the name of his sugar plantation), whose ability to marshal the support of factional leaders and their clienteles eventually propelled him to national leadership, could find himself appointed to the presidency of a province precisely in order to lessen the power of these private fiefdoms. In 1859 he reported from Pernambuco on his conversation with a local boss:

I had occasion to make that *coronel* understand that the Imperial Government and I had no reason to doubt that he was among those dedicated to order and the respecters of Law; . . . that to be always on my good side it would be a good idea for him to be very scrupulous in the choice of his *agregados* and hand over to local authorities any criminals that may be at his sugarmills; . . . and that I told him this so that I would not find myself faced with the need some time to send forces into his mills, which would surely displease him. He promised to do what I said."

Saraiva added that this "*coronel* . . . may gradually lose his propensity to act as a strongman [*valentão*] and his prestige as total boss.

If I had enough forces I would place a good part of them at his side a little distance away, and that would be enough to make him . . . accept politely all the necessary changes in his existence as a citizen." [19] Presidents, however, did not have enough forces to do that.

The concern to maintain the paraphernalia of liberalism meant, furthermore, that opponents could not be cleared out from all positions at once. That meant judges, for instance, if allied to the "outs," might still have enough independence to frustrate a president's effort to bring local leaders to heel. Saraiva then turned his report into a jeremiad, lamenting the lack of support he received from other authorities. The Regional High Court, for instance, had granted a writ of habeas corpus on behalf of an indicted criminal. "With such good men in as judges, the action of the administration and the police will never produce an effect, and those who dominate the land [*donos da terra*] will be the lawyers and scribes with their backs guarded by the millowner bullies [*senhores de engenho valentões*]." [20] The language is that of a struggle between civilization and barbarism; but Conservatives who had appointed those judges would sound the same theme, simply applying the invective to a different set of landowners and local bosses.

The kaleidoscopic shifting of local allegiances, combined with alternations in the ruling party at the national level and every party's attempt to mollify the losing faction with an appearance of fairness, meant that other representatives of officialdom (the National Guard commandant and the delegados, for instance) could also be at odds with each other. To some degree such tensions served to perpetuate the larger system by keeping information about local strength constantly flowing. Otherwise a swelling faction might burst out in unpredictable ways. Because Conservatives and Liberals had information both on who currently led local politics and on who threatened to come to the top, they could alter appointments, shift their ground, and thus appear to maintain both fairness and order. The commandant and the delegado could both claim—and did claim—to be speaking for the government, for law and order, and for the preservation of the system, and to be imposing their authority against the "turbulent" or "disorderly ones," the violators of the electorate's will, those "unfavorable to the liberty of the voters," and the propagators of "disorder." [21] In truth they always spoke for one faction or another, each with its patron-chief.

A common task for a provincial president consisted of gingerly arranging compromises among rival local factions, allowing both to participate in the spoils of office. If well conceived, this accomplishment had the advantage of preventing violence while maintaining control. Thus in 1851 the president of Sergipe turned in a list of proposed appointments to the National Guard drawn from two rival groups and urged the central government to make sure to appoint a mixture so that neither group could claim victory over the other. In exchange he demanded that the rival local leaders present him with a unified ticket of Deputy candidates representing both groups before he would throw his support to any one running for the office. Four years later a Minister of Justice noted that where there were two battalions of the National Guard in one locality, commissions as officers should go "to the leaders of both sides." Such initiatives could prevent a parish boss from needing to use extralegal means to demonstrate the strength of his position.[22]

For in his effort to demonstrate that strength, a local chief could encourage his faction to denounce acts of fraud or, sometimes, to perpetrate acts of violence. The contradictory demands of order, freedom, and hierarchy resulted in nuanced and shifting emphases in local elections that ranged from the exercise of rigid control by the faction that held the positions of constituted authority, through enough leniency to permit the opposition to charge fraud, to such clear weakness that a challenger believed he could successfully resort to violence in order to impose his will or at least assert the right to be noticed. When the dominant group held firm control, the election took place in perfect peace, and legal means—even if blatantly one-sided—proved sufficient to ensure victory. If opponents of the dominant faction won any votes at all, they had the good grace or political acumen to recognize their success as a gift to be received with gratitude. Each election, however, could put the relationships of local power at risk. As the Minister of Justice recognized, the majority party on electoral boards, "desiring many times to win no matter what or to *display an influence beyond their real one,* . . . are led to practice acts that threaten the political rights of the voting citizens and provoke dangerous conflicts." If a rival chief increased his following, he demanded a voice in local politics; that seemed only just. "If there was violence," one participant reminisced, "and many times there was, the winners were always the majority; that is, whoever had more people and therefore more force." Therefore, as a provincial president explained, "fraud and disturbances" often accompanied each other.[23]

On the other side also, fraud and force went together. Fraud was backed by the force of the dominant faction, that is, by the threat of force that succeeded in preventing the undoing of a fraudulent practice. We know nothing about cases of fraud that truly "worked"; the great bulk of electoral board minutes read dryly and properly, and the losers perhaps did not think it had occurred or more likely felt too weak even to protest. Such weakness could result either from the leader's lack of men to vote and bear arms, that is, his failure as patron, or from the tenuousness of his connections upward to the Cabinet, his failure as client. In any case most fraud left no trace; in the challenges to fraud, the historian gets only a glimpse of a much larger reality at which to guess.

In short, rival groups always counted on violence: either by the legally sanctioned force of the National Guard, Police Corps, and Army, which ensured that certain voters, whether truly in the majority or not, would emerge victorious at the ballot box; or by armed voters who would contest that power and establish their own right to control the election. Only a thin line separated the legal control of elections by the Cabinet, acting through its loyal agents and relying on the governmental monopoly of legitimate force, and the illegal violence or fraud exercised by local patrons. And in either case, the same goal obtained: to demonstrate electoral superiority and thus win new or further governmental support.

Fraud

Fraud or, rather, the allegation of fraud in the official documents had its roots in the threat of violence. A challenger could thus secure the right to lodge a complaint against the alleged dishonesty practiced by the majority of the electoral board, and such a statement could be placed in its minutes. Or if the electoral board had already fallen into the hands of the challengers, fraud could be denounced by those still allied with the formerly dominant chieftain. Such actions would simultaneously acknowledge the significant strength of each faction, preserve the aura of legitimacy, and exemplify proper behavior by placing the decision in the hands of higher authorities, ostensibly outside the boundaries of the conflict.

Denunciation of unfair practices could also be made before judges or other officials. In the seesaw of parish dominance, letters poured into the president's office from delegados, justices of the peace, county judges, and district judges, each describing the same events from a distinct perspective. Such letters did not get written only to be filed away; they were intended to draw attention to a faction's presence, to one's leadership of it, and to one's candidacy for posts of still greater local authority.

As a first step toward victory, a challenging group attempted to disqualify the chairman of the electoral board. Although this required the action of constituted authority, it could be considered foul play if those in control at a still higher level disagreed with the result. The law of 1846 specified that the chairman should be the man who received the most votes at the last election for justices of the peace even if he had meanwhile been suspended from his duties or been indicted for administrative malfeasance. That left open, however, the possibility of indicting him for another kind of crime. A district judge, acting in the interests of a local faction, accused the chairman of the electoral board of having altered the registration rolls; indicted him for the "crime of falsification"; and so removed him from the board, thus allowing a leader of a rival faction, the first runner-up for justice of the peace, to take his place. The judge held no genuine hope of making the charge stick; he only needed to have the chairman under indictment at the time of the election. Two other means of replacing the chairman of the electoral board emerge from a single case in which the incumbent had died: one could poison him; or one could merely claim he had been poisoned and charge his successor with the crime, thereby allowing still a third person to take over the electoral process.[24]

As a newly emergent chief sought publicly to demonstrate his power, no better occasion could present itself than the moment at the election when his rival's clients came to vote. At that point when the electoral board decided on the identity of voters, a majority of the members could refuse to recognize that a voter was who he claimed to be, "despite the affirmations to the contrary of respectable people." In one parish "nothing counted for the recognition of the identity of voters, not the parish priest, not the subdelegado, not the [other] justice of the peace or the ward inspectors. They were nonentities for information in this regard." The true holder of local power was clearly in doubt. Majority members of another board announced publicly that they would not recognize the identity of voters from the other faction, even those who had had their qualifications as voters affirmed by a Regional High Court. When one voter—"well known in the parish"—moved forward toward the ballot box, the others greeted him with loud shouts and repeated epithets of *phosphoro*. One aggrieved party claimed that a board allowed a "sixteen-year-old boy, . . . unknown in these parts," to vote when they called the name of a man who, "according to the list [of registered voters], is forty-eight." The board could also eliminate voters because their names did not appear exactly as written on the rolls, "for the lack of a dot on the i," said one witness. Thus "on frivolous pretexts" a board denied voters their rights.[25] Especially galling to the citizen thus excluded could be the choice of a person of lower class to take his place as the rightful voter:

We know of one election in which, when a *Comendador* belonging to two [imperial honorific] orders, the owner of several rural establishments and a millionaire, appeared to vote, the board decided that he was not the registered individual whose name had been called, taking their whimsy to the point of allowing the local jailer to vote in his presence! At this same election, in place of a real-estate owner and lawyer, the board allowed a freedman to vote, and instead of the provincial tax collector, a black street urchin [*um moleque*] whom they had called in for this purpose and to whom they gave a few coins."[26]

Some alleged that even slaves substituted for legitimate voters in 1840.[27] Thus the faction that had gained control of the board rubbed in the ignominy of their rival's defeat; who could be the client of a man who had been defied in this way and let it pass?

One way to achieve victory was to have the voter drop more than one ballot into the ballot box. In order to end this abuse, the government issued instructions in 1856 that ballots "shall be closed on all sides." Furthermore, the slit in the ballot box should be only wide enough to allow one ballot to be inserted at a time. "When, in the act of counting the votes, more than one ballot is found inside the same covering, all such ballots shall be destroyed." Later the law specified that the ballots should be "closed on all sides with wafers, sealing wax, or another appropriate substance." If electoral boards found a ballot enclosed within another, they were to consider the outer one an envelope if it had names scratched out or changed, but otherwise both ballots should be considered invalid.[28] News of these legal provisions had apparently not reached the far frontier in Rio Grande do Sul. In 1861, according to some members of one board there, when they opened the ballot box they "found large ballots that, closed on themselves, hid other, smaller ones, and in these others still smaller. The smaller ballots were introduced along with the larger ones, which the falsifiers doubled in two, using a flatiron over them; thus the smaller ones were false." This alleged fraud had been easy to practice because of the "very small ballots . . . of fine white tissue paper . . . an inch and a half long by one [inch] wide," enclosed in larger ones "three-quarters of a hand long and one hand wide." Other members of the board, however, alleged that the majority simply wished to throw out those ballots not written "on the paper used by their party." In response to these practices, lawmakers in 1881 specified that voters should use "white or bluish paper that shall not be transparent or bear marks, signs, or numbers."[29]

Rival factions found endless means of fraud. A board member could deliberately misread a ballot and announce the name of another candidate. Or the numbers written down by a chosen name could be increased. The minutes of the electoral board could be altered. One subdelegado publicly boasted "right in the church" that he had done this, defying anyone to do something about it. To lessen the chance for such alterations, the law specified that the numbers written into the minutes should be spelled out, not entered as digits. Sometimes alterations could be detected by comparing the number of lines on different pages of the minutes or the handwriting of the page numbers, or by noting that some pages had not been initialed by all members of the electoral board. Finally, all voters could be "excused from voting, [and] the minutes drawn up in private houses in the absence even of the individuals mentioned therein as being members of the board." This technique became known as election by *bico de pena* (point of a pen), a phrase still in use today.[30]

Even as practitioners violated the spirit of the law, they paid attention to legal niceties that bespoke their curiously forensic ethos. In one locality members of the losing party could not vote because, although the Regional High Court had sustained their appeal against exclusion from the registration roll, a justice of the peace publicly announced that before election day "he would not open any official correspondence addressed to him" so as not to receive the notification of the court's action.[31] Although he did not lack other means to the same end, his preference for this one is revealing: no matter that he was going to exclude legitimate voters, he would observe the letter of the law and preserve the legal ground on which to defend his action later. Furthermore, the most assuredly legal actions could be used in fact to defend the interests of one side alone.

Often rival groups would each organize an election and simultaneously prepare distinct sets of electoral board minutes. "Duplicate" minutes became a leitmotiv of political discourse and the constant target of reformers. The law itself foresaw that rival electors could show up at the Electoral College, each holding a set of minutes as his credentials. Sometimes two entire Electoral Colleges met to represent a single district, and the County Council that tallied their vote, although required to forward results from both, would throw its weight behind the one it considered most legitimate. Even these Councils could split, and one group form a rump session, so that two Deputies could arrive in Rio de Janeiro, each with credentials supplied by a single, though divided, Council.[32]

Bribery was a much more serious crime than any of the practices discussed so far. It violated the acceptable standards of behavior, for it suggested that a leader lacked the ability to marshal followers simply through his magnetism, verve, or social position. In one sense all voting *agregados* received bribes, since on voting days their patron treated them to food and gave them shoes; but this did not constitute bribery as it was then understood. One critic of the electoral system, in discussing the practice, displayed more concern about "the fortunes that were ruined" than with its morality. A coffee planter complained that a local election "has already cost and will cost much money for both sides, estimated at 20 *contos* [U.S. $10,400] for each one. . . . Here in Sta. Thereza [Valença] the opposition provides money to the voters and is said to be ready to spend whatever it takes to win, or at least to bother us."[33] Outright payments of cash to electors, however, seem to have been just too much and met with disapproval from the Council of State. Perhaps such bribes subverted the dignity appropriate to the squires who typically formed the Electoral Colleges. Indeed relatively few accusations of open bribery surfaced. One politician confided to another, however, that in constructing the party slate, he had given preference to Arthur. "It's necessary to use certain *indicated means* (financial ones). Arthur is ready to employ them on his own account and is personally going throughout the district." Undated lists of names can be found in another leader's private papers with significant amounts of money next to each; these he boldly labeled "List of voters to whom I gave money" and "Various who received money for the elections." [34]

The above descriptions of fraud reveal two problematical dimensions that made elections gripping. First, would a challenge be offered to the dominant faction? And, then, how would it be done? A challenger might aim only at a better place in the local hierarchy, for instance, having his protest recorded, perhaps securing a high enough rank among those chosen as substitute electors to sit on the next electoral board; but even that small aim could signal defiance of the formerly dominant boss. As to the means, which ones would the dominant faction choose? Would it get away with it? If not, would the challenger resort to more forceful means in asserting his strength? Suddenly, the contest could become one not of will and personality, but of guns and knives.

Force

If fraud failed contenders turned to force. Local violence proved as endemic as its condemnation. A member of Parliament referred to the "use of force, not of public force, but of force from outside, of men known by the word *capangas*." A nineteenth-century dictionary defines *capanga* as "a bully who is paid as bodyguard for someone or for electoral services; but in this case he is more than a wardheeler, he is a club-wielding rowdy, sometimes an assassin." A milder but ironic voice described him as "someone who throws himself into electoral struggle in search of a salary and even more because he likes it." The definition of *capanga* depended on who authored the document. In the view of some, *capangas* could even be led by government officials: one county judge spent his time "going through the various sections of Caçapava accompanied by armed *capangas*, ordering the voters to vote with his group." Because one faction did not always hold all the positions of authority, the line between order and violence depended on the observer.[35] Weapons varied. In Rio de Janeiro voters exchanged "blows with clubs." They drove "sharp instruments" through one voter's back. According to a Conservative leader in 1872, "they used the dagger and the club, ... Zacharias, Octaviano and *tutti quanti* in the churches urging the *capangas* on." Partisans also hurled bricks and stones at each other, in one place seized from the very walls of the church. "Occasioned by the elections," reported the Minister of Empire, "a lot of weapons" were being shipped from Pernambuco to the neighboring province of Alagoas. When one delegado arrested a voter found "with a dagger in the midst of the church," a "serious tumult followed," and the delegado thought better of his actions, releasing his prisoner on seeing that his friends were "armed with small carbines, knives, clubs, etc." Physical force could be applied to enemies even without weapons. One man was "thrown down the front steps of the parish church, so that he was very bruised and had to be carried away in a hammock."[36]

Conflicts at the voting place could easily spread throughout the town. When a group of armed men gathered on the "patio of the church" in a town in Ceará, prepared "to knock downs its doors," the delegado went to them to talk it over. They would not even hear him out, and killed him with two shots. But the delegado had not gone alone, being accompanied by "some friends" and at least nine members of the National Guard, and a battle then raged between the two groups, resulting in the death of seven besides the delegado. In 1886 the provincial president of Bahia wired the Prime Minister about events on the fifteenth and sixteenth of January in the interior town of Lençois as the Electoral College was preparing to meet:

City invaded on 14th *capangas* and criminals. Board illegally constituted, majority protests. On 15th armed *capangas* clash police force. Attempted invasion of city chambers stopped by police force. No election held. Liberal electors shielded immense mass of *capangas* at residence of Liberal chief. Volleys and shots from this point on city. Three injured. . . . Police force only ten first-line men. I ordered immediate dispatch tomorrow 30 men of the line . . . to reestablish order."[37]

The threat of force—from either side—could be as effective as its actual use, for one faction could thus get the other to abstain from voting. To do so, however, it had to propagate the view that it

BOLLETIM ELEITORAL
As eleições correram tranquillamente em todas as freguezias; apenas em algumas houve pe-
quenos passatempos como pão de crear bichos, nuvens de murros; gyrandolas de bofetadas, chu-
veiros de descomposturas, tudo temperado de ponta de faca e gume de navalha, com que se
apagou o calor de alguns phosphoros.

Violent Elections, 1872

would use violence and use it more effectively than its rivals. "I am
sure," wrote one delegado, "that these terrifying rumors are spread
principally to instill terror in the weaker spirits or the more pacific
ones, and make the population [read: opponents?] abstain for fear
of some kind of conflict, rather than seeing themselves involved in
it." In the struggle for local supremacy, each opposing group strove
to frighten the other; as an election approached the agents of each
leader "crossed the territory of this jurisdiction in every direction,
lining up people who will turn up at the election. The parties must
enter the city in close order so as to better display their strength."
If bloodshed occurred in an election for justices of the peace and
county councilmen, the subsequent voting for electors to choose
national Deputies could be entirely peaceful, since the opponents
would not dare even to organize alternative electoral boards to pre-

pare duplicate minutes and send in rival delegates to the Electoral College: "There were no duplicates because their loss of much blood, the great violence they had suffered, . . . taught them to abandon the field." [38]

Violence at election time revealed one of three failures of the dominant faction: failure to dominate the opposition so completely as to keep it quiet; failure to yield enough ground to appease a rival leader, to maintain, in short, the appearance of fairness; or failure to recognize that conditions had changed and it should acquiesce in the dominance of a new group. The manipulation of the process by the dominant faction could be so outrageous, the force of constituted authority so arbitrarily employed, that violence seemed a logical and only recourse. As one majority member who prepared the minutes of the electoral board put it, "the turbulent ones, . . . knowing they are defeated," resort to violence. Now, as we have seen, whoever dominated the electoral board always won the election, so this statement has to be seen as the recognition that not even the appearance of fairness had been maintained. Since the result of an appeal could also be foreseen, violence appeared as the only alternative for the outs: "The Liberals, having abandoned the process of registration, now resort to intimidation." The use of force anticipated defeat. The election of justices of the peace indicated who would preside over the voting for Deputies; so "If this election is not annulled," wrote one district judge in October 1860, "you may count on the spilling of blood during the one in December [for Parliament]." Sometimes challengers put it plainly: when one group realized it would lose, its leaders met privately with the majority members of the electoral board and announced that either the board would agree on "a division of the election [that is, to share electors] or the spilling of blood was inevitable." [39] Violence also displayed a challenger's mistake in not making his power (and his will to use it) understood beforehand or in overestimating the likelihood of his military victory.

To have the necessary force at hand meant that the local chief had to rely on the loyalty of *agregados* and *moradores*. In this sense they may have held the advantage, for they could bargain and yield that loyalty to the patron who offered the most in terms of protection and benefits. But an *agregado* who chose the wrong side had sacrificed all, often even his life. The vote itself cost the *agregado* nothing, but because violence was part and parcel of elections, he gave up much to secure a patron's care. And he could not avoid choosing. When faced, for instance, with the threat of arbitrary recruitment into the Army as an alternative, it became logical for him to fight valiantly on his patron's behalf, since as one commentator put it during the Paraguayan War, at least then you died fighting near home, whereas if you lost the elections you were recruited like sheep "to the slaughterhouses of the South and the swamps of Paraguay."[40]

It should also be remembered that even violence could not affect a party's ultimate parliamentary strength. The point of using force consisted not in having enough electors to choose a Deputy, but in asserting who had strength in the parish. For this reason Cabinets to a large degree allowed local events to take their course until the rival factions, tired of fighting, appealed upward. As with fraud, so with violence: "order" meant looking the other way and then appointing to local positions of authority those who had already won in the field of battle, for either side might be useful in the next election. Even a Councilor of State recognized that "in an election the thing to do is to win, since once an election is won it will always be approved." Since Cabinets could call on only a relatively few men in the Army and the Police Corps, they did not spread them all over the national territory and took care to use them only selectively. For one thing, even if troops went in, those elected under their protection could fear reprisal the day the troops left: as one delegado reported, things now seemed peaceful, "due to the presence of the commander of the garrison [destacamento], but very serious rumors have surfaced that in the absence of those soldiers there will be a terrible reaction."[41]

So winners had a free hand. Writing in 1860, one district judge accusingly reported that four years earlier a local strongman, "along with various criminals, surrounded the parish church at dawn and from it expelled the electoral board, suffering no punishment for this act." According to one Liberal account of events in Uberaba (Minas Gerais), the Conservative Cabinet rewarded "all the individuals who took part in the acts of violence" in the elections of January 1886 by appointing them to the positions of delegado, first and second substitute delegados, subdelegado, public prosecutor, imperial tax collector, and county tax collector; and two others were made notaries. The victorious local leaders thus felt encouraged a few months later to persecute the previous county boss, "head of the Liberal Party, [National Guard] Lieutenant Colonel Antonio Borges Sampaio, a person of quality, distinguished lawyer, and exemplary *pai de família*." They "expelled him from his home by threats of death, [issued] with the backing of armed *capangas* in the midst of scenes of the greatest savagery." Since the Cabinet had not yet moved the county judge to another place, the new faction forced him to resign and "leave the city." It also set a deadline for the district judge to do the same. Local factions, through violence, gained Cabinet backing for their excesses and thus perpetuated their authority. Fraud or even violence could later find legal justification.[42]

The ideal of order sometimes dictated another course, however. To prevent even so much as the appearance of anarchy, the government occasionally decided to back one faction, but it did so cautiously, hoping to avoid taking sides until the natural victor could be determined. When one superior commandant of the National Guard publicly announced that he intended to win the election "at any cost, that he had a lot of ammunition and a lot of arms to repel his adversaries from the church," the provincial president forwarded to the district judge papers relieving the commandant of his post and ordering the new one "to gather immediately all weapons and ammunition that may have been distributed for the National Guard." Yet at the same time and most significantly, in his cover letter the president instructed the judge to keep these orders secret if there were any prospect of arranging a peaceful election and to use them only if nothing else worked. By taking this deliberate approach, the president allowed the threat of violence to frighten away opponents, since a "peaceful" election did not necessarily mean a fair one. The government worried most about the appearance of tranquility, and it much preferred to back the faction that could win without an overt use of force.[43]

The government frequently pursued the course of seeking an electoral compromise. In 1860 the president of Ceará "had the pleasure of reporting" that at one location where he had feared violence, "all fears have evaporated . . . because the two parties have come to an accord to divide the number of electors evenly between them."[44] A district judge, faced with two clashing factions led by the first and third justices of the peace, suggested that the second justice of the peace take over as chairman of the electoral board; when both groups rejected that alternative, he managed to persuade them at least to hold their elections in separate rooms and submit duplicate minutes, and this, he boasted, they had done "without the least confusion or agitation."[45]

The condemnation of violence characterized public discourse both because it contradicted the belief in order and because it threw into question the legitimacy of Brazilian liberalism. Residents of the European-oriented capital city found electoral violence especially disgusting. After the 1872 election the bishop of Rio de Janeiro bewailed the violence inside church buildings. "Still warm is the Brazilian and Catholic blood spilled within the pacific walls of the temples of God; . . . instead of the temple of the sainted Jesus, reverently guarded by priests, one sees a ballot box surrounded day and night by soldiers and partisans." He then came to the point: "In this opulent and populous capital live a large number of foreigners. . . . What will they say seeing that periodically [the temples of God] are transformed into battlegrounds where elections are fought? . . . And what will the Protestants say? . . . What will they say of our churches on election days?" And he concluded: "If at the capital there are such excesses even where good manners and gentility reign, at a place noteworthy for the politeness of the residents, the high social position of so many inhabitants, the presence of the highest authorities of the country, and the connections with foreigners from the most cultivated countries, what is to be feared in the rest of the Empire?"[46] In short, such actions affronted the standards of Europeanized behavior.

If scandalous to some city residents, electoral violence survived, was expected by most Brazilians, and did not truly shock. Violence was a necessary part of political struggle, for how else could an aspiring local leader call attention to his rising strength? Because relationships of power among the few locally rich constantly shifted, elections had to be held frequently so one had the opportunity to measure one's strength. If one were delegado, substitute county judge, or National Guard commandant, one's clientele automatically expanded, and electoral results could be secured with ease. So leaders of local struggles, although directly intending to win elections, indirectly intended to occupy the positions of local dominance—which in turn served to win elections. The road to such appointments lay along the course of violent action. The denunciation of fraud in official documents already signified some degree of strength for an aspiring chief and offered a middle step toward local dominance, but force was the only genuine source of power. Contemporaries commonly explained electoral violence in terms of ins and outs: "The official positions are occupied by those belonging to one faction [while] the side that is outside the official positions" formed the opposition; or, "One party, the Liberal one, had in its favor the *delegacia de policia* and the county judge-ship."[47] Violence logically followed. Whereas any one location might enjoy peace and stability for some stretch of time, every year violent struggle raged someplace in Brazil. Foreign observers, like some subsequent historians, too easily accepted the version the men in Rio de Janeiro so desperately wished to believe, that Brazil formed a land of staid and dignified elections and orderly political transitions. Reality was quite the contrary.

Men of wealth locally sought official positions for themselves, their family, and their clients by working through politicians and bureaucrats all the way to Cabinet Ministers. A Breves, a Lacerda Werneck, a Lins, or a Dantas counted on the reward of such placement for himself or his followers to aggrandize his already substantial authority. By gaining such positions these men extended their clientele and expanded the resources available to their family. Verily, the local chiefs struggled to *be* the government.

SIX

Faction and Party

AT FOUR IN THE MORNING of election day, Sunday, December 30, 1860, the plantation house of José Dutra de Faria bustled with activity. Over the past week, some 300 Conservative partisans under the leadership of Francisco Alves Moreira, another local landowner, had gathered there in preparation for an armed struggle to help Justice of the Peace Faria gain control of the parish church in the nearby village of Caçapava, 100 kilometers east of São Paulo. For too long, they felt, one of Faria's neighbors, the Liberal Venancio Felix da Rocha, had succeeded in keeping the Conservatives out of power by relying on hired guns and the abuse of his position as county judge. Rocha had been aided in these schemes, they charged, by his close friend the delegado, João Moreira da Costa, a lieutenant colonel in the National Guard and brother of the Liberal chieftain in the more important neighboring county of Taubaté. Costa had even, on various pretexts, they said, arrested several of Faria's fellow party members on Christmas Day and locked them up in the village jail to keep them from voting. But now Faria believed he had received official sanction from the district judge in Taubaté, a Conservative, to "secure the aid of private citizens if needed to make your authority respected"; and so he was counting on the armed might of his followers to restore a proper balance to local political life.[1] Faria's enemies, however, alleged that instead of local citizens his men included "deserters and other criminals from various counties," and "employees and *capangas*, blind and abject instruments of half a dozen caudillos."[2]

Faria and his men set off at the earliest break of a summer dawn, with Faria wearing the green and yellow sash of his office, intending to enter the town while its residents still slept and take up positions on the patio of the church. But as they neared the village, they found some of its inhabitants alert, and armed men at the street corners. That did not intimidate Faria, for he knew his men outnumbered their opponents. He paused at the head of his troop and dramatically raised his arms to cry, "Long live Peace! Long live the Emperor!" Others later claimed he had shouted, "Down with authority! Down with the *delegado*!" Whatever his words, they were met, he later said, by the cry, "Here's some lead [*aqui vai balla*]!" and a salvo of bullets.[3] Faria's men sought cover and began to fire back. Soon, as he expected, their superior numbers brought them victory and, half an hour later, after freeing those held in the jail, Faria proceeded on to the church. Three people lay dead and five others gravely wounded, including the wife of one of Faria's own supporters, who had come to the door of her house to help the injured. The dead included two members of the provincial Police Corps, whose chance passage through town had allowed Costa, the delegado, to press them into service on the side of his greatly outnumbered forces and at least put up a fight. Rocha, who at the time of the struggle was belatedly gathering his forces on his plantation, fled on foot to Taubaté, thirteen kilometers away, while his supporters hid in the woods. Thus the two Conservatives Faria and Moreira had bested their Liberal rivals Rocha and Costa. The delegado and the county judge had lost to the justice of the peace.

Despite the bloodshed, Faria proceeded during that day and the next to conduct the election in the normal fashion, acting in his capacity as the legally constituted chairman of the electoral board. The voters chose ten electors, who later, at the Electoral College, unanimously supported the Conservative ticket.[4] When the voting ended Faria mounted his horse and confidently set out for the provincial capital to report the misdeeds of his Liberal adversaries to the Conservative provincial president.

What was his surprise, however, to be met on January 3, two-thirds of the way to São Paulo, by the provincial chief of police and thirty Army soldiers with orders from the president for his arrest. The chief of police took Faria back to Caçapava, "in order not to hinder his defense," and put him in the very jail from which he had so recently freed his partisans.[5] The Conservative president, who had on December 31 ordered police troops put under the command of the Conservative district judge, now accused that same judge of unduly interfering in the election by illegally siding with one faction against the other, and ordered all troops to take commands henceforth only from the chief of police.

This story exemplifies several qualities of Brazilian political life already discussed in earlier chapters. The delegado and members of the Police Corps pitted themselves against bullyboys led by a local boss anxious to assert his strength. The leaders on both sides owned land. They struggled to gain positions of authority, and they appealed to higher-ups for approval. If the instruments of political control had worked to perfection, there would have been no incidents such as this one in Caçapava, for the hopelessness of electoral struggle would have been clear; both sides believed their superiors would back them, however, so they clashed, each sure their excesses would be overlooked. Neither faction undertook to oppose those above them in the chain of authority leading to the Cabinet. While Brazilian political leaders genuinely wanted elections to be orderly and fair, the very links between court and village—because messages could be misunderstood—produced flare-ups of violence. Such tendencies, as I have shown, were common.

Here, however, I wish to use these events to discuss two other characteristics that define Brazilian politics. First, citizens divided politically not because of party loyalties, much less ideological considerations, but because of personal ties, making party labels seriously misleading at both the local and the national level. Second, power flowed simultaneously "downwards" from the Cabinet through the provincial president and "upward" from local bigwigs to the president and Cabinet in eddies and swirls that defy simple summary. It is a complex task to identify its course.

That complexity explains the difficulty Cabinets encountered in exerting discipline over Deputies, in creating party loyalty among them. Candidates for election to Parliament had to be endorsed by both Cabinets and local chiefs. Only when a political leader made it to the Cabinet did he become interested in party discipline, that is, in having clear lines of command with which to muster easy majorities; until then politicians paid equal attention to their vicinal patrons. For all the lip service to the value of national parties, building them posed almost insurmountable difficulties. Consequently, "party" simply meant an affiliation among Deputies, and not a lasting commitment to program or policy. Parliamentary parties formed, split, and reformed, taking surprising and apparently contradictory positions on major issues right up to 1889. This precarious quality of the political parties goes far to explain the seeming contradictions in Brazilian political history that saw Conservatives supporting liberal causes and Liberals voting conservatively. Historians have stubbornly insisted on ignoring these realities, with the result that much of what has been written about political life during the Empire is necessarily confused and confusing. Keeping in mind the influence of the local chief on the Deputy can clarify the meaning participants saw in political events of their time. It can also suggest how the Empire prefigured practices often associated with the First Republic (1889-1930) and even those of today.

Personalistic Politics

Caçapava had been administratively separated from the county of Taubaté only five years before the bloody events of 1860. Although this area along the Paraíba River had long been a fattening ground for cattle coming from the South for sale in the city of Rio de Janeiro, after 1830 landowners there had begun to plant coffee. The number of coffee plantations in the county of Taubaté (then including Caçapava) had risen from 86 to 240 between 1836 and 1854, with a resulting jump in production from 770,000 pounds to 11.7 million. The population of the county of Caçapava in 1872, twelve years after the events narrated above, numbered 8,969. Nearly a fifth of these people were slaves, and only 1,423 free men were old enough to vote, of whom 860 were registered in 1870. Newly prosperous men on the rise struggled to assert their dominance over what must have been a growing and shifting population. Social flux impelled the struggle as much as uncertain political standing.[6]

Sharp political divisions characterized the county. In commenting on the election of 1860, the winning Conservative Deputy declared that the "Conservative Party is very large there, but always divided and, in the elections, the Liberals sometimes join one faction and sometimes another." Costa, the delegado, had probably been more honest, however, when he spoke of "the two political or, rather, personal factions here." The district judge in Taubaté agreed that one faction could be called "Conservative," whereas the other was composed of "some who call themselves Liberals and others who say Conservative, but all linked by ancient hatreds and a shared private enmity toward the others." In the records of past elections, the same names alternated in the minutes of the electoral boards back to 1842.[7]

A principal reason for the sudden outburst of violence in Caçapava in 1860 was the belief that the government would sanction the Conservative appeal to arms. The fact that a Conservative Cabinet ruled in Rio de Janeiro encouraged that belief. So did the party affiliation of the district judge. When he later saw the suddenly altered reaction of the provincial president, the judge hastily denied he had taken sides. He claimed that he had stayed totally aloof from electoral rivalries, and that only an accidental bureaucratic relationship—regarding signatures on a petition to him from the County Council—had linked his name to that of Moreira, the local Conservative chieftain. He admitted, however, that he had recommended to the provincial chief of police the removal of Rocha as delegado, and that "this became known, I know not how," so that in the public's mind his own name had become firmly linked with Faria's group. Others saw it differently. The president of the province later accusingly reported on the "lively interest that the district judge . . . took in the election of one candidate for Deputy."[8] Yet the provincial president himself had at one point berated that very judge for not being even more forceful, that is, more partisan. When Justice of the Peace Faria first wrote to the district judge reporting on the allegedly arbitrary actions of the delegado, the judge replied that all he could do by law was to write the delegado, advising him to do his duty; adding significantly, as we have seen, that if necessary the justice of the peace could summon the help of citizens to maintain his authority. The district judge explained to the provincial president on December 27 that he did not feel he should "interfere . . . in a struggle of unhinged passions at the risk of not being properly obeyed and of being misinterpreted." When the president heard of this four days later, he soundly castigated the district judge for his pusillanimity. A district judge, he insisted, had the right to "inspect and instruct" the locals, and the president ordered him to go at once to Caçapava and initiate a legal process to bring Rocha and Costa to trial for abusing their authority. The district judge cautiously (and wisely, as it turned out) avoided doing so, explaining that he needed more evidence and a formal charge by a police officer. Meanwhile, the provincial president on December 31 ordered troops put under the district judge's command, especially welcome news to the judge, since otherwise, he complained, he had no "public force" with which to enforce the law.[9]

Suddenly the signals changed. The president now accused the district judge of wanton partiality, removed the command of troops from him, dispatched the chief of police to Caçapava to enforce order, and issued new instructions calling for the arrest not of Rocha and Costa but of Faria instead. The reason for this sudden reversal lay in a letter the president received on January 2 from Marcelino José de Carvalho, a Conservative chieftain in Paraibuna. Paraibuna neighbored Caçapava, and their county seats were only 50 kilometers apart. There Carvalho owned at least five agricultural properties, including a coffee plantation called Fartura (Plenty) that he inherited through his mother from a colonial royal land grant. He claimed another plantation and ranch through squatters' rights established more than forty years earlier.[10] Carvalho had been elected a provincial assemblyman and held the rank of colonel in the National Guard. Everyone described him as a Conservative leader. His daughter, however, and here is the key, had married Rocha, head of the Liberals in Caçapava. On December 29, the day before the election, Carvalho went to Caçapava, either, as Rocha explained, "with the sole intention of conciliating the two factions" or, as Faria saw it, to "put himself at the head of [Rocha's] group directing things in a manner unfavorable to the freedom of the voters."[11]

Carvalho, "a man of recognized influence in the province," advised his son-in-law Rocha not to allow armed men to enter the parish church, and Rocha tried to follow his advice. In this action Rocha probably drew encouragement from his own close friendship with the Taubaté public prosecutor, the son-in-law of a large Caçapava landowner, who was also related to the principal political family in Taubaté. Rocha further counted on support from the brother of his ally Costa, a Liberal leader in Taubaté and a man of "important prestige." With these endorsements, Rocha doubted his opponents would resort to force. This miscalculation resulted in bloodshed. Even Carvalho would have fallen victim to the firing, "had he not quickly fled." [12] So two converging lines of authority now clashed: some counted on the district judge, presumably on good terms with the provincial president and thus with the Cabinet, while others relied on the bosses of both parties in neighboring counties. The villagers ended up dead and wounded. The president of the province abruptly changed sides when the Conservative Carvalho wrote him in support of the Liberal Rocha. The influence of such chiefs could not be ignored. Having first encouraged the district judge to intervene, the president later accused him of unduly using his influence.

The Minister of Justice, João Lustosa da Cunha Paranaguá, later visconde and then marquês de Paranaguá, the only Liberal in an otherwise solidly Conservative Cabinet, had probably been chosen precisely because of what some considered his spinelessness. The barão de Cotegipe later wrote of "the weakness of his spirit in any matter that would mean commitment, especially if he needs the support of those he might hurt." When the provincial president's report arrived in Rio de Janeiro, the chief bureaucrat in the Cabinet, noting the direction of events after Carvalho's intervention, suggested an immediate investigation of the Conservative district judge. The Liberal Minister of Justice, although agreeing, indicated that the role of the Liberals Rocha and Costa also demanded examination. Party labels had little effective meaning in the day-to-day work of winning elections and gaining public office. [13]

When Parliament met, although dominated by Conservatives, the Credentials Committee recommended against recognizing the legitimacy of the Conservative electors chosen in Caçapava by Faria's group and succeeded in getting the election annulled. This action had no effect on the choice of Deputies, since the electors from Caçapava did not have enough votes to influence the overall outcome one way or the other. The choice of electors, however, had much to do with who would rule locally. A new election in Caçapava, held in August 1861, returned only Liberal electors; among the voters who did not show up were Francisco Alves Moreira and José Dutra de Faria. [14] The action of Parliament could be taken as a demonstration of its commitment to fairness, had not other elec-

João Lustosa da Cunha Paranaguá (1821-1912),
later visconde and marquês de Paranaguá, 1861

tions in 1860 proved the contrary; its decision displayed rather the
permeability of party. The support for the Liberals of Caçapava
offered by the Conservative Parliament, Conservative Cabinet, and
Conservative president sheds much light on the party history of
nineteenth-century Brazil.

Loyalty to person, not to party or program, predominated. The
illiterate *agregados* who gathered at Faria's house, we may presume, knew little and cared less about such issues as tariff law or
currency policy. Whether they believed delegados should surrender
their judicial role to county judges we do not know, but in Caçapava delegado and county judge joined to lead the other faction.
Programs did not mobilize the ordinary man. Though loyalty may
be too strong a word—or suggest Faria's point of view rather than
that of his followers—these men looked to him for protection, the
use of land, and social place. For him they died. Even more directly,
personal connections linked family members. The County Council

included nephews, uncles, cousins, and in-laws. Parties as such held only a tenuous claim on those in Caçapava. As it was there, so it was throughout Brazil. Forty years earlier an Englishman had noted of elections that "those festive occasions are more especially selected by the *valentoens* [sic], or rustic bravos, for the purpose of wreaking their vengeance on the devoted heads of each other." Contemporaries often identified parties by the names of the candidates while other labels lay forgotten: "The two parties, Vasconcellista and Teixeirista, are energetically engaged in the struggle," said a president of Minas Gerais. Or, as he explained a few days later, "In this capital [city] the party of Dr. [Francisco Diogo Pereira de] Vasconcellos has won in one parish, and that of Manoel Teixeira de Souza in the other, each getting 11 electors." [15]

Everywhere local chiefs held the key to the election of Deputies. These chiefs were often electors themselves and certainly determined who would become one. They ordered the ballots with the list of names prepared and passed them out to their supporters. Certainly the electors so chosen knew to whom they owed their selection, and betrayals provoked shocked comment. A letter writer in Bahia, after referring to one elector as "the creature of Luiz Antonio who named him," went on to describe the behavior of another, "Augusto França, . . . who knew how to fool Pedro Brandão, who had placed him on his ticket. But França had already been bought by [Manuel Pinto de Souza] Dantas; only when they voted on the organization of the [Electoral College's presiding] board did he reveal his true colors, voting against the protest of Luiz Antonio." Normally, however, electors followed the instructions of the bosses who had placed them in the College, if they were not themselves those chiefs. As one Deputy disgustedly exclaimed, there were some districts "in which the majority of voters is made up of Indians, to put it plainly, savages, who will lend themselves to making electors anyone whom Tom, Dick, or Harry indicates. The electors (in certain places) do not know the political and social mission they should carry out; on the contrary, . . . having written on their ballot [for Deputy] the name given them by the *potentate* of the place, they judge they have fully satisfied a sovereign political right." [16]

Candidates for Deputy, therefore, directed their entreaties to electors or their patrons, not to ordinary voters. The personalistic nature of party politics meant that campaigning centered not on establishing a program, but on drawing on the loyalty of particular individuals. This appeal took place either in person or through letters. When an experienced provincial president advised a young candidate to write "a few little letters" to the locally prominent, he expressed a significant dimension of political reality: those chiefs would determine the outcome. The letters were brief and to the point: "You will much honor and oblige me by supporting me in the College of Valença," wrote one candidate. Sometimes the candidate resorted to mere form letters, having a secretary copy them out over and over again, with a vague appeal for "the efficacious support of your deserved influence in that Electoral College." The prospective Deputy did not spare the flattery. One referred to the addressee as "among the best-known and distinguished electoral influences" that "represent our real force in the province." Hinting at his own possible future role in securing patronage, he added, "I place myself and my friends at your disposal wherever I may be," and closed with the phrase, "your fellow party member, friend, and servant [*servo*]," a somewhat more humble expression than usual.[17] The local bigwigs in some places expected the candidate to visit them: "I have already been to Santa Rita [do Rio Negro], [S. Sebastião do] Alto, and Sta. Maria Magdalena. I arrived early this morning and this afternoon I go on to S. Francisco [de Paula]. I will be at least a substitute [Deputy] and there is hope of even more. Only by about August 6 will I have finished my pilgrimage."[18]

If candidates for election to Parliament did not contact electors in person, they relied on a third party, a friend or relative of both the candidate and the county boss, or on a chain of such contacts. One such middleman reported that he had written on behalf of a candidate to his friends, "who have connections in the district and ascendancy over the Gomes, father and son, of Brejo Grande. I did as much in Poções, etc., for [another candidate, Luis Acyoly Pereira] Franco, where a *Jew* called Fortunato, who is dedicated to me, exerts much influence." The personalistic character of the campaign meant family ties towered in importance. And just as women played an important role in preserving property within the bonds of family, they supplied the contacts to all the "in-laws" to whom politicians so regularly appealed. Women joined in the effort to bring electoral victory to their menfolk by drawing on their family

connections and writing on their behalf. Women also wrote letters
to secure appointments for office seekers, usually with political purpose in mind.[19]

So the Deputies in Parliament were chosen through elections
dominated by local chiefs driven by local rivalries. If they then
formed alliances with other Deputies and called themselves Liberal
or Conservative, their loyalty remained tied to the bosses who had
elected them. Most Deputies did not themselves head clienteles, although they could be related to the local bosses. Almost by definition they held law degrees. Their education and urban experience
distanced them from the rural bosses who controlled the Electoral
Colleges. The *bacharel* often expressed his disdain for those men,
all the more so because he depended on them for his own success.
In Parliament the Deputy could display his learning, his wit and
urbanity, his knowledge of the world beyond Brazil; but in campaigning he felt the weight of his sometimes illiterate patron. At the
same time, as long as he managed to secure positions of local authority for the county chief, the Deputy often enjoyed considerable
latitude in his legislative behavior and found the freedom to take up
philosophical positions according to his wishes.[20] In Parliament,
however, he encountered another constraint: the influence of the
Cabinet itself, where all appointments were decided.

The major interest of the local elites who chose the Deputies was
patronage. As we have seen, the county bigwig desired and, to some
extent, required appointment to positions of official authority in
order to maintain his following. While Deputies, Ministers, presidents, and judges all decried boss control, local potentates derived
their power from those very men by being appointed delegados or
National Guard officers. The vice-president of the province of Sergipe reported in 1851 on João Gomes de Melo, barão de Maroim,
"a robust fellow, a little over 40 years of age, active, with a cheerful
disposition and anxious to please," who, because of his wealth,
headed the provincial faction or party called Camondongo. "Up to
now the barão, whatever the ruling party, has sought to be in its
good graces," for "what the barão prefers above all else is to see his
relatives and friends in official positions; what he wants to avoid at
all costs is to find himself *cheated out of* the town of Maroim (those
are his very words)." The barão de Maroim himself ran for Deputy
and won election (or, should one say, elected himself?) in 1853,

going on to become a Senator in 1861. Perhaps most bothersome in all this to other Deputies as well as administrators were Maroim's "defects of education." By 1885 a politician expressed some relief that "although his [Maroim's] influence had once been worth much, it has somewhat declined lately." They had nothing to fear, however; throughout his political life Maroim's loyalty went not to party but to the Ministers who could assure him local control. As the president of Sergipe explained more generally in another letter, the support for the Conservatives came from men of property, "who have something to lose and thus they tend toward order. But above these tendencies, there is the blind love for local influence: when its preservation depends on an alliance with a Cabinet of opposite belief, they will probably sacrifice those tendencies for these desires." And he spelled out how it worked in still another letter: once the Conservatives took power in Rio de Janeiro, the members of a provincial faction had changed their party label and declared themselves Conservative and proceeded to "list in a book those who shall be considered Conservatives in Sergipe . . . and declare that such and such individuals shall not be Conservatives, . . . baptizing their opponents as Liberals."[21]

When a Cabinet faced Parliament, it sought support from Deputies for its legislative bills. If parliamentary sessions proved acrimonious and the Deputies cast their votes unpredictably, the Emperor might question the Prime Minister's effectiveness as leader. As Pedro II once explained to his daughter, "If the opposition were such that it slowed the work of a Conservative Cabinet, I would call the Liberals to the government."[22] The Cabinet, therefore, strove constantly for party discipline, that is, to ensure that Deputies supported its program. On the other hand, since the Emperor would sooner or later place the opposing party in power anyway, local chiefs had to guard their flanks and make sure they did not go so far in their loyalty to the current office holders as to make it impossible for them to support the opposing party at a later date. Cabinet members, in their turn, faced the challenge of managing a team in double-harness, using one set of reins to direct the Deputies and the other to guide the local bosses into supporting the right candidate. In both cases patronage was crucial. A Deputy depended on the Cabinet to secure appointments for the local chief and his clients, appointments that would enhance the chief's might at election time.

At the same time the Cabinet had to make clear to the parish boss that positions of local authority for himself and his clients required his support of a chosen Deputy. Encouraging this team of chief and Deputy to pull together challenged the coachman-skills of the best Prime Minister.

In general the aspiring politician who wished to become a Deputy for the first time sought endorsement from whichever Cabinet held power. As one contemporary noted, "to be the government's candidate is the ardent desire of every person who wishes a seat in Parliament; to proclaim himself as such and be so recognized is his first and principal concern."[23] If a candidate did not receive that endorsement, he could still turn to the local boss. For the future he found it useful to demonstrate his strength, that is, his ability to get electors to back him anyway. Thus, if victory could not be hoped for, at least one tried to make one's mark: "I think Rodolpho will win; but Cicero may perhaps be able to present a complaint to the Chamber of Deputies." Indeed, in that election for the ninth district carried out under a Liberal Cabinet, Rodolpho Epiphanio de Sousa Dantas defeated Cicero Dantas Martins, barão de Geremoabo. Although the result for Cicero had been a foregone conclusion, he considered it important to show his capacity to challenge the winner. At the next election carried out under a Conservative Cabinet (1886), his effort paid off: he won.[24] Not exceptionally a politician remarked, "We only want to salvage our honor in defeat." "I'll be content," he added, "if we don't disappear from the *map*."[25] Only the support of parish chiefs, despite their probable but temporary loss of positions of authority, could make that possible. So the Deputy stood at the intersection of two planes of power, one dominated by the Cabinet, the other by the village boss. *

---

* The ambiguity of the Deputy's impulse has to be kept constantly in mind, since personal loyalties also tied him to Cabinet members and, if a Cabinet were dismissed, he could not switch his allegiance to the new Prime Minister without endangering his credibility as a serious politician and man of character. The two planes of power were inadvertently captured by the statement that "the elected Deputies, instead of representing the opinion of the country, do not in fact represent anything but the whims of partisan ministries with their president-levers and their hamlet potentates": Braz Florentino Henriques de Souza, *Do Poder Moderador: Ensaio de direito constitucional contendo a análise do título V, capítulo I da Constituição Política do Brasil*, 2d ed. (1st 1864) (Brasília, 1978), p. 134.

Party affiliation played a relatively minor part in this struggle. If local factions struggled among themselves to be recognized as the legitimate receivers of patronage and political office from whoever controlled the central government, the Cabinet desired electoral support from whatever local faction would be most likely to win, that is, whoever exerted most strength. It was therefore irrelevant which party label a local faction adopted. In Caçapava a Conservative Cabinet could uphold a "Liberal" faction, especially if by so doing it would cement the loyalty of a chief in a neighboring county. The Conservative government had no difficulty in supporting the barão de Maroim in Sergipe, even though he and his followers had changed party labels four times in accordance with national trends and had received equivalent protection from Liberal governments.[26] When a Liberal Cabinet came to power, it would count on the same supporters. "In general," wrote one political commentator, "our [local] parties have been favorable to the central government, and only declare war on it when they totally lose hope of securing its support." As an example, he cited an Electoral College in which all members agreed to cooperate with each other in naming a Deputy, but nevertheless strung out their work for two days until they knew who had won in the provincial capital so their choice would be the same.[27] Frequently the rivalry and violence of local politics lay not between two groups bearing distinct party names, as happened in Caçapava, but between two factions both claiming to belong to the party then in power.

This reality clashed with the idealized view of party and government held by the politicians themselves. Brazilian leaders tended to look to Europe (as they did later to the United States) for models of action, for categories into which to put their own experience. Whether correct or not, they thought of European parties as disciplined, cohesive bodies that were divided along clearly demarcated boundaries of program, policy, and ideology. None of these qualities characterized Brazil, and the very men who rose to power by ignoring such precepts then bemoaned their absence. One celebrated contemporary student of the political system, Francisco Belisário Souza, claimed that "no one who has reflected on the parliamentary system anywhere in the world can ignore the utility of united and compact political parties with their own distinct ideas and known tendencies, directed by the most eminent men of politics. They are, in the phrase of Bulwer-Lytton, the nerves of parliamentary liberty." To this ideal the author contrasted "the parties dividing into groups, into conventicles of half a dozen individuals, without a connection or link, without common interests or traces of union." As one Senate committee concluded, "unfortunately, party means faction." When some attacked the "conciliation" Cabinet of 1853 as aiming to destroy the political parties, especially the Liberal Party, a Conservative replied: "If by parties you mean the old regiments of gladiators, the permanent social alarm, the ferocity of cannibalistic programs, . . . oh, yes, there may well be 'conciliation' to destroy such a plague; but one does not call these things the party and the partisans, but rather the faction and the factious." Curiously, no one suggested that parties themselves by their divisiveness posed a threat to national survival and should be avoided as unpatriotic, as had earlier happened in the United States. In 1854 a law school student, doubtless reflecting the views of his elders, wrote that "in the representative system there is a need for a constant and constitutional opposition." [28]

Party Building

One reason to deplore local factionalism came from the desire, once a man got into power at the center, for clear lines of command. The rivalries of local groups made his work harder, even if he had himself risen by exploiting them. Some of the obsession for order and harmony discussed earlier may actually reflect the politician's personal desire for a smooth ride. He wanted one county chief, one provincial group to support, not several. [29] Out of this concern grew attempts at party building, that is, attempts to discipline members of Parliament, to form firm and continuing alliances among them and so expand the authority of Prime Ministers and Cabinets. In effect national leaders tried to make Deputies more beholden to them than to the local chiefs. This effort also drew on and enhanced the idea of a nation, for it started from the premise that all of Brazil formed one domain within which political struggle would take place. In a nation the myriad local pyramids of patronage would give way to two large ones facing each other. Just as a village chief extended his following from family to faction, so a national one built on local factions to form a party. It hardly needs saying that building this kind of party did not imply elaborating a program, much less one that would endanger the established social order.[30]

The party boss in a province—sometimes the president, sometimes another—faced a tough task, for he had to contend with "the greatest difficulty, which is the candidates, by their number and indiscipline. . . . They spring up like mushrooms." When all the electors in a College wanted to support the Cabinet, wrote one observer, one would think that they would proceed with "peace and harmony"; but since there were fifteen candidates for five places, the majority party would immediately split. The Cabinet had to decide among candidates for election to Parliament, all claiming to share its views, and all drawing on the support of at least some electors. Then a president would take forceful action, and only losers complained: "at the presidential palace, clubs were organized, directed by the president, to designate the candidates who deserved the support of the government."[31]

An extensive series of letters survives between two Conservative leaders, João Maurício Wanderley, barão de Cotegipe, and João José d'Oliveira Junqueira Júnior, who took turns leading the party in Bahia and working in Rio de Janeiro. They struggled to fashion a disciplined party. "I cannot fail," wrote Cotegipe from Rio de Janeiro, "to thank you in the name of the party and in my own for the initiative you have taken in giving useful direction to the struggle that will take place."[32] Throughout their correspondence they confronted the basic problem of how to maintain the loyalty of Conservative candidates and prevent them from fighting each other rather than yielding and compromising among themselves in order to win victories against the Liberals. To do this the winners must be made to recognize that they owed their election to the endorsement they received from the party chiefs and not just the endorsement of the local bosses. In this effort one can see the limits of the electoral control exercised by the Cabinet. When, in the early 1870s, the Conservatives in Parliament split over the law freeing all future children born to slave mothers, the party leaders became particularly sensitive to the issue of loyalty. In considering who should be endorsed from Bahia, Cotegipe, now acting as provincial party captain, noted that among the three Deputies from the second district, two had supported the government program and the third "did not go to Parliament and took no stand. There are suspicions against him among our supporters and personal enmity on the part of some. . . . Would it be good to exclude him? I think not. . . . Foreseeing this difficulty I sounded him out and he said that if he is favored, we can count on his support." The Cabinet member Junqueira replied: "Has he joined our ticket? It is indispensable that he be explicit." The Cabinet was not prepared, Junqueira added, "to suffer any unwelcome surprise—for instance [his] election without a previous agreement with us and his later boasting of a victory that no one tried to deny him." A few years later, in 1881, with Cotegipe in Rio de Janeiro and Junqueira in Salvador, they again addressed the issue of choosing candidates to endorse. Two men in the eighth district of Bahia sought party approval. Junqueira wrote that "Innocencio [Marques de Araújo Góes Júnior] has some defects, and I myself have sometimes suffered his ingratitude, but he has rendered some services to the party, and there is a *certain circle* that supports him." Cotegipe thought that José Augusto Chaves would more likely win, "even though Innocencio has votes that are his *exclusively* and not of the party." They thus acknowledged the power of Innocencio's patron, and perhaps for this very reason Cotegipe preferred Chaves, who would be more beholden to the Cabinet.[33]

Even national leaders did not put loyalty to a program, or for that matter, to an abstraction such as "party," before individual, personal connections. To begin with they undermined their own efforts to create party institutions by allowing their private preferences to interfere. The main problem in June 1881 occurred in the district formed by the provincial capital, where two Conservatives wished party endorsement. One of them was Junqueira's *compadre*. Junqueira had tried to persuade the other man to run in the sixth district, "where we have some strength and there are two angry Liberal candidates" competing against each other, but the candidate did not want to run in that district. Junqueira could not summon the party leaders because one of the would-be candidates sat on the party directorate and its other members were candidates elsewhere; but more important, Junqueira did "not think we should give them so much power." Thus he himself preferred personal connection—his own—to institutionalized party apparatus. The relatively abstract goal of party victory blurred with the ambition to advance one's friends. Cotegipe as well, despite frequent talk of

João José d'Oliveira Jun-
queira Jr. (1832-88),
1861

João Maurício Wanderley,
barão de Cotegipe
(1815-89), 1861

party goals, had to confess that he personally could not support one candidate because he "profoundly offended me. I will abstain, although I admit that politically he is preferable."[34]

Cotegipe had long tried to establish party discipline not only in Bahia but throughout the country. In 1876 João Alfredo Correia de Oliveira wrote to him from his home in Pernambuco that, with other Conservative leaders there, he had arranged "an accord for the proper direction of the party." Now he would "come to an understanding with other friends" and work out a party ticket "in accord with the ideas that I brought from there [Rio de Janeiro]." In such work João Alfredo had much experience. Six years earlier, when he had been posted to the province of Pará, he had reported that "the Conservative Party of Pará is deeply divided and, as presently organized and directed, is not a party on which the government can confidently rely." Indeed, its leaders "fight like fishwives [*briga de comadres*]." João Alfredo finally managed, nevertheless, to "get them to agree, [and we] prepared the list of future members of the Provincial Assembly." All one could hope for, he added, was "the appearance of unity, which does not seem to me possible to convert into sincere peace, solidarity, and cohesion. I search for the Conservative Party of Pará and do not find it." In Rio Grande do Sul conditions appeared no better. The president of the province reported in 1871 that the Conservative Party consisted of two groups, "the wolves and the sheep." Their division did not spring from "ideas or aspirations" or from a "political cause," but arose through "purely personal" considerations. To a later president of Rio Grande do Sul, Cotegipe ranted, "The Conservatives are becoming ungovernable, and so will lose."[35]

Liberals suffered the same indiscipline as Conservatives. Their candidates in Rio de Janeiro, even during the crucial election of 1860, sometimes fell to fighting each other around the ballot box. From Rio Grande do Sul an observer reported in 1871, "The so-called Liberal Party ... is divided into as many little factions as there are different chiefs aspiring to lead the party." It had fallen into "complete disharmony." In response to these conditions, some Liberals met in Rio de Janeiro in 1875, determined to imitate the Conservatives in their organization. They now urged the creation of party directorates in each province because, said the meeting's chairman, "party discipline requires the most complete uniformity of effort, cohesion, and harmony." When they regained power, Liberals in fact devoted much energy to this end. Manuel Pinto de Sousa Dantas, a Cabinet member in 1880, spent some time ironing out differences among the Deputies from Pernambuco, in order to "reestablish in that province the unity of the Liberal Party." Of a senatorial election in Ceará, Prime Minister José Antonio Saraiva noted, "The division of the Liberal Party is an evil that greatly contributes to the lack of necessary regularity in the elections." He wrote to the provincial president that he did not want to "seem inclined toward one faction of the Liberal Party," but went on to bemoan the "deplorable consequences of a division in the party." Similarly, Affonso Celso de Assis Figueiredo, visconde de Ouro Preto, worked feverishly as Prime Minister in 1889 to get some would-be Liberal candidates to give up the race to ensure the victory of others. As he explained to a politician in Minas Gerais, "We cannot do without a numerous and disciplined majority in the next Chamber. We will reach this goal if in each district there is *only one candidate* recommended by the [party] directorate." Even the Republican Party faced this problem, and its leaders kept careful track of the allegiance of electors.[36]

From the point of view of the young aspiring politician, party discipline naturally held few attractions, and the support of a local patron seemed quite satisfactory. In 1875 one of them asked the Liberal Center (Centro Liberal) in Rio de Janeiro to approve his name as a candidate for Deputy from Minas Gerais. He considered his trump card the local support he enjoyed, so much so that if he had not had to run province-wide, he stressed, he would not have bothered to get party support. Since elections no longer took place just within districts, however, he could only issue threats: in case he did not find a place on the ticket, "I will abstain from participating in the election in my county, which will probably mean a total defeat [there] for the Liberals." At the same time he grumbled to another friend about the "nepotism" of the tickets organized at the party Center. The next year he went further: "It displeases me immensely the way they want to make candidates into supplicants before the panjandrums in Rio." A few months later he bitterly complained that "in tickets organized at the [party] Center we provincials enter only to fill a place." On the other hand, if the central party chiefs did nothing, candidates complained as well. One Conservative railed against the "indifference and abandonment of our paunchy [leaders] in Rio, who show no sign of life!" [37]

Liberals, like Conservatives, found their own reliance on personal connections an impediment to building a disciplined party. Manuel Pinto de Sousa Dantas, the Liberal Prime Minister, faced the constraints of family ties and friendships. In 1884 he sent his son to Bahia to iron out party differences and, among other things, place their good friend Ruy Barbosa as a candidate in the most securely Liberal district, the ninth. Dantas's cousin, however, son of the landed boss of the area, wanted that position for himself, and succeeded in getting it. Barbosa had to be content to run in the eighth district, which he lost. [38] Dantas's own fickleness probably harmed the principle of party loyalty, for he sometimes yielded to the pull of personal connections—or animosity—and sometimes worked for more abstract party goals. In 1881, in order to defeat his "most pitiless enemy," he supported the normally Conservative Joaquim Elísio Pereira Marinho, barão de Guahy, but three years later, apparently judging other claims more important, he threw the government's support behind that very enemy to defeat Guahy. [39]

The ambiguity of motivation in electoral behavior surfaced in the campaigns of two candidates. In 1878 a local boss in Bahia indicated he would support Ruy Barbosa for election because Barbosa's name had been "included in the list sent me by our friend Dr. Zama." Then he added that he would certainly support Barbosa "not only as a distinguished fellow party member but as a relative." Personal ties merged with party ones, and program did not appear important. When the abolitionist Joaquim Nabuco campaigned in 1885 as a Liberal in Pernambuco, a provincial chieftain confessed that "Nabuco's electoral campaign is over, and I took an active part in it, *not because I am in agreement with his ideas*, but because I could see we needed to lift up our Party. . . . The result of the election was such that it surprised a lot of people, principally the Conservatives." [40] Plainly the writer of those words did not support a program. But when he spoke of party, did he mean loyalty to party chiefs who placed Nabuco on the ticket? Or did he mean to strengthen the claims of Liberal bosses in the parishes in their demands for patronage? His true meaning remains unclear.

Party Inconstancy

When a party gained power, it rarely stuck to its preannounced program, such as it was, to the disgust of those few members of Parliament who actually expected to enact it. Dantas had to reassure Ruy Barbosa in 1878, telling him that "a Cabinet's program cannot include all the program of the ruling party." Barbosa should go ahead, said Dantas, and speak up, but though he criticized the government in the press, he should vote with the Cabinet: they could disagree "in economic and administrative questions, but let us not forget our political duty."[41] Political duty had to do not with program but with loyalty, and ultimately that loyalty remained personal. The power the Cabinet held over a Deputy lay in the patronage it would or would not dispense to his local patron. The Deputy, in turn, had to weigh the support of the patron against his own devotion to high-flown principle. With such a fragmented party system nationwide, it is not surprising that Deputies, once they arrived in Rio de Janeiro, formed only temporary alliances, or that party labels meant relatively little as far as program was concerned.

The party system, or rather the lack of a system, facilitated communication among the political elite. Government could still be an arrangement among friends. By not dividing themselves too rigidly into distinct parties, they could keep talking across party lines, bringing information to the Cabinet essential for its success. Dantas had begun his political career as a protégé of the Conservative chieftain Cotegipe. Later he became leader of the Liberals, but he could still count on Cotegipe, for instance, to time the Senate discussion of the budget as Dantas wished. Meanwhile, Cotegipe, when in the opposition, could expect a Liberal provincial president to take some interest in protecting the local interests of the Conservative Party for the sake of their friendship.[42] Similarly, a fellow Conservative in Salvador wrote Cotegipe asking him to speak to the Liberal Prime Minister Lafayette Rodrigues Pereira on behalf of a customshouse employee in Salvador who was being persecuted for having aided the Conservative in his political campaign: "It would be good for you to warn Lafayette, if that's not too difficult." On the other hand, the rivalry for positions and authority could also mean that politicians missed opportunities to undertake measures that would benefit the country, since if one party supported a certain action, the other would oppose it regardless of its merit.[43]

In locking up loyalty to the Cabinet, patronage provided the key. First, the connection between provincial and national "party" mirrored the relationship between local faction and central government, for electoral victory in the province won the right to patronage from Rio de Janeiro. That fact is clearly reflected in two closely spaced letters from Junqueira (then a Cabinet member) to Cotegipe, the party chief in Bahia. In the first Junqueira congratulated Cotegipe on the electors chosen and thanked him for the promise of their support: "You are a great general." Two weeks later Junqueira added, "You may be certain that we will do nothing regarding Bahia that will displease you, for I consider you the recognized and natural chief of the party."[44] Second, patronage from the central government could be used as a carrot and a stick directly to discipline candidates and shape a ticket that would ensure a cooperative Parliament. In 1884 a prospective candidate wrote to Cotegipe that perhaps his rival for the party's nomination could be persuaded to desist if Cotegipe were to promise him, "yourself, some immediate or early compensation; . . . he will pretend to be unhappy, declaring he will retire to private life, but down deep he will greatly thank you for it because he will thus free himself from [running in] the first district, which frightens him." When, a few months later, the Conservatives announced their party ticket, that candidate continued "to pretend to be upset," but did agree to run in another district. This change, however, had displeased a county boss, who thought his son had a right to the seat: "a small encouragement from you would comfort him some."[45]

A provincial president found himself in a doubly difficult position. On the one hand, he had to channel central government patronage to respond to the genuine strength of a dominant local faction. Therefore, he required the full cooperation of the central authorities in appointing or dismissing people according to a local leader's will and with knowledge of which chief led the biggest clientele. Yet at the same time, the president had to be able on occasion to switch government support from one faction to another to produce the election of the right Deputies. Then he had to use other levers, apply official force, dismiss some delegados and National

Guard officers, or even annul elections. In arranging endorsements for candidates, he had to do so "in such a way as not to create difficulties for the government or [stimulate] the opposition of [the province's] Deputies at the next session."[46] The president of São Paulo knew that no real contradiction existed between his general assignment to produce a Conservative victory and his specific task of backing a winning faction in Caçapava; only the measurement of local strength befuddled him, for he had at first not considered family connections across county boundaries. The important thing was to maintain the authority of the real boss in the region.

Many historians have noted with implied astonishment that in imperial Brazil the Conservative Party carried out liberal reforms and Liberals enforced conservative measures. This behavior derived from the very nature of party politics as Brazilians practiced it and does not merit surprise. The agglomerations of politicians in Parliament lacked strong links to each other or to separate, alternative, and self-sustaining electoral machines, much less to ideologically defined movements or disciplined electorates.[47] Several important politicians abandoned the Liberals to join the Conservatives, and vice versa; and only a few became identified with a particular reform, steadfastly held to a principled view, or took unwavering stands on controversial issues. As one observer put it, "parliamentary majorities are not formed by convictions but by passwords that Cabinet Ministers say they bear [from the Emperor]. Groups congregate and disperse like sand in the breeze."[48] They adopted party labels with little consistency, and much provincial- and parish-level struggle occurred within and not between the so-called parties. To be sure, when out of power the minority members of Parliament, led by the Senators of their party, would take up somewhat more doctrinaire positions, but even then, not rigidly. And it is true that in the cities voters began to identify more and more with particular stands and cast their votes for electors with the name and party of Deputies in mind. But there were few cities.

A look at several well-known political events of the period confirms the permeability of party, the inconstancy of party loyalty, the tendency toward party fragmentation, and the relative unimportance of party program. Alliances formed and dissolved, and the same Deputies were sometimes "Liberals" and sometimes "Conservatives." Historians have tried to impose a vision of party drawn from other places or other times, but the use of party labels should be always imagined as if written with quotation marks.

The weakness of party ties became apparent in the 1840s in Pernambuco, where the Liberal Party displayed deep splits.[49] One group of Liberal politicians, led by sugar planters and headed by Antonio Francisco de Paula Holanda Cavalcanti, had close family ties to the province's Conservative leaders and often worked with them in the Provincial Assembly while opposing the Conservatives in the national Parliament; another group, also depending on sugar planters for support but centered in the city districts and led by Antonio Pinto Chichorro da Gama, cooperated with the Conservatives in Parliament while fiercely opposing the Conservatives in the Provincial Assembly. In 1841 the Conservative Cabinet offered patronage appointments to the branch of Liberals led by Chichorro da Gama, in exchange for its acceptance in Parliament of the laws creating the delegados and centralizing power in Rio de Janeiro. This branch of the party accepted the offer and refused to join the Liberal revolt that broke out in 1842 in Minas Gerais and São Paulo, making defeat there all the more certain. As soon as the revolt ended, however, the Conservative Cabinet withdrew its patronage from Chichorro da Gama's faction and granted positions instead to the Conservatives of Pernambuco. As "his" Liberals lost their posts they tended to unite with the other Liberals—so much so that when the Conservative government finally fell, the new Liberal Cabinet of 1844 included representatives of both wings of Pernambuco's party.

That unity proved tenuous, and the Liberals soon fell to fighting again, precisely over the appointment of Chichorro da Gama as the president of Pernambuco. When his friends in the Cabinet were squeezed out, his Liberal allies in Parliament began voting against the Liberal Cabinet. The Cabinet then moved even further and dismissed Chichorro da Gama as provincial president. Tempers rose. The breaking point came with the Emperor's appointment in 1848 of a new Cabinet led by a Conservative Pernambuco planter, Pedro de Araújo Lima, visconde de Olinda, one-time Regent of the Empire. The Chichorro da Gama faction in Pernambuco rebelled. Taking their name from the beach street on which their newspaper office was located, the Praieiros did not find unconditional support among Liberal sugarmill owners of the interior and certainly little sympathy among the Liberals of Minas Gerais and São Paulo they had so recently disdained; their revolt soon collapsed. Yet both they and their opponents continued to call themselves Liberals. Their struggle had centered on patronage, not on political philosophy.[50]

The Conservative Party did not hew to a conservative program, even when it seemed most united. Although the Conservative Cabinet of 1848, headed at first by the visconde de Olinda, pushed through a number of measures to complete the strengthening of the central government and the position of the Rio de Janeiro coffee planters within it, many of the measures it undertook had been advocated by Liberals in the past and could have been supported by Liberal Deputies, had there now been any. Most notably the government suppressed the international slave trade. The measure had been advocated by a Liberal Cabinet in early 1848.[51] This Cabinet also pushed through the Commercial Code, first introduced in Parliament by Liberals in the 1830s, which helped merchants within Brazil mesh with the international economy. It began, moreover, to move toward free trade, a goal defended at least by some ideologically inclined liberals, if not particularly by Liberal politicians. Finally, it asserted Brazil's claim to influence over the nations bordering its southwestern frontier, thus defending the local interests of cattlemen in Rio Grande do Sul who, calling themselves Liberals, had only five years earlier been in revolt against central authority.

Fragmentation and shifting ties among members of Parliament are again starkly exemplified by a split among Conservatives in the early 1870s. In 1868 the Emperor appointed an arch-Conservative Cabinet led by the planter-oriented Joaquim José Rodrigues Torres, visconde de Itaborahy. For the first time since 1842, Liberal politicians formed a sharply defined party group. In May 1869 their Reform Club issued a manifesto calling for a thoroughgoing reform of the Constitution, the repeal of the law of 1841, an end to the National Guard as it then existed, the abolition of the system for dragooning soldiers, and the gradual emancipation of the slaves.[52] Some former Conservatives signed the document; and some party members, feeling that Itaborahy had gone too far in manipulating the election of 1868 by excluding all opponents, also opposed him, despite calling themselves Conservative. Because of these criticisms, the Cabinet did not long survive and, after an intervening one, the

Emperor named José Maria da Silva Paranhos (the elder), visconde do Rio Branco, Prime Minister in March 1871. His Liberal start in political life and his participation in the "conciliation" Cabinet (1853-58) augured moderate positions. Few, however, could have been prepared for his impressive political skill, his farsightedness, and his disinterested statesmanship.

In quick succession the Conservative Rio Branco pushed through a series of strikingly innovative measures that Liberals could only applaud. He began by finally separating some police and judicial functions, restricting the delegados' judicial role. The law he urged and passed limited to minor crimes the police's responsibility for hearing witnesses, preparing the case, and drawing up indictments, and, further, totally removed from the police the right to judge such cases. County judges would henceforth exercise these functions, and Rio Branco strengthened the judges' tenure. He removed the National Guard's assignment as a police force and recruiter for the Army; only the provincially paid police forces or, if they proved insufficient, the Army itself could now be called on to maintain order, with the National Guard to be summoned only in times of national emergency declared by act of Parliament. Rio Branco also suggested the need for proportional representation in elections, thus encouraging the study of reforms that eventually resulted in the electoral law of 1875, discussed earlier, passed by a later but still Conservative Cabinet. Most surprisingly, he persuaded the Council of State to back his effort to push through the Law of Free Birth, granting freedom to all children subsequently born to slave women. By these measures Rio Branco satisfied both liberal opinion and many of the Liberals in Parliament, while driving a wedge between his followers and the right wing of his party. That wing campaigned hard against him in 1872 but won few seats; Rio Branco ably wielded the power of patronage to secure the election of Deputies loyal to him.[53] When, in 1878, the Emperor finally called on the Liberals once again to head the government, not much remained of their original program of 1868 that had not been accomplished. In short, Rio Branco's government had firmly occupied the predominant center, breaking with fellow Conservatives, supporting so-called Liberal measures, and again demonstrating the meaninglessness of party labels.[54]

José Maria da Silva Paranhos (the elder; 1819-80),
later visconde do Rio Branco, 1861

In the 1880s an even more devastating split developed among
Liberal Deputies over the disturbing issue of slavery. Compelled by
the rising force of abolitionism in the cities, by the weakening commitment to the institution both in western São Paulo and in the
Northeast, and by slave unrest, Prime Minister Manuel Pinto de
Souza Dantas introduced a measure calling for freeing without
compensation those slaves reaching the age of sixty. Many of his
fellow Liberals in Parliament rushed to oppose him, and one of
them actually introduced a bill of no confidence. Even though Liberals enjoyed a clear majority of 65 to 46, only 52 Deputies supported him, and this included four Conservatives. New elections

resulted in the same division: despite the presence of 77 Liberals, Dantas suffered another parliamentary defeat in 1885, 52 to 50.[55]

That defeat, even with the Dantas Cabinet's close supervision of the election, reflects the political system's inability to cope with issues over which the Deputies' landed patrons were divided. Like all previous ones, the election itself had centered on the issue of patronage. On this score Dantas won handily. It was only Dantas's program that went down to defeat. Emancipation, in the eyes of some, threatened the very existence of their class, while for others, including many slaveholders, it stood as the only hope of their survival. The elected Deputies were Liberal but not emancipationist. One abolitionist complained at the time that the election had not been conducted on the issue of slavery.[56] This parliamentary vote uncovered some of the limits to the Cabinet's power to control elections and bring to Rio de Janeiro men who would back the government's legislative program. For all the levers of power at its command, the central government could not act autonomously, disregarding the interests of the propertied who formed the other plane of patronage to which Deputies responded. Most of the time the laws passed in Parliament did not directly impinge on the interests of local chiefs; but when they did, the Deputies ceased to be the obedient clients of the Cabinet. The historian Robert Conrad has persuasively argued that regional differences between the Northeast and the coffee-producing Center-South greatly affected parliamentary divisions because representatives of the Northeast tended to support emancipation.[57] Still to be examined, however, are the characteristics of particular electoral districts and the predilections of county bosses. Moreover, if it is striking that many Deputies chose to risk losing their seats rather than support the government's program, it is equally notable that so many Deputies voted for Dantas on an issue whose eventual outcome was in doubt. Precisely measuring the relative weight of ideological commitment, personal allegiance to the Prime Minister, and cautious obedience to local patrons remains a task for the future.

The slavery issue continued to expose the fragility of party alliance. After the fall of the Dantas Cabinet, the Emperor called on the Liberal José Antonio Saraiva to find a middle way. He altered the Dantas bill in many respects to make it palatable to slavocrats, including the provision that sixty-year-old slaves should work another three years as compensation to their masters, before being genuinely freed. The bill as altered garnered the support of most Conservatives, but was now opposed by the Liberals who had previously supported the Dantas measure. It narrowly passed in the Chamber of Deputies. Saraiva found himself too weak politically to continue and, with the Liberals now too fragmented to form a new government, the Emperor logically turned to the Conservatives, naming the barão de Cotegipe Prime Minister.[58] The Conservative Cotegipe then oversaw the final passage of the Dantas-Saraiva bill through the Senate, thus once again suggesting that party rubrics had little meaning. Cotegipe also supervised new elections that, relying on the forceful use of patronage, succeeded in extracting from the same electorate an overwhelmingly Conservative majority.

Finally, in 1888, when the Conservative Cotegipe refused to put through the final abolition of slavery, his longtime faithful ally, the equally Conservative João Alfredo Correia de Oliveira, did the job instead. In this, he worked with the same Parliament as had Cotegipe, a Conservative one. When accused of being disloyal to the Conservative Party, João Alfredo replied, "No one has ever accepted in the organization of [Brazilian] political parties the existence of an infallible authority with power over all, to decree who is in the party and who is outside it." Paulino José Soares de Souza (2º), the son of the visconde de Uruguay and a staunch Conservative like his father, disappointed at not being named Prime Minister so he could include indemnification to slaveowners in an abolition bill, joined the Liberals on another matter to bring the Conservative João Alfredo government down. The divided Conservatives, both in 1871 and in 1888, nevertheless got the credit for the passage of major liberal reforms. As one caustic observer remarked, "The Conservative Party is the party of reforms . . . because . . . if this country marches, it marches ass-end first."[59]

These patterns of party history resulted directly from the fact that thoughout the years of the Empire parties had no consistent programs and simply represented momentary alliances of men in Parliament around particular questions. Members owed their election not to their defense of issues but, on the whole, to the combined support of the Cabinet and local chieftains interested in patronage. Some politicians might try to build party unity and discipline, but that never became a goal in itself, and these very same men often broke their principles when it suited them, that is to say, when the expectations of their culture required it. For almost fifty years parliamentary parties had formed, split up, and reformed, but governments had succeeded in maintaining political stability and unity, adjudicating differences among the members of the economic elite and keeping the poor in their place. In short the parties worked well enough just as they were to maintain the hegemony of the propertied.

The Social Base of Party

Before concluding this chapter we may usefully consider the social base of party alignments. Since I have just shown parties to have been inconstant and transitory, it may seem odd to take the matter up. But allegations have been made that deserve specific examination. The claim is that a middle class of urban professionals, public employees, merchants, and tradesmen flocked to the Liberal Party, a party presumably seen as a group of voters, not of legislators.[60] Like most myths, this one contains some grain of truth. In the cities, where voters could be less easily controlled and appeals to program could prove more effective, those of middling wealth both had a greater voice in politics and found the ideology of individual rights more attractive than in the countryside. In the 1840s, for instance, the leaders of the Praia wing of the Pernambucan Liberal Party drew enough strength from an urban group that felt insecure financially to take on opposition to Portuguese merchants as part of their program. Equally, landowners in the newest regions, engaged in carving their estates out of virgin forest, in areas where individual ambition had freer reign, where most settlers had arrived only recently, where men held their property more precariously and land concentrated less massively in the hands of the few, these men may have chafed at the control exerted by politicians at the center even if, or perhaps because, in appointing delegados and National Guard officers, the choice fell on one of them, that is, on a rival who had not yet clearly constructed a clientele on his own hook. More provincial autonomy might have lessened the national reach of the wealthiest coffee planters in Rio de Janeiro and of the most firmly established sugar magnates around Salvador and Recife, that is, of men who had direct access to such political leaders as the marquês do Paraná, the barão de Cotegipe, and the marquês de Olinda. It should be remembered that "liberalism" in Brazil principally meant favoring local elites over national ones. In this sense Liberal Party candidates for Parliament may have appealed to men of lesser wealth, although one would not normally describe these planters as "middle class." Sometimes contemporaries themselves alleged that a difference in wealth led to differing political interest: a planter said he joined the Conservatives because "I had something to lose." A justice of the peace in Crato, Ceará, claimed that the Conservatives had been defeated by "the Liberal Party, smaller in number and wealth, but fuller of arrogance and animosity, led by men [of] ambition but lacking in fortune."[61]

The evidence presented in this book makes clear why, on the whole, neither Liberals nor Conservatives could be described as middle class or bourgeois. Men of substance locally, counting on their *agregados*, extended family members, and other dependents, formed the bulwark of both parties, and might even alternately support them, as did the barão de Maroim. Both Liberals and Conservatives in Caçapava owned land, apparently in equally large properties. As we have seen, Joaquim José de Souza Breves, the coffee planter of Piraí, whom no one would describe as of middling wealth, led the Liberal Party in his county, while the barão do Paty do Alferes in neighboring Vassouras firmly defended the Conservatives. Both took up their political positions while that region could still be described as a frontier. Similarly, sugar planters of equivalent wealth led each side in Pernambuco, for instance, Holanda Cavalcanti, a Liberal, and Araújo Lima (marquês de Olinda), a Conservative. In contrast, neither small landowners nor city residents controlled *agregados* in large enough numbers to make a difference. And parties won or lost elections in the countryside, not in the city.

Moreover, the leading merchants, perforce engaged in export trade, were in intimate contact with the planting class; coffee planters often became partners in the firms of coffee factors and sometimes organized these houses themselves. Planters also lent money to other planters, and some became bankers, while rich merchants typically purchased land with their profits. On major policies—such as slavery, immigration, public lands, and federalism—planters and merchants would normally be found on both sides.[62]

Finally, since the Liberal Party did not truly hew to a liberal program (whether seen in terms of individual rights or decentralization), if urban voters and ambitious planters turned to it, they did so only for lack of an alternative. Certainly few Liberals ever spoke deliberately on behalf of the poor, although a few attacked the very wealthy. Outsiders scornfully noted, as did Miguel Lemos, the Positivist leader, that Parliament was "an assembly of planters or of agents for planters."[63]

Even Republicans came from the same kinds of family and sometimes from the very same families as the Liberals and Conservatives. In the 1880s Joaquim José de Souza Breves Júnior became a Republican, as did two grandsons of Francisco Peixoto de Lacerda Werneck, the barão do Paty do Alferes. In Pará, an active center of Republican agitation, the Republicans belonged to the same families as politicians in the major parties, although joined by the petty bourgeoisie. Under these circumstances it is not surprising that Conservatives and Republicans often cooperated during the last months of the Empire.[64]

The Deputies themselves, regardless of party, did not necessarily come from families of great wealth or tradition. A professional career could be carved out by sons of middle-class urban families, especially if they could secure the protection and benevolence of a wealthy patron. With a law degree in hand, contacts with sons of prominent families, a sharp intelligence, and an eye for the main chance, a man of modest means might very well make it into Parliament. If he performed well as public prosecutor, judge, provincial president, or Deputy, he could receive a choice appointment in a Regional High Court or even enter the Cabinet. Journalism sometimes proved a path to the same end. Some journalist-Deputies chose to serve those who urged reformist causes, but for every example of such a tendency—Ruy Barbosa, for instance—others could be found to contradict it—like Francisco de Sales Torres Homem, the visconde de Inhomerim, who became the paladin of retrograde policies after a rebellious youth. No statistical study of the Deputies has ever been undertaken attempting to link class background to political position. Though their credentials stated their occupation, this was often merely listed as *bacharel*, that is, law graduate.[65] Judges formed a large number, especially at midcentury. Occupation, even when more specific, tells us little about wealth and its source, and even less about connections. On the whole members of Parliament acted as clients of local bosses or as spokesmen for their own wealthier relatives, even as they obediently served the Cabinet.[66] Those who pushed liberal reform successfully did so only when backed by a significant segment of the propertied. Surely real success as a politician, entrance into the Cabinet, for instance, meant in Brazil, as in most places, a record of avoiding the advocacy of measures that would radically alter the social system.[67]

Political life also implied an easy familiarity with other men of influence, typically men of wealth. Major politicians maintained houses appropriate for entertaining, and their homes served as the informal venue for political decision making—their homes or the offices of the party newspaper. As Cotegipe, himself a sugar planter, wrote to his protégé João Alfredo Correia de Oliveira: "Today I am in my new home on Marquês de Abrantes Street. If you are free, come today at 5 o'clock to share our dinner"; he would also invite another politician, and "we will talk." When together in Rio de Janeiro, Junqueira invited Cotegipe to "have soup *without the least formality*" on Junqueira's birthday. In Salvador the merchant-politician barão de Guahy invited Cotegipe for dinner "with us and with Dr. Eduardo Ramos, completely 'en famille.' Our afternoon meal is usually served at 5, more or less." Younger men did the same. A youthful merchant in Salvador sent a note to Ruy Barbosa: "Rodolpho [Dantas], Chico, and Juca, dine today with us at 5:30 with the family; [please come and] complete the clique [*panelinha*] of such good friends." Soup, dinner, birthday parties, all suggest servants, a relatively large house, proper manners, standing among the right people, a rare position within a society where so few held property.[68] (Such practices also imply a close connection between politics and the family; these were not two separate spheres, but one. And politics would be talked about at table with the women present, women who often took a lively interest in extending family resources, whether material or political.)

Regardless of what minor tendencies there may have been for Liberals to speak for the interests of an urban group or for those of less than preeminent wealth, or for the Conservatives to win elections in the more established, wealthier regions, the Deputies shared a common social background, and the predominant direction of both parties pointed toward the real issue: the patronage of village chiefs. The landed bosses of Caçapava, Liberal and Conservative, divided over that essential matter and none other. Local leaders did not particularly care to achieve some goals that to a later generation may seem instinctive. The question of revenues did not surface forcefully as long as those leaders got their control over positions of authority. Even if the revenues from which local appointments were paid went first to the central government before returning, that would not disturb the local boss, whose power did not depend on a constituency potentially unhappy with the level of taxation (which fell mainly on imports anyway). As long as he could name his clients to all the posts in the public service and there was no rival font of placement, he did not demand an increase in positions and thus an increase in revenue. Moreover, he and many of his clients were interested in such positions more because of the authority they conferred than because of the salaries they brought.

Parliament did not divide over conflicting demands of interest groups or social classes. Insofar as slightly different nuances of emphasis occurred within it—for example, along regional lines—they manifested themselves within parties and not between them. Liberals and Conservatives focused equally on their rural base, North and South. And since in rural areas almost by definition the local factions were led by large landowners, we can see why no measure was ever undertaken that upset all such men at once. The abolition of slavery in 1888 took place only when a large slice of landowners either no longer cared (as in the Northeast generally) or were actively in favor of abolition. The authority of the rural bosses remained untouched. As one observer had much earlier remarked, "Let us see if the Cabinet can dismiss and transfer the planters from their estates." [69]

Parish and county factions lay at the base of political division in nineteenth-century Brazil, and the instability of party alignments among Deputies logically flowed from that reality. Personal loyalty, personal connection, made every Deputy in Parliament beholden to two masters: the village chief whose friends and relatives were electors, and the Cabinet member who named that chief to the coveted position of delegado, National Guard commandant, or substitute county judge. At the local level "two parties or rather two gangs [bandos]," or rival groups "of all sizes, names, and qualities," competed for dominance.[70] Out of these factions emerged the electors who chose the Deputies. Despite vigorous efforts by some leading politicians to build national parties, factions remained more significant. No wonder parliamentary politics constantly made allies out of former enemies, and party labels were put on and taken off almost as easily as a set of clothes. To be sure some politicians seemed more attuned to policies designed to protect individual rights, advance provincial autonomy, and lessen the Emperor's prerogatives, but no party steadfastly advocated such measures. Indeed the Conservatives were as likely to pass liberal legislation as were the Liberals. For a Deputy's constituency had voted not for a defender of a program or even for an obedient party agent, but for a man who could secure positions from the Cabinet. In every locality, if there were "ins" there must be "outs," and the essential question, as in Caçapava, revolved around who would get the official posts. That question remained paramount throughout the Empire, even after a reform in the electoral system, and indeed retained its importance well into the twentieth century.

SEVEN

Electoral Reform

SOCIAL AND ECONOMIC CHANGE IN the 1860s and 1870s impelled some alterations in Brazilian political culture, with accompanying effects on electoral institutions. The impact of electoral reform on such issues as personal loyalty and factional strife proved minimal, but the altered understandings of society such reform reveals are striking. The larger changes can be briefly summarized. First, the railroad increased the pace and shifted the center of economic life. By 1868 rails had reached inland from Rio de Janeiro to the Paraíba River valley and from Santos to the highlands of São Paulo. Railway building greatly accelerated thereafter, from 522 kilometers constructed in the 1860s to 2,653 during the next decade, allowing coffee production to spread into new areas, especially in the province of São Paulo. The total value of coffee exports from Brazil grew sevenfold between 1841 and 1881. Second, increasing export trade encouraged the rise of urban interests. A growing number of city dwellers administered the additional banks, transport companies, and insurance corporations organized to serve the rising demands of the coffee trade. Expanding governmental revenues, derived from coffee, also financed a proliferating urban-centered bureaucracy. Even smaller towns in the coffee region gained importance as distributing centers for foodstuffs and imports. Third, the larger urban market and spreading fan of railway lines, combined with the effects of military procurement for the Paraguayan War (1865-70), stimulated some manufacturing, especially in Rio de Janeiro city. By the mid-1870s iron foundries, textile mills, breweries, shoe factories, and the hat industry had all attained some significance, so that urban residents now had more varied interests, and an industrial working class began to appear. Finally, the end of the African slave trade in 1850 and passage in 1871 of the law freeing the children of slave mothers pointed clearly if belatedly to the end of slavery. By 1879 voices in Parliament began to demand more rapid emancipation if not immediate abolition.[1]

Both city dwellers and wealthy planters, for different reasons, pressed for reforms in the electoral system. Urban groups, although ultimately dependent on the export economy, now questioned some older patterns of political life. Educated city dwellers especially criticized the excessive political power of the rural boss, a power that blocked any attempt to increase their own weight in the political process. Living in the cities, bureaucrats, merchants, industrialists, engineers, and professional men, now more than ever, looked to Europe for standards of political behavior. They began to consider the county oligarch indicative of Brazil's backwardness and barbarism, a point of view shared by many *bacharéis*, even sons of landed bosses.[2] Because these men saw the illiterate *agregados* as giving the rural bosses an unfair advantage in elections, they suggested that voting should be restricted to the literate and the propertied, by which they principally meant themselves. By this means they also wished to set themselves off from the urban masses, since rubbing shoulders with the city's working poor in chaotic elections offended their sensibility. Moreover, with the increasing pace of economic activity and the spread of standards that placed a premium on economic success, men of middling wealth began to accept the idea that the ownership of property proved a person's virtue. From that belief a short step took one to its corollary: the poor lacked virtue and therefore did not deserve to vote. Literate Brazilians began to be told that the "evils" of the electoral system resided in its inclusiveness.

Some planters, in their turn, feared the emergence of a large group of freedmen enjoying political rights. As they considered the effect of the 1871 free-birth law, they doubted (at least momentarily) their own capacity to maintain control over the newly freed as they did over *agregados*. While many planters viewed emancipation itself without trepidation, they had forebodings about the political role of the former slave. The end of slavery proved worse in the anticipation than in the fact. With hindsight the historian knows that the technique of combining violence and selective benevolence continued to work after the abolition of slavery in 1888, just as it did before; at the time, however, slaveholders could not be sure. As a Northeasterner put it, the "sugarmill owners, rentiers, and all of us, . . . the most important class, the first guarantee of public order, [are] weighed down with the imminent expropriation of our instruments of work." A politician captured the fearful mood of the times when, in 1883, reflecting back on the changes since 1871, he called for additional police, saying, "More than ever is felt the lack of local forces . . . ready to lend their support to maintain personal security and public order. The social transformation that is taking place and every day inevitably speeds up demands them."[3] At least at that moment, some planters and ranchers preferred to rely on citified *bacharéis* rather than on *agregados*, and became willing to countenance an increase in the influence of the lettered elites in elections if freedmen could be excluded.

This chapter considers, first, the criticisms leveled at the old electoral system of indirect elections and, then, the legislative process that created a new one. The class prejudices that informed the rising fear of *agregados* and freedmen found undisguised expression in the various proposals for reform. The electoral law of 1881 reduced the number of those who voted from over 1,000,000 to some 150,000, yet curiously—and symptomatically—this law has often been misinterpreted, then and later, as a democratic measure, hailed as a great victory for enlightenment and freedom. The truth is that the fear of an expanding number of free workers who might misuse their voting rights overshadowed the possible gains that had earlier justified a wide electorate as witness to a hierarchical drama. That ritual no longer seemed worthwhile. Increasingly, the laboring classes appeared as dangerous classes.

The Attack on Indirect Elections

Urban growth and the impending freedom of slaves created the classic tension between liberalism and democracy, leading to the exclusion of the masses from the polling places. "Liberty and equality," wrote one commentator, "are diametrically opposed and only go together in the mouths of demagogues or tyrants." Ruy

Barbosa, an energetic young publicist, agreed, contending that the main threat to freedom lay in the "tyranny . . . exercised by democracy against the individual." Emphasizing the importance of "the human molecule, the vigorous, educated and free *individual*," he stressed that political equality was relative, depending on the "inequality of social conditions" and the "inequality of natural aptitudes." To demand equality for all reflected the "corruption that comes from socialist error." Ninety years after the French Revolution, a speaker in Parliament blamed it for introducing "the principle of equality, the greatest danger to be found in society." Another writer added that "God created men free, and thereafter inequality grew between them because of their good or bad use of natural liberty: thus social inferiority and superiority." The current rules on elections, however, "deny all this and dare to correct the work of God, . . . wishing all men to be equal in order to be free!" Such distrust of democracy reflected a renewed fear of the poor. A Conservative ideologue asked, "What? Shall we say to the illiterate, the idiot, the beggar, that his opinion and his vote weigh as much as those of the wise man, the property holder, the distinguished citizen?" That would be like "the feet dictating laws to the head."[4]

Both liberals and conservatives—ideologically defined—now found themselves in agreement that only the propertied should vote. José Antonio de Figueiredo, a prominent liberal reformer, maintained that "every good electoral system should have as its goal that the greatest possible number of proprietors participate in choosing a Deputy; that all those interests on which institutions rest should be represented; [and] that [only] those citizens who are . . . distinguished by their education, morality, enlightenment, or management of business . . . should be called [to the ballot box]." A conservative chimed in: "There is no society where the lowest and most numerous part of the population enjoys the slightest share in the division of power; everywhere it is the numerical minorities that dictate the law." These were "the innate tutors of their fellow citizens." Another conservative, the novelist-politician José de Alencar, elaborated: "Dignity and electoral independence cannot exist in the masses," for "the rural worker, the factory worker, the man of the people, has a very limited horizon; his spirit does not rise above petty local squabbles. These classes are unable [*inhabeis*] to choose a national representative." Still another writer insisted that the only solution to corrupt elections would be to turn them over to "the less numerous class, the less needy, the less dependent, less ignorant, less given to scenes of violence—freer, therefore, of inclinations toward anarchy." An increasing number of voices began to plead for direct elections with a stiff property qualification.[5]

Figueiredo also spoke of the dangers implied in the existing electoral system, dangers to order posed by the lower classes. Noting the low property qualifications then in force, allowing virtually everyone to vote, he wondered how the country could keep operating with an electoral system that, "instead of calling to the ballot boxes the capable ones, the intelligent and superior classes," did just the opposite. After describing the poor as "incapable" of electoral independence, he went on: "In political society they are, with reason, regarded [in the same way] as are *minors* in domestic society." The result has been "this general lack of prestige that undermines the principle of authority. Yet nothing is more frightening or more prejudicial to society than to encourage contempt for those in power." Figueiredo sarcastically declared himself astounded to find as defenders of the existing system some Conservatives "who say they are faithful and exclusive sectarians of the principle of authority and friends of order." Allowing such a broad spectrum of the population to vote, Figueiredo said, was "truly communist, for it confers on all the same political rights without distinction as to capacity." The existing electoral laws relied on "principles most subversive of order, of morality, and even of religion"; their real danger lay in their potential for "compromising social order." Another liberal firebrand, José Ignacio de Abreu e Lima (2°), also warned against any system that "turned over the most sacred and important duty of society to those who most need watching."[6]

Urban criticisms of voting practices equally attacked the county chief and the lowly voter. Figueiredo decried the electoral system for "perpetuating the dominion of village bosses [*mandões de aldeia*]." He despised these rural potentates: "individuals who have no position and no merit, are good for nothing except to be electors or justices of the peace." Turning to those who defended the electoral law, he asked, "What do you offer instead? . . . The reign of blindness, of fury, of corruption, of disorder—the imprudence of the wage-earning class! . . . What you want is that a small class of potentates, helped on by a servile, blind, and improvident clientele, should exclusively control elections." Figueiredo only grudgingly admitted landowners to the group to be endowed with political rights: "urban real-estate owners, capitalists, farmers above a certain level [*agricultores de certa ordem*], medical doctors, Navy and Army officers, *bacharéis*, lawyers, priests, etc." In contrast, professionals and businessmen merited his special attention, for their "important rights shine out," requiring others to respect them wherever they were: "in court, in the pulpit, in the banks and business world, in teaching, in the Army and Navy, and in the government."[7]

The debate provoked some writers to defend the existing system. It exemplified, they said, the corporate unity of society, the solidarity of the patriarchal household, and the principles of paternalism. These conservatives argued that the system worked well, that property qualifications would drive apart "classes and individuals," whereas a broad suffrage brought "them together by virtue of . . . the mutual dependence Providentially established between all classes and individuals." Men who prized status and dominion condemned a high property qualification for voters, since it would make government representative not of "the nation" but of the "rich class." It would "degenerate the government into an aristocracy of money, of all kinds the worst." All this, let us remember, in defense of a two-tiered electoral system that clearly safeguarded an unequal social structure! José de Alencar in fact defended the old system precisely because it did exclude the poor from exercising real power. The Progressive Party in 1862, holding that universal suffrage was impossible, had specifically dismissed direct elections from its program as necessarily requiring a "distinction between social classes," a measure that would deprive "many Brazilian citizens of their political rights."[8]

The urban emphasis of the reform impulse can be found in many of the specific proposals for change. The Liberal Party, founded in 1869 under the leadership of José Thomaz Nabuco de Araújo, suggested in its program that a clear distinction be drawn between rural and urban districts. In cities of over 10,000 population, all those with an income sufficient to qualify as electors under the existing law should be allowed to vote directly, but everywhere else the electoral system would remain unchanged. Cities of this size, besides being centers of commercial and manufacturing wealth and congregating a sizable number of professionals, would have included only provincial capitals with numerous public employees. Nabuco de Araújo explained that in the cities "there is democratic force, the influence of opinion, publicity, the possibility of inspecting, independence. Direct elections in the interior would be a thousand times worse than indirect ones." Setting appropriate property qualifications there would be impossible, "since there is no land tax," whereas in the cities the existing real-estate tax could be used as a guide. If a law extended direct elections to the countryside, he said, "the great seigneurs [would] not require intermediary influences; with *capangas* they could make Deputies."[9]

Another proposed reform would have automatically added certain members to the Electoral Colleges beyond those chosen by the voters. Several Liberal and Conservative Deputies joined in co-sponsoring a bill in 1868 that would have included in every Electoral College all clergymen, officers of the armed services, graduates of establishments of higher education, and primary and secondary schoolteachers, plus anyone who paid in advance a rent above a certain figure. The proposal went to committee and remained forgotten, but its bias in favor of professionals is clear. The Conservative Minister of Empire in 1870, a member of a prominent landed family in Rio de Janeiro, countered that suggestion by appealing to an old colonial formula: as additional members of the Colleges, he recommended "*os homens bons* [literally, the good men, that is, the men of standing] of all parties," plus "the citizens who possess the presumed characteristics of independence and intellectual development above the ordinary level." He thus leant his weight to the inclusion of planters and men of rural property, however vaguely defined.[10] These ideas suggest the alternative forces pushing for reform of the existing electoral rules.

Among those who advocated direct elections for a limited few stood Francisco Belisario Soares de Souza, whom contemporaries called Belisario. A member of an ultra-conservative political family rooted in the plantations of the province of Rio de Janeiro, and a nephew of the visconde de Uruguay, he had opposed Rio Branco's drive to pass the Law of Free Birth. In winning election in 1872, Belisario had had to overcome Rio Branco's influence, that is, the opposition of the moderates in his own party, and that betrayal (as he saw it) left him embittered. He understood the source of the government's control of elections as deriving from the power it

Francisco Belisário Soares de Souza (1839-89)
and His Book, 1873

wielded over ignorant voters. He rushed into print with a series of
articles calling for limited, direct suffrage. When gathered into a
book that same year, those articles came to exercise a major influence on those who considered the problem of elections throughout
the next decade. An illustrated humor magazine soon published a
cartoon showing Belisario holding his book as he peered through a
window at voters engaged in a violent free-for-all on the stairs leading into a church.[11]

Belisario expressed deep contempt for the lower class and a close
identification with the interests of men of property. In describing
the elections in the city of Rio de Janeiro, he scorned "the nomadic
laborer who works here today and there tomorrow, the flunky in a
public office, . . . the peddler, the itinerant slave trader." Perhaps his

emotional commitment to electoral reform arose in fear that emancipation could only provoke chaos, for he stressed that "universal
suffrage is an immense danger at times of social crises or during
popular commotions." He railed against "the *popular* passions, in-
flammable, unreflective, and often brutal." Regardless of what electoral laws existed, he went on, if one turned elections over to "the
lowest segment of society, to the most ignorant and dependent,"
one would succeed only in creating a travesty. Under the present
system, "the voters are the great mass enrolled in the registration
lists, a turbulent rabble, ignorant, undistinguished, and dependent." The voting process drew "the unknown multitudes, blind
instruments—either of individual passions or of the authorities."
As he saw it, "For the ignorant and illiterate individual who inhab-
its our country, it matters little whether Peter or Paul is Deputy." If
"the *popular* masses, alternatively indifferent or impassioned and
furious," got their way, no electoral law could save society.[12]

Another persistent advocate of electoral change was Aureliano
Candido Tavares Bastos. Despite some contradictory impulses, he
generally defended the interests of São Paulo coffee planters in the
newer regions. An ardent believer in free trade and the need to attract foreign capital to railroad enterprises, he always pushed measures that would expand Brazil's exports. Though he wished to encourage immigration from Europe, he held a low view of Brazilian
working men—one is left to speculate whether for him the principal difference between Brazilian and foreign workers was their race.
If so, the specter of freedmen voting could only have filled him with
foreboding. In 1873 he published a fiery pamphlet in which he denounced the role in "our elections [of] the most brutish classes of
our population, these barbaric hordes who live in vice and crime."
He then appealed to both the planters and the urban classes by
alleging—in an amazing twist of reasoning—that the existing system made the poor lazy and unwilling to work: "This right of voting . . . keeps them in idleness and dependence on the rich and powerful."[13] In a few years planters would themselves say much the
same thing.

Legislation

The Rio Branco Cabinet, though it came to power in 1871 expressly to push through a series of other reforms, also took up elec-

toral ones. By then several advocates of change had gone well beyond the Liberal program of 1869 and now asked for direct
elections nationwide, in the countryside as well as in the city, limited, of course, to those with property. Others remained more cautious. They felt that alterations in other areas—diminishing the
power of delegados, creating a lottery in place of forced recruitment, removing the police duties of the National Guard and further
restricting the government's power to move judges—would solve
the problem of controlled elections. Moreover, these more timid
spirits, including the Emperor, feared that instituting direct elections would require amending the Constitution and so open the
door to other, more far-reaching and potentially dangerous changes
in the entire political structure.[14] In the end Rio Branco, in addition
to his many other reforms, did introduce a bill to alter the electoral
law in several respects. The Conservative Cabinet that succeeded
him pushed through the law of 1875 based on that proposal. It
included provisions allowing for proportional representation of minority interests, as I have already noted.

This law of 1875 introduced several other innovations that established important precedents, although falling far short of the goals
set forth by most reformers. First, it called for the permanent registration of voters rather than the annual procedures by which last
year's voters could find themselves excluded, while new voters became legitimate. Second, the list of registered voters, although prepared by the local registration boards as before, would only be
completed by Boards of Revision chaired by the county judge acting
with two other citizens chosen by the County Council. Third, the
law specified that a numbered registration certificate (*título de
eleitor*) would then be issued to each voter, bearing his signature (if
he knew how to write) and his age, civil status, profession, income,
and parents' names. Fourth, no voter would be denied the right to
vote so long as his signature matched the one on the certificate in
his possession; if the members of the electoral board entertained
any doubt about his identity, they should not reject his ballot but
accept it and keep it separate from the rest.[15]

Most important, the law of 1875 specified how the would-be
voter would establish that he had the requisite income of 200 milreis. Although it still left the door open to many poor people, it
made it much more difficult to establish one's annual income. No
longer would this be left to sworn statements of casual spectators.

Positive proof was now required. The voter could, for example, present receipts for taxes paid that year or a copy of an officially recognized contract for a three-year lease on land "that he cultivates." Alternatively, he might present a copy of a judicial act in which he had proved his income. At the same time, however, the law opened up exceptions for several groups, permitting men to establish their income simply by virtue of their occupation or status, such as "advocates, solicitors, doctors, surgeons, pharmacists," officers in the armed services, clerics, merchants registered at the Board of Trade, plantation or factory owners, captains or licensed pilots of merchant ships, and anyone with a diploma from any of the Empire's institutions of secondary or higher education. The voter now had to undertake a considerable amount of paperwork; in a volume of documents regarding appeals from men who had been excluded from the initial registration process, we find stacks of affidavits from third parties on income, place of residence, age, and rent paid.[16]

In keeping with the spirit of the law, the Emperor instructed his daughter, whom he left as Regent when he visited the United States in 1876, to insist with the Cabinet that it take measures to assure proof of income and make certain that its subordinates did not "contradict its desire for . . . a faithful execution of the law." He went on to suggest the need for a new measure that would exclude illiterates from voting. As he later commented, "It's not the dress that will turn Messalina into a vestal virgin, but the [improved] culture of the people and thus of the government." In saying this, he faithfully captured the biases of the propertied against the ignorant.[17]

Demands for further electoral reform grew louder, and in January 1878 Pedro II finally dismissed the Conservatives (in power for ten years) and summoned a Liberal leader, João Lins Vieira Cansansão de Sinimbú, to form a Cabinet.[18] Sinimbú then supervised elections designed to bring to the capital a Parliament ready to collaborate with him in his announced intention of reforming the electoral law, although we may note at this point that the measures he proposed would draw support from many Conservatives and opposition from many Liberals—as in other matters, parties did not stand for programs. It is ironic that a Cabinet wishing to pass a law that would theoretically restrict the power of the government to control elections did not hesitate to use the customary means to ensure its own success.

While this electoral campaign took place, Sinimbú, acting as Minister of Agriculture, convened Brazil's first agricultural congress. He had summoned it to consider the needs of export agriculture in the South-Central region, and almost all the delegates were coffee planters; it quickly became caught up with the hotly debated question of electoral reform. Most delegates wanted the electorate restricted to a narrow layer of society that would vote directly for the nation's representatives. As one planter put it, the only solution was to exclude "from the ballot box the scum of the people." "It is undeniable," added another, "that in order to display great political influence in their county, many of our fellow countrymen sacrifice their own agricultural interests, turning a large part of their lands over to lazy and idle men." He concluded that "it is necessary to repel from the ballot box the ignorant mass that has joined in to pervert national representation." A planter from the Paraíba Valley suggested that specific measures be adopted "forbidding the *agregado* from being a voter." Another argued instead that the propertied should be forbidden to take in free Brazilian workers "as *agregados*, except to use them in cultivation." Only two speakers objected to these views. One denied that planters kept *agregados* for electoral purposes: "Brazilians in general are generous; landowners, since they are benevolent, accept these poor men, who then work for them, attaching themselves to the household. It may be that they become an element in elections, since they may understand it to be their duty to accompany their patrons; but that does not make them thugs." The coffee planter and Liberal politician Joaquim José de Souza Breves Júnior also argued against limiting the right to vote. He alleged that such a measure would discourage the immigration of rural workers from Europe, although one may wonder whether he did not fear more for his own political machine in Mangaratiba. Behind all their debates loomed the fear of the impending end of slavery.[19]

Meanwhile, the newly formed Sinimbú Cabinet encountered difficulties throughout 1878 in resolving its internal disagreements on electoral reform.[20] Most of the members wished to restrict the vote, while one, Gaspar Silveira Martins, stood firm to extend it. That fiery leader came from Rio Grande do Sul, increasingly an area of small properties farmed by European immigrants, often Protestant, although he was himself a large rancher.[21] When the new Parliament convened in December, the government had still not prepared its bill on electoral reform, despite eleven months of work. Finally, on February 5, 1879, Silveira Martins left the Cabinet, and within a week the government proposed direct elections with restricted suffrage.

As the Cabinet was struggling over its internal divisions, the Council of State also met to consider the matter. It unanimously agreed that the system should be altered, and most members believed the vote should be restricted to the literate. On almost every other issue, however, it divided. Several Councillors urged measures to define "net income" more precisely. The crucial problem for the Council, however, was the fact that the system of indirect elections lay enshrined in the Constitution, promulgated by Pedro I himself in 1824. Even the property qualification had been spelled out there. The electoral system could not be changed without tampering with that text, an alarming thought. A Parliament empowered to pass a constitutional amendment could also alter other institutions. Some members suggested that perhaps an assembly summoned to consider the reform of one article of the Constitution could be dismissed if it took up other issues. The Council reached no decision on the matter.[22]

And when the Cabinet brought forth its proposed electoral reform in February 1879, it did in fact call for a constitutional amendment. It proposed that Deputies to the next Parliament be charged with altering the nation's basic charter so as to institute direct elections and limit suffrage to those whose income equaled that already required of electors. The bill implied that this amount would be set only as a lower limit, and could later be raised by law. Furthermore, illiterates would not be allowed to vote (nor would Protestants), regardless of income.[23]

Silveira Martins now joined the opposition, along with several other Liberal dissidents, in demanding instead a widening of the electorate by abolishing all property restrictions. One speaker went so far as to threaten that if so many lost their right to vote, they "[could] only oppose force with force." These speakers denied that the lower class alone tended toward corruption: the poor man could be bought "with money, but [so could] the lawyer with administrative contracts, the courtier with titles, the businessman with subsidies and privileges, the ambitious with jobs and positions." Much more "scandalous" than allowing illiterates to vote was blaming them for fraudulent registration processes or false and duplicated minutes of electoral boards, matters that were carried out, after all, only by those who could read and write.[24]

Others, also Liberals, defended the bill. They expressed the views of their class in contrasting the ignorance of the poor and the wisdom of the propertied. Ruy Barbosa said those who wished to maintain the vote of illiterates "defend the sovereignty of ignorance, mother of misery, mother of subservience, mother of immorality, mother of all social ruin." One former Republican, now a member of the Liberal Cabinet, asked rhetorically, "Do ignorance and blindness, because they are widespread, abundant, and generalized, thus acquire the right to govern?" And he answered, "If eight-tenths of the population of the Empire is illiterate, then these eight-tenths should be governed by the two-tenths who know how to read and write."[25] If the propertied felt these illiterate voters now posed a threat but had not earlier, one can conclude that the change came from their understanding that slavery was ending.

Although Sinimbú had earlier argued to Silveira Martins that restricting the vote was a necessary concession to ensure the Senate's approval of direct elections, the Senate turned the measure down. A powerful Conservative Senator—Cotegipe—pointed out that, without changing the existing system, a Cabinet willing to "maintain the most scrupulous impartiality and moderation during an election [could] diminish if not totally eliminate" the system's deficiencies. "When the general tendency [in the world] is toward widening the circle of those interested in public affairs to the largest possible number," it seemed strange to him to "run counter to the principles so highly proclaimed by our Constitution more than half a century ago, and this at a time when education is more diffused, wealth is greater, communication is easier, and there is more knowledge of things and of men." In addition the exclusion of illiterates might strike at many important persons, patrons of the legislators themselves. A Senator reflected the scorn of the planter for the urban intellectual, arguing that "he could present many examples of men who, not knowing how to read or write, had accumulated vast fortunes; and these men certainly had more interest in the welfare of society than others who passed their time reading romances and are good for nothing else."[26] The real reason for senatorial opposition, however, is not hard to find. The bill called for the next Parliament to be given constituent power, and Senators could not have been unaware of the frequently voiced demand to end their life tenure. They saw any tinkering with the Constitution as an even greater danger to the Empire than popular participation in elections. The suggestion that the Constitution could so easily be altered frightened them. The Sinimbú Cabinet, weakened by the opposition to this measure in the Senate, found itself further debilitated when the growing discontent of urban interests over other issues found expression in a riot protesting a minor tram-tax in the city of Rio de Janeiro. The government's indiscriminate use of force to subdue the rioters completely discredited the Cabinet, and it quickly fell.[27]

It was replaced by another Liberal Cabinet, led by José Antonio Saraiva, in March 1880. Saraiva also supported electoral reform but set out to push it through by law instead of by constitutional amendment. Saraiva proved a much abler politician than Sinimbú and had been an established party leader much longer. Always known as a conservative Liberal, he came from a landowning family and possessed a sugar plantation himself.[28] His proposed bill aimed at restricting political participation to the few; he engaged in enough give-and-take, however, to win support even from many legislators who desired universal suffrage. Thus, for instance, to Silveira Martins, from a province with many immigrants, he offered a provision that would open the polls to Protestants and even allow them to be elected to Parliament, though this measure was opposed by most members of the Council of State.[29] At the same time Saraiva attracted support from Conservatives by carefully eschewing other reform measures being pushed by a new generation of politicians, such as the complete emancipation of the slaves.

In the boldest stroke of all, Saraiva actually agreed to lower the income requirement of electors by half, making it equivalent to the constitutional requirement for voters and thus collapsing the distinction between them. Henceforth the law would refer only to electors (*eleitores*) and not to voters (*votantes*),* and elections for

---

* A practice I shall follow, even though Electoral Colleges no longer met.

José Antonio Saraiva (1823-95), 1861

Deputy and Senator would be direct. But Saraiva specified a list of extremely complicated documents needed to prove the requisite annual income. Although, as we have seen, virtually everyone would have enough income, very few would be able to produce these particular proofs. Saraiva argued that "the proof of income will be vitiated once you admit proof by sworn testimony or any other except by documents, and documents that are trustworthy." He insisted that on this question of the proof of income he would not yield; and he did not.[30] Because he had not deprived anyone of his constitutional right to vote, Saraiva maintained that no constitutional amendment need be passed. The reform could be instituted through an ordinary law.

Saraiva roughly sketched out the provisions he envisioned even before leaving Salvador to accept the post of Prime Minister. He

asked Manuel Pinto de Sousa Dantas to enlist Ruy Barbosa's language skills in drafting the law, but Saraiva must get the credit or
blame for its provisions. Even without altering the rules on who
could qualify as a voter, he thought, much could be done to place
power in the hands of the propertied. Some measures he suggested
that did not enter the final law indicate his bent of mind. The electoral boards, for instance, could be organized by the "electors with
the most income in the parish." Another idea, later also dropped,
called for a Senator to be chosen by all the Senators, Deputies, and
assemblymen from his province, plus 50 electors chosen from
among the men with the most income in each parish.[31]

As finally enacted, the law clearly expressed the class biases of its
creators in the specifications it set for proof of income. Because
these specifications are central to understanding its import, they are
worth examining in detail. The list of required documents needed
to prove the requisite income was exceedingly precise:

One set of proofs, for instance, referred to income from real property. There were only three acceptable proofs: (1) for a rural
property occupied by the owner, proof of title with a price of
purchase that would, at 6 percent, yield the requisite 200 milreis,
or a judicial evaluation establishing that value; (2) for a rural
property leased to another, a lease contract that specified the
rental value, properly registered at a notary public; and (3) for
urban properties a certificate from the tax office that the property
had been assessed as having an annual rental value of not less
than 200 milreis.

A renter needed a ruling from a district judge based on tax office
documents, rental contracts, *and* receipts that he paid 200 milreis
a year for a rural property or a variable amount on a sliding scale
for an urban property, ranging up to 400 milreis in the city of
Rio de Janeiro.

Merchants had to present proof of their inscription in the Board
of Trade also demonstrating sufficient capital investment to
yield 200 milreis in annual income. The same was true for ship
captains.

Owners of factories or shops also had to prove they had capital
sufficient, if invested at 6 percent, to provide the requisite annual
income.

Managers of factories or head cashiers of commercial establishments were to prove that the enterprise in which they worked had
a capital sufficient to produce twice the required annual income.
Only payment of certain specific taxes would establish these sources
of income, in itself extremely modest, and all proofs had to bear
a date one year previous to voter registration. As Saraiva explained it, only taxes on property and on business would do;
otherwise someone could come along and pay taxes for twenty
or thirty people all at once and thus make them electors.
Stockholders in banks and other companies or depositors in gov-
ernment-run savings institutions had to submit certificates showing their capital or savings to be sufficient to produce the necessary income.
Public servants had to show various documents regarding their
salaries, but other types of employees could not rely on salaries
at all as proofs of income.
Exempted from providing any proof of income were several classes
of public servants, from Ministers of State, Senators, and Deputies to provincial presidents, judges, clergymen, upper bureaucrats in specified offices, delegados, subdelegados, and officers in
the armed services.
In addition any graduate of a legally recognized school who could
show his diploma, public school teachers, professors, and administrators, and teachers in publicly inspected private schools
would be exempted from presenting proof of income.[32]

Thus, quite clearly, the ability to produce certain proofs of property ownership or occupation substituted for a higher level of income in ensuring that only the elite would vote, whether rural or
urban. The law barred the way to the ballot box for the great mass
of the people. As Joaquim Nabuco put it, it placed Brazilians "between two aristocracies: one of diplomas and one of capital."[33]

The registration process now passed entirely into the hands of
judges. Every would-be elector presented to a county judge a written request for registration. The judge drafted a list of registered
electors in each parish and passed it on to the district judge, who
would issue the final and official list. The district judge would also
then sign an electoral certificate for each elector and send these to
the county judge for distribution.[34] The control over elections ex-

ercised by electoral boards made up of planters, ranchers, and their allies ended with this measure. And judges, whether themselves men of property (or beholden to a landed patron) or truly independent, could be expected in either case to keep out the *agregado*.

These provisions of the law as enacted demonstrate the prejudices of the legislators. Further evidence can be found in Saraiva's speech introducing his bill. Universal suffrage, he believed, would mean the dominance of the poor over people with property and education, a group that naturally held a greater interest in the preservation of public tranquility and the proper functioning of institutions. "Votes for everyone," he later added, "will not produce true democracy, only demagoguery or absolutism." Yet his bill, he claimed, would encourage the deserving poor to struggle upward. Virtuous behavior could secure the ballot: "The worker who today earns 800 milreis, 1,000 milreis, 2,000 milreis, [and who cannot] easily present [one of these] documents, with a little saving can in two or more years have an elector's certificate [*título de eleitor*]. If [by then] he does not have a small building, a small tailor's or shoemaker's shop through which he pays some [acceptable] tax, he will save something, depositing it in the savings bank, and he will become an elector."[35]

Despite many criticisms, Saraiva had carefully constructed the necessary majority to pass the law. He had gotten each group to give way on one point after another. He abandoned his own earlier interest in demanding literacy for all electors, and even gave up a clause that the elector always had to sign his electoral certificate himself; but to satisfy those who desired a literacy test, he included a provision specifying that after the first registration, people subsequently added to the registration lists would have to be literate.[36] Saraiva had included in the government's bill an assurance that freedmen could be electors (earlier they could be voters but not electors) and even be elected to Parliament.[37] This step raised such objections that he then omitted specific mention of freedmen, wording the law in such a way, however, that freedmen—assuming they could meet all the other requirements of income and proof—could in fact vote.

The same device allowed Protestants not only to vote but to be elected to the highest offices, provided they swore allegiance to a Constitution that made the "Roman Apostolic Catholic religion . . .

the religion of the Empire."[38] Here, however, is a symbol of a secularization too complex to be adequately discussed in a few lines. By the last quarter of the nineteenth century, the earlier taken-for-granted identification of the state with religion had been undermined. I do not refer necessarily to a decline of religious sentiment, but to a growing acceptance of the concept of separate spheres, of the view that religion formed a set of beliefs, not the definition of society. Catholic Christendom was no longer coterminous with the authority of the King. For this reason churches ceased to be the location for elections under the new law. In 1868 the Conservative José de Alencar, himself the son of a priest, had criticized the practice of holding elections in the churches, not only because it lowered the prestige of religion, but because "there is no right to demand that a Jewish citizen should enter the Christian temple to vote." Good Catholics found other reasons: the bishop of Rio de Janeiro in 1872 petitioned the Minister of Empire, saying, "Brazilians are religious, Sir; it is already well known that for a long time they have found it ugly and indecorous that elections take place in churches." Although Saraiva's original bill still called for elections in churches, he readily gave way on this point. According to the law finally passed in 1881, "only in the absolute absence of other buildings can religious temples be designated" as their locale.[39]

Churches no longer needed to be the location for elections because of the abandonment of most electoral rituals. Now that the great mass of the population would not be summoned to participate in a drama of hierarchy, the elaborate theater could be abandoned. As the law curtly stated, "The religious ceremonies are dispensed with." To avoid any remaining possibility of pushing and shoving, a railing to separate the electoral board from the electors would remain in place throughout the election, and each elector would pass beyond that barrier only as the chairman called his name. The election would now take place in one day, and could in fact begin at 9 A.M. and end by 12:30, a stark and businesslike procedure. One voter in 1887 nostalgically remembered the earlier tumult of crowded churches that so sharply contrasted with the elections "we have now, in which a few dozen citizens, registered with the greatest difficulty and all wearing ties and socks [vote and], without even lingering to learn the results of the counting, leave to go tend to their business."[40]

The reaction to the law proved generally mild, even though, according to one count, and this bears repeating, in all Brazil only some 150,000 electors managed to register under the new law, in contrast to the more than one million voters registered in 1870.[41] Even some of the propertied found themselves excluded from the electoral process. At the first registration several district judges asked the central government what to do about landowners who owned their land only through squatters' rights (a common practice). These men lacked any documents on its value. Others had bought their land years earlier when it consisted only of "virgin forests," and their titles therefore spoke of very low values, although the properties were now worth enormous sums. These questions, referred to the Council of State, received an unequivocal reply: the law clearly excluded those who could not prove their income in the specified ways. Such men of property, the Council added, despite "the guarantee, as indicated by their income, that they would circumspectly exercise their right to vote," were still suspect "in view of the abuses of such proofs in the previous [1875] legislation." The lawmakers, the Council added, had preferred to exclude these men than to "widen the holes in the net through which those voters of the previous lists could enter the new registration lists, thus discrediting the effort." [42] Some, nevertheless, slipped through at first, finding clever ruses. For instance, colluding lessors signed lease agreements for the "sole purpose" of providing the necessary qualifications to "electors who live in poverty, never paid taxes, never held public posts, and do not have the means to pay such leases"—a technique that soon produced new and even more detailed regulations to guard against it.[43]

Results

In the first election held under the new law, Saraiva insisted on the scrupulous observance of its provisions and made a genuine attempt to avoid imposing the government's will. Indeed several government candidates lost their seats, including a Cabinet member. In 1881 one Liberal politician who not six months before had agreed with Saraiva that elections should by all means be fair, even if that did not benefit "our party, which fortunately it will," now complained, as the president of a province, that the Conservatives were taking advantage of the restrictions Saraiva had placed on Liberal officials: "It seems to me unjust that we hold back our friends, tolerating this shamelessness of Conservative functionaries led by Senators and Conservative chieftains." For him, at least, it was clear that law or no law, nothing substituted for victory. Even before its enactment, politicians maneuvered to draw district boundaries to their advantage. And they immediately perceived that registration would be a central step, even more so than under the previous law. As a politician wrote a friend from the interior of Bahia, "I could not meet you at the [provincial] capital to give you an *abraço* and have you stay with me, because I was here taking care of registration. You know that it is the most important and serious work of the [new] law; and he who does not have his friends and allies will have lost the election." From a town in Minas Gerais, a Liberal politician reported: "The electorate here will be made up of 450 to 470 electors, of which only 60 or 70 Conservatives. Almost all the registration was carried out by me, for I presented [in court] more than 400 petitions." Still, many believed the law had deeply altered political practice. In 1882 a speaker boasted that the earlier "tumultuous scenes" had, "to the honor of our country, been forever expurgated from our political contests by direct elections."[44]

If the restraint of the government made the elections of 1881 among the most honest Brazil had known, the effect would not last. As one perspicacious observer noted, it was not the nature of the law, but the behavior of the government that made the effort a success. The same restraint, if it had been applied under the previous law, would also have led to the defeat of some government candidates. "Others will come" who will not be so forbearing.[45] By the time of the next election, carried out by a new but still Liberal Cabinet in December 1884, the temptation for politicians to work their will seemed overwhelming. One Conservative complained from Bahia that "a growing number of *phosporos*" were being included in the registration lists. And when the Conservatives carried out the next election in early 1886, many made the same allegations of fraud as had been so frequent formerly: the illegal registration of electors, "illiterates voting in place of registered electors who were absent," and "tumultuous elections."[46] The resulting Parliament proved overwhelmingly ready to back the Cabinet. During the 1880s, for a Chamber of Deputies that varied in size from 122 to

125 members, the opposition elected 47 in 1881, 55 in 1884, and only 22 in 1886. Reportedly the last Parliament elected, held under the Liberals, would have had hardly any Conservative representatives had it ever sat; but the overthrow of the Empire prevented that demonstration of the futility of such electoral law-making.[47]

In any case the power of large landowners in rural counties remained unscathed, even if urban points of view could now find greater representation in Parliament. District judges proved sympathetic to the interests of the wealthiest. Delegados and subdelegados still emerged from the squirearchy, although reportedly landowners became less generous toward their *agregados*. In the end the already powerful had little difficulty gathering the necessary documents, voluminous though they were.[48] The return in 1881 to single-member districts, moreover, gave some rural chiefs greater access to Parliament, as had happened in 1856. It allowed, for instance, a few Republican coffee planters in São Paulo to concentrate their forces in 1884 to elect two Republicans to the Chamber of Deputies, as well as greatly increase their strength within the São Paulo Provincial Assembly. At the same time other, more radical Republicans complained that the system continued to perpetuate "the demeaning conditions of dependence and protectorate" in the countryside, with "*les coqs de village*" in control, a condition that only "universal suffrage" would correct.[49]

Some brave souls continued to demand broader suffrage, but when they did, they encountered such remarks as this one: "I am a liberal, but I do not wish to widen the suffrage because I do not want elections carried out by the police." Some saw through this kind of liberalism, like the Conservative who declared on the floor of the Chamber that the law seemed anything but liberal "unless you want to give this name to a law that wrenched the right to vote from nine-tenths of those who exercised it for better or for worse." He went on to say that he liked the law, but objected to the "pharisaic zeal" with which the Liberals claimed to be defending the "so-called rights of the people."[50] By 1887, when the Conservatives controlled the Cabinet, a Liberal spokesman, the son of the visconde de Figueiredo, noted in Parliament:

Any reform of the [electoral] law . . . must begin by widening the vote, so sacrificed in 1880 [*sic*] to the needs of the moment. Circumstances obliged the [Liberal] Cabinet then to make concessions to its adversaries. . . . The demands of the law . . . for the citizen to acquire his electoral certificate [*título de eleitor*] are exorbitant—taxes, capital, and a most severe proof—so that at times it is impossible. Its rigor has been so excessive that there are not a few counties in the interior of the Empire where the number of electors is less than 30, so that there are not enough citizens there to fill the public posts for which one must legally have the qualifications of an elector.[51]

In 1889 that speaker's father—who in 1880 had alleged that the lower classes had to be excluded from the polls because of "the ease with which our population allows itself to be seduced, corrupted, or intimidated"—now as Prime Minister called for a small "widening of the vote, maintaining the present registration but considering as proof of legal income the fact of a citizen knowing how to read and write, with the only restriction that he should exercise some licit profession and enjoy civil and political rights."[52] The recognition had spread that a literacy test would be quite sufficient to exclude the unwanted masses.

Later lawmakers, in the Republic, also understood that only literacy need be required to keep elections firmly under the control of the propertied, and in 1892 they made that the sole prerequisite.[53] And since, as before, electors desired from the government mainly local authority, they continued to back candidates for Deputy or Senator suggested by those in power at the center. At first some hesitated. A disillusioned politician, a newly converted Republican, expressed his fears, saying "with statewide elections and universal suffrage, one would have to be absolutely ignorant of our social condition to think that the officially sanctioned tickets of previous times will win out." He was wrong: many people alleged widespread interference by the authorities even in the election of 1890 for the new Constituent Assembly, and government candidates won easily. Subsequent elections soon repeated, perhaps with greater scandal, the manipulations of earlier times. A monarchist then blamed "universal" suffrage, "the victory of the incompetent multitudes," which he contrasted with the healthy reform of 1881 that had "excluded from the vote the illiterate and proletarian classes." Defenders of the Republic, however, continued to claim that the 1881 law had been nothing more than a "pseudo reform."[54]

For all the mutual recriminations, the two electoral laws—Imperial and Republican—pointed in the same direction: excluding the propertyless from the polls. Social and economic changes occurring by 1880 impelled the search for a different electoral system. Driven by a fear that freed slaves would overwhelm the mechanisms of electoral control, rural chiefs acquiesced in measures that removed most voters from participation, even though this step somewhat lessened their own power in comparison to that of the politically active urban professionals. Property now clearly set off the voting citizen as it had not done before. The dramatic performance that demonstrated the hierarchy of society no longer centered around the ballot box. The ex-slaves joined the *agregados* and most of the small farmers among those who played no official part in the electoral process, although as part of a clientele they still lent strength to the imposing physical and symbolic power of the patron. Whether or not the urban professional increased his relative weight in the affairs of government at the center, the local authority of the rural bosses remained unquestioned. And for them the search for positions remained central to political life.

PART THREE

THE PRACTICE OF
PATRONAGE

EIGHT

Patterns of Patronage

THE VERY FIRST ACCOUNT of the discovery of Brazil, written as a letter to the Portuguese King by Pero Vaz de Caminha in 1500, ended with a plea for a pardon on behalf of Vaz de Caminha's son-in-law. Such a request or *pedido* birthmarked Brazil's polity, and the exchange of patronage for service or loyalty has remained a visible sign to this day. The earliest colonial proprietary governors expressly received the authority, delegated from the King, to dispense patronage within their domain. When the Portuguese court-in-exile arrived in Brazil in 1808, it came with an extraordinary number of public employees, and the Prince-Regent, acting as "a true father to his vassals," rewarded them, said one witness, for "such a great sacrifice, according to their *condição*, worth, and capacity." He also extended his "generous liberality . . . profusely to the inhabitants of Brazil, . . . granting knightly insignias and distinctions to some, posts and offices to others, to these titles and employment, to those honors and benefices; to all love and paternal solicitude." He provided employment even for those Portuguese artisans who had accompanied him by creating "royal" factories, that is, publicly financed manufacturing enterprises to employ them. The revolt in 1831 that drove Pedro I to abdicate the throne centered on the large numbers of Portuguese who still held positions of public employment; Pedro complained that the movement's main purpose was to "grab jobs." The Additional Act of 1834 reforming the Constitution intended, among other things, to increase the patronage of the provincial authorities, and so the law of 1841 may be understood as returning that patronage to the central government.[1] Certainly the number of public employees continued to grow throughout the rest of the century.[2] Rather than seeing patronage as a hindrance to effective government, Brazilians understood that expanding such opportunities formed the state's very reason for being.

This chapter focuses on the channels of patronage. The electoral reform of 1881 had no visible effect on it, and I here consider the pattern of patronage both before and after that date. Particularly important is an analysis of nearly 600 private letters of recommendation written on behalf of office seekers. Politics took form and the transactions of power occurred through this kind of correspondence—outside the formal institutional framework. The most frequent letter writers were members of Parliament, who wrote to Cabinet members on behalf of others. Writing such letters was one of a Deputy's central activities. Office seekers aspired especially to be named judges, but also sought positions as police and National Guard officers, members of the armed forces, or bureaucrats. Personal connections between office seeker and letter writer and between letter writer and recipient remained crucial, lending a regionalistic flavor to the system, despite the spreading network of correspondents throughout all Brazil. The *bacharéis*, whether judges or members of Parliament, did not act only or even chiefly as agents for the imposition of public authority as against private dominion, but rather bound together the national and local spheres of government with powerful ties of friendship, family connection, and personal loyalty. Mapping the lines of patronage can make that clear.

The Channels of Patronage

He who held authority literally possessed it and could legitimately grant it, or part of it, to another. Public office thus became a resource to be drawn on like any other. It could be "owned," bestowed, or withdrawn. He who received an office, received it as a gift. In 1808 a governor acknowledged that theoretically the best bureaucracy was one in which employees were "subject to being expelled as soon as they fail to fulfill their obligations." "But this observation," he added significantly, "is not intended to restrict the generosity of the sovereign." Brazilians often referred to someone as the "proprietor" of an office, especially in the early part of the century, but at least as late as the 1860s. When someone took office, he was said to have "taken possession [*tomou posse*]" of it, a locution still used today, and he paid a stamp tax at that moment, as one would be expected to do on acquiring other property. By 1889 the didactic compiler of a dictionary, with a keen sense of changing standards, indicated that although the word *mercê* (mercy or grace) had as one of its meanings the grant of employment, "if it is for a public post, the term is today improper, for the principle cannot be accepted that what the law prescribes shall be given through merit should be conceded as a favor." Improper usage, however, continued to reflect the common view.[3]

Not only could authority be subdivided, but some people held only the channels of its passage, as it were, while it cascaded from ultimate giver—the Emperor—to ultimate receiver—the office holder. Brazilians considered the power to oversee the distribution of the gift second only in importance to the power to give it in the first place. To be able to distribute positions made one automatically a patron and greatly facilitated the business of building a following. For the grant from the sovereign included not only the authority to command, but most particularly a claim on the loyalty and deference of clients. Although the Emperor theoretically granted most positions himself, he did so on the recommendation of his Cabinet, and few positions could therefore rival a Minister's in its potential for increasing a clientele. Some descriptions of Cabinet politics cast it explicitly in terms of bowing and scraping before the Emperor in order to gain the coveted power to appoint.[4] With each Minister at its apex, a pyramid of patronage was built on successive layers of distributors.

Many intermediaries, moreover, had the legal right to present the names of persons for appointment, that is, *nomear* them. For instance, the subdelegado presented the names of ward inspectors to the delegado for appointment, the delegado presented the names of subdelegados to the chief of police, the chief of police presented the names of delegados to the president of the province, the presidents presented the names of chiefs of police to the Minister of Justice, and the Minister proposed the names of presidents to the Emperor. Appointments of National Guard officers followed the same pattern. The practice, in fact, characterized almost every appointment;

for example, the Minister of Justice appointed notaries public on the presentation of their names by provincial presidents, who were required to "declare explicitly whether the candidates deserve the investiture [*provimento*]." The right to nominate held special importance because those so presented could serve temporarily (*interinamente*) until actual appointment and thus enjoy immediately the perquisites of the post. For a local chief working systematically to build up his following, his appointment as delegado or National Guard commandant held obvious appeal, allowing him immediately to present the names of his clients and have them take possession of their posts.[5]

The power to dismiss accompanied the power to appoint. The holder of an office with legal authority to present someone for appointment could also later suspend that person while forwarding a recommendation for his formal dismissal to the next level. For example, a delegado had the right to suspend a jailer, although only the chief of police could dismiss him. One subdelegado, as soon as he took over the position, suspended all the ward inspectors his predecessor had named.[6] Dismissals, like appointments, could be used to build a following and assert one's strength, not only against political opponents but against personal enemies. When a complaint was raised about some of his dismissals, a provincial president—Manuel Pinto de Sousa Dantas—replied, "They could have been no other unless I were to adopt the principle that certain offenses should be not only forgotten but rewarded by my own hands. They are not merely political offenses, but personal ones that demand *vengeance*." Ten years earlier, as a candidate for election and relying on informal channels, he had written, "I've heard that ——— hopes to be transferred to ———. I ask you to place him somewhere else, because such an appointment would not be agreeable to me—just because relations are not good between him and me and you can see that if I can succeed in preventing him from going there, it will be better for me." Denying any request could be a way of punishing those who did not demonstrate their loyalty.[7]

The building of a clientele operated as intensely at the national level as at the local one. A man who would soon enter the Cabinet himself titled a chapter in an 1876 book "Employmentmania": "This sickness—endemic in Brazil—is one of its great ills. It derives principally from the fact that Ministers and provincial presidents believe the most efficacious and secure means of developing and consolidating a clientele is to establish lifetime or temporary incomes on behalf of the sons, sons-in-law, relatives, or protégés of [local] political magnates."[8] João Mauricio Wanderley, barão de Cotegipe, described how he once used the appointment power simultaneously to punish and reward. A district judge in Paraíba had dared to organize a coalition of some dissident Conservatives and Liberals to defeat the government's candidate. Since there were complaints about him from the provincial president, his transfer could be justified as "an administrative measure" but would be rightly seen in that locality for what it was, a political punishment. At the same time the transfer could be carried out to political advantage elsewhere, since the judge was an *afilhado* (godson) of a Deputy from the neighboring province of Rio Grande do Norte, who would be pleased to see him return to his home province, to a vacant district judgeship of higher rank. Finally, that would leave the man's position in Paraíba to be filled, thus resolving still another major problem: there were several office seekers whom two Deputies and two Senators—one a baron and one a viscount—wished to protect. One candidate had much in his favor: not only was he the son of a former Deputy; he was poor and burdened by a large family, and had already served three four-year terms as county judge. Thus the multiple transfer could be carried out "with satisfaction for these his friends and benefit to the public service."[9] Cotegipe yielded simultaneously to the impulses of patronage and paternalism. Controlling government patronage could in itself make one a patron and extend one's clientele to include the patrons of others.

If I have here indicated that patronage flowed from king downward to the office seeker, earlier chapters make clear that another pyramid intersected that one on a different plane and bore down even deeper. The family and household relied on and built up pervasive relationships of dependence and deference. The patron's entire retinue, his immediate followers as well as those who rendered loyalty and obedience to him as an employer, landlord, or moneylender, sought from him protection and support. If the outward symbol and particular means of his power lay in the control he exercised over local offices, whether through the official right to nominate candidates or the unofficial expectation that he would recommend them, an equally rich source of power centered on his possession of physical resources such as land, slaves, or cattle. He could make office seekers depend on him, even candidates for Parliament. The locally rooted patron played on the national system of patronage as much as those in the national system played on him. The intersecting planes of patronage are reflected in a letter from the young João José de Oliveira Junqueira Júnior, then running for Deputy for the first time, in which he bragged that a local bigwig "has committed himself to making me a Deputy. It will be enough that the government has no other candidates and lends me a shadow of support or moral approval and does not distribute this district to another candidate." It is not surprising, therefore, to find that a Cabinet member kept detailed lists of the local people of influence in each electoral district, for he depended as much on them as they on him. Even for a Prime Minister, local potentates became the ultimate patrons.[10]

Yet a parish or county chief did desire office, which made him also dependent on the government. With such an appointment he could, for instance, go beyond dispensing access to some fragment of his property to *agregados* and begin extending the largesse of his special political resources. Whether he struggled to be recognized as the head of a single extended family or as the patron of a large clientele, positions of authority were crucial. Dispensing gifts or meting out punishment could then receive official reinforcement. A funeral orator praised a deceased planter because, "when his party was in power, the kindly influence that he exercised . . . was used only to benefit and protect whosoever pled for his protection."[11] The statement indicates the patron's ability to withhold his protection, the efficacy of his intercession at least part of the time, and the threat to his position when his party fell from power.

The formal structure of patronage found precise reflection in the informal sphere. In countless letters of recommendation sent outside official channels, patrons in effect "presented" the names of office seekers. Sometimes they addressed such letters directly to those with the power to appoint; at others they requested that the recipient present the name of the candidate. Just as formally the right to present a name meant in reality the right to appoint, certain letters of recommendation may have had equivalent power. Political actors spent much time writing such letters or soliciting them and, in that display of social confidence, revealed once again how political power lay exclusively with the literate. The filling of positions for an entire country as big as Brazil required that the nationwide network of patrons and clients rely heavily on private correspondence to transact the exchange of deference for favors. The fact that the network spanned the whole country was a consequence of the very centralization that worked to create national unity.

Historians have sometimes noted to each other, with some dismay, that the "papers" of prominent Brazilian political leaders of the past often consist of little more than drawers full of *pedidos*, that is, letters asking for employment and other favors either for the writers themselves or their clients. Yet the presence of so many letters directed to this purpose points to their importance for politicians; they indicate an aspect of political behavior not captured in official correspondence that requires attention. I have chosen to examine in detail such letters received by four men whose political life spanned the reign of Pedro II. Pedro de Araújo Lima, marquês de Olinda (1793-1870), had served in several Cabinets before 1840 and even as Regent from 1837 to 1840. Pedro II named him Prime Minister four times, in 1848, 1857, 1862, and 1865. João Lustosa da Cunha Paranaguá, marquês de Paranaguá (1821-1912), held portfolios in four Cabinets in addition to being Prime Minister in 1882. Franklin Américo de Menezes Dória, barão de Loreto (1836-1906), served in only two Cabinets and never became Prime Minister; but as the son-in-law of Paranaguá, he shared the latter's access to the Emperor and thus to various Cabinets. Finally, Affonso Augusto Moreira Pena (1847-1909) was a member of three imperial Cabinets before going on to cap his career as President of the Republic from 1906 to his death in 1909. These four politicians received 577 *pedidos* during the Empire.[12]

In the most common pattern, the author of the letter, as Vaz de Caminha had done, wrote not on his own behalf but on behalf of a third party who sought a particular favor or job. Only 68 of the letter writers (12 percent) wrote to secure something for themselves. In a significant number of cases (10 percent), the letters reveal still another layer of relationships, for their authors did not write for someone who had approached them directly but for the friend of a relative, a relative of a friend, or a friend of a friend. Naturally, this practice of writing letters at the instigation of an-

other sometimes led to the granting of a position to a totally un-
suitable candidate. One letter writer defended himself by saying "I
don't know the person involved; if I recommended him it was at the
request of his close relative here, who is our strong ally in the party
[*correligionario nosso muito firme*]." Sometimes the office seeker
delivered the letters himself: "Each one appears with . . . a stack of
letters of recommendation from influential people."[13]

Politicians received more letters as they moved up the ladder of
power themselves. The four men whose papers I examined for this
study received more recommendations when they served as Minister of Justice (26 percent of the total) than they received in any other
Cabinet post. The two who became Prime Minister received another 19 percent, and *pedidos* also showered on them when they
were simply members of the Chamber of Deputies (18 percent).
When they served as Minister of Agriculture and Public Works,
they received as many as when Minister of War (10 percent). As
presidents of provinces they received only 8 percent.[14] As Prime
Ministers, politicians received letters from occupants of all other
major government positions; such a breadth of clientage was never
true before they reached that rank.

The system hinged on members of Parliament, who worked diligently to recommend office seekers or others desiring favors. As the
accompanying chart suggests, over a third of all letters received
came from Deputies and Senators, compared with only 16 percent
from provincial presidents and 9 percent from judges. Over time
the proportion of letters from legislators increased, and that of
presidents declined.* This change suggests a growing role for
Deputies in the network of clientage precisely at a time, as I will
show in the next chapter, when party considerations rose in importance. Although newspapers in Rio de Janeiro paid much attention
to goings-on in Parliament, where elaborate customary rules guided
procedures, debates drew crowds, and a maiden speech loomed as
a great occasion, it is clear from an examination of *pedidos* that
a major if not principal task for lawmakers lay in mending the
network of clients and patrons. As one sardonic observer alleged,

---

* Deputies accounted for 25 percent of the letters during the period 1850-69, but
for 44 percent in the next 20 years; the proportion of letters from presidents declined
from 22 percent to 11 percent in the same period.

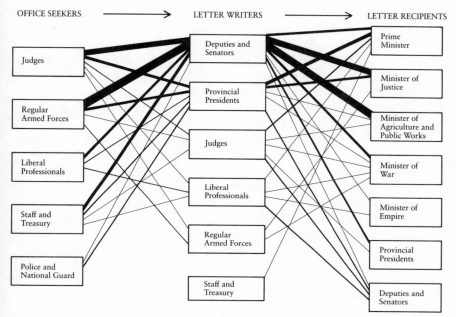

The Flow of Clientage

the Deputies "have their sons, brothers, and relatives, and, as clients, all their mistresses and the relatives and suitors of their mistresses." [15]

It was the Deputy's job to know to whom to send the request. Of the letters from Deputies, almost three-quarters went to occupants of three posts: the Prime Minister, the Minister of Justice, and the Minister of Agriculture and Public Works. Only a tenth of the Deputies' letters went to provincial presidents. In deciding on the target for his letter, a Deputy had to know not only who had the legal right to make certain appointments, but who had the actual power; it also meant knowing who could be counted on. A letter recommending a candidate for appointment to the bureaucracy at the central or provincial level went with greatest likelihood to the Prime Minister himself, and only then to the Minister of Agriculture and Public Works. On the other hand, if the office seeker desired a judgeship, the most appropriate recipient was the Minister of Justice, and only then the Prime Minister. And if one's client aimed for a police office or a commission in the National Guard, the best person to address after the Minister of Justice was a provincial president. Such decisions required both political insight and sensitivity to the nuance of social place. To be sure geographical proximity also played a part. One contemporary remarked that although presidents made the lowest level appointments, "the strongest influence is that of the Deputy. But since he may not always be in direct contact with the provincial president [to present requests], for any ridiculous post he turns up with a sackful of letters before the Minister" at the capital. When the Deputy was not in Rio de Janeiro, however, he was certain to pester the president in his home province: "not a day passes that he does not appear with a package of requests," wrote the president of Pará of one Deputy.[16]

Next to the Deputies, provincial presidents penned the most letters of recommendation. Since presidents were chosen by the Prime Minister, they had a direct link to the government, and petitioners readily perceived this important fact. As one of them put it, "You know it never hurts to be in the good graces of the president, especially if one lives in the sticks." No sooner did a newly appointed president arrive at a province than he was besieged with "constant calls of felicitation" that interrupted his work; they made their purpose clear enough since, "having received immense courtesies, [welcoming] deputation, dinner, ball, etc. etc.," he did not feel that he could break with the dominant faction from one moment to another. Whether the office seeker should go through the president or the Deputy in Rio de Janeiro, however, remained an open question. One member of the Chamber told a letter writer in reply to his request: "As long as Sinimbú is Prime Minister, you will succeed more easily through Lourenço [Cavalcanti de Albuquerque, the provincial president]."[17]

Although letter writers simultaneously played the parts of patron and client, as a man grew older he could expect to be more frequently patron than client. An examination of their ages and positions indicates that as letter writers entered their thirties they were less often judges and more often Deputies. And whereas Deputies wrote one-quarter of their letters on behalf of judges, among those in this sample no judge ever wrote on behalf of a Deputy. Judges sometimes wrote on their own behalf; Deputies never did.

Positions Sought

The most frequently sought office was that of judge (see Table 3). Letters asking for judgeships arrived from every region of Brazil. Positions as county or district judges were the most desired (see Table 4), but a goodly portion of job seekers sought profitable places as probate judges. A few asked to be substitute judges, for which no training in law was required; but even these petitioners needed to have a patron. A table of substitute judges from Rio Grande do Sul lists them by district and county with the following data: in the first column are such annotations as "capitalist," "medical doctor," "rich merchant," and "wealthy landowner"; in the second are their former services, such as "county councilman," "provincial deputy," "lieutenant colonel in the National Guard," and "former substitute judge"; finally, and tellingly, the third indicates their patron: "presented by the district judge," "presented by the commandant of the National Guard," or "presented by *bacharel* so-and-so." [18] Equally, a judgeship could increase the judge's following and make him the patron of others.

Many men asked for other offices connected with judicial activity. Over 5 percent of the 577 letters had to do with positions as *tabeliães* and *escrivães*, posts with responsibilities somewhat like those of a notary public, court secretary, and registrar of contracts

TABLE 3
Positions Requested

Position	Number	Percent
Judicial office	164	28.4%
Bureaucratic post	109	18.9
Liberal profession	62	10.7
Commission in regular armed forces	69	12.0
Police position and commission in National Guard	40	6.9
Other	133	23.1
TOTAL	577	100.0%

NOTE: A scattering of the letters examined here recommended people not for positions but for titles of nobility, aid in elections, or other favors. These are included in the category "Other."

TABLE 4

Judicial Offices Requested

Office	Number	Percent
Regional High Court judge	1	0.6%
District judge	46	28.0
County judge	47	28.7
Other judge	13	7.9
Judges asking for unspecified promotions	14	8.5
Public prosecutor (*promotor*)	13	7.9
Notary (*escrivão, tabelião*)	30	18.3
TOTAL	164	99.9%

NOTE: Percentages in this and subsequent tables do not necessarily total 100 because of rounding.

all rolled into one. The *escrivão* and *tabelião* performed key tasks in every legal action. They could even block criminal investigations, and not a few wrote the judges' decisions for them.[19] So, as one Deputy in Rio de Janeiro complained to Parliament, "if a little post of notary [*um lugarzinho de partidor ou escrivão*] falls empty in a village or city, 40 or 50 candidates immediately appear here at the capital."[20]

A little under one-fifth of the posts requested stood within the bureaucracy itself. In this category I have included members of each Ministry's secretariat, the staff of the provincial presidents, all Treasury officials, and postal workers (see Table 5). All bureaucratic positions brought benefits beyond a salary or even the opportunity for graft; most important, they allowed the exercise of power over others. A man on the staff of a Ministry or of a provincial president was in a position to select whose petition would move forward or

TABLE 5

Staff Positions Requested

Position	Number	Percent
Central government staff	37	33.9%
Provincial government staff	18	16.5
Treasury	48	44.4
Post Office	6	5.5
TOTAL	109	99.9%

languish in a pigeonhole.[21] Three days after a new Minister of Empire had been named, a member of his staff received a letter from "a dear friend" saying, "Now is the time, as I see it, for you to help me"; the petitioner clearly understood the power of the bureaucrat. Treasury positions offered ample opportunity for illegal gain and were always attractive. One Treasury official himself admitted in an 1862 investigation of earlier malfeasance that at the customshouse "all merit consisted then, as today, in the importance of one's patron; aptitude and honesty were measured as they are measured [now] on the scale of the protectors." A businessman at the beginning of the Republic noted that for a position at the customshouse the Treasury now required someone who would be "most of all *honest*"; he proposed a candidate who "was one of the few who in past times did not steal public revenues."[22] In a system like Brazil's, in which patron-client relations so deeply permeated all positions, the Post Office was not a particularly desirable place. As one Minister of Empire reported, since agents got no salary, but only a percentage of the income from their Post Office branch, good workers could not be attracted to the position, and in any case they would have to live from something else. Nevertheless, his predecessor informed a Cabinet colleague in 1853 that he should send along the papers on "the candidate for the position at the mails. . . . It will not do to delay the presentation of names because the candidates are swarming [*formigam*]. From everywhere I have already received an immense number of recommendations, and they grow every day." Perhaps the political role of postmasters was the magnet that drew them: one letter writer, in making a recommendation, noted, "This is a post with much importance for local politics because at election time the postmasters tie up the communications of their adversaries, slowing the dispatch and delivery of their letters."[23]

As Brazilians have long recognized, the government was and is the chief employer of liberal professionals. In this category I have not included the judges and Deputies, almost all of whom held law degrees, or the public prosecutors (*promotores*), who normally hoped for promotion to a judgeship. I do include requests for other positions as lawyers (3), however. The rest of the positions requested were as doctors or pharmacists (19), professors or staff members of the law and medical schools (15), other teachers (12), students (2), a newspaperman, and ten assorted others. Together these positions accounted for nearly 11 percent of the total. Letters from São Paulo were twice as likely to ask for such positions as the average; those from the extreme South hardly ever aimed at them. Doctors filled many government posts that did not require their particular skills, as well as some that did. The government-owned iron factory in Ipanema, São Paulo, for instance, needed a resident physician, and they also served as health inspectors at the ports. Doctors and lawyers highly prized faculty positions in the law and medical schools, no doubt partly because of the political role they could then play. Candidates multiplied for such positions, wrote Cotegipe. Some wanted only minor jobs at these schools as sinecures: the head of a provincial secretariat in Bahia wished to be moved to a position on the medical school's administrative staff so that he would have the time to manage a newspaper advocating the cause of the Progressive League. One critic alleged that "party spirit, always a bad counselor, often rejects as a candidate for or even as the holder of a teacher's post a good and capable man in favor of an inept person."[24] I have already noted how patronage could assure admission to the law and medical faculties, so letters for students made sense. From other correspondence it becomes clear that passing the bar examination required letters of recommendation so that a favorable examining board would be appointed. Similarly, for a medical student to get a position as a resident at a military hospital required "pull," as did admission to the prestigious Pedro II secondary school in Rio de Janeiro or to the school for the blind. Even admission to mental hospitals depended on a letter of recommendation.[25]

The search for positions in the regular armed forces accounted for almost an eighth of all the requests. It was a common practice for the Navy and War portfolios to be held by promising young politicians and, of the four letter recipients I studied, only the visconde de Olinda did not occupy the Ministry of War at some time or other. Despite measures encouraging the professionalization of the armed services and the granting of promotions by reason of seniority or special training, letters of recommendation continued to flow on behalf of officers, even for those in the lowest ranks.[26] In one case a proposal that an Army lieutenant be cashiered accompanied the recommendation for someone to take his place in that battalion. One first lieutenant got both his father-in-law and his brother-in-law to use their political influence to get him a promotion. In keeping with what one might expect from the concentration of armed forces in Rio Grande do Sul, there were more letters from the South asking for positions in the regular armed forces than from any other region, outside the capital.[27]

Two kinds of positions specifically brought authority without a salary: National Guard officers and police officials. Nearly 7 percent of the requests were for these positions. Of course names were presented in the normal way as well; but the Minister of Justice and presidents enjoyed the right to appoint candidates who had not been officially presented. The letters I examined consisted of private, not official, correspondence, and sought to influence the decision outside the regular channels. In 1872 the Minister of Justice wrote, "I have named and am naming [officers] for the National Guard in Bahia. I suspect that no Minister of Justice since 16 July [1868] has named as many in such a short time for this and other provinces. They are already labeling me a reactionary. The burdens of office!"[28]

Although most of the requests involved positions as judges, bureaucrats, liberal professionals, and officers in the armed forces, police, or National Guard, many dealt with a variety of other positions and benefits. The Church and the foreign service offered potentially prestigious careers. Fifteen of the office seekers were churchmen. As the new Navy Minister, the Bahian Cotegipe received a letter from the Minister of Empire asking him to get the archbishop of Bahia to act on the Minister of Empire's presentation of a certain priest to a parish. "I like Padre ———," the Minister of Empire added, "and a cherished friend of mine is pushing him [*por elle se interessa*]." This letter suggests that bishops did not always jump to appoint a Minister's nominees, and that regional ties and personal connections also remained important in Church affairs. Eight men sought positions as foreign service officers. Often they desired a transfer to a more favorable location. One counted on the support of his son-in-law, the close friend of the newly appointed Foreign Minister, to get him out of Lima, Peru. As the younger man wrote, "Is there no way, with the vacancy at St. Petersburg, to move someone there and rest [*encostarem*] my old father-in-law in Lisbon or Buenos Aires?" As it turned out, the "old father-in-law" had to be satisfied with Asunción.[29]

Securing even the seemingly most minor positions required patronage. Four office seekers from the group I examined hoped for the lowly position of *porteiro*, literally doorman, although the occupant would also be the archivist of the office in question, in charge of searching for papers relating to petitions and receiving commensurate emoluments from the interested parties. One Deputy recommended the "son of my employee" for the position of museum assistant. The protector of a would-be administrator of the public theater in Salvador reminded a friend in Rio de Janeiro of his "promise": "one little word from you to the new president and everything will be arranged." The same patron complained bitterly, however, that even for the "music for the church festivities" he had had to write letters of recommendation, and he wondered whether it would be possible to divide the music for the traditional "feast of Bomfim" between two contenders.[30] Such minor requests, along with those seeking appointments in the Church and foreign service, six asking for support in elections, and those requesting a variety of other favors, accounted for nearly a quarter of the letters (see Table 3).

In seven cases letters of recommendation indicated that promotions were requested simply to make room for another. Indeed, finding places for new appointments probably explains most dismissals. A complicated transaction in the 1880s involved the post of customshouse inspector. A letter writer in Salvador tried to help the local inspector get a transfer to the city of Rio de Janeiro. The obstacle to the transfer was the occupancy of that position in Rio de Janeiro by a man named Pires. Pires would like to retire at his present salary, the letter writer explained, but despite his thirty years of service, he had not been in his present position long enough to do so, according to the rules; were Pires to be promoted to a still higher position, however, he would be entitled to retire immediately at his current salary. If he could only be promoted (and here is the point) that would open up a vacancy for the office seeker. Not successful in that proposal, the correspondent returned to the same issue a year later, noting that another position had fallen vacant through retirement and suggesting that it could be given to the head of the customshouse, thus opening up a place for Pires, who would then vacate the position of inspector. Incredibly, the same letter complained that the government had transferred a clerk from the customshouse in Salvador to Corumbá in the far-western province of Mato Grosso, commenting that "they were really very hard on this employee, who by his social position [*categoria*] had a right to a bit more consideration, and the transfer was all the more odious because one knows perfectly well that it was done only to open a vacancy for an *afilhado*."[31]

One contemporary claimed that "in this sorry country . . . the English precept 'the right man in the right place' is entirely unknown." At least Brazilians preferred to create the right place. Effective patronage often required the expansion of government posts. In some cases the candidate himself proposed that a new position be instituted. One critic described it with heavy scorn: "Since the posts needed for the governance of this plantation are not enough for all the high protected ones, a lot of places are created without any necessity whatsoever."[32]

Some positions, as we have seen, were much more sought after than others. The desirability of judgeships is relatively clear from the documents. As a young man, Junqueira Júnior wrote the barão de Cotegipe from Salvador, noting that he had been county judge in nearby Cachoeira and was now public prosecutor (*promotor*) in Salvador, but would prefer to be county judge in Salvador or, "better yet," to be a Deputy in the national Congress. His contemporary Dantas, who already occupied a position as county judge, sought transfer to a better location, "unless by some miracle, as happened to —— and others, I were named district judge, in which case I would accept the worst district in the Empire, because afterwards we would arrange things [*dariamos o geito*]." Thirty years later, now acting as a patron in his own right, Junqueira asked for a district judgeship for a friend in the interior of the province of Bahia. "Should this not be possible, I would suggest you give him an administrative assignment, the presidency of a province that he can handle, or even any job that could be given." At one time, as Minister of War, Junqueira remarked: "I wanted to give some presidencies to able young men of that province [Bahia] and so I asked —— and ——, whose names had already been accepted by the Cabinet and by the crown; but they did not want to accept, preferring to be judges. Is there still anyone who would accept and has the necessary qualifications?"[33] Whereas 29 percent of the *pedidos* I examined requested judicial offices, only 1 percent referred to a place as provincial president. By comparing the position already held with the one requested, I found that in almost all categories there were some office seekers who wished to be judges, including a fifth of all police and National Guard officers. Since, as I have noted, these officers tended to be drawn from the ranks of prominent property holders, it is not surprising to find that none of them wanted to be bureaucrats, or vice versa. No bureaucrat, judge, or police or National Guard officer asked to enter the military. No judge wished a position that could be classified as liberal professional.

Over time some changes occurred in the positions requested. As the law schools continued to churn out graduates, entering the judiciary became more difficult, and discouraged candidates apparently did not even ask. In comparing two twenty-year periods before and after 1870, I found that the proportion of requests for judgeships dropped from 32 percent to 27 percent, while the proportion seeking places as liberal professionals rose sharply, from 6 percent to 14 percent.[34] The Paraguayan War (1865-70) and the subsequent reduced role of the National Guard also had an effect on the requested positions. Requests for police offices and National Guard commissions fell from 11 percent to 4 percent, while those for places or promotions in the regular armed services rose from 11 percent to 13 percent.

Equally noticeable, however, is the *lack* of change over time in the proportion of requests for positions in the bureaucracy, a figure that remained at between 18 percent and 19 percent throughout the entire period. Some writers have argued that, with the decline of coffee in the Paraíba Valley, a great flux of impoverished aristocrats moved to the city in search of government employment. Yet the steady proportion of requests for bureaucratic positions seems to belie that claim. Although it is true that more of the office seekers in the coffee-rich provinces of Rio de Janeiro sought appointments in the city of Rio de Janeiro than was the case nationwide, that can be explained by their proximity to the capital. It was a constant characteristic regardless of economic upturns or downturns. Such unchanging patterns also cast doubt on the argument of the political scientist Hélio Jaguaribe, who has suggested that the declining economy of the Northeast sent office seekers to Rio de Janeiro. In short the decline of an elite group meant exactly that: when lacking economic resources, its members also lacked political force. Patronage was for winners.[35]

In 1899 a commentator maintained that the low level of economic development in Brazil fueled the struggle for positions. Basing his argument on observations made in 1854 by Auguste van der

Straten-Ponthoz, he went on to say that "the violence of elections is one of the results of the tendency for public salaries to become the dominant principle. . . . The electoral impulse is derived not from the interests of classes . . . but from the attraction of the budget. Elections are carried out to secure employment or to preserve it." A recent historian has echoed this view, contrasting the Brazilian situation with that of Jacksonian America, in which a prosperous middle class used the spoils system as a weapon against a Virginia aristocracy. Whereas in the United States there were even better jobs for the capable, and the circulation of public jobs could be predicted by the regularity of elections, in Brazil, he maintains, there were few alternative positions, and public employment virtually created the middle class.[36]

This interpretation is thrown into question, however, by the fact that the search for staff positions—as measured by letters of recommendation—did not alter in times of economic prosperity and did not characterize depressed regions more than prosperous ones. The difficulty lies in the equating of public employment with a salary. No doubt salary was the primary concern for many would-be bureaucrats, and in fact 10 percent of the letters referred to the candidate's poverty (or to his old age or the large family he supported). * But this compares with more than 40 percent for positions made attractive mainly by the authority they carried, although their holders sometimes also received some salary: judges, public prosecutors, police officers, members of the National Guard, or notaries public (notaries were paid set fees, but the chief source of their wealth came from money received for influencing the outcome of judicial matters). Even wealth would be relatively useless without some degree of authority: the enmity of a probate judge, for instance, could delay the settling of a large estate and thus deny the surviving spouse the right to mortgage property and borrow funds. The desire for authority characterized the search for appointments, as it had in colonial times and was to do during the later Republic.[37] This was the goal. Elections were directed at securing employment, but did not threaten the budget. To be sure limited economic development often made state employment the only hope for salaried or

---

* Another 3 percent mentioned the pretendant's wealth or the prominence of his family.

"white-collar" work and, in a slave society, that was crucial for the maintenance of status if one had to earn a living. But the system of patronage aimed much higher.

Regional Ties

The personal nature of patronage lent a powerfully regionalistic flavor to the correspondence. Letters of recommendation came disproportionately from people whose regional roots coincided with those of the recipients. They also often recommended office seekers who were in that region. Even when the addressee reached the highest rungs of his career, his ties remained markedly stronger with the home province where he had personal connections than with other places. Recognizing this tendency partially corrects the view of some historians that the systematic movement of politicians led them to acquire a permanent clientage in all parts of the country; they did acquire some clients elsewhere, and that is significant, but their principal ties continued to be to their place of origin. Certainly no cadre of "mandarins" acted independently "of regional economic and family interests."[38] Olinda, the sugar planter from Pernambuco, received one-third of his letters from people primarily identified with Pernambuco and also one-third about office seekers there, with the next largest group being at the capital. The *baiano* Loreto received 45 percent of his letters from *baianos*, although the office seekers concerned were almost as frequently in Pernambuco or at the national capital as in Bahia. Pena, who hailed from Minas Gerais, received 61 percent of his letters from *mineiros*, although they referred not only to petitioners in Minas and Rio de Janeiro city (26 percent each), but also to candidates in São Paulo (12 percent). Paranaguá, who came originally from Piauí but generally identified himself with Bahia, where he began his career as a district judge, received 29 percent of his letters from people identified with Bahia and 16 percent from those who hailed from Pernambuco; even so the largest proportion of office seekers involved in the letters he received (20 percent) were in the obscure province of Piauí. Seven percent of all the letters, furthermore, specifically referred to the office seeker as the writer's *conterraneo*, that is, as originally coming from the same place. Although it is true that politicians established contacts in other areas, they maintained strong ties to their own regions.

Contemporaries clearly recognized the regional connections that linked aspiring office holders to Cabinet members. A politician in Bahia rejoiced "as a *baiano*" that Cotegipe had become a member of the Cabinet, for Cotegipe had "always struggled on behalf of the interests of Bahia." The "interests" to which he referred turned out to be in appointments. Other Cabinet members from Bahia could also be expected to show loyalty to their home state and appoint *baianos* to posts there.[39] Or, if they did not, the fact could be noted and protested in Parliament. Similarly, given that there were two Cabinet members from Pará, the Senator from that province found it inexplicable that the Minister of the Treasury wished to suspend work on a customshouse and prevent raises going to the Treasury personnel there.[40] As one disgruntled politician wrote just after the end of the Empire, "I know how things are, and I know that [Minister of Justice Manuel Ferraz de] Campos Salles does not know anything about the affairs of Bahia; thus the actions of the Minister of Justice must be inspired by someone else. . . . Since you are a Cabinet member and *baiano*, it is natural that I should think you have had a direct and immediate role in all those [actions]."[41]

Putting together a Cabinet required sensitivity to regional balance. As soon as José Antonio Saraiva was asked to form a Cabinet, he wrote to a leading politician in Minas Gerais saying, "I wish to have in the Cabinet a representative from Minas, an important province whose interests I do not know well. . . . I ask you to think on this and give me a name that would best suit the province of Minas." As word spread that the Emperor had chosen Saraiva, others began to speculate on their chances and his regional choices. "I believe that once again we will not have a Minister from Pernambuco," wrote Manuel Buarque de Macedo to Luis Felipe de Souza Leão. "I have suggested your name, but the fact that you desire the position may be an obstacle. . . . I do not think they will consider me because my personal friends Dantas and Saraiva know I would not do as a Minister. . . . In any case, rest assured that if that should happen, I will not accept, and I will take the occasion to suggest one of you." The documents are silent on how Buarque de Macedo explained the fact that when Saraiva announced his Cabinet, he was the new Minister of Agriculture and Public Works. As it turned out, the Cabinet included no one from Minas Gerais. Eight years later, when João Alfredo Correia de Oliveira organized a Conservative Cabinet, a Liberal from Minas Gerais maliciously pointed out that the Prime Minister "had thought little of [Minas Gerais], since no Senator or Deputy of that party from Minas was judged suitable to hold a portfolio, whereas São Paulo and Rio de Janeiro furnished two each."[42]

The regional emphasis in the correspondence also testifies to the enduring centrality of the personal ties between client and patron, for we find that as a letter writer moved about, he wrote mostly on behalf of people in the area where he found himself. Aside from the letters originating in the national capital, from 70 percent to a full 100 percent of the letters coming from a region referred to requests for favors to be granted in that region.

Most office seekers sought positions in the same provinces in which they were then located (see Table 6). The difficulties of travel contributed to the desire to remain at home. In appointing High Court judges, for instance, consideration had to be given to the problem of getting to the regional seat: to Goiás you could only send bachelors, because of the long trip on horseback, whereas Mato Grosso meant a long trip by sea and river, but at least "you don't put your foot in a stirrup"; to Rio Grande do Sul you could send family men. Certainly few job seekers wished to go west: not one asked to go to Mato Grosso, and only one wished a job in Goiás. When an office seeker did ask to move to another province, it could be because, as one district judge explained, "[I am] persuaded that I would be in closer contact with the capital of that province, where my family is." The same impulse even affected candidates for election to Parliament. One of them wrote saying, "You know I aspire to a seat in Parliament, and I could be elected in more than one province, needing only for you to blow softly in that direction; but I have a particular predilection for Sergipe . . . where I have friends and connections."[43]

In general people also wanted a position in a place of the same level (capital or interior) as the one where they currently served, particularly if they were located in the national capital or in some foreign country (see Table 7). Of those in the provincial capitals who did not wish to stay there, more wanted to go to the interior than to the national capital; the attraction of judgeships explains their preference. Office seekers at the national capital, however, *never* asked to be placed in a position in the interior. These choices reflect career ambitions. Someone who already held a judgeship but

TABLE 6

Office Seekers' Preferences by Area

(*Number and percent of references*)

Current location	Total	Not wishing to move	
		Number	Percent
North	15	13	86.7%
Pernambuco	43	40	93.0
Bahia	27	26	96.3
Other Northeast	38	29	76.3
Espírito Santo and Rio de Janeiro provinces	12	7	58.3
Rio de Janeiro city	21	20	95.2
Minas Gerais	14	10	71.4
São Paulo	15	13	86.7
South	9	8	88.9
Foreign country	10	10	100.0
TOTAL	204	176	86.3%

TABLE 7

Office Seekers' Preferences by Administrative Level

(*Number and percent of references*)

Current post	Total	Wishing to stay at same level	
		Number	Percent
Foreign country	10	10	100.0%
National capital	23	22	95.7
Provincial capital	96	80	83.3
Interior	65	51	78.5
TOTAL	194	163	84.0%

hoped to become a Deputy, for instance, would probably seek an office in the provincial capital, which, as one of them put it, "is the great center of provincial politics."[44] The older the office seeker grew, the more likely he was to request a job in the national capital, and the less likely to seek a transfer to the interior. *

Of all a patron's gifts for clients, the most desired were those granting them positions of authority, especially that of judge. To this end someone had to write letters on the clients' behalf, and

* With the exception that after age sixty, as the number of letters declined sharply, the proportion of men asking to go to the interior increased.

Deputies did this more than anyone else. Political life depended on this exercise or on effective action to respond to letters received. A successful run for Parliament meant the Deputy's supporters—be they his patrons or clients—would then receive, for themselves appointments from the Cabinet to judgeships or commissions in the National Guard, and for their protégés bureaucratic posts in the Treasury or in other bureaus. Or they might be rewarded with promotions in the Army or positions at the customshouse, on the medical school faculty, or in the Church. A good Deputy could manage all this.

Patronage both sustained the paraphernalia of the state and became its raison d'être. If electoral gain seemed to contemporaries the major purpose of patronage, winning elections was also the best way to secure or keep positions. A county judge, "one of the most influential local chiefs," understood this plainly, wishing to win an election because "he says an election is the best way for him to reach a district judgeship." A member of Parliament alleged that judges inevitably "throw themselves into politics principally in order to hold onto their jobs."[45] Ultimately all positions were used to advance elections. Thus patronage fed the patron-client system much as a towering tree of the Amazon forest draws sustenance from its own decaying leaves as soon as they fall to the ground. Patronage thrived on itself. And the circle of patronage-elections-patronage strengthened the values of the client system itself, based on the exchange of gratitude for benevolent care.

As they moved up the career ladder, the men involved in this correspondence were spread out over an immense area, establishing patron-client ties that helped weld all of Brazil's territory into a single system of patronage, despite its regional currents. Year in and year out, close personal ties proved crucial, and this meant proximity, direct knowledge. That far-flung system stretching across thousands of miles was bound together by requests for favors and by the resulting correspondence between and among office seekers, letter writers, and dispensers of patronage. Seeking government positions depended on manipulating a wide network of connections, so that in a sense the state helped form the nation. Again it can be said, patronage begot Brazil.

NINE

Anxious Connections

THE RANKED ORDER of Brazilian society shaped the practice of patronage, and individual mobility within that order gave it direction. Among the politically active, each participant nervously sought to preserve or improve his place, while reaffirming, legitimizing, and expressing his commitment to a system characterized by relationships of superiority and inferiority. Every letter written to recommend another or to seek a position for oneself revealed relative status. Most also suggested specific links between individuals, links that seemed important to participants, whether family connections, ties of clientele, or the pull of party loyalty. Beyond expressing their general belief in the appropriateness of clientage, letter writers advanced arguments on behalf of office seekers that stressed the virtues of paternalism and the preeminent importance of social standing. The first part of this chapter explores the connections between those who wrote letters of recommendation and those who received them and between office seekers and letter writers—whether relatives, friends, or fellow party members. Variations in these patterns shed much light on the structure of patronage. Next, since participants in the exchange of letters established and constantly reiterated their relative position of patron or client, it is necessary to acknowledge the deep anxiety suffusing all that correspondence. Finally, the grounds adduced for recommending an appointment reveal the premium placed on social place, deferential behavior, and constant loyalty.

Relationships

The patronage system rested first of all on the basic unit of society—the family. Of the *pedidos* I examined, a full third took pains to note the kinship between the letter writer and the office seeker. Doubtless other family ties remained unstated. Since Brazilians viewed the holding of a position as an important resource, they logically advanced the interests of their families by seeking official places for their relatives. A family would wish to have members as judges, bureaucrats, and, most of all, representatives in Parliament in order to secure still more appointments, commissions, and sinecures, and thus project its standing into the next generation. In 1848 José Antonio Saraiva effectively mobilized his relatives to secure the position of *promotor* for himself, as was probably the case for most of those who never became famous enough to have their correspondence saved. A law school graduate who had a father in the judicial or political elite was at least twice as likely to make it into the same circle as a classmate who did not. The interests of the family could extend to fictive kin and household members as well. To secure a place for an *afilhado* as parish priest in Paraíba do Sul, the powerful coffee-planting Werneck family joined in an effort to have the incumbent removed. The "family and relatives" went so far as to refuse to attend mass until they got their way.[1]

Women played an important if unrecognized role in politics—as they did in a family's effort to build up other property. It was they who connected all the in-laws referred to in so many recommendations, and they often penned letters of recommendation themselves (3 percent of the total). In the early part of the century, a young woman's parents made her break off an engagement because the prospective groom was now "outside the Cabinet and, without the Emperor, could no longer grant titles and favors." The barão de Maroim, having married a rich widow, "has known how to make good use of his fortune, generously dispensing his income most of all in favor of his relatives, the majority of whom owe the good [official] positions in which they find themselves to him. . . . To this fortune he [therefore] owes his place of influence in the party."[2]

Favors bestowed on one person could win the loyalty of his entire family—or alienate those who had been forgotten. Patronage and honors were bestowed "to preserve the gratitude of his family, which is large and influential and of Liberal origin," or "to entwine the Castro e Silva family relations with the government." Families left out of the stream of patronage felt that exclusion as a threat. The president of Minas Gerais advised his superiors in Rio de Janeiro that it would not be advisable to appoint a certain candidate to the position of National Guard commandant in Pitanguí because "the predominance of his family owing to the accumulation of many public offices is already allegedly a motive or pretext for unhappiness among other prominent and influential persons in the county."[3]

Nepotism did not constitute a shameful practice; there was nothing to hide. In 1884 the president of Pernambuco frankly explained that he wished to promote a public prosecutor to a county judgeship to open up a place for his own son. Rather, it was more common to recognize the existence of family loyalty and simply try to curb its most flagrant abuses. By law "father, son, brothers, or brothers-in-law" could not serve together on a County Council. The electoral law of 1846, at a time when electors still signed their ballots, specified that they could not vote for their ancestors or descendants or for their brothers, uncles, or first cousins. Even the rules limiting nepotism, however, were frequently sidestepped. One observer complained that the authorities ignored the "legal incompatibility" that should have prevented one treasury judge from having an uncle on the Regional High Court, another as probate judge, and a son as public prosecutor, all in the same district. Such laws only set certain limits to nepotism without regarding the basic impulse as condemnable. One rural patron, in recommending several men for appointment, explained why family ties were best: these "are my relatives, which fact you will weigh, but . . . I should say what I believe and so indicate those who merit my entire trust by the personal knowledge that I have of them." A man who refused to use his public office to aid a relative would be thought to have violated a basic precept of social life.[4]

Next to family came clientele. Most of the time the word *amigo*, literally friend, meant either patron or client. The patron was the client's friend, and the client the patron's.[5] A popular saying of the time went, "He who is everyone's *amigo* is either very poor or very rich." It was therefore a "lopsided friendship," to use Pitt-Rivers' apt phrase. Brazilians used the word *amigo* in this sense unselfconsciously and, I suspect, still do. Even when used as between seeming equals, it commonly implied the exchange of favors and not necessarily the sharing of intimacies or deep feelings. As one letter writer put it in reverse, "I have not maintained a friendship with him nor has he asked me for anything [*Não tenho relações de amisade com elle e nem elle nada me pediu*]." One aspiring politician clearly saw that "no young man will gain advantage in political life if he does not have to sustain him, to protect him, an *amigo* who occupies a position in the nation as high as the one you happily occupy."[6] In the relationships between the three tiers of patronage—office seekers, letter writers, and letter recipients—the word *amigo* occupied a prominent place.

Amigos offered one more tool through which a person marshaled resources, but since *amigos* were not literally linked to property, the tie to them remained more tenuous and ephemeral than that to family members. A member of Parliament explained, "in politics there are no *amigos*," meaning you could not count on them. One politician, confessing his "hope" to be elected Senator, went on to say, "I don't know whether I will succeed, but I have greatly improved my chances. However, . . . my adversaries write from there that my own *amigos* oppose me, among whom they cite your relatives." He thus expected relatives to have influence on each other, even as *amigos* could prove false. A popular saying emphasized the common view of the comparative reliability of family over patrons by stating its opposite: "A good *amigo* is worth more than a relative or cousin." Nevertheless, even if they believed them less reliable than relatives, political leaders spent much effort building networks of *amigos*. Provincial presidents, it was said, spent their time "almost exclusively taking care to recruit affections, placing *amigos*, and making proselytes." João Mauricio Wanderley, barão de Cotegipe, insisted that he never allowed friendship to interfere with the public good, although "when I see that there is a political advantage, and that I could help those with whom I am in contact, it would be weakness and perhaps something worse to abstain just because I am an *amigo*."[7]

In another and related meaning, *amigo* signified fellow party member or supporter of the same political cause, also called a *correligionário*. Politicians frequently used *amigo* in this sense in their private letters to each other. Whether authors of letters of recommendation—most of which were very brief—also meant it this way is hard to tell. Because of the nature of elections and of parties as described earlier, more often than not a fellow party member was indeed either the speaker's patron or his client. The fact that the two terms often appeared in the same letter does not mean the writer had consciously made a distinction between them: he may have been merely using two expressions for the same relationship. In general, I think "fellow party member" had an immediate instrumental purpose, while an *amigo* could be one's patron or client for other purposes as well.

A summary of all the relationships specified in the letters of recommendation I examined appears in Table 8. As it makes clear, family connections were much more important at the first or lower level of the patronage system than at the second, whereas party ties were most important between the letter writer and his addressee. Since the most frequent letter writers were Deputies, and most recipients Cabinet members, it is not surprising to find party ties looming large in this "upper" part of the network. Table 8 also shows *amigo* as an equally valid tie in both directions: "downward" to the office seeker and "upward" to the recipient of the letter. As always in this analysis, I rely entirely on relationships specifically mentioned in the letter: for instance, I know of some family connections that the correspondents did not mention, but I have not included them in the table.

It could be hypothesized that the earlier in time and the farther from the center, the more frequently would correspondents appeal to family connections, and that the later and closer to the center—that is, the more "modern"—the more frequently would they write of party and interest.[8] Insofar as party meant principally faction or clientele and not a program, the argument becomes somewhat academic. Nevertheless, a closer examination of the relative frequency with which Brazilians used these terms is worthwhile precisely because of the insight to be gained about political culture. In considering the issue it is important to distinguish between the two layers of patronage, that is, between the office seeker and his

TABLE 8

Stated Relationships Between Patrons and Clients

Relationship	"Downward" between letter writer and office seeker		"Upward" between letter writer and recipient	
	Number	Percent	Number	Percent
Family member	82	34.6%	22	4.0%
Amigo	103	43.5	199	36.6
Fellow party member	38	16.0	232	42.6
Co-worker in government	11	4.6	91	16.7
Other	3	1.3	—	—
TOTAL	237	100.0%	544	99.9%

NOTE: Letters often mentioned more than one relationship.

immediate patron and between that patron and *his* patron to whom he wrote. Speaking only of the "lower" level of patronage, we do in fact find a drop in the proportion of those who appealed to family ties from 42 percent in 1850-69 to 31 percent in 1870-89, and a slight rise in party mentions, from 16 percent to 17 percent. However, from an examination of a further 127 letters written during the first twenty years of the Republic—mostly to Affonso Pena—I know that references to party connection then fell off substantially (to 3 percent), while family connections once again increased to 35 percent. That fact throws into question whether the earlier change had much to do with altering ways of life and changing values. Furthermore, at the second level of patronage, that is, between letter writer and recipient, both categories—family and party— declined in importance, although only slightly, even during the Empire. Meanwhile, references to *amigos* greatly increased at both levels. Such an increase in clientage and personal ties contradicts any alleged "modernization."

Is it true that the farther from the center, the less candidates tended to note party connections? At the lowest level of patronage, definitely not. The party ties of the office seeker received the most attention in letters coming from the North and Northeast, and those letters made far less frequent reference to *amigos* than was true for Brazil as a whole. In contrast letters from São Paulo and Rio de Janeiro, relatively close to the national capital, had the highest incidence of references to family. In the upper part of the network, between letter writers and recipients, the hypothesis would be true only if it applied to the extreme South, whence 19 percent of the letters referred to family, well above the average of 4 percent.[9] The least frequent mentions of party ties are found in the letters from São Paulo and the other Southern provinces, and the capital itself. Evidently neither proximity nor a supposedly "modern" outlook led to emphasis on party. In the Northeast, usually considered traditional, letter writers referred to their family connections to the recipients only 4 percent of the time, compared with 46 percent for party ties.

If by greater distance from the center, one means the interior as opposed to the provincial and national capitals, the hypothesis is wrong again. Family was less likely to be mentioned as the connection between a letter writer and an office seeker desiring a post there than at either the provincial or the national capital (see Table 9). In contrast letters requesting positions in the interior mentioned party much more frequently than the others. One can conclude that the hypothesis of political modernization has little validity for Brazil in the nineteenth century. Similar notions regarding the relationships of patrons and clients permeated all regions and did so throughout the period.

Significant variations do occur, however, in the connections emphasized by letter writers according to the position they held, as can be seen from Table 10. Deputies appealed upward primarily on the basis of party connections but related downward as *amigos*. They mentioned the party ties of their clients relatively seldom. None of them referred to their family connections with the letter recipient, but 9 percent allowed that they were related to the office seeker. Provincial presidents, being the appointees of the Cabinet and sharing its political purposes, referred just as often to their work together in government as they did to their party connection. They were generally cautious in calling the Cabinet member *amigo*, but used the term for roughly three out of every ten office seekers. Presidents had considerably more family connections to the candidates than did Deputies, but like them, they tended not to have family connections with the addressee. About a third of the time they referred to the office seekers' party ties, that is, twice as often as the Deputies did, perhaps because they knew such loyalties

TABLE 9

Relationships of Letter Writers to Office Seekers
by Administrative Level of Requested Post

(*Number and percent of references*)

Relationship	National capital		Provincial capital		Interior	
	Number	Percent	Number	Percent	Number	Percent
Family member	17	44.7%	27	39.1%	9	17.3%
Amigo	14	36.8	32	46.4	22	42.3
Fellow party member	3	7.9	8	11.6	19	36.5
Co-worker in government	4	10.5	2	2.9	2	3.8
TOTAL	38	99.9%	69	100.0%	52	99.9%

NOTE: The location of the desired post is not mentioned in many letters.

would be seen as aiding the political fate of the Cabinet and not theirs alone. Judges, in referring to their connections with letter recipients, called them *amigo* more than half the time, but used that term to refer to those they recommended only 8 percent of the time, although the office seeker's party alliance—another kind of clientage—appeared with overwhelming frequency in their correspondence. Judges were also much more beset by claims of family among their clients than were Deputies or presidents. Liberal professionals were the most likely group to be related to the letter recipient but, mostly, they were unabashedly their *amigos*. And when they wrote on behalf of another, they called him *amigo* over half the time.

Among office seekers—rather than letter writers—the group most likely to be recommended on the basis of family connections were members of the armed forces (see Table 11). When recommending judges, letter writers tended to lay greater stress on their party connections than they did for other categories of office seekers. Every group relied on *amigos*, but letters about liberal professionals mentioned this tie most frequently.

Rarely can the historian know what action was taken to respond to a letter of recommendation. The official gazette did not name all holders of government positions in one place. Sometimes in the archive itself, from marginal notes or from a subsequent letter, one can deduce the result. I was able to do this for a mere thirty-two of

TABLE 10

Relationships of Letter Writers to Recipients and Office Seekers by Position of Writer

(*Percent of references*)

Relationship	Position of letter writer			
	Deputy	President	Judge	Liberal professional
"UPWARD" TO RECIPIENT				
Family member	0.0%	3.2%	0.0%	6.3%
Amigo	30.4	9.6	52.8	75.0
Fellow party member	49.7	43.6	47.2	12.5
Co-worker in government	19.9	43.6	0.0	6.3
TOTAL	100.0%	100.0%	100.0%	100.1%
	(n = 171)	(n = 94)	(n = 36)	(n = 16)
"DOWNWARD" TO OFFICE SEEKER				
Family member	9.1%	19.0%	30.8%	28.6%
Amigo	72.7	28.6	7.7	57.1
Fellow party member	16.4	33.3	61.5	0.0
Co-worker in government	1.8	19.0	0.0	14.3
TOTAL	100.0%	99.9%	100.0%	100.0%
	(n = 55)	(n = 21)	(n = 13)	(n = 7)

TABLE 11

Relationships of Letter Writers to Office Seekers by Position of Office Seeker

(*Percent of references*)

Relationship	Position of office seeker				
	Judge	Bureaucrat	Regular armed forces	Liberal professional	All groups (n = 104)
Family member	30.4%	16.7%	47.1%	18.2%	30.8%
Amigo	30.4	50.0	47.1	72.7	43.3
Fellow party member	34.8	8.3	5.9	9.1	17.3
Co-worker in government	4.3	25.0	0.0	0.0	8.7
TOTAL	99.9%	100.0%	100.1%	100.0%	100.1%

the 577 letters. Of these thirty-two, eight were successful in their aspirations. If this small group is indicative of the larger trend, one could conclude that one-quarter of all these letters succeeded in their purpose, although almost all positions seem to have been filled through the process of recommendations. Six of the thirty-two letters do not indicate the tie between the letter writer and the recipient (the upward connection); of the remainder, letters indicating a family relationship had the highest success rate (38 percent). For only nineteen cases do we know both the success rate and the "downward" relationship between the office seeker and the letter writer. Five of these succeeded in landing a position: three *amigos* of the letter writer, one family member, and one party stalwart.

Anxiety

Whether *amigos* or relatives, whether office seekers or letter writers, all participants engaged in an exchange laden with apprehension. As in any personal encounter, the patron-client correspondence provoked complex emotional responses. Politics provided one more arena in which to assert the qualities of leader, of *pai de família*, of patron. At stake lay power, self-esteem, and family survival. No two persons, even of the same "class," stood absolutely equal: one always depended on the other; one always requested while the other granted or denied. In addition relationships did not remain fixed and regularly required testing. The writing of a letter of recommendation established the relative position of three people at that moment, suggesting the unequal standing of everyone. And in seeking to establish status, one emotion predominated: anxiety. The office seeker naturally suffered as he awaited appointment; but the man who wrote on his behalf also needed to show he could succeed, for otherwise doubt would be cast on his position as patron. The patron might opt to deny his client's request that he write a letter, but that choice could not be exercised without risk that the client would turn to someone else, and do so successfully. Similarly the patron's patron could be anxious to please the letter writer and apologetic if he could not accommodate him, although he too could take the risk and say "no." In each case some area of concern could provoke uncertainty about social place.

The office seeker himself, while trying to maintain an appearance of strength, tensely awaited the outcome of his effort to line up protectors. One letter of recommendation asked that some position, any position, be granted while the man awaited appointment to a possible provincial presidency, "so that it will not appear that he is in Rio as a candidate in expectation." The would-be president sought to avoid displaying his dependency, his weakness, his status as client. A measure of the apprehension permeating the system is that thirteen letter writers asked only that the subject be maintained in his current position. And as new appointments were made to places along the channel of patronage, others down its course had reason to tremble. When a new provincial president arrived, "no one feels secure since it is well known that the one who [really] decides is Affonso [Celso de Assis Figueiredo, a Cabinet member], whose family and adherents are all taken care of and whose enemies are punished by the hand of the government." [10]

The strain felt by a young man in search of the Cabinet's support in coming elections is especially clear. As an aspiring politician, João José de Oliveira Junqueira Júnior confessed to Cotegipe, "I trust a lot, a lot, in [you] the Cabinet Minister, the Senator, and most of all the—*amigo*. My future depends on my election this year." A month later he seemed to threaten his patron with possible desertion while simultaneously vowing perpetual fealty: "What result will all my effort, all my work, have if it does not bring me an election? That would be really discouraging. You, only you, can lift me out of this anxious and uncertain state and, I will not say make me a more dedicated *amigo*, but create in me one of those obligations that are never broken because they determine my future." Shortly he added, "Do not abandon a dedicated *amigo* like me or allow the Chapada District to become the prize of an ingrate, or worse." His patron, however, put him off with promises of alternative rewards and persuaded him to run for the position of substitute Deputy. Once the election was over, Junqueira wrote again, saying that he did not expect the incumbent to give him a chance to take the seat in Rio de Janeiro as substitute, and asking Cotegipe "to fulfill the other proof of your consideration. . . . It would be painful to me to see my contemporaries and classmates get ahead of me (for some will go to the Chamber) without my having any other compensation." Then, thanking his patron for "the promise of an early realization of a proof of consideration from the Imperial Government," he insisted, "Now is the most appropriate time since once the Chamber convenes, ambitions and demands will appear." Soon he had his reward, and he thanked Cotegipe effusively for having named him president of the province of Piauí. That did not satisfy him for long, however, and in less than a year he requested the creation of a new electoral district in which he could run: "Complete your beautiful work by placing me in the Chamber of Deputies." Junqueira's worry and tension are predominant in all this correspondence.[11]

In a culture of genuine paternalism, the recipient must see himself as a child, with cloying gratitude for a father's benevolence that cloaks enormous relief at escaping punishment. Manuel Pinto de Souza Dantas, as a young politician, acknowledged Cotegipe's care in these words: "The kindness with which you distinguish me authorizes me to think that I am worth something—and, therefore, that you take me as a *padre* takes certain children." Later he compared himself to a bush below an oak tree. His expressions of gratitude apparently kept the gifts coming, for in less than two years he could jubilantly exclaim: "I am a Deputy and to you I also give my congratulations for such a result."[12] Anxiety had its reward.

At other times a self-deprecating stance camouflaged the real anxiety permeating the relationship between client and patron. The writer shielded himself from feeling diminished if the request were not met. "My brother-in-law . . . wrote me to say he wished to be county councilman. . . . If this can be done *without the least inconvenience or upset* to the general plan, would you do it?" A young politician desiring party endorsement addressed two men, referring to each of them as "most eminent" party leader and pretending to seek advice on whether he "had sufficient achievements [*títulos*] for such an elevated goal." By suggesting he might not, he in effect asserted that he did; but his needing to make the assertion discloses his deeper doubt.[13]

Sometimes a whining tone can be discerned in the correspondence, revealing both a keen sensitivity to the imbalance of power between patrons and clients and a belief in its injustice. A letter from José Bento da Cunha Figueiredo, president of Pernambuco

(1853-56) and former president of Alagoas (1849-53), so clearly reveals this sentiment that it is worth quoting at length:

As you know, it has been seven years that I have been tied to the yoke that the government placed on me. I abandoned my family and severed all my personal interests, so that I am now poorer than I was, whereas I should have acquired by the sweat of my brow a modest fortune to leave to my nine children were I working for them and not for the country. You know I have done this out of an excessive desire to accommodate the Cabinets under whose orders I have been; that I have never asked for anything for me or a relative; that I have not demanded reward or the salary that I lost as Deputy when I was ordered to stay in Alagoas with the sad salary that presidents then received, which was not enough to support even me, much less the family I left in Pernambuco. Just for not wishing to abandon the cause of the government in Alagoas, I suffered the unpleasantness of losing my election in Pernambuco. . . .

Now I am still tied to the yoke and I hear that, speaking of electoral districts in Rio, they say, "Would José Bento still want to be a Deputy?" Well, what do they want me to be? Not a Senator, for that is for finer stuff [*beiços mais finos*], and I admit that I am somewhat limp [*mole*]. But do they not even wish me to be a Deputy? Thus they repay love with ingratitude. [Do they think being president is] a bed of roses? . . . What is this, João? Do you mean it is in doubt whether I wish to be Deputy? I want to, yes sir; what I don't pine for is to be president.[14]

The two planes of patronage sometimes caught a young county judge in an excruciating vise between his local patrons and the Cabinet members who appointed him. "Thus you will understand," wrote the young José Antonio Saraiva in 1849, "that it is impossible for me to betray the government that so trusts in me, and yet the opposition [candidate] has been recommended by *amigos* who should know, and yet forget, my position. How will I support the government? How serve my *amigos*?"[15] These anguished questions doubtless kept many politicians, old and young, awake nights.

The position of petitioners intensified the possibility of resentment on both sides. A prominent coffee planter had asked a provincial assemblyman to support a request before the government. The assemblyman had done nothing. The planter wrote him:

I feel much hurt by you, and my reason is the *pedido* I addressed to you. . . . These reasons would bother you too if you were in my place, considering our friendship [*amizade*] since 1868. . . . As you can see, I trusted too much in our friendship. . . . If you had taken my *pedido* seriously, you would have written to explain the reasons why you could not satisfy my request. . . . But you treated me not as the dedicated *amigo* that I have always been or as the fellow party member who is always ready to sacrifice himself for your party, but as an importunate and ordinary job seeker or some minor actor. As you see, these are reasons enough to irritate any man who has dignity and character.[16]

A politician from Bahia reported on the disgruntlement of local bigwigs in the interior toward a Deputy, "for having paid little attention to his *amigos*." A member of Parliament later recalled how the electors of the interior "believed the Deputy should be a kind of attorney or factor for all errands, even the most private. . . . They write often and demand a prompt reply." Another Deputy bewailed the practice whereby "we have the Deputy depending on the caprice or ill-will of an [Electoral] College that he has always served; because, unfortunately, they forget all his services and the benefits received, owing to one [request] alone that finally cannot be granted."[17]

Sometimes the deep irritation at this necessary subservience to rural patrons translated into a supercilious attitude toward country bumpkins who lacked urban polish. One Deputy complained that his role was constantly to secure favors from the government for constituents, attending to "the little frivolities that characterize village life." There may also have been a bit of generational conflict, to the extent that men who belittled the values and customs of the country often at least unconsciously attacked their fathers or their fathers' friends.[18] As we have seen, the career of a judge who would be Deputy often began in a remote village, where the philosophical issues that had excited him in law school found scant response. João Lustosa da Cunha Paranaguá, later visconde de Paranaguá, remembered that "there are posts where a judge can be considered a true exile. The man accustomed to a somewhat more polite social ambience finds himself there separated from everything that could nourish his spirit, deprived of all comforts of life. That judge, furthermore, is prevented from conscientiously exercising his duties because he is almost always subject to the prepotency of one or another individual." The last sentence makes the relationship clear: dependence along with secret contempt, making that dependence all the more intolerable. A district judge in the interior of Ceará bewailed: "How a Judge must suffer who has self-regard but the ill-luck to live in the sticks."[19]

From a minor judgeship a *bacharel* might go on to a provincial presidency, where once again he felt the power of those he deemed his intellectual inferiors. A president's disgust at the behavior of the locals cloaked not a little discomfort over his own status. A president in Rio Grande do Norte maintained, for instance, that "there is no province more ungovernable than this one." An inability to govern must mean that power lay elsewhere. Braggadocio would poorly substitute for calm assurance: in Sergipe the president described the men who surrounded him as "stupid men and at the same time proud, intriguers, liars, false, and corrupted, but governable because besides all this they are cowardly and afraid."[20]

To escape the constant tension created by his double dependency—on the Cabinet and on the village chief—the Deputy had to choose: either retire from politics or pursue it to a lifetime seat in the Senate, where he could enjoy peace at last. As one observer put it, "He who is not a Senator is a nobody." Indeed, some preferred a Senate seat to a Cabinet post.[21]

Certainly a position in the Cabinet did not bring peace. In 1856 perhaps the wealthiest man in Brazil, Antonio Clemente Pinto, barão de Nova Friburgo, a coffee planter in the Paraíba Valley, had asked the Minister of Empire, a politician rooted in the province of Rio de Janeiro, to expedite an allegedly routine matter at the Treasury. The Minister referred it to his newly appointed colleague at the Treasury, but added that "if you cannot grant the request, please at least return by the bearer a letter I can show my *amigo*, one that will justify me to him." Two weeks later, however, he felt forced to write the Treasury Minister again: the barão, "suspicious at the delay of more than a month [sic] that such a simple matter—which everyone says is merely routine—has had at the Treasury," had written him, "excusing me from the trouble that he supposes I have had, . . . and asking me to return the papers enclosed with his request, which will be enough to content him, perhaps because, not trusting any longer in my intervention, he wishes to entrust someone else with the same papers. I have much felt the outcome of this business." It is hard to know whether the Minister of Empire suffered more in contemplating his response to the coffee planter than did the Treasury Minister as he scrambled to get control of his new office.[22]

The complications of crossing lines of patronage and conflicting loyalties could be considerable, and Cabinet members could easily quarrel with each other over such appointments, for on them depended the survival of their personal followings. As a gossipy critic of the system explained in 1864, "From these different intercessions from Deputies, Senators, courtesans, presidents, and high feminine personages are born little rivalries that the Cabinet . . . accommodates, or big ones that cannot always be contained and that produce the fall of ministries."[23] The collapse of the Itaborahy Cabinet in 1870 resulted from such friction. Besides the close family relationship of the Prime Minister to the Minister of Empire (father and son), complications arose because the Minister of War's daughter was married to a Deputy from Espírito Santo. As Cotegipe, who was in the Cabinet, related the story, the Minister of War insisted that the Cabinet appoint three friends of his son and son-in-law to provincial presidencies. Then, when the Minister of Justice became ill and the Minister of War temporarily took his place, the son-in-law became chief aide at the Justice secretariat, and "appointments to judgeships flowed toward the same interests"; the same happened for the National Guard. Even worse, "[other] Cabinet members were no longer sought after in the Chamber of Deputies," that is, they lost their control of patronage. Finally, according to his account, Cotegipe successfully demanded that the Cabinet resign.[24] Dispensing patronage required much skill from Cabinet members even when more circumspectly practiced. Firing someone else's client took special care. When one public servant not only failed to perform his duties but did not appear for many months on end, his supervisor in the Cabinet wrote to José Antonio Saraiva, "Knowing your interest in ——, I did not wish to take any step regarding this employee's irregular behavior without first consulting you."[25] Patronage thus proved crucial not only in securing jobs, but in keeping them.

One cannot attribute apprehension only to the client. A patron constantly encountered challenges to his position, to his ability to maintain the loyalty of clients. Junqueira warned Cotegipe that in Bahia several people wished to lessen Cotegipe's position as patron: "The plan of Sr. Martins is to boast that he made ten or twelve

Deputies and to enter the New Year as chief or director of the Bahian delegation." A few weeks earlier Junqueira had himself prodded Cotegipe to action, reporting a rumor that Junqueira's rival would be given the Cabinet's nod to run in the district: "What right does he have? They say it is Counselor Martins who protects him." Thus the ability to get one's clients elected and success at securing other positions for them measured one's position as a patron.[26]

A patron had to be able to protect his clients and foster their welfare; otherwise, he would cease to be their patron. But in exercising such protection, he found himself forced to become a client of others, and thus came to share the clients' nervousness. One letter writer confessed to his wife, "I am most unfortunate in my *pedidos*" on behalf of others. Cotegipe, momentarily out of the Cabinet and in Bahia but with an entourage to protect, wrote to his former protégé Junqueira, now Minister of War, to inquire after his earlier recommendation of a man wishing to receive a promotion in the National Guard: "As I have already said, I do not have any personal interest of friendship in this business; but since I proposed the man and I did not suppose there would be any doubt, I assured him that he would be chosen. Now how does it stand? He is capable and the richest individual in the parish. . . . The way his nomination has been checkmated is already less than flattering to me. I do not want to appear as a petitioner [*pretendente*] in such a minuscule matter."[27]

The patron feared as well that potential clients might make their requests through another, rather than joining his following. In recommending a candidate for a job, one letter writer in Salvador added that the appointment "would greatly suit me to give a lesson to someone in Rio de Janeiro who is persuaded that without his action . . . my *amigo* will obtain nothing." If patrons often complained of all the requests they received from their clients, they also encouraged them as a way of expanding their clientele. Thus the already prestigious Cotegipe could write in 1870 to the energetic and ambitious João Alfredo Correia de Oliveira: "Perhaps you do not know how much I like you now that I know you better; I tell you this so that you will not spare me if you see that I can render you some service."[28]

The patron also became a captive of the client. Clearly the patron was not as bound as the client, and certainly not in the same way.

Yet as a commentator noted, "There is no one here who enjoys liberty of action; they are all patrons and clients." One politician said that he did not want to run in the provincial capital district because there were so many electors there, all close together and "almost all public employees with aspirations." He hoped to lessen dependence on his own clientele. Another candidate for Deputy agreed, saying he found himself in the especially delicate position of sending in many *pedidos*, since in a district embracing the provincial capital "public employees place us on a real treadmill." With the advent of direct elections, he later added, "the Deputy is so identified with the elector" that only many favors could secure his reelection.[29] In some sense the frequent complaints about the number of letters that had to be written reflected this loss of independence, as well as being a boast on their numerous clients. As one candidate for Deputy exclaimed, "I'm surviving as best I can the pain in the ass that *amigos* cause me without pity [*Vou alliviando como posso o sacco que os amigos vão enchendo sem dó*]."[30] The pain only increased once one entered the Cabinet. Junqueira despaired of the "claims of people from our province who arrive in mass." Later he added: "You know well how hard it is to satisfy the Deputies, who are always going about complaining. The hardest task that Cabinets face is appointments. We are holding up as best we can."[31]

If a client's request could not be met, he had to be informed of this gently, by a patron concerned to keep his loyalty despite the failure. One Cabinet member wrote a long letter to Cotegipe in the 1850s, telling him he could not give his *afilhado* a position as clerk at the Post Office, explaining the obstacles to the appointment, and assuring him that a new and better-paid position would soon be opening up in another bureau. He suggested that "your *afilhado* wait." Almost twenty years later the Minister of Foreign Relations had to confess to Cotegipe that "I was much embarrassed by your repeated request in favor of your special *amigo*, the barão de Penedo. You should believe that I wish to serve you and, if in this case . . . I am not able to do so, I hope you will not attribute this to my ill-will, something that is quite impossible." A Cabinet member who took two months to appoint someone recommended by a Senator felt the need to explain that he could not do it sooner "for lack of an opening and ancient facts regarding his life as a public servant. . . . Paranaguá [another Cabinet member] can tell you how I worked to satisfy you." Worried patrons sought to assuage hurt feelings or wounded pride.[32]

Only a few stood sufficiently outside the system to avoid its tensions. A local political leader and member of a dominant family in Paraná wrote: "Asking nothing for myself, aspiring to nothing, I can maintain greater prestige." To accept a position as director of the government savings bank, he said, would lessen "[my] moral force and my political position in the province." To some the blandishment of public employment did not prove attractive. One landowner in the early Republic wrote from the still coffee-rich Paraíba Valley to "say with pride to my *amigo* Dr. Braz that I do not require the support of the government in order to have on my side my fellow party members and loyal *amigos* of electoral struggles, because hardly any of them needs a public position, and they do not depend on the government's soup kitchen [*das sopas do governo*]." It was, he added, the government that needed them, those of "[us] who defend the ideas of the present regime, [to fill] local positions." Twenty years earlier a member of a political family in Minas Gerais had declared, "I gave up that career [in politics] to dedicate myself to agriculture; I now prefer to see coffee sprout; it is the more independent life."[33] The true measure of patrons and clients may be found in the degree of their independence. Pedro II, who appeared to be at the top, in truth depended on others; once he was gone, they went on as before. Yet each of them also counted nervously on clients and suffered collective anxieties that found expression in the repeated appeals to family, following, and hierarchy.

Grounds for Recommendation

In a letter of recommendation the writer expressed attitudes he expected the recipient to share, touching on those points whose referents lay at the nerve center of the political culture. And in appealing to a jointly held regard for kin, friendship, and social ranking, these letters not only advanced the chances of a candidate's appointment, but also strengthened the validity of those principles themselves, lest they be doubted. When a letter writer pointed to his family relationship to the office seeker, he unconsciously reiterated the importance of the family as a basic unit of society. He also acknowledged an intense interest in preserving the resources of his family, a concern he expected the recipient of the letter to understand and endorse. Similarly, when he called the office seeker his *amigo*, he appealed to a shared belief in the appropriateness of building a clientele. Underlying the entire enterprise lay collectively held assumptions pointing to ranked order in society with family and clientele as its cement. Given the emotional charge embedded in the simplest letter, it is instructive to attend to those characteristics of the office seeker that the letter writer deemed potent and effective.

The measure of a man lay not in one quality, but in many. True, the relationships between office seeker and letter writer often seemed quite enough to secure appointment: to say he was a relative or *amigo* often stood as the reason for expecting the request to be granted. Sometimes the letter writer pointed to still further extensions of the patron-client network as a sufficient justification, saying the office seeker had "respectable connections" or had been recommended by someone else. The fact that in 121 of the 577 cases I examined the letter writer advanced no argument on behalf of the petitioner suggests that he considered his own place as patron or client quite adequate grounds.[34] In the pages that follow, however, I have ignored these letters, although I have noted a few others that said enough to imply that the writer's authority was reason enough for granting the request. In still other cases the letter writer merely described the candidate as "qualified," meaning that he met the minimum standards set by law. In five cases the writer frankly admitted that he had no knowledge of the office seeker's qualifications. Most letters, though, included some reasons why the recipient should make the appointment or present his name to someone who would. In these justifications one can perceive the larger concerns that permeated the political community.

The loyalty of a candidate or of his family counted heavily. Contemporaries considered faithfulness, whether political or personal, one of the most important virtues, and a man who held office could be expected to be loyal to his allies. A provincial president could explain in 1860 that, although he had "dismissed not a few police delegados and subdelegados" for political malfeasance, "one cannot reasonably expect that individuals who occupy the positions of police authorities, magistrates, and National Guard officers should suddenly break their commitments and affections." A good man remained "faithful to his sworn flag." Some believed that urban or commercial life eroded such virtue: "Despite the perfidy of supposed *amigos*, betrayals and conspiracies among disloyal partisans, I am in second place in the list [of those elected], and if the backlands are not yet contaminated by the hypocrisy of large centers and still observe the traditions of loyalty, [I will be elected]." The interior, however, did not always prove to be so virtuous: one parliamentary candidate confessed his exasperation at the electors in the district of Jacobina, deep in the dusty interior of Bahia, where "I did not receive a single vote, despite reiterated promises and offers from my *amigos* and the county judge." Also, political loyalty had to last: a Prime Minister returned one letter of recommendation with the remark, "The information from the Treasury does not endorse him; to be a Conservative *now* does not endorse him." [35] Of the grounds advanced for appointment in the letters of recommendation, 10 percent referred to political reliability. Such attention implies also doubt. One had to assert the loyalty of the candidate, else it would be a source of worry.

It is true that a good number of the reasons proffered in justification of the *pedido* had to do with the particular merit of the office seeker. His past performance was exemplary or his expertise needed; his conscientiousness might be praised or his education noted. Letter writers referred to the candidate's honesty with some frequency. They would sometimes describe him as being apolitical to stress that the reasons for the appointment resided in his qualifications. In recommending a nominee to a Conservative Minister, a writer acknowledged that the candidate "may have Liberal ideas, but I can assure you that he has not been active for a long time, and does not act politically [*não faz política*] as a magistrate." [36] Sometimes letter writers maintained that candidates deserved the appointment out of equity, that is, they had been passed over for the sake of less-qualified men because of favoritism; now the candidate should be restored to his rightful place. Alternatively, nominees were said to be entitled to a position by their seniority over other candidates or by their many long years of service. As Pedro II recommended regarding judges, the best policy was "a lot of care on first choice and then seniority for promotion." [37] Of course a system impersonally dependent on seniority would not require any letters of recommendation at all, and even impersonal grounds could be raised to back a personal request. A father wrote about his son, who hoped for a faculty position in the law school, that he was "a doctor of cap and gown, the oldest candidate, with the most seniority." [38]

In attempting to prevent some of the worst abuses of the patronage system, Brazilian lawmakers determined that for certain positions examinations would be required; but that did not erase the importance of securing a patron. In 1872, for example, candidates for positions in the provincial treasury of Bahia had to be tested on commercial bookkeeping, arithmetic, and handwriting. Before a candidate could even take the test, however, he prepared an application that more resembled a petition. One applicant mentioned his poverty and large family, as well as his service in the Paraguayan War, appealing to the paternalism of those who would allow him to take the test. In addition he had persuaded ten different notaries to go through their records to attest that no judicial actions stood against him, and secured from both the subdelegado and the parish priest statements praising his good conduct, virtually letters of recommendation. In short, to be admitted to the exam depended on the goodwill of many to whom he would thus owe favors, that is, it required an intelligent and energetic effort to line up patrons. The law also required the would-be notary public to pass a test administered by a legally trained judge; yet over 5 percent of the *pedidos* I examined asked for positions as notaries, witness to the inefficacy of performance alone as a means of securing such positions. Other posts, ostensibly filled by a *concurso*, or public contest—where the candidates presented their credentials and sometimes, as for positions on the faculties of law or medicine, performed—still relied on favoritism, and a letter of recommendation could overturn the results. Cotegipe, for instance, maintained that one *concurso* had been won "owing to protection" and went on to argue for the appointment of the runner-up. [39]

It is impossible to be sure that political and personal purpose did not similarly inform decisions that writers of *pedidos* justified for other reasons. Nevertheless, if all references to the candidates' external and measurable qualifications—past performance, expertise, conscientiousness, honesty, education, seniority, years of service, equity, apoliticality—are summed, they account for only a quarter of the reasons given for making appointments. Letter writers understood it best to concentrate on other matters.

Some grounds for appointment appear at first to refer to qualities of performance but, on closer inspection, really deal more with the office seeker's social position. I came to this conclusion partly because of the vagueness that characterized the usage of certain terms and partly from the context in which they appeared both in the *pedidos* and in other documents of the era. I refer to such words as *habil, apto, capaz, talentoso,* and *competente* (literally, able, apt, capable, talented, and competent). In no case were these words used to describe ability, aptitude, capability, or competence for a particular task or position. Rather, they appear to have referred to the qualities inherent in the class of people who could be properly considered for public employment. Thus, aside from being an in-law of the letter writer, the sole qualification of a man who wished to be warehouse superintendent at the public works department in Salvador consisted in being "apt," while "great ability" justified the proposed appointment of a secretary to the president of Ceará, and "great talent" was all that described a man suggested as administrator of a normal school.[40]

The word *inteligente* (literally, intelligent) also implied the proper background and the qualities emphasized in the education of a *bacharel*; it meant a shared rhetorical culture, smooth and elegant speech, and the social skill to entertain polite company, at least as much as any quickness of mind or the ability to solve problems. The word did not apply to the lower orders of society. A nineteenth-century dictionary begins its definition of intelligence by characterizing it as a "quality of the soul"; to be *inteligente* was to have "elevated qualities of spirit."[41] Similarly, from context and comparison with other contemporary evidence, I have concluded that even *bom carater* (good character), *carater purissimo* (purest character), *honradez* (honorability), and *probidade* (probity) did not refer so much to a firmness of moral principles as to behavior suitable to the propertied and their friends. Character was something the upper class had and others did not. In contrast *moralidade, honestidade,* and *integridade* (morality, honesty, and integrity) did refer to particular moral qualities needed for jobs where, for instance, money would be handled.

A number of adjectives clearly referred to the gentility of the candidate: *homem de bem* (man of good [qualities]), *estimavel* (estimable), *muito conceituado* (very well regarded), *honrado* (honorable in the original meaning of the word in English), *digno* (worthy), *bom moço* (good young man), and the frequently used but never specified *boas qualidades* (good qualities). Even more clearly related to social position was *homem distinto*, which a contemporary defined as someone "who is not common: who is not of the people by birth, merit, or degrees; who has noble qualities of character."[42] Writers of recommendations also pointed to the candidate's excellent manners or said he was polished or well behaved (*excelentes costumes, polido, bem educado*). It is probably true that references to the candidate's general education also applied more to class than to his specific skills, but I have not counted them as such; I have interpreted education as referring to a genuine need in this position, even if the adjective was simply *formado* (has a degree) or the writer referred generally to the candidate's *illustração* (enlightenment).[43] Some letters referred specifically to the candidate's wealth and social prominence or those of his family (*abastado, homem importante, familia importante*) as grounds for the granting of a favor or a position. Wealth, by assuring an independence from temptations to corruption, could, I suppose, be considered an objective qualification for certain positions. The Treasury Minister received advice from a businessman against one appointment at the customshouse because the candidate owed ten *contos* to "approximately 48 creditors, almost all in commerce, storekeepers, etc. As a public employee placed in a fiscal office in direct contact with commerce, his reputation may be called into question."[44] Most of the time, however, wealth indicated proper social standing, not a specific quality useful in the job. Social position accounts for almost a quarter of the reasons advanced for granting someone an appointment.

The fact that so many letters spoke of these social qualifications reveals a generalized anxiety. Too much mobility had occurred, and could occur, for one simply to assume that every office seeker came from the right background. And the importance of social standing had to be reiterated for the sake of both the letter writer and the recipient.

Finally, one set of arguments appealed to the shared preference for paternalistic modes of conduct. The fact of his having a large family to support was often offered as a reason for recommending a candidate. With some frequency those writing letters expressed their care for someone old or poor, although the person also needed to be humble and loyal. A man whose party loyalty was unclear should nevertheless be kept on: "if later on it is necessary to place one of our *amigos* in his position, we will work out a practical way to harmonize party needs with the *excessively precarious* situation of the functionary, who has a large family and has behaved well toward me."[45] Thus benevolence purchased loyalty and obedience.

References to an office seeker as a *bom pai de família*, or good family man, good father, had the same purpose. On the one hand it meant that he provided for his family, cared for his dependents, may even have been a kind father. But it also meant that he exercised control over his family and held himself responsible for the members of his household and their actions. He fulfilled the expectations of a patriarchal culture. A firm leader of a household shored up the base of the social structure. Not by accident did one patron link these qualities of the office seeker: he "is a cooperative citizen and good *pai de família*." Several nominees were recommended because they wished to be near their families and kin, as for instance, in a letter on behalf of a physician in the municipal sanitary corps of Rio de Janeiro who desired a transfer to Salvador: "This young man is a relative of people whom I very much wish to serve and has a mother and family who expect from him the aid they need"; away from home and thus dividing his income, "it will be difficult for him to comply with the duties of a good son." Insofar as the family stood as model for the state, the practice of familial virtues became central to the preservation of authority and thus of society, and so merited patronage.[46]

Table 12 shows the reasons advanced in behalf of a favor seeker by category and subcategory. The many references to social place emphasized the hierarchies of society at large, while assuring the recipients of the letters that the person in question stood among those entitled to their support. Insofar as he did not have such standing, a letter writer could fall back on the paternal values that ensured control: he who needed help stood as a child to the dispenser of largesse. The connections built up by patronage contributed to the same end, for they emphasized the appropriateness of the "lopsided friendship" and of family ties in the search for public

TABLE 12

Grounds Advanced by Letter Writers on Behalf
of Candidates for Positions or Favors

(n = 1,360[a])

Grounds		Percent
Relationship		16.1%
Amigo	8.7	
Family or household	7.4	
Patronage system itself		7.1
Good connections	2.6	
"Qualified"	4.1	
Authority of letter writer	0.4	
Political loyalty		9.3
Merit of candidate or impersonal qualities		25.6
Performance or expertise	7.5	
Conscientiousness, honesty, morality	4.3	
Education, general or specific	4.5	
Seniority or years of service	5.3	
Equity	3.2	
Apoliticality	0.8	
Social place		23.5
"Hábil," "inteligente," etc.	9.8	
Gentility ("homen de bem," etc.)	9.6	
Wealth or social status	4.1	
Paternalistic values of letter writer		12.1
Candidate poor	5.5	
Candidate with large family to support	4.0	
Candidate old or sick	1.0	
Candidate good family man	1.6	
Other		6.3
TOTAL		100.0%

[a]Many letter writers advanced more than one reason for recommending the appointment or favor.

office. Only a quarter of the reasons broached involved the merit and skills of the candidate or impersonal bureaucratic criteria for advancement.

The broad categories of Table 12 are those of the historian, not of contemporaries. To the letter writers, those qualities that I have identified as indicating social position constituted as much a legitimate claim to the appointment or other benefit as did his expertise or education. Being a good family man seemed as relevant as his honesty, for in either case his principal task was to set an example.

One letter aptly sums up the qualities desired in a public servant. João Alfredo Correia de Oliveira, president of Pará in 1870, was soon to leave for Rio de Janeiro to take his seat in the Chamber of Deputies, as would two of his vice-presidents. Concerned about the fitness of the four remaining vice-presidents who would, in their order, succeed him if no alterations occurred in the list, he sent a confidential letter to the Minister of Empire discussing the suitability of each. From his criticism of them, one may glean the qualities sought for in a president and to some degree admired in every public servant, qualities that João Alfredo understood as valid and knew the Minister would recognize as such.

All four of the vice-presidents lacked the combination of characteristics João Alfredo thought necessary or had qualities he found positively distasteful. One enjoyed the necessary social distinction (*homem honrado*) but was very old, required an assistant to guide him in his acts, and on previous occasions had proved weak and easily "fooled"; in fact, he was always "surrounded and pressed by *amigos*" who, disagreeing among themselves, left him "not knowing what to do." Another, although "reputedly an honest person," was also too malleable and eager to please, "without the strength to free himself from *amigos*." When he had acted as an aide to the old man, "he had given in even more readily than the old man himself." The third in line "was once a Liberal and is now hated by his former party colleagues." Furthermore, he sold his influence to the highest bidder, "accustomed to receiving favors and money . . . from those requesting [positions]." Neither political friends nor enemies held him in any regard, and he simply lacked what was most necessary in a provincial president: "the moral force that will gain the good opinion of the public." Finally, the fourth man was "honorable" and dutiful, but of the opposing Liberal Party and "a declared and excitable opponent of the government." He often, furthermore, lost his temper and "has struck a man in the public square."

In contrast to all these unlikely candidates, João Alfredo proposed the installation of a new vice-president in a position to become the chief administrative officer automatically whenever João Alfredo was away from the province. The "honest young man" he had in mind, besides being sensible, prudent, and *inteligente*, was "a dedicated Conservative." In addition, as the brother of a Deputy from Maranhão and the son-in-law of a prominent Pará politician

João Alfredo Correia de Oliveira (1835-1919), 1861

and Senator, he belonged to an influential family. He was also, even more importantly, "my *amigo* of many years." As a district judge, finally, he had performed well; although known not to be a "political judge," during elections he had "carried out important and delicate commissions." His appointment, without displeasing the Liberals, would satisfy the three warring factions of Conservatives. He would know how to "attend to the legitimate interests of the party . . . while correcting and containing the bad tendencies and pretensions of *amigos*." If, while altering the list of vice-presidents, the Minister of Empire were also to get rid of the crooked one—for the sake of "morality"—or the Liberal one—for the sake of "politics"—João Alfredo had still another candidate to suggest, a man who besides his "honest character" and "moderate" politics, was a "rich landowner [and] commandant of the National Guard."[47]

An ideal appointee, therefore, would have not just one desirable quality but several. The office seeker should be conscientious in the performance of his duties yet also have the necessary social graces and garner the respect of other men, be *inteligente* and *honrado*. He should have clients, yes, but also the strength to withstand their importunings (not allowing them to become the patrons), and should simultaneously be a loyal client himself. He would be steady in his political loyalties, yield them to the letter writer's party, and yet win the respect of his adversaries through prudence and moderation. He should enjoy good family connections and preferably wealth. Since the combination of all these qualities would be hard to find in one individual, some of them would naturally have to be sacrificed in the case of lesser appointments. For a vice-president who was not expected ever to become even acting president, social position and wealth would be sufficient in themselves. João Alfredo did not mention a knowledge of the law, the developmental needs of Pará, or budgetary skills. His *amigo* got the position, no doubt because in writing on his behalf, João Alfredo had known how to touch the right chords, sensing and sharing societal anxieties regarding leadership, power, and social standing. *

Perhaps the most surprising feature of the qualities mentioned in the *pedidos* I examined is their consistency over time. The frequency with which writers referred to the particular abilities of the office seeker never varied significantly. There was some proportional decline in references to social position in the last two decades of the Empire (from 29 percent in the 1850s and 1860s to 20 percent), but looking ahead to the first twenty years of the Republic, I have noted that recommendations once again stressed social place (25 percent). The frequency with which letter writers mentioned the relationship between the writer and the office seeker, especially their party connections, varied inversely to references to the candidate's social position. Most important, despite the passage of time, merit gained no weight as a ground for appointment.

Significant variation did occur, however, according to the posi-

* And when João Alfredo became Minister of Empire a few months later, he appointed the same "honest young man" president of Pará, Miguel Arcanjo Galvão, *Relação dos cidadãos que tomaram parte no govêrno do Brasil no período de março de 1808 a 15 de novembro de 1889*, 2d ed. (Rio de Janeiro, 1969), p. 147.

tion requested. Candidates for promotions in the regular armed forces, for instance, had their specific abilities mentioned almost twice as frequently as the average for all office seekers, whereas class remained less significant for them. In contrast, those seeking appointment in the National Guard or as police officers were far less likely to have their skills noted than was the rule: for them party connections loomed largest in importance. While for all letters taken as a whole, class and merit stood about even in prominence, those who sought positions in the bureaucracy were more likely to have their social standing noted than their competence for the job by a ratio of 3:2. These observations confirm what one would predict of men in the armed forces, generally believed not to have come from families of the best social positions; and what I have explained in this book about the role of police officials and National Guard officers likewise makes the short shrift given to their skills unsurprising.

Some regional variation also appears in this correspondence. For example, whereas specific qualities fitted to the job accounted for 25 percent of the grounds mentioned for the whole group, the figure rose to 38 percent in São Paulo and 40 percent in the South (whence most military job seekers appeared). It was not the traditional North and Northeast or the province of Rio de Janeiro that pulled the average figure down; in fact the references to such qualifications somewhat exceeded the average in letters from those areas. Letters from the capital city itself and from the province of Minas Gerais account for the difference, with mentions of a candidate's merit falling to lows of 16 and 12 percent, respectively. Letters written from Minas Gerais were twice as likely to mention personal connections as those from the rest of the country. Since the Northeast differed so markedly from Minas Gerais in this regard, I do not believe the pattern in Minas can be simply attributed to the supposed traditionalism of its society.

The reasons adduced for placing a candidate for office reflect the way in which Brazilians judged and categorized each other. The quantitative analysis of these letters brings specificity to what we could have imagined: social position, the relationships of clientage, and the pull of paternalism account for three-quarters of the reasons advanced for recommending placement. Letter writers saw the specific qualifications of the candidate for a position as merely complementing these other characteristics. The crucial consideration for a letter writer was to mesh the reasons he adduced with the values of the recipient. The importance of one's social standing as a qualification for appointment to bureaucratic and political positions suggests a relationship between the state and society that has heretofore not been sufficiently stressed. The bureaucracy was deliberately filled by men from a certain class because their public function was precisely to link that class to government, not to act independent of it. In this regard at least, it is difficult to see any basis for a conflict between the state and Brazil's dominant classes.

In writing *pedidos* men who simultaneously acted as patrons and as clients uncertainly worked their way to a better place in the social scale. In building their own clientele, patrons chose to stress not only the ties of family and friendship, but also the appropriate social place of the office seeker and his political loyalty, along with his merit. The reiteration of these qualities throughout the imperial period reflects the uncertainties not only of the letter writers, but of society at large. Letter writers also carefully weighed the relationships appropriately mentioned in such requests. These differed sharply according to whether they referred to those connections the author claimed to the recipient of the letter or to those he had with the office seeker: on the whole the writers of *pedidos* believed family ties, party alliances, and bonds between *amigos* to be the most important. Every person sought to establish his relative position, claiming friendship if family ties did not suffice, building a following, solidifying the structure of gradations while clambering over its sharp edges, hoping to reach the next level or at least avoid plunging down to another.

Epilogue

On November 15, 1889, military officers in Rio de Janeiro overthrew the Brazilian Empire. Coffee planters in São Paulo took over the government of their state on that same day in the name of the new Republic. Landowners elsewhere did nothing, some because they did not care, others because they blamed the old regime for the end of slavery in 1888. In the city of Rio de Janeiro and in other capitals many rejoiced. These events have been much studied, and their causes are still debated; I do not intend to enter that debate here. Yet recognizing the central place in Brazilian politics of efforts to build a following can broaden our understanding of those factors that encouraged a change in regime. Whether we consider *paulista* coffee planters, military officers, or disgruntled urban groups as chiefly responsible for bringing down the Empire, patronage was one of their central concerns.

In São Paulo, as the railroads began to spread into the interior after 1868 and coffee prices surged, acquiring land became crucial. Success in that effort depended on force, whether measured in the number of clients that could be mustered for actual battle or in the positions of legal authority controlled by each family. Planters jousted for leadership within their local spheres and pursued the business of building a clientele as frenetically as that of making money. Yet the number of *paulistas* in the Cabinet on whom they or their Deputies could call for help in securing appointments and other favors lagged far behind the province's wealth. The key positions of Prime Minister and Minister of Justice did not once fall to a *paulista* after 1871. Just as the direction of *pedidos* depended on ties of family and *amigos*, so the lack of men in the Cabinet to whom one had personal connections could prove a major weakness. In turn, for the central authorities to remain effective in São Paulo, they needed to be responsive to the rapidly changing relative position of rivals there and build close connections between themselves and local elites. They failed to do either. True, many planters objected to the fiscal or monetary policies pursued by the imperial government (although such objections remained vaguely expressed and contradictory). But planters in the newer regions of São Paulo may also have resented the difficulty they encountered in transmitting a sense of their local power to the imperial government. Given the economic weight the new coffee regions could place behind their protest, their interests should have been attended to. Just as centralizing forces had won out in the 1830s and 1840s once the immediate hinterland of the national capital had gained economic predominance, so the loss of that predominance undermined the ability of the central government to withstand centrifugal tendencies.

Military officers also found that the imperial government ignored their search for positions and places. For them the end of the war with Paraguay in 1870 concluded a period of rapid promotions and expanded opportunity. Professional advancement then slowed to a snail's pace. Salaries remained stagnant while the cost of living steadily increased. Successive governments strove to reduce the size of the Army, and vacancies became rare. With years of accumulated resentments, the officers' discontent mounted.[1] Certainly, once the Army gained power in 1889, it is difficult to find a consistent plan in execution except one: the new government quickly doubled the size of the Army. To be sure, a nationalist rhetoric and a Positivist ideology colored the thinking of military leaders, but the failure of patronage formed the core of their deep and growing hostility toward the old regime.

Another source of malaise for the Empire centered on its inability to expand the number of public positions open to *bacharéis* as rapidly as candidates for them appeared. In the decade 1830-39 the law schools produced only 710 graduates; by 1880-89 the number of newly minted lawyers reached a peak of 1,966.[2] Some of the steadily mounting excess had once been absorbed by simply expanding the number of judicial districts, but that expedient was no longer sufficient to handle the avalanche. As the rate of advancement within the judicial and political hierarchies slowed, disenchantment with the Empire spread among the younger generation of liberal professionals. And *bacharéis* were energetic in providing various intellectual justifications for abolishing the monarchy, whether they stressed democracy, republicanism, and federalism, or industrial progress, scientific advance, and strong, authoritarian government.

Other urban groups may have genuinely felt hampered by the Empire in their struggle to assert their economic interests. As with electoral reform, the growth of cities impelled significant political changes. Expanding ports had meant an ever-larger population of urban professionals and workers, from railroad magnates to warehousemen, from bank managers to tradesmen. Their interests were certainly not those of landowners. Yet patronage had extended readily to protecting the financial and entrepreneurial ventures of some, and one may wonder, therefore, to what extent the political structure of the Empire actually stood in the way of industrialists and other businessmen. When some scholars argue that the 1889 change in regime resulted (even in part) from the demands of new interest groups, they are, at least implicitly, arguing that the imperial practice of granting benefits to the favored few according to personal ties provoked a demand for evenhanded policies that would make public resources equally accessible to everyone or at any rate to everyone within a certain economic sector. What I suspect, however, is that many who supported the Republic desired not the end of such partiality, but their own share of the benefits. Certainly, whether as coffee planters or *bacharéis*, military officers or industrialists, men looked to government as a means to an end and counted on their personal relationships to help them toward that goal.

Finally, there had always been demands for a decentralization of the power of patronage. Bringing that power home to the provinces would be especially furthered if provincial presidents were elected rather than appointed from Rio de Janeiro. That had been a longstanding desire of various reformers. The Liberal-Radical manifesto of 1868 had included elected presidents among its demands. Manuel Pinto de Sousa Dantas, bewailing the alleged misdeeds of a provincial president of Bahia in the 1870s, had asked a friend, "Is reform not urgent—federal autonomy or something like it?" In

1882 Francisco Octaviano de Almeida Rosa proposed that presidents should at least be nominated in provincial elections, for eventual appointment by the Emperor.[3] Even the very monarchist Affonso Celso de Assis Figueiredo, later visconde de Ouro Preto, had recognized in 1883 the strength of this demand for "federalizing" patronage, and urged that the appointment of county and district judges be placed in provincial hands. Several provincial legislatures expressed their desire to name county judges, priests, public health functionaries, secretaries of the chiefs of police, and jailers.[4] With the Republic they got their wish. Almost the first act of the new government was to give the state presidents the right to "create jobs, fill them, . . . and set their salaries."[5]

Although the Republic reversed the tendency toward the centralization of appointments begun in 1837, it did not weaken the reliance on patrons. National expenditures on staff remained roughly at the pre-1889 level. The federal President was the chief dispenser of patronage, so it is no surprise to learn that the political elites of São Paulo and Minas Gerais—then economically the strongest centers—soon agreed to take turns in naming him. Moreover, prosperous states like São Paulo now enjoyed new taxing powers of their own with which to increase revenues and thus expand public employment. Voting for state presidents and county executives (*prefeitos*) intensified the electoral struggle to gain local appointive power, and the creation of state courts increased opportunities for the swelling number of law school graduates. Many of the political practices of the Empire quickly revived. No sooner did Quintino Bocayuva, a leading propagandist for the Republic, enter the Cabinet in 1889 than he transferred his son-in-law from county judge in northern Rio de Janeiro to chief of police in the Federal District; it was not long before the young man secured the post of district judge, then probate judge. As one politician later observed, "The Republic was born with son-in-lawism [*genrismo*]." An American diplomat in 1890 succinctly described the new regime as "a military government tempered by nepotism."[6]

The resulting system of government, firmly in place by 1898, has been dubbed *coronelismo*.[7] The county boss, or *coronel*—the rubric derived from the imperial National Guard—usually a landowner, received carte blanche to make decisions locally and wield a heavy hand against his opponents, as long as the electoral results from his county favored the candidates chosen by party leaders. The presidents of each state similarly enjoyed great leeway, but bore the responsibility for seeing that the *coronéis* produced compliant electorates. And elections quickly became subject to the same forces as before: the local boss and the central government in symbiotic relationship, linked by the state president, relied on and strengthened each other. Thus, as before, an intricate web of mutual influence connected local and central governments.

One factor, however, had been omitted in the new formula: politicians could no longer count on someone at the top to act as arbiter of their disputes, as the Emperor had done. Political machines now became longer-lived, and no technique existed to alternate the dominant faction or to arrange for the peaceful adjudication of differences among political leaders. As a result violence may have become even more common at the local level; certainly military actions punctuated the history of the next four decades. Finally, in 1930, Getúlio Vargas, himself a product of the *coronel* network in Rio Grande do Sul, unhappy with São Paulo's insistence on extending its hold on the national presidency, and ably drawing on various sources of dissatisfaction within the First Republic, overthrew it. His papers are chock full of *pedidos*.

In this book I have argued that the intertwining of patronage and elections most directly served the interests of the propertied class. Although the link between leader and follower did not erase the tensions between haves and have-nots, it made it possible to contain them. The early regional struggles for local supremacy gave way to a centralized Empire because it suited the few who saw themselves surrounded by the many—by slaves and the free poor. The well-off then used elections as dramatic acts to send a clear message to minor participants, identifying for them the grand persons to whom they owed deference and to whom they should render loyalty and obedience. Nevertheless, since the participants in the first level of those indirect elections could prove a numerous and boisterous crowd and the impending end of slavery threatened to send a flood of freedmen to the ballot boxes, the electoral "reform" of 1881 drastically reduced their number.

In retrospect the historian may be tempted to think of Brazilian elites as paranoid in their constant fear of disorder—since, in fact, no Revolution occurred. But this nonoccurrence may be seen, rather, as a great tribute to their skill at combining persuasion and force. For a constant movement of people, a repeated questioning of the individual's place, and a steady tremor of minor protest against violations of the paternalistic code regularly jarred Brazilian social and political life. The little challenges repeated throughout Brazil a thousand times in any one moment could well leave any elite perpetually on edge. The system of patronage, by bringing some benefit to clients, prevented the accumulation of these tensions and dampened potential animosities. The ethic of the *amigo* worked to prevent the sympathetic vibrations of minor conflicts from creating a major one.

The principle of leadership depended on winning elections. Political challenges from below, if successful, could have endangered the acceptance of hierarchy as appropriate and proper in every relationship. A Cabinet always secured a majority in any Parliament whose election it supervised; and a local leader only lost an election when already out of power as measured by less formal but more forceful means. Political events, whether in the rural village or at the capital, can be understood only in light of the ideology of inequality that gave purpose to political action. Yet elaborate legalisms surrounding elections and the repeated attempt to legislate fair elections ensured that losers, rather than abandoning the system and overthrowing it, would feel caught up in it and accept its rules. Such efforts blunted the sense of injustice that might otherwise have occasioned generalized intra-elite violence or even encouraged radical social change. Yet firmness in controlling elections, along with the appearance of generous evenhandedness, resulted not from Machiavellian plots among a few politicians, but from taken-for-granted standards of behavior applicable as much within the family and on the *fazenda* as in politics. If political culture was shaped to benefit some and not others, culture itself set limits to action.

Parties became vehicles for gaining and dispensing patronage. Much of the political history of the Empire can be explained by taking into account that fundamental basis of party life, in which votes were exchanged for official positions. Members of the Chamber of Deputies played a crucial role in making possible such transactions along two planes, one headed by the Prime Minister, the other by the county potentate. The Deputy assured the flow of positions of authority to the locally prominent and simultaneously conveyed to the Cabinet the shifting balance of power among rural bosses on whom it ultimately depended. In playing that role, Deputies wrote endless letters, appealing to shared understandings of social rank and paternal care, and extending patronage to cover the entire farflung nation. The fact that everyone in this exchange acted in some sense as both patron and client animated the constant search for political and social advantage. Indeed the central goal of obtaining public place and position and the clients' dependence on the benevolence of a patron proved enduring even after the fall of the Empire.

For no waning of the patronage system accompanied the change of regime in 1889. New groups among the propertied rose to prominence without abandoning that practice. This point needs particular attention because it runs counter to the position of those theorists who see all societies as progressing unilinearly toward "rational," impersonal, and impartial government. Some historians, for instance, have argued that the coffee planters in the older regions of Rio de Janeiro and the sugarmill owners of the Northeast held more seigneurial, less entrepreneurial attitudes than the agricultural elite of São Paulo, and that this difference explains why the former backed the old-fashioned clientelistic Empire, while the more modern, business-oriented planters of São Paulo supported the shiny new impersonal institutions of the Republic.[8] But the barão do Paty do Alferes, one of the most business-oriented and successful coffee planters, backed the centralizing Empire wholeheartedly—out of political acumen every bit as sharp as that of his *paulista* successors a half century later. Planter-businessmen in both places and both times sought to use the instruments of patronage to their own purpose, and neither group wished to damage such useful levers. The system of patrons and clients did not represent a "stage" in Brazil's history except in the sense that it served the interests of a class whose life is not, one hopes, eternal.

Brazilians, moreover, had always criticized the patronage system. During the Empire they attacked its "corruption," its favoritism, its reliance on *filhotismo* or family ties, and everyone's perpetual dependence on personal connections. They thus suggested their ability to stand outside it, to view the state as having the larger purpose of serving all the people equally and impersonally. Yet they whole-heartedly participated in the solicitation and distribution of favors and appointments, taking no effective measure to combat the general reliance on patrons who, by definition, first protected their own clients. By their actions Brazilians signaled that for them an impersonal state remained a pipe dream, that the provision of employment and the distribution of authority constituted the true and lasting function of the state. The state advanced the interests of the propertied principally by reproducing and maintaining the patron-client system itself. One can conclude that only deep alterations in the structure of society could significantly modify such practices. Even then no sudden change can be expected, for new groups may use old tools to exert their dominance, and culture does have a life of its own. Certainly, as the decisive tool in nineteenth-century Brazilian politics, as predominant expectation, as unself-conscious pattern of action, patronage provided the major link between society and state.

NOTES

Notes

In citing the letters of high bureaucrats and judges, I have adopted the convention of using hyphens between the abbreviated name of the correspondent's office and his jurisdiction. Thus PP-ES refers to the provincial president of Espírito Santo. For lesser officers, I do not indicate the jurisdiction unless they are the recipients of correspondence or write from a place other than the seat of their jurisdiction. The Brazilian National Archive's use of superscripts in its cataloguing system poses special challenges to typists and printers, so I have used a hyphen instead; thus IJJ⁵30 is rendered as IJJ 5-30. Published works are cited in full at the first occurrence in each chapter and in short form thereafter. To keep the notes as compact as possible, I provide only the information needed to track a work down: author, title, place and date of publication; particulars on monograph series, number of volumes, and the like are given in the Sources Cited, pp. 349-68. The following abbreviations are used in these Notes:

ACMRJ	Arquivo da Cúria Metropolitana do Rio de Janeiro
AGCRJ	Arquivo Geral da Cidade do Rio de Janeiro
AESP	Arquivo do Estado de São Paulo
AHI	Arquivo Histórico do Itamaraty
AIHGB	Arquivo do Instituto Histórico e Geográfico Brasileiro
AL	Alagoas
AM	Amazonas
AMIP	Arquivo do Museu Imperial, Petrópolis
AN	Arquivo Nacional, Rio de Janeiro
APEB	Arquivo Público do Estado da Bahia
APEP	Arquivo Público do Estado de Pernambuco
APERJ	Arquivo Público do Estado do Rio de Janeiro
ASCM-BA	Arquivo da Santa Casa de Misericórdia, Bahia
BA	Bahia
BCCD	Brazil, Congresso, Câmara dos Deputados
BCS	Brazil, Congresso, Senado

BN/SM	Seçao de Manuscritos, Biblioteca Nacional, Rio de Janeiro
CC	Coleção Cotegipe
CE	Ceará
Cotegipe	João Mauricio Wanderley, barão de Cotegipe
CP	Chefe da Polícia
CRB	Casa de Rui Barbosa
"Decreto, 1855"	*LB*, Decreto 842 of 19 Sept. 1855
"Decreto, 1860"	*LB*, Decreto 1,082 of 18 Aug. 1860
"Decreto, 1875"	*LB*, Decreto 2,675 of 20 Oct. 1875
"Decreto, 1881"	*LB*, Decreto 3029 of 9 Jan. 1881
GN	Guarda Nacional
GO	Goiás
Guahy	Joaquim Elisio Pereira Marinho, barão and then visconde de Guahy
ES	Espírito Santo
HGCB	Holanda, Sérgio Buarque de, ed., *História geral da civilização brasileira*
JD	Juiz de Direito
JM	Juiz Municipal
JP	Juiz de Paz
Junqueira	João José de Oliveira Junqueira Jr.
LB	Brazil, *Colleção das leis do Imperio do Brasil*
"Lei, 1846"	*LB*, Lei 387 of 19 Aug. 1846
MA	Maranhão
MF	Ministro da Fazenda
MG	Minas Gerais
MGuerra	Ministro da Guerra
MI	Ministro do Império
MJ	Ministro da Justiça
MM	Ministro da Marinha
MN	Município Neutro
MT	Mato Grosso
PA	Pará
PB	Paraíba
PE	Pernambuco
PI	Piauí
PM	Prime Minister (Presidente do Conselho)
PR	Paraná
PP	Presidente da Província
Rio	Rio de Janeiro (city)
RJ	Rio de Janeiro (province)
RN	Rio Grande do Norte
RS	Rio Grande do Sul
SAP	Seção de Arquivos Particulares, Arquivo Nacional
SC	Santa Catarina

SE   Sergipe
SP   São Paulo (province)
SPE Seção do Poder Executivo, Arquivo Nacional
SPJ Seção do Poder Judiciário, Arquivo Nacional
VPP Vice-presidente da Província

Introduction

1. Fernando Henrique Cardoso and Enzo Faletto, *Dependency and Development in Latin America* (Berkeley, Calif., 1979), especially pp. 89-91.
2. Joaquim Nabuco, *Um estadista do império*, [3d ed.?] (Rio de Janeiro, 1975); *HGCB*, no. 7.
3. Caio Prado Júnior, *Evolução política do Brasil e outros estudos*, [? ed.] (São Paulo, 1957). An even more mechanistic relationship between class interest and government policy is advanced by Nelson Werneck Sodré, *História da burguesia brasileira* (Rio de Janeiro, 1964). Although working from somewhat different premises, Décio Saes comes to the conclusion that slaveowners dominated the Brazilian state during the Empire; see his *A formação do estado burguês no Brasil (1888-1891)* (Rio de Janeiro, 1985).
4. Nestor Duarte, *A ordem privada e a organização politica nacional (Contribuição á sociologia politica brasileira)* (São Paulo, 1939), p. 137.
5. Francisco José de Oliveira Vianna, *Instituições políticas brasileiras*, 2 vols. (Rio de Janeiro, 1949).
6. Raymundo Faoro, *Os donos do poder: Formação do patronato político brasileiro*, 2d ed., 2 vols. (Pôrto Alegre, 1975); this is a much expanded version of the original, published in 1958.

Chapter 1

1. Peter L. Eisenberg, *The Sugar Industry in Pernambuco: Modernization Without Change, 1840-1910* (Berkeley, Calif., 1974), pp. 3-62; Moacir Medeiros de Sant'Ana, *Contribuição à história do açucar em Alagoas* (Recife, 1970); J. F. Normano, *Brazil, a Study of Economic Types* (Chapel Hill, N.C., 1935), pp. 19-27.
2. Affonso d'Escragnolle Taunay, *Pequena história do café no Brasil (1727-1937)* (Rio de Janeiro, 1945); C. F. van Delden Laerne, *Brazil and Java: Report on Coffee Culture in America, Asia and Africa to H.E. the Minister of the Colonies* (London, 1885); Stanley J. Stein, *Vassouras, a Brazilian Coffee County, 1850-1900* (Cambridge, Mass., 1957); Emília Viotti da Costa, *Da senzala à colônia* (São Paulo, 1966). On the replacement of sugar by coffee in central São Paulo, see Maria Thereza Schorer Petrone, *A lavoura canavieira em São Paulo. Expansão e declínio (1765-1851)* (São Paulo, 1968), p. 224.
3. Francisco Peixoto de Lacerda Vernek [i.e., Werneck, later 2° barão do Paty do Alferes], *Memoria sobre a fundação de huma fazenda na provincia do Rio de Janeiro, sua administração, e épocas em que se devem fazer as plantações, suas colheitas, etc., etc.* (Rio de Janeiro, 1847) (the

latest edition has a valuable Introduction by Eduardo Silva; Brasília, 1985); Eduardo Silva, *Barões e escravidão: Três gerações de fazendeiros e a crise da estrutura escravista* (Rio de Janeiro, 1984), pp. 47-85; Stein, *Vassouras*, p. 21n.

4. Brazil, Instituto Brasileiro de Geografia e Estatística, *Anuário estatístico do Brasil*, 1939-40, p. 1381; Sebastião Ferreira Soares, *Elementos de estatistica comprehendendo a theoria da sciencia e a sua applicação á estatistica commercial do Brasil* (Rio de Janeiro, 1865), I, 133, II, 53, 72, 116, 166, 181, 194, 248, 260; Joan E. Meznar, "Deference and Dependence: The World of Small Farmers in a Northeastern Brazilian Community, 1850-1900" (Ph.D. diss., Univ. of Texas at Austin, 1986); Alice P. Cannabrava, *Desenvolvimento da cultura do algodão na província de São Paulo (1861-1875)* (São Paulo, 1951).

5. Sebastião Ferreira Soares, *Notas estatísticas sobre a produção agricola e a carestia dos generos alimenticios no Imperio do Brasil* (Rio de Janeiro, 1860), pp. 63-100, 111-20; Soares, *Elementos de estatistica*, I, 104; Domingos Soares Ferreira Penna, *A região occidental da provincia do Pará: Resenhas estatisticas das comarcas de Obidos e Santarem* (Pará [Belém], 1869), pp. 186-200; Barbara Weinstein, *The Amazon Rubber Boom, 1850-1920* (Stanford, Calif., 1983), pp. 9, 38-52, 53; Moacir Fecury Ferreira da Silva, "O desenvolvimento comercial do Pará no período da borracha (1870-1914)" (M.A. thesis, Univ. Federal Fluminense, 1978).

6. Soares, *Elementos de estatistica*, I, 104, II, 99; [José Hildebrando Dacanal and Sergius Gonzaga, eds.], *RS: Economia & política* (Pôrto Alegre, 1979); the classic account of the contrast between the Southern and Northeastern cattlemen is found in Euclides da Cunha, *Rebellion in the Backlands* (Chicago, 1944), pp. 89-110; also see Daniel Parish Kidder and James Cooley Fletcher, *Brazil and the Brazilians Portrayed in Historical and Descriptive Sketches* (Philadelphia, 1857), pp. 348-51, 521-22. On the relationship between the trading patterns of Rio Grande do Sul and its revolutions, see Spencer L. Leitman, *Raízes socio-econômicas da Guerra dos Farrapos: Um capítulo de história do Brasil no século xix* (Rio de Janeiro, 1979).

7. Joaquim Norberto de Souza Silva, *Investigações sobre os recenseamentos da população geral do Imperio e de cada provincia de per si tentados desde os tempos coloniaes até hoje . . .* (Rio de Janeiro, 1870), p. 102; Brazil, Directoria Geral de Estatística, *Recenseamento da população do Imperio do Brazil a que se procedeu no dia 1° de agosto de 1872* (Rio de Janeiro, 1873-76); Brazil, Directoria Geral de Estatística, *Synopse do recenseamento de 31 de dezembro de 1890* (Rio de Janeiro, 1898) (by the seven largest cities I refer to the urban parishes of the Município Neutro and to the counties of Salvador, Recife, Belém, Pôrto Alegre, São Paulo, and Curitiba); Nicolás Sánchez-Albornoz, *The Population of Latin America: A History* (Berkeley, Calif., 1974), pp. 178-79. No accurate measure of urbanization or population density is possible because the Brazilian censuses presented population figures by parishes within counties without

differentiating between urban and rural areas, and no one has yet calculated the area of each parish or county at any one time.

8. For the extensive literature on this subject, see Robert Edgar Conrad, *Brazilian Slavery: An Annotated Research Bibliography* (Boston, 1977). Especially useful are Stein, *Vassouras*; Costa, *Da senzala*; Warren Dean, *Rio Claro: A Brazilian Plantation System, 1820-1920* (Stanford, Calif., 1976); Robert Wayne Slenes, "The Demography and Economics of Brazilian Slavery, 1850-1888" (Ph.D. diss., Stanford Univ., 1975); and Robert Edgar Conrad, *The Destruction of Brazilian Slavery, 1850-1888* (Berkeley, Calif., 1972). On urban slavery, see Sandra Lauderdale Graham, *House and Street: The Domestic World of Servants and Masters in Nineteenth-Century Rio de Janeiro* (Cambridge, Eng., 1988); Mary C. Karasch, *Slave Life in Rio de Janeiro, 1808-1850* (Princeton, N.J., 1987); and Luiz Carlos Soares, "A manufatura na formação econômica e social escravista no Sudeste. Um estudo das atividades manufatureiras na região fluminense: 1840-1880" (M.A. thesis, Univ. Federal Fluminense, 1980). On rural slavery outside plantation areas, see Roberto Borges Martins, "Growing in Silence: The Slave Economy of Nineteenth-Century Minas Gerais, Brazil" (Ph.D. diss., Vanderbilt Univ., 1980).

9. *Filhos-familias* were defined as "sons of whatever age while under their father's power" and can be contrasted with the paterfamilias: Candido Mendes de Almeida, ed., *Codigo Philippino; ou, Ordenações e leis do reino de Portugal* (Rio de Janeiro, 1870), Liv. IV, Tit. LXXXI, par. 3, Tit. XCVII, pars. 17, 19; Liv. V, Tit. XXXVI, par. 1, Tit. XCV, par. 4. A father could grant permission to a son-at-home to trade on his own account from age 18, provided he did so in writing: *LB*, Lei 556, 25 June 1850 [Codigo Commercial], Tit. I, Cap. I, art. 1, par. 3.

10. Brazil, *Constituição política do Império do Brasil*, art. 92, par. 2; José Antonio Pimenta Bueno, *Direito publico brazileiro e analyse da Constituição do Imperio* (Rio de Janeiro, 1857), p. 193; Pedro Autran da Matta e Albuquerque, in Antonio Herculano de Souza Bandeira, ed., *Reforma eleitoral, eleição directa: Collecção de diversos artigos sobre a eleição directa dos quaes são autores os seguintes senhores* ... (Recife, 1862), p. 236. In 1831 a bill was introduced in Parliament, without success, to grant "widowed mothers" (*mães de famílias* or materfamilias) the right to vote "through one of their sons, sons-in-law, grandsons, or any [male] relative if these are lacking": BCCD, *Reforma eleitoral: Projectos offerecidos á consideração do corpo legislativo desde o ano de 1826 até o anno de 1875* ... *colligidos na secretaria da Camara dos Deputados* (Rio de Janeiro, 1875), p. 10. Women could not engage in commerce without their husbands' permission: *LB*, Lei 556, 25 June 1850 [Codigo Commercial], Tit. I, Cap. I, art. 1, par. 4.

11. Antonio de Moraes Silva, *Diccionario da lingua portugueza*, 8th ed. (Rio de Janeiro, 1889-91). Brazilian scholars have long noted the importance of the family; see Gilberto Freyre, *The Masters and the Slaves (Casa-Grande & Senzala): A Study in the Development of Brazilian Civilization*

(New York, 1956); Francisco José de Oliveira Vianna, *Instituições políticas brasileiras* (Rio de Janeiro, 1949), especially I, 235-74; and Edmundo Zenha, *O município no Brasil (1532-1700)* (São Paulo, 1948), pp. 131-40. See also Stein, *Vassouras*, pp. 147-49.

12. Almeida, *Codigo Philippino*, Liv. 4, Tit. LXXXVIII, pars. 1, 4, 5, Tit. XCVI; Alida C. Metcalf, "Families of Planters, Peasants, and Slaves: Strategies for Survival in Santana de Parnaíba, Brazil, 1720-1820" (Ph.D. diss., Univ. of Texas at Austin, 1983), p. 4.

13. Brazilian consul in Paraguay to MJ, Assunción, 14 Feb. 1870, CP-Corte to MJ, Rio, 1 Mar. 1870, 2 Apr. 1870, all in AN, SPE, IJ 6-518; examples of black-bordered letters are Junqueira to Cotegipe, Rio, 19 Jan. 1886, AIHGB, CC, L31, D115, and subsequent letters from him; they could be multiplied by the hundreds.

14. Unidentified newspaper quoted in José Antonio Nogueira de Barros, *Tributo de gratidão á memoria do capitão João Pinheiro de Sousa* (Rio de Janeiro, 1860), p. 11; João José de Oliveira Junqueira (father) to Cotegipe, Salvador, 8 Dec. 1856, AIHGB, CC, L30, D152; Antonio José Centeno to PP-RS, São João de Camaquã, 8 June 1872, AN, SAP, Cx. 781, Pac. 2, Doc. 11; Manuel Pinto de Souza Dantas to José Antonio Saraiva, Rio, 29 Jan. 1885, AIHGB, L272, D42. The same cohesion could be expected from commercial families in the city of Salvador, thus belying any particularly rural quality to this tendency: Joaquim Elisio Pereira Marinho, barão de Guahy, to Cotegipe, Salvador, 25 Sept. 1884, AIHGB, CC, L38, D9. Also see Joaquim Nabuco, *Um estadista do império*, [3d ed.?] (Rio de Janeiro, 1975), p. 67. Political hostility between one family and another could last through several generations: L. A. Costa Pinto, *Lutas de famílias no Brasil (Introdução ao seu estudo)* (São Paulo, 1949), pp. 73-132; Billy Jaynes Chandler, *The Feitosas and the Sertão dos Inhamuns: The History of a Family and a Community in Northeast Brazil, 1700-1930* (Gainesville, Fla., 1972); Eul-Soo Pang, *Bahia in the First Brazilian Republic: Coronelismo and Oligarchies, 1889-1934* (Gainesville, Fla., 1979), p. 40.

15. Rufino Eneas Gustavo Galvão, visconde de Maracajú, to Cotegipe, Belém, 29 July 1883, AIHGB, CC, L25, D83; Manuel Pinto de Souza Dantas to Cotegipe, Salvador and Santo Amaro, 31 May, 18 July 1856, ibid., L19, D14, D19. Uncle José Dantas Itapicurú was also the candidate's *padrinho*: Dantas to Cotegipe, Salvador, 24 June 1856, ibid., L19, D17. "Uncle João" is a reference to João Dantas dos Reis, who sometimes added Portatil Júnior to his name: J. C. Dantas Júnior, "O capitão-mór João d'Antas e sua descendência," *Revista Genealógica Brasileira*, 1: 2 (2d sem. 1940), 387-88, 395-96, 406. Since an effort to establish links with all major contenders for local power impelled marriage strategies, a certain intra-family hostility inevitably emerged, as is pointed out by Linda Lewin, *Politics and Parentela in Paraíba: A Case Study of Family-Based Oligarchy in Brazil* (Princeton, N.J., 1987), pp. 156-57.

16. For an example of how contemporaries described their family as including slaves, see Actas da Mesa Parochial de Pirassinunga, 7 Sept.

1872, copy encl. in PP-SP to MI, São Paulo, 25 Nov. 1872, AN, SPE, IJJ 5-30. Having cut the slaves off from their own kin, the planter expected to become the most significant person in their lives, and thus a kind of kin; see John W. Blassingame, *The Slave Community: Plantation Life in the Ante-Bellum South* (New York, 1971), especially chap. 3; and Mieko Nishida, "Negro Slavery in Brazil: Master-Slave Relations on the Sugar Plantations in the Northeast," ms in possession of the author. On the linking power of family and household, see Emmanuel Le Roy Ladurie, *Montaillou, the Promised Land of Error* (New York, 1978), pp. 49, 52. Also note similar structures in Hungary reported by Edit Fél and Tamás Hofer, "Tanyakert-s, Patron-Client Relations and Political Factions in Átány," *American Anthropologist*, 75: 3 (June 1973), 796-97.

17. For examples of family members as *agregados*, see LB, Decisões 1848, Additamento, Aviso, 1 Feb. 1848; Brazil, Directoria de Estatistica, "Arrolamento da população do municipio da Corte (São Cristovão) 1870," ms at Instituto Brasileiro de Geografia e Estatística (Rio de Janeiro), Departamento de Documentação e Referência, householder Januario [illegible] da Silva, Casa 11, rua do Campo de S. Christovão, 1º quarteirão, and householder Francisco Ferreira Pitança, Casa s.n., rua da Feira, 2º quarteirão. In this district of Rio de Janeiro (São Christovão), 68% of all households held *agregados*, and 6% of the *agregados* were relatives of the householder, according to an analysis carried out by Sandra Lauderdale Graham. On similar patterns in small towns, see Mappa dos habitantes existentes na 1ᵃ companhia das ordenanças da villa de Guaratinguetá . . . 1829, AESP, População, no. 55, L55, households 70, 76, 138, 150, 164, 169, 181, 262. A useful study is Eni de Mesquita, "O papel do agregado na região de Itú—1780 a 1830," *Coleção Museu Paulista*, 6 (1977), 13-121. The meaning of the term in the documents I have seen extends to a much larger group than those strictly so called by census takers; see Maria Luiza Marcílio, "Crescimento demográfico e evolução agrária paulista, 1700-1836" (Tese de Livre-Docência, Univ. de São Paulo, 1974), pp. 178-79. The *agregado*'s contribution to the family economy in urban settings customarily resembled that of an apprentice or domestic servant.

18. Luiz Peixoto de Lacerda Werneck, *Idéias sobre colonização, precedidas de uma sucinta exposição dos princípios que regem a população* (Rio de Janeiro, 1855), p. 36; Laerne, *Brazil and Java*, p. 309n; James W. Wells, *Exploring and Travelling Three Thousand Miles Through Brazil from Rio de Janeiro to Maranhão* (London, 1886), p. 168; speech of Joaquim José Alvares dos Santos Silva, in Congresso Agricola, *Congresso Agricola: Coleção de documentos* (Rio de Janeiro, 1878), p. 156; speech of Barbosa Torres, in RJ, Assembleia Legislativa, *Anais*, 1880, p. 593, quoted in Ana Maria dos Santos, "Agricultural Reform and the Idea of 'Decadence' in the State of Rio de Janeiro, 1870-1910" (Ph.D. diss., Univ. of Texas at Austin, 1984), p. 126; Stein, *Vassouras*, pp. 32n, 57n, 58; Maria Sylvia de Carvalho Franco, *Homens livres na ordem escravocrata*, 2d ed. (São Paulo, 1974), pp. 94-107.

19. João da Rocha Fragoso, Report, in Brazil, MF, *Relatorio*, 1891, Vol. 2, Anexo C, pp. 4-5.

20. Herbert H. Smith, *Brazil—the Amazons and the Coast* (New York, 1879), pp. 402-3; Imperial Instituto Bahiano de Agricultura, "Relatorio," in Brazil, Ministerio da Agricultura, *Relatorio*, 1871, Appenso C, p. 7; Stuart B. Schwartz, "Elite Politics and the Growth of a Peasantry in Late Colonial Brazil," in *From Colony to Nation: Essays on the Independence of Brazil*, ed. A. J. R. Russell-Wood (Baltimore, Md., 1975), pp. 144-54; Manuel Correia de Andrade, *A terra e o homen no Nordeste* (São Paulo, 1963), pp. 93-95. As I will show below, an *agregado* could change patrons and move about, giving him some bargaining power.

21. Speech of Moreira de Barros, Congresso Agricola, *Coleção*, p. 190.

22. The nature of the relationship was not particular to Brazil or even to "Catholic" countries, as Glen C. Dealy would have it: *The Public Man: An Interpretation of Latin American and Other Catholic Countries* (Amherst, Mass., 1977), pp. 9, 12-25. Useful bibliographies on client-patron relationships are James C. Scott, "Political Clientelism: A Bibliographical Essay," in *Friends, Followers, and Factions: A Reader in Political Clientelism*, ed. Steffen W. Schmidt et al. (Berkeley, Calif., 1977), pp. 483-505; and Luis Roniger, "Clientelism and Patron-Client Relations: A Bibliography," in *Political Clientelism, Patronage and Development*, ed. S. N. Eisenstadt and René Lemarchand (Beverly Hills, Calif., 1981), pp. 297-330. The importance of family and clientele in the electoral politics of ancient Rome is ably summarized by H. H. Scullard, *Roman Politics, 220-150 BC* (Oxford, Eng., 1951), pp. 12-30. Contemporary Latin America has been the focus of many studies of the topic; see, for example, Arnold Strickon and Sidney M. Greenfield, eds., *Structure and Process in Latin America: Patronage, Clientage, and Power Systems* (Albuquerque, N.M., 1972).

23. PP-BA to MJ, Salvador, 24 Oct. 1848, as quoted by Fernando Uricoechea, *O minotauro imperial: A burocratização do estado patrimonial brasileiro no século XIX* (São Paulo, 1978), p. 208; denuncia perante o Juiz Municipal, Pirassinunga, 20 Sept. 1872, copy encl. in PP-SP to MI, São Paulo, 23 Jan. 1873, AN, SPE, IJJ 5-30. Also see Thomas Flory, *Judge and Jury in Imperial Brazil, 1808-1871: Social Control and Political Stability in the New State* (Austin, Tex., 1981), pp. 72-73.

24. Antonio José Machado to Subdelegado, Freguezia do Monte (termo de S. Francisco da Barra do Sergipe do Conde, Comarca de Santo Amaro), [1857], and enclosures, APEB, Presidência, Polícia, Subdelegados, M.6231.

25. Here I differ from those theorists who argue from the vertical ties of patronage to an absence of class interests. Their view is summarized (and criticized) by Michael Gilsenan, "Against Patron-Client Relations," in *Patrons and Clients in Mediterranean Societies*, ed. Ernest Gellner and John Waterbury (London, 1977), pp. 167-82. Also see Peter Flynn, "Class, Clientelism, and Coercion: Some Mechanisms of Internal Dependency and Control," *Journal of Commonwealth and Comparative Politics*, 12: 2 (July 1974), 133-56.

Notes to Pages 22-26   283

26. See, for example, Camara de Villa Viçosa to PP-BA, 1 Sept. 1842, encl. in PP-BA to MF, 9 Dec. 1842, AN, SPE, IJJ 9-338. On land-tenure law and its application, see Warren Dean, "Latifundia and Land Policy in Nineteenth-Century Brazil," *Hispanic American Historical Review*, 51: 4 (Nov. 1971), 606-25; Emília Viotti da Costa, *The Brazilian Empire: Myths and Realities* (Chicago, 1985), pp. 78-93; Franco, *Homens livres*, pp. 80-94; Stein, *Vassouras*, pp. 13-17; and Thomas H. Holloway, *Immigrants on the Land: Coffee and Society in São Paulo, 1886-1934* (Chapel Hill, N.C., 1980), pp. 112-14.

27. Luiz Peixoto de Lacerda Werneck, *Le Brésil. Dangers de sa situation politique et économique; moyens de les conjurer. Lettre à son fils. . . . Ouvrage posthume revu par F. P. de Lacerda Werneck* (Rio de Janeiro, 1889), pp. 26-30; Stein, *Vassouras*, pp. 224-25.

28. I have particularly profited in writing this paragraph from the insights of Sandra Lauderdale Graham.

29. Henrique Pereira de Lucena to Zilia (his wife), Rio, 3 June 1887, APEP, Col. Lucena, 661; André Peixoto de Lacerda Werneck, *A lavoura e o governo, II° apelo aos fazendeiros. Artigos publicados no "Jornal do Commercio" de 15 a 21 de junho de 1890* (Rio de Janeiro, 1890), pp. 6-9; Stein, *Vassouras*, p. 134.

30. Compare the similar uses of paternalism in England: Douglas Hay, "Property, Authority and the Criminal Law," in *Albion's Fatal Tree: Crime and Society in Eighteenth-Century England*, ed. Douglas Hay et al. (New York, 1975), pp. 52, 61-62.

31. José Thomaz Nabuco de Araújo, quoted by Nabuco, *Estadista do império*, pp. 101-2; L. P. L. Werneck, *Idéias sobre colonização*, p. 36.

32. Luiz Alves dos Santos, "Discurso pronunciado no dia 9 de julho de 1882 pelo vigario . . . ," in [Manoel Peixoto de Lacerda Werneck], *O visconde de Ipiabas, Peregrino José de America Pinheiro: Perfil biographico, acompanhado do retracto do finado e seguido de algumas allocuções pronunciadas por ocasião de seus funeraes* (Rio de Janeiro, 1882), p. 30; Barros, *Tributo de gratidão*, pp. 10, 15; Francisco Peixoto de Lacerda Werneck, 2° barão do Paty do Alferes, to José Maria Pinto Guerra, Patí do Alferes, 11 Sept. 1858, AN, SAP, Cód. 112, v. 3, fl. 42. See also Dean, *Rio Claro*, p. 123.

33. F. P. L. Werneck, *Memoria*, p. 17; Luis Peixoto de Lacerda Werneck, quoted by E. Silva, *Barões e escravidão*, p. 214; M. P. L. Werneck, *Visconde de Ipiabas*, p. 15.

34. The literature on slave resistance is relatively extensive, and the issue is controversial, at least for other slave societies; as starting points for Brazil, see Clovis Moura, *Rebeliões da senzala (quilombos, insurreições, guerrilhas)* (São Paulo, 1959); and José Alípio Goulart, *Da fuga ao suicídio (aspectos da rebeldia dos escravos no Brasil)* (Rio de Janeiro, 1972).

35. Henry Koster, *Travels in Brazil in the Years from 1809 to 1815* (Philadelphia, 1817), II, 191-96, 215; Robert Walsh, *Notices of Brazil in 1828 and 1829* (London, 1830), II, 342, 350-51, 365-66; Kidder and

Fletcher, *Brazil*, p. 133; Mary Wilhelmine Williams, "The Treatment of Negro Slaves in the Brazilian Empire: A Comparison with the United States of America," *Journal of Negro History*, 15: 3 (July 1930), 328-34; Frank Tannenbaum, *Slave and Citizen: The Negro in the Americas* (New York, 1947), pp. 57-58; Herbert S. Klein, "Nineteenth-Century Brazil," in *Neither Slave nor Free: The Freedman of African Descent in the Slave Societies of the New World*, ed. David W. Cohen and Jack P. Greene (Baltimore, Md., 1972), p. 314.

36. *Honras funebres em memoria do . . . visconde de Inhaúma, Gran-Mest. . . . do Gr.º. Or.º. e Sup.º. Cons.º. do Brasil* (Rio de Janeiro, 1869), p. xiv; Agostinho Marques Perdigão Malheiro, *A escravidão no Brasil. Ensaio histórico, jurídico, social*, 3d ed. (Petrópolis, 1976), I, 132. For the application of this law, see "Letter of Freedom," 23 Aug. 1827, in Robert Edgar Conrad, *Children of God's Fire: A Documentary History of Black Slavery in Brazil* (Princeton, N.J., 1983), p. 320. The provision on ingratitude was revoked by the Law of Free Birth (*LB*, Lei 2040, 28 Sept. 1871, art. IV, par. 9), but conditional freedom remained legal and was sometimes still granted: see Locação de serviço, AN, SPJ, Cartório do Primeiro Ofício, Escrituras, 1871, Liv. 313, fls. 125-26, 363, and Cartório do Segundo Ofício, Escrituras, 1880, Liv. 245, fls. 5v-6, 71, 82v, 120. See also Sandra Lauderdale Graham, "Slave Prostitutes and Small-Time Mistresses: The Campaign of 1871 in Rio de Janeiro," ms.

37. CP-Corte to MJ, Rio, 5 Jan. 1855 (also see 16 Mar. 1855), AN, SPE, IJ 6-219; Delegado do 3º districto, Engenho de S. Luiza, to CP-BA, 17 Jan. 1855, APEB, Presidência, Polícia, Delegados, M.6188; JM-Cachoeira to PP-BA, Cachoeira, 1 June 1840, APEB, Presidência, Juizes, Cachoeira, M.2273; Subdelegado de Lagoa to CP-Corte, Rio, 3 Jan. 1872 [i.e., 1873], AN, SPE, IJ 6-518.

38. Domingos de Souza Leão to Pedro de Araujo Lima, marquês de Olinda, Recife, 21 Aug. 1865, AIHGB, L207, D72; Sociedade Auxiliadora da Agricultura de Pernambuco, *Trabalhos do Congresso Agricola do Recife em 1878 comprehendendo os documentos relativos aos factos que o precederam* (1879; facsim., Recife, 1978), p. 136. Significantly, the Paraguayan War made it easier for sugar planters to find free laborers for hire: Eul-Soo Pang, *O Engenho Central do Bom Jardim na economia baiana. Alguns aspectos de sua história, 1875-1891* (Rio de Janeiro, 1979), p. 52. On the lottery, see Nabuco, *Estadista do império*, pp. 852-55; William S. Dudley, "Institutional Sources of Officer Discontent in the Brazilian Army, 1870-1889," *Hispanic American Historical Review*, 55: 1 (Feb. 1975), 60 n.42; and *HGCB*, no. 7, pp. 168, 172. Being drafted remained the lower class's constant fear into the 1890s if not beyond: [Afonso Henrique de] Lima Barreto, *Triste fim de Policarpo Quaresma*, 7th ed. (São Paulo, 1969), pp. 184-85.

39. CP-Corte, Mapa Semanal, 26 Jan. 1859, AN, SPE, IJ 6-842, no. 4; *Diario Novo*, 21 Jan. 1845, quoted in Nancy Naro, "The 1848 Praieira Revolt in Brazil" (Ph.D. diss., Univ. of Chicago, 1981), p. 49 (in 1845

15 milreis would have been worth U.S. $7.80). Even the gathering of all the necessary documents to prove legal exemption from conscription could be burdensome for the poor: CP-BA to Delegado-Maragogipe, Salvador, 26 July 1869, copy, APEB, Presidência, Polícia, Delegados, Registro, M.5802.

40. Hastings Charles Dent, *A Year in Brazil, with Notes on the Abolition of Slavery, the Finances of the Empire, Religion, Meteorology, Natural History, Etc.* (London, 1886), p. 287. Descriptions of deserters almost always referred to a "mulatto" or a "freed black"; see, for example, CP-BA to Delegado do 1º districto da capital, Salvador, 11 Dec. 1868, copy, APEB, Presidência, Polícia, Delegados, Registro, M.5802.

41. MGuerra to PP-MG, in *LB*, Aviso 317 (Guerra), 27 Sept. 1856; Antonio Alves de Souza Carvalho, *O Brasil em 1870, estudo politico* (Rio de Janeiro, 1870), pp. 43, 45. Also see, on the conditions among recruits, Jeanne Berrance de Castro, *A milícia cidadã: A Guarda Nacional de 1831 a 1850* (São Paulo, 1977), pp. 38, 56 n.13.

42. Commandante Superior da GN to PP-RJ, n.p., 21 Feb. 1842, and Commandante Superior da GN to PP-BA, Ilhéus, 11 Nov. 1867, both quoted by Uricoechea, *Minotauro*, pp. 205, 207; Subdelegado-Lagoa to CP-Corte, Rio, 3 Jan. 1873, encl. in CP-Corte to MJ, Rio, 3 Jan. 1872 [i.e. 1873], AN, SPE, IJ 6-518; Francisco Peixoto de Lacerda Werneck to CP-RJ, Monte Alegre, 3 July 1852, quoted in E. Silva, *Barões e escravidão*, p. 76. On National Guard officers protecting their men from the draft, see Tenente Coronel da GN to PP-BA, Salvador, 6 Sept. 1855, APEB, Presidência, Militar, GN, M.3583. On the purpose of the draft, compare the provision adopted in Salvador after a revolt, ordering freed Africans either to pay a hefty tax or to find a patron who would assume responsibility for their behavior: João José Reis, *Rebelião escrava no Brasil: A história do levante dos malês, 1835* (São Paulo, 1986), p. 277.

43. L. P. L. Werneck, *Idéias sobre colonização*, p. 28; JD-Valença to Subdelegado-Santarém, Santarém, 7 Sept. 1857, copy, APEB, Presidência, Polícia, Subdelegados, M.6231; 2º barão do Paty do Alferes to João Batista Leite & Cia., Conceição, 12 Sept. 1859, quoted in E. Silva, *Barões e escravidão*, p. 77; Cristiano Benedito Ottoni, *O advento da republica no Brasil* (Rio de Janeiro, 1890), p. 79. The hierarchy in an elite household is portrayed in José de Alencar's 1871 novel, *O tronco do ipê, romance brasileiro*. Hierarchy has served the same purpose elsewhere; see Louis Dumont, *Homo Hierarchicus: The Caste System and Its Implications*, rev. ed. (Chicago, 1980), p. 18. On the hierarchy of color in Brazil, see Carl N. Degler, *Neither Black nor White: Slavery and Race Relations in Brazil and the United States* (New York, 1971), pp. 88-112. Contrast the acceptance of complex social gradations in Brazil with the contention of James Oakes, *The Ruling Race: A History of American Slaveholders* (New York, 1982), that the majority of slaveholders in the U.S. accepted an ideology of equality—for the free.

44. Or, in a sense, re-created, since in colonial times landowners also

commanded a militia: F. W. O. Morton, "The Conservative Revolution of Independence: Economy, Society and Politics in Bahia, 1790-1840" (Ph.D. diss., Univ. of Oxford, 1974), pp. 80-87; Elizabeth A. Kuznesof, "Clans, the Militia, and Territorial Government: The Articulation of Kinship with Polity in Eighteenth-Century São Paulo," in *Social Fabric and Spatial Structure in Colonial Latin America*, ed. David J. Robinson (Syracuse, N.Y., 1979), pp. 181-226.

45. A. Carvalho, *Brasil em 1870*, p. 45. On the officers' property, see, for example, Proposta para as vagas dos officiaes do esquadrão nº 4, encl. in Commandante Superior da GN to PP-BA, Feira de Sant'Anna, 22 Aug. 1856, APEB, Presidência, Militar, GN, M.3583; and Commandante Interino do 30ᵃᵛᵒ Batalhão de Infantaria to Commandante Superior Interino de Angra dos Reis e Paratí, [Ilha Grande], 22 Dec. 1857, quoted by Uricoechea, *Minotauro*, p. 212 (also see pp. 172, 185).

46. PP-BA to MI, Salvador, 6 Aug. 1849, AN, SPE, IJJ 5-25; PP-SE to MJ, Sergipe, 3 Sept. 1851, AN, SAP, Cx. 783, Pac. 2; Basílio de Magalhães, "Note on the Term *Coronelismo*," in Victor Nunes Leal, *Coronelismo: The Municipality and Representative Government in Brazil* (Cambridge, Eng., 1977), p. xvi.

47. Commandante Superior da GN to VPP-RJ, [Niterói], 21 Apr. 1866, and Coronel Chefe to VPP-RJ, Valença, 11 Sept. 1839, both quoted by Uricoechea, *Minotauro*, pp. 186, 206; A. Carvalho, *Brasil em 1870*, p. 45; *LB*, Lei 602, 19 Sept. 1850, arts. 12, 14; recruitment board to MJ, Rio, 26 July 1858, quoted by Antonio Edmilson Martins Rodrigues, Francisco José Calazans Falcón, and Margarida de Souza Neves, *Estudo das características histórico-sociais das instituições policiais brasileiras, militares e paramilitares, de suas origens até 1930: A Guarda Nacional do Rio de Janeiro, 1831-1918* (Rio de Janeiro, 1981), pp. 360-66; Uricoechea, *Minotauro*, pp. 168-71, 178 n.39.

48. José Mascarenhas Salles to Francisco Peixoto de Lacerda Werneck, Pau Grande [near Valença, RJ], 5 Sept. 1838, AN, SAP, Cód. 112, Vol. 4.

49. Speech of Saraiva, 4 June 1880, BCCD, *Anais*, 1880, II, 43.

50. For example, Raymundo Faoro, *Os donos do poder. Formação do patronato político brasileiro*, 2d ed. (Pôrto Alegre, 1975), and João Camilo de Oliveira Tôrres, *A democracia coroada (Teoria política do império do Brasil)* (Rio de Janeiro, 1957).

51. Archbishop-BA to PP-BA, Salvador, 12 Mar. 1845, APEB, Presidência, Religião, Arcebispado, M.5205; *O Brasil*, quoted by Flory, *Judge*, p. 169; Comandante Superior da GN to PP-RS, [Rio Pardo], 3 Jan. 1859, quoted by Uricoechea, *Minotauro*, p. 240. On the concentration of wealth, see Richard Graham, "Slavery and Economic Development: Brazil and the United States South in the Nineteenth Century," *Comparative Studies in Society and History*, 23: 4 (Oct. 1981), 644-48. Ilmar Rohloff de Mattos, in his *O tempo saquarema* (São Paulo, 1987), p. 117, draws attention to how contemporaries envisioned a tripartite division of society: those who did not possess even themselves (slaves); those who possessed only their own persons (the propertyless); and those who held property.

52. Rio de Janeiro, Prefeitura, *Codigo de posturas da Illma. Camara Municipal do Rio de Janeiro e editaes da mesma Camara*, nova edição (Rio de Janeiro, 1870), 2ª secção, Tit. IX, par. 22; João Gonçalves dos Santos to PP-BA, Salvador, 15 Nov. 1856, APEB, Presidência, Eleições, M.2794; statement of the defense, Moradores da Freguezia de São José do Rio Preto *v*. Pe. Manoel Florentino Cassiano de Campos, São José do Rio Preto (município de Paraíba do Sul), 1863, ACMRJ, Queixas contra padres, unnum. The priest also complained of their gross manners.

53. One muleteer who became exceedingly wealthy was Domingos Custódio de Guimarães (senior), who acquired several plantations around Valença (RJ) and secured the title of barão in 1854 and visconde do Rio Preto in 1867: Pierre Monbeig, *Pionniers et planteurs de São Paulo* (Paris, 1952), p. 84.

54. Richard M. Morse, "Some Themes of Brazilian History," *South Atlantic Quarterly*, 61 (Spring 1962), 169; José Alípio Goulart, *Tropas e tropeiros na formação do Brasil* (Rio de Janeiro, 1961); Luis C. Almeida, *Vida e morte do tropeiro* (São Paulo, 1971); Carlos Borges Schmidt, *Tropas e tropeiros* (São Paulo, 1932).

55. Quoted in Eisenberg, *Sugar Industry*, p. 195.

56. I have corrected a quotation found in Eisenberg, *Sugar Industry*, p. 148.

57. On the identification of a shifting population with a shiftless one, see Weinstein, *Amazon*, p. 43. On geographical mobility, see Chiara Vangelista, *Le braccia per la fazenda: Immigrati e "caipiras" nella formazione del mercato del lavoro paulista (1850-1930)* (Milan, 1982), p. 220.

58. Subdelegado to Delegado, Santo Amaro, 11 Apr. 1856, copy, and JD-Valença to Subdelegado-Santarém, Santarém, 7 Sept. 1857, copy, APEB, Presidência, Polícia, Subdelegados, M.6231; Vigario to Archbishop-BA, Valença, 5 Jan. 1873, encl. in Archbishop-BA to PP-BA, Salvador, 14 Jan. 1873, APEB, Presidência, Religião, Arcebispo, M.5205.

59. CP-PE to PP-PE, Recife, 3 Jan. 1852, APEP, Polícia Civil, 1852, 39; [Delegado] to PP-PE, Nazareth, 26 Dec. 1851; JP do 2º Districto to PP-PE, Santo Antão, 21 Dec. 1851; Director Geral dos Indios to PP-PE, Lage, 24 Dec. 1851, copies of all three encl. in PP-PE to MJ, AN, SPE, IJ 1-824; Delegado to CP-PE, Recife, 1 Jan. 1850; CP-PE to PP-PE, Recife, 3 Jan. 1852; Lt.-col. to CP-PE, Nazareth, 30 Dec. 1851, all three in APEP, Polícia Civil, 1852, 39; PP-PE to MJ, 30 Dec. 1851, AN, SPE, IJ 1-824; Paraíba, Presidente, *Relatorio*, 1852, p. 3. I owe all these references to Joan Meznar.

60. RJ, Presidente, *Relatorio*, 1858, pp. 3-4, as quoted by Stein, *Vassouras*, pp. 58-59.

61. Roderick J. Barman, "The Brazilian Peasantry Reexamined: The Implications of the Quebra-Quilos Revolt, 1874-1875," *Hispanic American Historical Review*, 57: 3 (Aug. 1977), 401-24; Meznar, "Deference and Dependence," pp. 190-243.

62. 2º barão do Paty do Alferes to Bernardo Ribeiro de Carvalho, Monte Alegre, 13 Feb., 21 Feb. 1857, quoted by E. Silva, *Barões e escravidão*, p. 84.

63. Paulino José Soares de Souza (2º) [Um Conservador], *Carta aos fazendeiros e commerciantes fluminenses sobre o elemento servil ou, Refutação do parecer do Sr. Conselheiro Christiano Benedicto Ottoni acerca do mesmo assumpto* (Rio de Janeiro, 1871), pp. 4, 6.

64. *O Despertador*, 5 Aug. 1839, quoted by Flory, *Judge*, p. 151; Associação Industrial, Rio de Janeiro, *O trabalho nacional e seus adversarios* (Rio de Janeiro, 1881), pp. 165-66.

65. PP-CE to JD, copy encl. in PP-CE to MJ, Fortaleza, 14 Dec. 1860, AN, SPE, IJJ 5-43; PP-BA to MI, Salvador, 6 Aug. 1849, ibid., 5-25; Brazil, Commissão Encarregada da Revisão da Tarifa em Vigor, *Relatorio . . . que acompanhou o projecto de tarifa apresentado pela mesma commissão ao governo imperial* (Rio de Janeiro, 1853), p. 342.

66. Speech of Sales Torres Homen, 11 Aug. 1859, BCCD, *Anais*, 1859, IV, 78; Pedro II quoted in Hélio Viana, *D. Pedro I e D. Pedro II: Acréscimos às suas biografias* (São Paulo, 1966), p. 158.

67. Petitioner quoted in Paulo Pinheiro Chagas, *Teófilo Ottoni, ministro do povo*, 2d rev. ed. (Rio de Janeiro, 1956), p. 47; PP-BA to MI, 19 Jan. 1850, AN, SPE, IJJ 9-339, 1850; Joaquim Pinto de Campos [Um Pernambucano], *Os anarquistas e a civilização: Ensaio politico sobre a situação* (Rio de Janeiro, 1860), p. 83.

68. On the purpose of inculcating deference, see E. P. Thompson, "Patrician Society, Plebeian Culture," *Journal of Social History*, 7: 4 (Summer 1974), 387.

69. Mesa Parochial to PP-BA, Vitoria, 19 Sept. 1860, AN, SPE, IJJ 5-25; Parecer das Secções de Justiça e Fazenda do Conselho de Estado, 9 July 1866, AIHGB, Coleção Senador Nabuco, L381, D4 (original numeration); José Bernardo Fernandes Gama to Euzebio de Queiroz Mattoso da Camara, Rio, Nov. 28, 1851, AN, SAP, Cx. 783 (labeled as being in Pac. 4 but found in Pac. 2).

70. Speech of Joaquim Nabuco, 10 July 1888, BCCD, *Anais*, 1888, III, 87; Nabuco, *Estadista do império*, pp. 83, 466 (quoted), 467, 942 (quoted).

Chapter 2

1. Charles R. Boxer, *Portuguese Society in the Tropics: The Municipal Councils of Goa, Macao, Bahia, and Luanda* (Madison, Wis., 1965), pp. 5-6, 72-109 (quotation from p. 6); Edmundo Zenha, *O município no Brasil (1532-1700)* (São Paulo, 1948); A. J. R. Russell-Wood, "Local Government in Portuguese America: A Study in Cultural Divergence," *Comparative Studies in Society and History*, 16: 2 (Mar. 1974), 187-231; Caio Prado Júnior, *The Colonial Background of Modern Brazil* (Berkeley, Calif., 1967), pp. 366-73; Richard M. Morse, "Brazil's Urban Development: Colony and Empire," in *From Colony to Nation: Essays on the Independence of Brazil*, ed. A. J. R. Russell-Wood (Baltimore, 1975), pp. 158-65; John N. Kennedy, "Bahian Elites," *Hispanic American Historical Review*, 53: 3 (Aug. 1973), 415-39; Kenneth R. Maxwell, *Conflicts and Conspiracies: Brazil and Portugal, 1750-1808* (Cambridge, Eng., 1973).

2. Kenneth R. Maxwell, "The Generation of the 1790s and the Idea of a Luso-Brazilian Empire," in *Colonial Roots of Modern Brazil. Papers of the Newberry Library Conference*, ed. Dauril Alden (Berkeley, Calif., 1973), pp. 107-44; Kátia M. de Queirós Mattoso, *A presença francesa no movimento democrático baiano de 1798* (Salvador, 1969); Fernando A. Novais, *Portugal e Brasil na crise do Antigo Sistema Colonial (1777-1808)* (São Paulo, 1979); F. W. O. Morton, "The Conservative Revolution of Independence: Economy, Society and Politics in Bahia, 1790-1840" (Ph.D. diss., Univ. of Oxford, 1974), pp. 113-45; Maria Odila L. da Silva Dias, "Ideologia liberal e a construção do Estado do Brasil," *Anais do Museu Paulista*, 30 (1980-81), 211-25. The image of "a miserable republic of Negroes as in Haiti" still evoked fear as late as 1853: Sérgio Teixeira de Macedo (Brazilian minister to England) to Lord Clarendon, London, 23 May 1853, copy encl. in Macedo to ME, London, 6 June 1853, AHI, 217/3/7, no. 12.

3. This paragraph and the following pages on events to 1850 are drawn, except where otherwise noted, from John Armitage, *The History of Brazil from the Period of the Arrival of the Braganza Family in 1808 to the Abdication of Don Pedro the First in 1831*, 2 vols. (London, 1836); Manuel de Oliveira Lima, *Dom João VI no Brasil, 1808-1821*, 2d ed., 3 vols. (Rio de Janeiro, 1945); José Honório Rodrigues, *Independência: Revolução e contra-revolução*, 5 vols. (Rio de Janeiro, 1975); Alan K. Manchester, "The Transfer of the Portuguese Court to Rio de Janeiro," in *Conflict and Continuity in Brazilian Society*, ed. Henry Keith and S. F. Edwards (Columbia, S.C., 1969), pp. 148-83; Emília Viotti da Costa, "The Political Emancipation of Brazil," in *From Colony to Nation: Essays on the Independence of Brazil*, ed. A. J. R. Russell-Wood (Baltimore, 1975), especially pp. 67-70; Basílio de Magalhães, *Estudos de história do Brasil* (São Paulo, 1940); Paula Beiguelman, *Formação política do Brasil*, II (São Paulo, 1967); Tobias Monteiro, *Historia do Império: A elaboração da independencia* (Rio de Janeiro, 1927); Tobias Monteiro, *História do Império: O primeiro reinado*, 2 vols. (Rio de Janeiro, 1939-46); HGCB, nos. 4 and 5; Carlos Guilherme Mota and Fernando A. Novais, *A independência política do Brasil* (São Paulo, 1986); and the summaries by Leslie Bethell, "The Independence of Brazil," and Leslie Bethell and José Murilo de Carvalho, "Brazil from Independence to the Middle of the Nineteenth Century," in *The Cambridge History of Latin America*, ed. Leslie Bethell (Cambridge, Eng., 1985), III, 157-96, 679-746. Also see Maria Odila Silva Dias, "The Establishment of the Royal Court in Brazil," in *From Colony to Nation: Essays on the Independence of Brazil*, ed. A. J. R. Russell-Wood (Baltimore, 1975), pp. 89-108; and Joaquim Nabuco, *Um estadista do império*, [3d ed.?] (Rio de Janeiro, 1975), pp. 1-75. Roderick J. Barman, *Brazil: the Forging of a Nation, 1798-1852* (Stanford, Calif., 1988), provides a detailed narrative.

4. Quoted by Bethell, "Independence of Brazil," p. 186.

5. Brazil, *Constituição política do Império do Brasil*.

6. Brazil, *Ato adicional [à Constituição política do Império do Brasil]*.

7. County ordinances and budgets fill the bulk of the pages of collec-

tions of provincial laws; even such matters as the prohibition of public bathing during the day or the funding of a local beggars' asylum constituted matters for deliberation by provincial lawmakers: Resolução, 25 Apr. 1862, Posturas de Canavieiras, and Lei 891, 22 May 1862, both in Bahia, *Colleção das leis e resoluções da Assembléa Legislativa e regulamentos do governo da Bahia, sanccionadas e publicadas no anno de* . . . , 1862, part I; also see letters dealing with bridges, churches, and other local matters in Camara Municipal to PP-RJ, Pirahy, 1844-46, APERJ, Col. 37, PP2/5, 22. Members of the Provincial Assemblies were in close touch with local bosses (and so were members of Parliament, as I will show in subsequent chapters), and the right to oversee the County Councils did not necessarily imply conflict between the Assemblies and those bosses, *pace* Maria Isaura Pereira de Queiroz, *O mandonismo local na vida política brasileira (da Colônia à Primeira República): Ensaio de sociologia política* (São Paulo, 1969), p. 41.

8. It should be noted that the County Councils had already in 1828 been stripped of the remaining judicial functions left them by the Philippine Code of 1603; the 1828 law further and specifically enjoined County Councils from deliberating on matters affecting areas beyond the county borders (that is, matters of national import), from making decisions "in the name of the people," and from interfering with the authority of provincial presidents: *LB*, Lei de 1 Oct. 1828, art. 24. A detailed analysis of the County Councils' legal status is João Batista Cortines Laxe, *Regimento das camaras municipais ou, Lei de 1° de outubro de 1828, annotada com leis, decretos . . . ; precedida de uma introdução historica e seguida de sete appensos . . .* , ed. Antonio Joaquim de Macedo Soares, 2d ed. (Rio de Janeiro, 1885). Also see João Martins de Carvalho Mourão, "Os municipios, sua importância politica no Brasil-colonia e no Brasil-reino. Situação em que ficaram no Brasil imperial pela Constituição de 1824 e pelo Ato Adicional," in Primeiro Congresso de Historia Nacional, *Anais* (Rio de Janeiro, 1916), III, 299-318; and Victor Nunes Leal, *Coronelismo: The Municipality and Representative Government in Brazil* (Cambridge, Eng., 1977), pp. 32-34. On the linkage of liberalism with provincial rather than individual rights, see José Murilo de Carvalho, "A composição social dos partidos políticos imperiais," in Minas Gerais, Universidade Federal, Departamento de Ciências Políticas, *Cadernos*, no. 2 (Dec. 1974), pp. 7-8, 24-25.

9. Octávio Tarquínio de Sousa, *História dos fundadores do Império do Brasil* (Rio de Janeiro, 1957), V, 251.

10. Angelo Muniz da Silva Ferraz (the prosecutor), quoted in João José Reis, *Rebelião escrava no Brasil: A história do levante dos malês, 1835* (São Paulo, 1985), p. 248 (also see p. 42 on the general fear of anarchy); MJ to CP-Corte, Rio, 1 Nov. 1835, quoted in Gizlene Neder, Nancy Naro, and José Luiz Werneck da Silva, *Estudo das características histórico-sociais das instituições policiais brasileiras, militares e paramilitares, de suas origens até 1930: A polícia na Corte e no Distrito Federal, 1831-1930* (Rio

de Janeiro, 1981), pp. 191-92. Also see MJ to PP-BA, 27 Feb. 1835, quoted by Thomas Flory, *Judge and Jury in Imperial Brazil, 1808-1871: Social Control and Political Stability in the New State* (Austin, Tex., 1981), p. 234, n.20 (and p. 135 on earlier fears of slave rebellions as a consequence of liberalizing reform). The degree to which racial fears triggered a conservative reaction is explored by Thomas Flory, "Race and Social Control in Independent Brazil," *Journal of Latin American Studies*, 9: 2 (Nov. 1977), 199-224.

11. Spencer L. Leitman, *Raízes socio-econômicas da Guerra dos Farrapos: Um capítulo de história do Brasil no século xix* (Rio de Janeiro, 1979). In Pernambuco, by contrast, rivalries between elites could unhinge established social relations and seem to encourage disobedience from below: Nancy Naro, "The 1848 Praieira Revolt in Brazil" (Ph.D. diss., Univ. of Chicago, 1981), pp. 147, 150, 154, 156, 163, 171, 175, 188, 203.

12. Brazil, Instituto Brasileiro de Geografia e Estatística, *Anuário estatístico do Brasil, 1939-40*, p. 1374.

13. *O Sete de Abril*, 19 Nov. 1838, quoted by Bethell and Carvalho, "Brazil from Independence," p. 712.

14. Ilmar Rohloff de Mattos, *O tempo saquarema* (São Paulo, 1987), pp. 43, 106-7. Throughout his book Mattos insightfully analyzes the forces that impelled the centralization described in this chapter. The Roman law tradition of Brazilian leaders trained in Portugal has been emphasized as an element of imperial unity by José Murilo de Carvalho, "Political Elites and State Building: The Case of Nineteenth-Century Brazil," *Comparative Studies in Society and History*, 24: 3 (July 1982), 378-99. There were, of course, still other, principally economic, considerations that figured in the elites' desire for a strong state: Luiz Felipe de Alencastro, "Le Traite négrière et l'unité nationale brésilienne," *Revue Française d'Histoire d'Outre-Mer*, 66: 244/245 (3ème/4ème tri. 1979), 415-16. But I am not persuaded that the wish to maintain a single market for slaves could have been prominent among them, as Décio Saes argues in *A formação do estado burguês no Brasil (1888-1891)* (Rio de Janeiro, 1985), p. 170.

15. *LB*, Lei 261, 3 Dec. 1841; *LB*, Regulamento 120, 31 Jan. 1842. For a useful summary of this legislation and its antecedents, see Lesley Ann Williams, "Prostitutes, Policemen and Judges in Rio de Janeiro, Brazil, 1889-1910" (M.A. thesis, Univ. of Texas at Austin, 1983), pp. 20-52.

16. Joaquim Rodrigues de Souza, *Systema eleitoral da Constituição do Imperio do Brazil* (São Luiz, 1863), p. 32 (quoted); Aluísio de Almeida [Luís Castanho de Almeida], *A revolução liberal de 1842* (Rio de Janeiro, 1944); José Antônio Marinho, *História do movimento político de 1842*, 3d ed. (Belo Horizonte, 1977), especially pp. 74, 85, on the response to the electoral law; Francisco Iglesias, "O cônego Marinho e 1842," in Marinho, *História*, pp. 13-36; Victor M. Filler, "Liberalism in Imperial Brazil: The Regional Rebellions of 1842" (Ph.D. diss., Stanford Univ., 1976), especially pp. 64, 160, on how the Liberal cause weakened for fear of slave revolts. Also see Arnaldo Daraya Contier, *Imprensa e ideologia em São*

Paulo (1822-1842): (Matizes do vocabulário político e social) (Petrópolis, 1979), pp. 100-105.
17. Nabuco, *Estadista do império*, p. 945. A favorable view of this forceful centralization, which so benefited the upper class, has been perpetuated by generations of Brazilian historians. See, for example, Pedro Calmon, "Organização judiciária: (a) na Colônia; (b) no Império; (c) na República," in *Livro do centenário dos cursos jurídicos* (Rio de Janeiro, 1928), I, 95. The conscious and unconscious purpose of such acclaim has not received the attention it deserves.
18. V. Leal, *Coronelismo*, p. 139.
19. Contrast S. N. Eisenstadt, *The Political Systems of Empires* (New York, 1963), for example, p. 14. Also see Raymundo Faoro, *Os donos do poder: Formação do patronato político brasileiro*, 2d ed. (Pôrto Alegre, 1975), I, 332-36. Helpful discussions of related historiographical issues can be found in William Beik, *Absolutism and Society in Seventeenth-Century France: State Power and Provincial Aristocracy in Languedoc* (Cambridge, Eng., 1985), pp. 3-33; and Alfred Stepan, *The State and Society: Peru in Comparative Perspective* (Princeton, N.J., 1978), pp. 3-45.
20. See the weekly reports on Cabinet meetings, Abaeté to Pedro II, Feb.-Apr. 1859, AMIP, CXXVIII, 328. On the trivia that occupied his time, see Pedro II, diario, 1861-63, AMIP, Maço XXV, Doc. 1055 passim. For an example of his copy-editing changes to the reports and proposed legislation of Ministers, see Junqueira to Cotegipe, Rio, 5 May 1886, AIHGB, CC, L31, D136, and Pedro II to Affonso Celso de Assis Figueiredo, Rio, 22 Oct. 1879, L427, D5. On Pedro II's constant effort, always unsuccessful, to impose honest elections, see Heitor Lyra, *História de Dom Pedro II, 1825-1891*, 2d rev. ed. (Belo Horizonte, 1977), II, 293-94. The traditional view, then and later, whether in approval or condemnation, is that Pedro II held much power; see, for instance, Anpriso [Anfriso] Fialho, "Biographical Sketch of Dom Pedro II, Emperor of Brazil," in Smithsonian Institution, *Annual Report of the Board of Regents* (Washington, D.C., 1877), pp. 173-204; and Fialho, *Processo da monarchia brazileira: necessidade da convocação de uma constituinte* (Rio de Janeiro, 1885). Nabuco contradictorily claims that Pedro II had great power, and that he was frustrated by the power wielded by others: *Estadista do império*, pp. 937-45. Some students of the period have agreed with me that he held little real power, only to maintain that democracy was the rule, which is hardly my point: João Camilo de Oliveira Tôrres, *A democracia coroada (Teoria política do império do Brasil)* (Rio de Janeiro, 1957).
21. Martinho [Alvares da Silva] Campos, 23 Dec. 1874, Atas do Centro Liberal, 1870-76, AIHGB, L495, D6, fl. 12v; Affonso Celso de Assis Figueiredo, *As finanças da regeneração: Estudo politico offerecido aos mineiros* (Rio de Janeiro, 1876), p. iii; Henrique Augusto Milet, *Miscellanea economica e politica* (Recife, 1882), p. 75; Jozé [sic] Antonio Marinho, *Sermão que recitou na capella imperial . . . por occasião do baptisado da serenissima princeza a sra. D. Leopoldina Thereza . . .* (Rio de Janeiro,

1847), p. 15. A major critique of the principle of Moderative Power is found in Zacharias de Góes e Vasconcellos, *Da natureza e limites do poder moderador*, 2d ed. (Rio de Janeiro, 1862); and an impressive reply is Braz Florentino Henriques de Souza, *Do Poder Moderador: Ensaio de direito constitucional contendo a análise do título V, capítulo I, da Constituição Política do Brasil*, 2d ed. (Brasília, 1978).

22. José Honório Rodrigues, *O Conselho de Estado: O quinto poder?* (Brasília, 1978); João Camilo de Oliveira Tôrres, *O Conselho de Estado* (Rio de Janeiro, 1956); Mattos, *Tempo saquarema*, pp. 107-38; *LB*, Lei 1083, 22 Aug. 1860, arts. 1-2; *LB*, Decreto 2711, 19 Dec. 1860. For the Council's deliberation on the internal statutes of a railroad company, see Luiz Pedreira do Couto Ferraz to Cotegipe, [Rio], [Apr. 1855?], AIHGB, CC, L22, D115. On how the Emperor chose Council members, see Nabuco, *Estadista do império*, pp. 705, 1004.

23. Some historians have spoken of these speeches as if they represented the points of view of the Emperor himself; abundant evidence exists that they resulted from brief statements contributed by each Cabinet member, and that one of them, usually the Prime Minister, welded these statements together: see Luiz Pedreira do Couto Ferraz to Cotegipe, 4 May [1856], AIHGB, CC, L22, D130; speech of Zacharias, 18 July 1870, BCS, *Anais*, 1870, II, 120; speech of Rio Branco, 8 May 1871, BCS, *Anais*, 1871, p. 24; José Bento da Cunha Figueiredo to Cotegipe, Petrópolis, 1 Oct. [1875], Rio, 20 Jan. 1877, AIHGB, CC, L23, D132, D152; Pedro Leão Veloso to Pedro II, Rio, 27 Oct. 1882, AMIP, M.190, D.8634; Joaquim Delfino Ribeiro da Luz to Cotegipe, São Cristovão, 30 Apr. 1886, AIHGB, CC, L35, D140; Ambrosio Leitão da Cunha, barão de Mamoré, to Cotegipe, Rio, 27 Apr. 1886, AIHGB, CC, L18, D104; and Cristiano Benedito Ottoni, *O advento da república no Brasil* (Rio de Janeiro, 1890), p. 20.

24. José Murilo de Carvalho, *A construção da ordem: A elite política imperial* (Rio de Janeiro, 1980), p. 87. Brazilian biographical dictionaries are understandably reticent on the matter, so one may presume the proportion of the landed was even greater.

25. *LB*, Lei de 20 Oct. 1823, arts. 1-3, 24; Lei 40, 3 Oct. 1834, arts. 1, 5; Lei 207, 18 Sept. 1841; Caetano José de Andrade Pinto, *Attribuições dos presidentes de província* (Rio de Janeiro, 1865); Cotegipe to Henrique Pereira de Lucena, Rio, 3 Dec. 1885, APEP, Col. Lucena, 564; MA to PP-BA, Rio, 5 Feb 1875, draft, and MA to PP-ES, 7 Apr. 1875, draft, AN, SPE, IA 6-19; several requests for passports in APEB, Presidência, Polícia, Licenças, M.6403; petition from Cezario Telles do Carmo, Salvador, 10 Jan. 1855, APEB, Presidência, Agricultura, Pesca, M.4634; also see Tôrres, *Democracia coroada*, p. 325. On the reception of provincial presidents, see João Francisco Lisboa, *Obras*, 2d ed. (Lisbon, 1901), I, 82-84; and José Antônio Soares de Souza, *A vida do visconde do Uruguai (1807-1866) (Paulino José Soares de Souza)* (São Paulo, 1944), p. 49.

26. Miguel Arcanjo Galvão, *Relação dos cidadãos que tomaram parte no govêrno do Brasil no período de março de 1808 a 15 de novembro de*

1889, 2d ed. (Rio de Janeiro, 1969), p. 61; João Alfredo Correia de Oliveira to Cotegipe, Belém, 31 Jan. 1870, and Cotegipe to João Alfredo Correia de Oliveira, Rio, 23 Mar. 1870, typescript copy of draft, AIHGB, CC, L50, D84, D89; *LB*, Decreto 207, 18 Sept. 1841. On the length of the presidents' tenure, see José M. Carvalho, *Construção da ordem*, p. 95. On the local residence of vice-presidents, see Naro, "1848 Praieira Revolt," pp. 80, 118.

27. *LB*, Lei 261, 3 Dec. 1841, arts. 1, 4; *LB*, Regulamento 120, 31 Jan. 1842; *LB*, Lei 2033, 20 Sept. 1871, art. 1, para. 13, and arts. 10, 11; José Marcellino Pereira de Vasconcellos, *Roteiro dos delegados e subdelegados de polícia; ou, Colleção dos actos, atribuições e deveres destas autoridades* (Rio de Janeiro, 1862); Antonio Alves de Souza Carvalho, *O Brasil em 1870, estudo politico* (Rio de Janeiro, 1870), p. 21.

28. See, for example, Manoel José Gomes de Freitas, Lista para Piratinim, presented to PP-RS by J. Jacinto de Mendonça, n.p., n.d., AN, Cx. 781, Pac. 2, Doc. 9. I will say more about this preference in later chapters.

29. J. Vasconcellos, *Roteiro dos delegados*, p. 55 and passim; CP-BA to Delegado-Santo Amaro, Salvador, 10 Dec. 1868, copy, APEB, Presidência, Polícia, Delegados, M.5802; A. Carvalho, *Brasil em 1870*, p. 22; Cotegipe, [Pareceres . . . sobre a eleição direta], 1880, AIHGB, CC, L88, P28; Luiz Peixoto de Lacerda Werneck, *Le Brésil. Dangers de sa situation politique et économique; moyens de les conjurer. Lettre à son fils. . . . Ouvrage posthume revu par F. P. de Lacerda Werneck* (Rio de Janeiro, 1889), p. 73; L. Williams, "Prostitutes, Policemen and Judges," pp. 103-8. Since County Councils lacked executive officers, aside from the *fiscaes* who taxed, fined, and inspected, it was up to the delegados to carry out county ordinances: deposition of Antonio Ferreira Vianna, Rio, 29 Aug. 1889, AGCRJ, 61-4-12, fl. 104; V. Leal, *Coronelismo*, p. 58. Contemporaries understood the King to be principally a judge, thus blurring any distinction between judicial authority and enforcement or police functions: Joaquim Pinto de Campos [Um Pernambucano], *Os anarquistas e a civilização: Ensaio politico sobre a situação* (Rio de Janeiro, 1860), p. 40.

30. Delegado to CP-BA, Inhambupe, 15 Aug. 1855, and Subdelegado to CP-BA, Frequezia de S. Anna [Salvador], 13 Aug. 1858, APEB, Presidência, Polícia, Delegados, 1855-56, M.6188, M.6231. The chief of police submitted daily or weekly reports to the president on occurrences in the province based on reports he received from the delegados: see, for example, CP-BA to PP-BA, Salvador, 8, 9, 12 June 1857, APEB, Presidência, Polícia, Chefes, M.2953. In Rio de Janeiro the chief sent his weekly report to the Minister of Justice: Mappa Semanal, Secretaria de Policia da Côrte, 1855, AN, SPE, IJ 6-219. Similar reports can be found for most provinces; see Thomas H. Holloway, "The Brazilian 'Judicial Police' in Florianópolis, Santa Catarina, 1841-1871," *Journal of Social History*, 20: 4 (Summer 1987), 733-56.

31. Subdelegado to CP-BA, Santo Amaro, 20 Oct. 1857, APEB, Presidência, Polícia, Subdelegados, M.6231. On the matter of passports, also see AGCRJ, 62-1-28, fls. 336-37; and L. P. L. Werneck, *Brésil*, pp. 73, 76.

32. João Francisco Alves de Carvalho to CP-BA, Salvador, 4 June 1856, APEB, Presidência, Polícia, Licenças, M.6403; Commissario da Hygiene to PP-BA, Feira de Sant'Anna, 11 June 1878, APEB, Presidência, Saúde, M.1589; Subdelegado-S. Pedro to CP-BA, [Salvador], 30 Nov. 1858, APEB, Presidência, Polícia, Subdelegados, M.6231.

33. Tristão de Alencar Araripe [CP-ES], "Instruções provisorias para os inspectores de quarteirão dos termos da provincia do Espirito Santo, 22 May 1857," in J. Vasconcellos, *Roteiro dos delegados*, pp. 235-36; Delegado to Inspector de Quarteirão, Pirassinunga, 25 Aug. 1872, encl. in PP-SP to MI, São Paulo, 23 Jan. 1873.

34. Inspector do 11° quarteirão to Subdelegado-Freguesia do Sacramento, Rio, 18 Jan. 1855, encl. in CP-Corte to MJ, Rio, 24 Jan. 1855, AN, SPE, IJ 6-219; Richard Graham, *Escravidão, reforma e imperialismo* (São Paulo, 1979), pp. 90-93.

35. For example, Acta da Junta Parochial de Alistamento, 16 Aug. 1887, parish of Sant'Anna, Salvador, copy encl. in PP-BA to MI, Salvador, 15 Nov. 1887, AN, SPE, IJJ 9-354.

36. Registro da correspondencia expedida para subdelegados, [Nov.-Dec.] 1859, APEB, Presidência, Polícia, Subdelegados, M.5737; Subdelegado-Lagoa to CP-Corte, Rio, 3 Jan. 1872 [i.e., 1873], AN, SPE, IJ 6-518; JD-Cachoeira to PP-BA, Cachoeira, 28 Nov. 1840, APEB, Presidência, Juizes, M.2273. National Guard officers were also given quotas of recruits to be filled: Commandante do 4° batalhão-parish of Riachão de Jacuipe to Comandante Superior-Feira de Sant'Anna, Jacuipe, 27 Aug. 1856, copy, APEB, Presidência, Militar, GN, M.3583.

37. A law of 1831 had authorized the provincial presidents to create these units: Paulino José Soares de Souza, visconde de Uruguay, *Estudos praticos sobre a administração das provincias do Brasil . . . Primeira parte: Acto Addicional* (Rio de Janeiro, 1865), II, 159-62ff; also see Brazil, *Ato Adicional*, art. 11, par. 2; Gustavo Barroso, *História militar do Brasil*, 2d ed. (São Paulo, 1938), pp. 57-58ff; and *HGCB*, no. 4, p. 501. For accounts of the forces in Rio de Janeiro and São Paulo provinces, see F. Silveira do Prado, *A polícia militar fluminense no tempo do império (1835-1889)* (Rio de Janeiro, 1969); and Heloisa Rodrigues Fernandes, *Política e segurança: Força pública do Estado de São Paulo. Fundamentos histórico-sociais* (São Paulo, 1974), pp. 53-145. These provincial corps were under the nominal command of the Minister of War, a fact that sometimes complicated their administration; see, for instance, PP-SE to MJ, Sergipe, 22 July, 1 Aug. 1851, AN, SAP, Cx. 783, P2. Though County Councils could also organize their own police forces, they mostly lacked the revenues to pay them. Only the city of Rio de Janeiro had a substantial force: Rio de Janeiro (city), Prefeitura, *Consolidação das leis e posturas municipais* (Rio de Janeiro, 1905), 1ª parte, unnum. decreto, 9 Nov. 1831, Decreto 2081, 16 Jan. 1858, Decreto 3598, 27 Jan. 1866, Decreto 9395, 7 Mar. 1885, Decreto 10222, 5 Apr. 1889; Neder et al., *Estudo . . . polícia na Corte*, pp. 126-33, 139-44, 161-71.

38. Acto do Governo, 12 Feb. 1862, in Bahia, *Colleção das leis*, 1862,

part II; CP-RJ to PP-RJ, Niterói, 4 Aug. 1860, encl. in PP-RJ to MJ, n.p., 7 Aug. 1860, AN, SPE, IJJ, 5-43; J. Vasconcellos, *Roteiro dos delegados*, p. 22; Manuel Alves Branco, quoted by Flory, *Judge*, p. 137. On the small size of this force in Rio de Janeiro, see Berenice Cavalcante Brandão, Ilmar Rohloff de Mattos, and Maria Alice Rezende de Carvalho, *Estudo das características histórico-sociais das instituições policiais brasileiras, militares e paramilitares, de suas origens até 1930: A polícia e a força policial no Rio de Janeiro* (Rio de Janeiro, 1981), pp. 134-65.

39. *LB*, Lei de 18 Aug. 1831, Lei 602, 19 Sept. 1850 (the quotation is from art. 1 of both these laws); also see Decreto 722, 25 Oct. 1850; and Brazil, Ministerio da Justiça e Negocios Interiores, *Noticia historica dos serviços, instituições e estabelecimentos pertencentes a esta repartição, elaborada por ordem do respectivo ministro, Dr. Amaro Cavalcanti* (Rio de Janeiro, 1898), chap. 6. On the transfer of entire National Guard units to Army duty, see Commandante do 22° batalhão de infantaria to Commandante da 3ª companhia, Valença, 17 Sept 1865, AN, SAP, Cód. 112, Vol. 6, Doc. 29. On city patrols, see CP-Corte to MJ, Rio, 3 Feb. 1854, AN, SPE, IJ 1-80. For the history and responsibilities of the National Guard, see Jeanne Berrance de Castro, *A milícia cidadã: A Guarda Nacional de 1831 a 1850* (São Paulo, 1977); *HGCB*, no. 6, pp. 274-98; Fernando Uricoechea, *O minotauro imperial: A burocratização do estado patrimonial brasileiro no século XIX* (São Paulo, 1978), especially pp. 130-40; and Antonio Edmilson Martins Rodrigues, Francisco José Calazans Falcon, and Margarida de Souza Neves, *Estudo das características histórico-sociais das instituições policiais brasileiras, militares e paramilitares, de suas origens até 1930: A Guarda Nacional no Rio de Janeiro, 1831-1918* (Rio de Janeiro, 1981), pp. 3-277.

40. P. Souza, *Estudos praticos*, II, 179; *LB*, Lei 2395, 10 Sept. 1873. In 1880 there were 918,017 National Guardsmen against just 7,410 provincial policemen: José Murilo de Carvalho, *Teatro de sombras: A política imperial* (São Paulo, 1988), p. 39.

41. *HGCB*, no. 6, pp. 235-58, especially p. 244; Morton, "Conservative Revolution," pp. 70-80, 313-21.

42. PP-PB to MGuerra, n.p., 11 Jan. 1850, PP-RN to MGuerra, Natal, 11 May 1850, AN, SAP, Cx. 823, Pac. 2, fls. 43, 273; *HGCB*, no. 6, p. 294.

43. Junqueira to Cotegipe, Rio, 4 Feb. 1886, AIHGB, CC, L31, D118; Henrique Francisco de Avila to Cotegipe, Rio, 3 Sept. 1887, ibid., L7, D41 (quoted); William S. Dudley, "Institutional Sources of Officer Discontent in the Brazilian Army, 1870-1889," *Hispanic American Historical Review*, 55: 1 (Feb. 1975), 44-65.

44. *LB*, Aviso (Imperio), 21 Oct. 1843, quoted in P. Souza, *Estudos praticos*, I, 180n; "Parecer da commissão" in BCCD, *Reforma eleitoral: Projectos offerecidos á consideração do corpo legislativo desde o anno de 1826 até o anno de 1875 . . . colligidos na secretaria da Camara dos Deputados* (Rio de Janeiro, 1875), p. 553. On the place of the Church, see

Candido Mendes de Almeida, comp. and ed., *Direito civil ecclesiastico brazileiro antigo e moderno em suas relações com o direito canonico ou, Colleção completa . . . a que se addicionão notas historicas e explicativas, indicando a legislação actualmente em vigor e que hoje constitue a jurisprudencia civil ecclesiastica do Brasil* (Rio de Janeiro, 1866), Tomo I, Vol. 2, especially pp. 563-608; João Fagundes Hauk et al., *História da igreja no Brasil: Ensaio de interpretação a partir do povo. Segunda época: A igreja no Brasil no século XIX* (Petrópolis, 1980), pp. 81-95, 200-205. Clergymen allegedly fostered the peasants' threat of violence against the attempted implementation of a civil registry in 1851: PP-PE to JDs, circular, Recife, 24 Dec. 1851, copy, AN, SPE, IJ 1-824; I owe this reference to Joan Meznar.

45. Brazil, Ministerio da Justiça e Negocios Interiores, *Noticia historica*, chap. 7, pp. 46, 88; José A. S. de Souza, *Vida*, p. 626; Nabuco, *Estadista do império*, p. 290; A. Carvalho, *Brasil em 1870*, p. 29.

46. *LB*, Lei 261, 3 Dec. 1841, arts. 14, 117, 118; *LB*, Regulamento 120, 31 Jan. 1842; *LB*, Decreto 559, 28 June 1850, and the debate on it, first, on 7 and 16 Mar. and 16, 17, and 18 Apr. 1850 in BCCD, *Anais*, 1850, II, 77, 160, 335-48, 351-63, 365-75, and, then, on 25 May and 1, 3, 4, 20, and 21 June 1850, in BCS, *Anais*, new ed. (1978), sessões de maio 1850, pp. 97-100, and sessões de junho, 1850, pp. 10-79, 254-318; A. Carvalho, *Brasil em 1870*, pp. 27-29. Until 1871 county judges sometimes combined their duties with those of the delegado; see, for example, APEB, Presidência, Polícia, Delegados, 1855-56, M.6188; and Exeguente: Lucas Iezler, executado: José Ribeiro Pereira Guimarães, Cachoeira, 1860, n.9, APEB, Judiciario, M.1662. On the profitability of a probate judgeship, see JD to MJ, Jacobina, 10 Sept. 1862, AN, SPE, IJ 1-922. In 1871 still more authority passed to the district judges at the expense of the county judges, but some authority previously held by delegados went to the county judges, and one man could not hold both positions: *LB*, Lei 2033, 20 Sept. 1871. For a survey of these changes, see Aurelino Leal, "História judiciária do Brasil," in Instituto Historico e Geographico Brasileiro, *Diccionario historico, geographico e ethnographico do Brasil* (Rio de Janeiro, 1922), I, 1107-1187; and Candido de Oliveira, "A justiça," in Affonso Celso de Assis Figueiredo, visconde de Ouro Preto, et al., *A decada republicana* (Rio de Janeiro, 1900), III, 7-148.

47. José Antonio Pimenta Bueno, *Direito publico brazileiro e analyse da Constituição do Imperio* (Rio de Janeiro, 1857), p. 330; Galvão, *Relação dos cidadãos*, p. 58. Provincial presidents could recommend the removal or demotion of a district judge, although the final decision would rest with the Council of State.

48. *LB*, Lei 261, 3 Dec. 1841, art. 19 (also see art. 13), Lei 2033, 20 Sept. 1871, art. 1, par. 3; JD-Taubaté to PP-SP, Caçapava, 3 Jan. 1861, copy encl. in PP-SP to MJ, 20 Jan. 1861, AN, SPE, IJJ 5-43; JD-Pombal to PP-PB, Villa de Pattos, 20 Feb. 1861, copy encl. in PP-PB to MJ, 9 Mar. 1861, AN, SPE, IJJ 5-43; Billy Jaynes Chandler, *The Feitosas and the Ser-*

tão dos Inhamuns: The History of a Family and a Community in Northeast Brazil, 1700-1930 (Gainesville, Fla., 1972), p. 51. County councilmen could serve as still lower-ranking substitute judges, "of second degree": Candido Mendes de Almeida, ed., *Codigo Philippino; ou, Ordenações e leis do reino de Portugal* (Rio de Janeiro, 1870), p. 372n.

49. Brazil, MJ, *Relatorio*, 1865, Anexo C; Brazil, Ministerio da Justiça e Negocios Interiores, *Noticia historica*, chap. 7, p. 88; Affonso d'Albuquerque Mello, *A liberdade no Brasil: Seu nascimento, vida, morte, e sepultura* (Recife, 1864), p. 111.

50. Eul-Soo Pang and Ron L. Seckinger, "The Mandarins of Imperial Brazil," *Comparative Studies in Society and History*, 14: 2 (Mar. 1972), 215-44; Roderick J. Barman and Jean Barman, "The Role of the Law Graduate in the Political Elite of Imperial Brazil," *Journal of Inter-American Studies*, 18: 4 (Nov. 1976), 423-50; Nanci Leonzo and Rita Maria Cardoso Barbosa, "As 'virtudes' do bacharelismo" in Sociedade Brasileira de Pesquisa Histórica, II*a* Reunião, *Anais* (São Paulo, 1983), pp. 125-28.

51. Unidentified to Bras Carneiro Nogueira da Costa e Gama, conde de Baependy, Saudade, 27 July 1860, AN, SAP, Cód. 112, Vol. 8, Doc. 36. For another example, see José Antonio Saraiva to Henrique Garcez Pinto de Madureira, São Paulo, 15 Mar. 1842, 13 May 1845, 5 Nov. 1845, in José Wanderley de Araújo Pinho, *Política e políticos no império* (Rio de Janeiro, 1930), pp. 12, 20, 21. Also see Roque Spencer Maciel de Barros, *A ilustração brasileira e a idéia de universidade* (São Paulo, 1959), p. 203.

52. Antonio Augusto da Costa Aguiar to Pedro II, São Paulo, 30 Jan. 1862, AMIP, CXXXI, 6422.

53. Barão Paty do Alferes to Manoel Peixoto de Lacerda Werneck, Monte Alegre, 31 Mar. 1854, AN, SAP, Cód. 112, V. 3, fls. 165-66.

54. Flory, *Judge*, pp. 181-99; Junqueira to Cotegipe, Salvador, 9 July 1856, AIHGB, CC, L30, D178; José M. de Carvalho, *Construção da ordem*, pp. 51-72. Note that when the propertied fell to quarreling over the value of perpetuating slavery in the 1880s, so did judges.

55. Bueno, *Direito publico*, p. 205.

56. João Manuel de Carvalho, *Reminiscencias sobre vultos e factos do imperio e da republica* (Amparo, 1894), p. 90; Raimundo Magalhães Júnior, *José de Alencar e sua época*, 2d ed. (Rio de Janeiro, 1977), p. 215; *HGCB*, no. 7, p. 139; Affonso Celso de Assis Figueiredo Júnior, conde de Affonso Celso, *Oito annos de parlamento. Poder pessoal de D. Pedro II. Reminiscencias e notas*, rev. [2d ed.?] ed. (São Paulo: Melhoramentos, n.d.), p. 126; José W. de Rodrigues, "Fardas do Reino Unido e do Império," *Anuário do Museu Imperial*, 11 (1950), 45-47; Lisboa, *Obras*, p. 84 (quoted); BCCD, *Manual parlamentar. Regimento interno da Camara dos Deputados* (Rio de Janeiro, 1887), p. 67n; Adolpho Hasselman to Ruy Barbosa, Salvador, 14 Nov. 1878, CRB, unnum. (on the uniform of a minor bureaucrat); Brazil, *Constituição*, art. 16; *LB*, Decreto 1482A, 2 Dec. 1854, Decreto de 2 Sept. 1825; MF, circular (to other ministries), Rio, 17 Apr. 1883, AN, SPE, IG 1-377. On the sash of office of delegados,

see *LB*, Decreto 584, 19 Feb. 1849, art. 2. Heated arguments broke out over such matters as whether the uniform of county councilmen could also be worn by the council secretary: PP-BA to MI, Salvador, 22 May 1843, AN, SPE, IJJ 9-338, 1843, fl. 5. Age was also considered to entitle one to precedence (Bernardo de Souza Franco to Zacharias de Góes e Vasconcellos, Rio, 14 Apr. 1867, AMIP, I-ZGV-14.4.867-Fr.o), but I find no evidence that status and honor were more valued in Rio de Janeiro than elsewhere, as Uricoechea, *Minotauro*, p. 236, contends.

57. For example, Fernando Henrique Cardoso and Enzo Faletto, *Dependency and Development in Latin America* (Berkeley, Calif., 1979), pp. 66-69, 89-91.

Chapter 3

1. Speech of Coelho Rodrigues, 26 Oct. 1888, BCCD, *Anais*, 1888, IV, 403.

2. José Antonio Pimenta Bueno, *Direito publico brazileiro e analyse da Constituição do Imperio* (Rio de Janeiro, 1857), pp. 389-489 (Pimenta Bueno, to be sure, knew he was not primarily describing a reality but defending an ideal). Although written in the 20th century, João Camilo de Oliveira Tôrres, *A democracia coroada (Teoria política do império do Brasil)* (Rio de Janeiro, 1957), pp. 245-52, faithfully captures the view of many 19th-century Brazilians, which the author takes at face value. Also see Roberto Schwarz, *Ao vencedor as batatas: Forma literária e processo social nos inícios do romance brasileiro* (São Paulo, 1977), pp. 13-25; Emília Viotti da Costa, *The Brazilian Empire: Myths and Realities* (Chicago, 1985), pp. 53-77; and Ubiratan Borges de Macedo, *A liberdade no Império* (São Paulo, 1977).

3. Pedro II, "Normas de D. Pedro II quanto a política interna e externa" (ca. May 1857), in Hélio Viana, *D. Pedro I e D. Pedro II: Acréscimos às suas biografias* (São Paulo, 1966), p. 158.

4. Joaquim Rodrigues de Souza, *Systema eleitoral da Constituição do Imperio do Brazil* (São Luiz, 1863), p. 33; José Thomaz Nabuco de Araújo, speech of 2 May 1853, BCCD, *Anais*, 1853, I, 138.

5. "Decreto, 1855," art. 1, par. 3. A bill to the same effect had been introduced in the Senate almost before the ink was dry on the 1846 law: BCCD, *Reforma eleitoral: Projectos offerecidos á consideração do corpo legislativo desde o ano de 1826 até o anno de 1875 ... colligidos na secretaria da Camara dos Deputados* (Rio de Janeiro, 1875), pp. 258-74. On these reforms in general, see Luiz Peixoto de Lacerda Werneck, *Le Brésil. Dangers de sa situation politique et économique; moyens de les conjurer. Lettre à son fils. ... Ouvrage posthume revu par F. P. de Lacerda Werneck* (Rio de Janeiro, 1889), pp. 48-49; Victor Nunes Leal, *Coronelismo: The Municipality and Representative Government in Brazil* (Cambridge, Eng., 1977), p. 119-20; Roderick J. Barman, "Brazil at Mid-Empire: Political Accommodation and the Pursuit of Progress Under the *Conciliação* Ministry, 1853-1857" (Ph.D. diss., Univ. of California, Berke-

ley, 1970), pp. 205-34; and José Murilo de Carvalho, *Teatro de sombras: A política imperial* (São Paulo, 1988), pp. 144-45, 155.

6. Bueno, *Direito publico*, p. 199.

7. Junqueira to Cotegipe, Salvador, 31 May 1856, AIHGB, CC, L30, D177. Also see J. R. Souza, *Systema eleitoral*, pp. 28, 30, 37. On the manipulation of elections fostered by a similar law in Italy, see N. A. O. Lyttleton, "El patronazgo en la Italia de Giolitti (1892-1924)," *Revista de Occidente*, 127 (Oct. 1973), 112.

8. Antonio Alves de Souza Carvalho, *O Brasil em 1870, estudo político* (Rio de Janeiro, 1870), p. 41. One historian, however, claims that despite the charge of government interference, at the next election, in 1856, the opposition Liberals elected an unheard-of one-third of the Chamber: Pedro Calmon, *História de D. Pedro II* (Rio de Janeiro, 1975), II, 550. But compare Francisco Belisário Soares de Souza, *O sistema eleitoral no império (com apêndice contendo a legislação eleitoral no período 1821-1889)* (Brasília, 1979), pp. 83-84, stating that only 12 of the 100 Deputies elected were Liberals. This inconsistency may be due to the ambiguity of party definitions, a subject I explore in a later chapter. The specific number of Liberals elected to Parliament is also discussed in Barman, "Brazil at Mid-Empire," p. 240.

9. "Decreto, 1860," art. 1, par. 2; the legislative history of this law can be found in BCCD, *Reforma eleitoral*, pp. 354-67.

10. Junqueira to Cotegipe, Salvador, 29, 27 Aug. 1868, AIHGB, CC L31, D9, D8, respectively; Americo Brasiliense [de Almeida Mello], *Os programas dos partidos e o 2° império. Primeira parte: Exposição de principios* (São Paulo, 1878), pp. 45-46; "Decreto, 1875," art. 2, par. 17; Martinho Campos, in Centro Liberal, "Atas" (meeting of 30 July 1875), AIHGB, L495, D6. José de Alencar, *Systema representativo* (Rio de Janeiro, 1868), p. 3, claims he had proposed the "two-thirds" measure in 1859; later in this book (p. 72) he proposes something like the Hare system of exactly proportional representation.

11. "Decreto, 1881," art. 17. Attempts to protect the rights of the minority finally led to a proportional voting system in the 20th century; see Joseph L. Love, *São Paulo in the Brazilian Federation, 1889-1937* (Stanford, Calif., 1980), p. 134.

12. JM to PP-SP, Caçapava, 30 Dec. 1860, copy encl. in PP-SP to MJ, São Paulo, 20 Jan. 1861, AN, SPE, IJJ 5-43; Affonso Celso de Assis Figueiredo, *As finanças da regeneração: Estudo politico offerecido aos mineiros* (Rio de Janeiro, 1876), p. iv. Anarchy was commonly identified with tyranny outside Brazil as well: Richard Hofstadter, *The Idea of a Party System: The Rise of Legitimate Opposition in the United States, 1780-1840* (Berkeley, Calif., 1969), p. 12. On the conflicting appeal of liberty and order for Brazilian leaders during the first half of the century, see Ilmar Rohloff de Mattos, *O tempo saquarema* (São Paulo, 1987), pp. 133-38.

13. PP-CE to delegados and subdelegados, circular, copy encl. in PP-CE

to MI, Fortaleza, 13 Aug 1860, AN, SPE, IJJ 5-43; Actas da Mesa Parochial de Pirassinunga, 7 Sept. 1872, copy encl. in PP-SP to MI, 25 Nov. 1872, ibid., IJJ 5-30.

14. PP-RJ to MJ, Niterói, 2 Jan. 1861, ibid., IJJ 5-43. Also see PP-BA to MI, Salvador, 6 Aug. 1849, ibid., IJJ 5-25.

15. PP-CE to MI, 13 Aug. 1860, ibid., IJJ 5-43.

16. Manuel Pinto de Souza Dantas to Ruy Barbosa, Salvador, 5 June 1876, in Manuel Pinto de Souza Dantas, *Correspondência* (Rio de Janeiro, 1962), p. 20; Affonso d'Albuquerque Mello, *A liberdade no Brasil: Seu nascimento, vida, morte e sepultura* (Recife, 1864), p. 90.

17. José Antonio de Figueiredo, in Antonio Herculano de Souza Bandeira, ed., *Reforma eleitoral, eleição directa: Collecção de diversos artigos sobre a eleição directa dos quaes são autores os seguintes senhores . . .* (Recife, 1862), p. 202.

18. Cotegipe to Henrique Pereira de Lucena, Rio, 17 Jan. 1886, APEP, Col. Lucena, 603.

19. Bueno, *Direito publico*, p. 256; Brazil, *Constituição política do Império do Brasil*, art. 101, pars. 5, 6; speech of Martinho Campos, 24 Sept. 1875, quoted by [Artur] Colares Moreira, "A Camara e o regimen eleitoral no Império e na República," in BCCD, *Livro do centenário da Camara dos Deputados* (Rio de Janeiro, 1926), II, 40; speech of Nabuco de Araújo, 17 July 1868, BCS, *Anais*, 1868, III, 115.

20. Paulino José Soares de Sousa to Firmino Rodrigues Silva, n.p., 27 Dec. 1852, quoted in Nelson Lage Mascarenhas, *Um jornalista do império (Firmino Rodrigues Silva)* (São Paulo, 1961), p. 172; Manuel Pinto de Souza Dantas to Zacharias de Góes e Vasconcellos, n.p., 15 Jan. [1866], AMIP, I-ZGV 15.1.866 Dan.c.; Affonso d'Escragnolle Taunay, "Prefacio," in Alfredo d'Escragnolle Taunay, *Homens e cousas do Imperio* (São Paulo, 1924), p. vii; João Lins Vieira Cansansão de Sinimbú to Aureliano Candido Tavares Bastos, 1874, quoted in Carlos Pontes, *Tavares Bastos (Aureliano Cândido), 1839-1875* (São Paulo, 1939), p. 347; Henrique Augusto Milet, *Auxilio a lavoura e credito real* (Recife, 1876), p. vi.

21. *O abolicionismo perante a historia ou, O dialogo das tres provincias* (Rio de Janeiro, 1888), p. 61; Aureliano Cândido Tavares Bastos, *Os males do presente e as esperanças do futuro ([e outros] estudos brasileiros)*, 3d ed. (São Paulo, 1976), p. 16.

22. F. B. S. Souza, *Sistema eleitoral*, p. 6; Pedro II, quoted by Joaquim Nabuco, *Um estadista do império*, [3d ed.?] (Rio de Janeiro, 1975), p. 1004; Pedro II to Cotegipe, Rio, 23 Jan. 1886, in Pedro II, *Cartas do imperador D. Pedro II ao barão de Cotegipe* (São Paulo, 1933), p. 268; Pedro II, marginal comment in Tito Franco de Almeida, *O Conselheiro Francisco José Furtado. Biografia e estudo da história política contemporânea*, 2d ed. (São Paulo, 1944), p. 100n. Also see Pedro II, *Conselhos à regente* (Rio de Janeiro, 1958), pp. 33, 60; but compare p. 67.

23. Ambrosio Leitão da Cunha to Cotegipe, Maranhão, 20 Sept. 1868,

AIHGB, CC, L18, D63; Junqueira to Cotegipe, Salvador, 4 July 1855, ibid., L30, D169 (Alvaro Tiberio de Moncorvo Lima was named PP-BA on 1 Aug. 1855).

24. PP-RS to PM, Pôrto Alegre, 9 Dec. 1871, draft, AN, SAP, Cx. 781, Pac. 2; PP-PA (João Alfredo Correia de Oliveira) to MM (Cotegipe), Belém, 9 Mar. 1870, AIHGB, CC, L50, D89; PP-MG (Pena) to MJ (Nabuco de Araújo), AIHGB, L365, P11.

25. PP-BA to MI, Salvador, 15 Nov. 1867, AN, SPE, IJJ 90-343, fl. 175; PP-CE to MJ, Fortaleza, 29 Dec. 1860, ibid., 5-43; enclosures in JM to PP-PI, Mamanguape, 7 Sept. 1860, encl. in PP-PI to MI, n.p,, 11 Feb. 1861, ibid., 5-43. A president's authority for acting as in this last case rested on his right to suspend any public employee for malfeasance of any sort: LB, Lei de 3 Oct. 1834, art. 5, par. 8.

26. Processos de Presidentes, Bahia, 1879, AN, Cód. 954, Vol. 19, fl. 87; "Lei, 1846," arts. 111, 118; CP-BA to Delegado-Alagoinhas, Salvador, 10 Dec. 1868, copy, APEB, Presidência, Polícia, Delegados, Registro, M.5802; PP-MG to MGuerra, Ouro Preto, 5 Mar. 1888, AIHGB, CC, L35, D172; MI to PP-CE, Rio, 22 Oct. 1860, copy, AN, SPE, IJJ 5-3, fl. 29; Darrell E. Levi, *The Prados of São Paulo Brazil: An Elite Family and Social Change, 1840-1930* (Athens, Ga., 1987), p. 226, n.15. When a president ruled the election of a County Council invalid, the previous Council would be reinstalled pending new elections: Consulta do Conselho de Estado, Seção Justiça, 28 June 1881, AN, SPE, Cx. 558, Pac. 3.

27. Junqueira to Cotegipe, Salvador, 4 Apr. 1876, AIHGB, CC, L31, D70; PP-MG to MGuerra, Ouro Preto, 5 Mar. 1888, ibid., L35, D172.

28. Guahy to Cotegipe, Salvador, 16 Oct. 1885, ibid., L38, D19; Luiz Pedreira do Couto Ferraz, visconde do Bom Retiro, to Cotegipe, Constantinople, 12 Oct. 1876, ibid., L22, D167.

29. PP-RJ to JD, [Niterói], 5 Dec. 1860, copy encl. in PP-RJ to MI, Niterói, 31 Dec. 1860, AN, SPE, IJJ 5-43; José Antonio de Magalhães Castro, *Refutação da exposição circumstanciada que fez o doutor Justiano Baptista de Madureira ... ao Presidente da Provincia da Bahia, sobre as elleições do Collegio de Villa Nova da Rainha* (Rio de Janeiro, 1857), pp. 6 (quoted), 8; [PP-RGS], Relação dos Juizes Municipaes da Provincia e seus Supplentes ... , Pôrto Alegre, [1872]; Domingos F. dos Santos to PP-RS, n.p., 10 Feb. 1872; plus unsigned, undated notes, all in AN, SAP, Cx. 781, Pac. 2. On a judge's effort to secure a compromise, see PP-CE to MJ, Fortaleza, 19 Dec. 1860, AN, SPE, IJJ 5-43. Appeals regarding the registration of voters came to the High Courts after hearings by the County Board of Appeals, made up of the county judge, the top vote-getter in the County Council, and the top vote-getting elector in the county's central parish ("Lei, 1846," arts. 33-38); JM to MI, Marianna (MG), 17 Sept. 1860, AN, SPE, IJJ 5-25. After 1875 district judges received added power, with the decision to make citizens excluded from the lists of registered voters appeal to them before turning to Regional High Courts ("Decreto, 1875," art. 1, pars. 14, 17, 18); at this time they also gained the authority, previously

held only by provincial presidents, to declare local elections for justices of the peace and county councilmen null and void (ibid., art. 2, pars. 30-32).

30. Guahy to Cotegipe, Salvador, 8 Oct. 1884, AIHGB, CC, L38, D13; speech of Olegario, 15 July 1880, BCCD, *Anais*, 1880, III, 290.

31. José Antônio Soares de Souza, *A vida do visconde do Uruguai (1807-1866) (Paulino José Soares de Souza)* (São Paulo, 1944), p. 626; Lenine Nequete, *O poder judiciário no Brasil a partir da Independência* (Pôrto Alegre, 1973), I, 102-3; Thomas Flory, *Judge and Jury in Imperial Brazil, 1808-1871: Social Control and Political Stability in the New State* (Austin, Tex., 1981), p. 184.

32. José Manuel de Freitas to João Lustosa da Cunha Paranaguá, São Luiz, 24 Jan. 1878, AMIP, I-DPP, 24.1.878, Fre-cl.4; Manuel Pinto de Souza Dantas to Cotegipe, Salvador, 24 June 1856, AIHGB, CC, L19, D17.

33. Alencar, *Systema representativo*, p. 118.

34. Speech of Martinho Campos, 24 Sept. 1875, BCCD, *Anais*, 1875, V, 209; José Antonio Saraiva to Franklin Americo de Menezes Dória, Salvador, 2 Jan. 1887, AIHGB, L173, D1, fl. 66; Junqueira (MGuerra) to Cotegipe, Rio, 22 Aug. 1872, AIHGB, CC, L31, D30.

35. PP-RJ to PM, Niterói, 19 Nov. 1881, AIHGB, L270, D8. Also see Junqueira to Cotegipe, Salvador, 6 Jan. 1884, AIHGB, CC, L31, D94.

36. PP-SP to MJ, São Paulo, 25 Mar. 1861, AN, SPE, IJJ 5-43; Cotegipe to Junqueira, Salvador, 26 Nov. 1874, copy of draft, AIHGB, CC, L31, D60; Guahy to Cotegipe, Salvador, 28 Dec., 23 Nov. 1885, AIHGB, CC, L38, D34, D26, respectively.

37. "Decreto, 1855," art. 1, par. 20. A step toward such incompatibilities had been proposed in 1845 but defeated: BCCD, *Reforma eleitoral*, pp. 153, 156. The principle had applied to County Councils since colonial times, and by the 19th century there was a long list of positions deemed incompatible with a seat on them: Lei de 1 Oct. 1828, art. 23 in "Additamentos" in Candido Mendes de Almeida, ed., *Codigo Philippino; ou, Ordenações e leis do reino de Portugal* (Rio de Janeiro, 1870), p. 372n. There was also the fear that as public employees those elected would too slavishly follow the government party.

38. Junqueira to Cotegipe, Salvador, 12 Oct. 1855, AIHGB, CC, L30, D171.

39. "Decreto, 1860," art. 1, pars. 13-14; "Decreto, 1875," art. 3; "Decreto, 1881," art. 11.

40. Joaquim Nabuco, *Eleições liberaes e eleições conservadoras* (Rio de Janeiro, 1886), p. 55; J. R. Souza, *Systema eleitoral*, p. 37; speech of Martinho Campos, 24 Sept. 1875, BCCD, *Anais*, 1875, V, 213. Also see Augusto Tavares de Lyra, *Esboço historico do regimen eleitoral do Brasil (1821-1921)* (Rio de Janeiro, 1922), p. 40; and José M. Carvalho, *Teatro de sombras*, pp. 147-53.

41. Statement of Jequitinhonha, 18 July 1868, in Brazil, Conselho de Estado, *Atas* (Brasília, 1978), VIII, 52; [Antonio Alves de Souza Car-

valho], *O imperialismo e a reforma, anotado por um constitucional do Maranhão* (Maranhão [São Luiz?], 1866), p. 41; Tomaz Pompeu de Sousa Brasil to José Antonio Saraiva, Fortaleza, [late 1880 or early 1881], AIHGB, L270, D6.

42. José Antonio Saraiva to José Thomaz Nabuco de Araújo, 24 Dec. 1868, quoted in Nabuco, *Estadista do império*, p. 675; JP to PP-SP, Caçapava, 1 Jan. 1861, copy encl. in PP-SP to MJ, 20 Jan. 1861, AN, SPE, IJJ 5-43; L. P. L. Werneck, *Le Brésil*, p. 78; A. Carvalho, *Brasil em 1870*, p. 23. Also see *O Brasil*, 18 Dec. 1848, cited in Flory, *Judge*, p. 226 n.40.

43. Subdelegado to PP-BA, Bom Conselho [da Amargosa] (termo de Geremoabo), 7 Aug., 13 Aug. 1863, APEB, Presidência, Polícia, Subdelegados, M.3005 [2005]; PP-CE to delegados and subdelegados, circular, copy encl. in PP-CE to MI, Fortaleza, 13 Aug. 1860, AN, SPE, IJJ 5-43. Also see PP-BA quoted in Mesa Parochial de Victoria to PP-BA, Victoria, 14 Sept. 1860, AN, SPE, IJJ 5-25.

44. Amaro Ferreira de Camargo Bueno to PP-RS, Passo Fundo, 11 May 1872, AN, Cx. 781, Pac. 2, Doc. 11.

45. Junqueira to Cotegipe, Salvador and Rio, 2 Aug. 1868, 6 July 1872, AIHGB, CC, L31, D7, D21. Presidents had the right to suspend National Guard officers and appoint replacements, pending approval from the Minister of Justice; in the meanwhile crucial elections could take place: PP-PA to MI, Belém, 24 Jan. 1861, AN, SPE, IJJ, 5-43; A. Carvalho, *Brasil em 1870*, p. 40. For a proposal that a president dismiss numerous officers, see Commandante Superior da GN to PP-RS, Cruz Alta, 7 Apr. 1863, quoted by Fernando Uricoechea, *O minotauro imperial: A burocratização do estado patrimonial brasileiro no século XIX* (São Paulo, 1978), p. 246.

46. PP-RS to PM, Pôrto Alegre, 9 Dec. 1871, draft, AN, SAP, Cx. 781, Pac. 2; *HGCB*, no. 6, p. 251; José Mariano Carneiro da Cunha to Affonso Pena (MGuerra), Rio, 6 Apr. 1882, AN, SAP, Affonso Pena Papers, L5, 1.2.314, L:C. For another example of an officer getting his subordinates to vote a certain way, see PP-ES to PM, Victoria, 15 July 1863, AIHGB, L207, D120.

47. *HGCB*, no. 5, p. 80; Paulo Pinheiro Chagas, *Teófilo Ottoni, ministro do povo*, 2d rev. ed. (Rio de Janeiro, 1956), pp. 465-74; MJ to CP-Corte, Rio, 5 Sept. 1860, draft, and notes regarding election of 1860, AN, SPE, IJJ 5-43. Ottoni also won in Minas Gerais.

48. PP-RJ to MJ, [Niterói?], 20 Aug. 1860; PP-ES, Instruções [to Army capt.], 28 Aug. 1860, encl. in PP-ES to MJ, Vitória, 28 Aug. 1860; PP-CE to MI, 13 Aug. 1860; JD to PP-PA, Macapá, 27 Oct. 1860, copy encl. in PP-PA to MJ, Belém, 26 Jan. 1861, all in AN, SPE, IJJ 5-43. Provincial presidents held authority over Army contingents within their provinces.

49. Acta da Mesa Eleitoral da Villa do Principe e Santa Anna de Caeteté, 21 Jan. 1858, ibid., 5-25; Presidente da Mesa Eleitoral da Parochia da Cidade to PP-BA, Barra do Rio Grande, 21 Dec. 1887, ibid., 9-355, Vol. I, fl. 53.

50. "Lei, 1846," art. 108; *LB*, Decreto 8213, 13 Aug. 1881, art. 240; F. B. S. Souza, *Sistema eleitoral*, p. 6.

51. Paulino José Soares de Souza, visconde de Uruguay, *Estudos praticos sobre a administração das provincias do Brasil. . . . Primeira parte: Acto Addicional* (Rio de Janeiro, 1865), II, 179; JD to PP-PA, Macapá, 22 Oct. 1860, copy encl. in PP-PA to MJ, Belém, 26 Jan. 1861, AN, SPE, IJJ 5-43. Also see PP-RS to MJ, Pôrto Alegre, 13 Apr. 1860, ibid.

52. "Lei, 1846," art. 108; JD to PP-SP, Bananal, 13 Sept. 1860, encl. in PP-SP to MJ, São Paulo, 25 Sept. 1860, AN, SPE, IJJ 5-43.

53. A. Carvalho, *Brasil em 1870*, p. 14. On how the war opened the way for increased electoral pressure, see JP to MI, Campanha (MG), 28 Feb. 1867, AN, SPE, IJJ 5-34; and Junqueira to Cotegipe, Salvador, 29 July 1868, AIHGB, CC, L31, D6.

54. A. Carvalho, *Brasil em 1870*, p. 44; PP-ES to MJ, Victoria, 22 June 1861, AN, SPE, IJJ 5-43.

55. Comandante Superior da 9ᵃ Legião to PP-RJ, Rezende, 4 May 1849, quoted by Uricoechea, *Minotauro*, p. 220 n.36; A. Carvalho, *Brasil em 1870*, p. 19; Manuel Luiz Osorio, marquês do Herval, to selected electors, circular, [1872], draft, AIHGB, L233, D7959.

56. Affonso Celso de Assis Figueiredo, *Reforma administrativa e municipal: Parecer e projectos* (Rio de Janeiro, 1883), pp. 72-73. In discussing the National Guard's electoral role, Uricoechea, *Minotauro*, does not sufficiently distinguish between the application of force and the way the government used commissions (highly valued for the social position they conferred) to reward electoral loyalty; this leads him contradictorily—but correctly—to say that the 1873 law both diminished and increased the Guard's importance in elections: pp. 244-45.

57. Guahy to Cotegipe, n.p., n.d., AIHGB, CC, L37, D106; Guahy to Cotegipe, Salvador, 25 Sept. 1884, ibid., L38, D9; José de Araújo Costa to José Lustosa da Cunha Paranaguá, Teresina, 21 Mar. 1872, AMIP, I-DPP, 21.3.872, Cos-cl.2; Dantas to Cotegipe, Salvador, 31 Jan. 1857, AIHGB, CC, L19, D36.

58. Guahy to Cotegipe, Salvador, 6 Sept. 1877, 19 Dec. 1882, AIHGB, CC, L37, D144, D165; Junqueira to Cotegipe, Rio, 16 Dec., 20 Dec. 1885, ibid., L31, D110, D111. It is instructive to contrast the Brazilian experience with that of the U.S. where office seekers also formed what Thomas Jefferson called "a numerous & noisy tribe"; but Jefferson struck a deal with his opponents, agreeing not to dismiss their appointees if he were elected: Hofstadter, *Idea of a Party System*, pp. 127, 133-34, 154 (also see pp. 126 and 163).

59. Junqueira (MGuerra) to Cotegipe, Rio, 30 Sept. 1872, AIHGB, CC, L31, D35; Comandante do Quartel do Comando do Corpo Policial to PP-RS, Pôrto Alegre, 20 Dec. 1871, AN, SAP, Cx. 781, Pac. 2, [Doc. 20]; Ambrosio Leitão da Cunha to Cotegipe, n.p., 4 Feb. 1887, AIHGB, CC, L18, D131.

60. Cotegipe (PM) to Henrique Pereira de Lucena (PP-RS), Rio, 3 Dec., 20 Nov. 1885, APEP, Col. Lucena, 564, 562; Junqueira to Cotegipe, Cachoeira, 2 Nov. 1855, AIHGB, CC, L30, D172.

61. Pedro II to Luiz Alves de Lima e Silva, marquês de Caxias, 1856, quoted in Viana, *D. Pedro I e D. Pedro II*, p. 145. Also see Heitor Lyra, *História de Dom Pedro II, 1825-1891*, 2d rev. ed. (Belo Horizonte, 1977), II, 269.

62. Progressive Party program in Brasiliense [de Almeida Mello], ed., *Programas dos partidos*, pp. 16-17; PM (Alves Branco) to PPs, circular, 1847, quoted in *HGCB*, no. 7, p. 82; speech of Pacheco, 18 Apr. 1861, BCCD, *Anais*, 1861, I, 20.

63. Lourenço de Albuquerque to Luis Felipe de Souza Leão, Engenho Velho, 1 Mar. 1885, AIHGB, L456, D48; Junqueira to Cotegipe, Salvador, 11 Oct. 1884, AIHGB, CC, L31, D99.

64. José Antonio Saraiva to José Thomaz Nabuco de Araújo, 24 Dec. 1868, quoted in Nabuco, *Estadista do império*, p. 676. Pedro II told his daughter that he too wished for free elections but thought them unlikely: Pedro II, "Conselhos à D. Isabel (1871)," in Viana, *D. Pedro I e D. Pedro II*, p. 241.

Chapter 4

1. *LB*, Decreto, 7 Mar. 1821, Decisão 57 (Reino), 19 June 1822, cap. 2, art. 6. Elections for county councilmen, of course, had long been familiar: Candido Mendes de Almeida, ed., *Codigo Philippino; ou, Ordenações e leis do reino de Portugal* (Rio de Janeiro, 1870), Liv. I, Tit. 67. On Bonifácio's effort to avoid direct elections, see Emília Viotti da Costa, "The Political Emancipation of Brazil," in *From Colony to Nation: Essays on the Independence of Brazil*, ed. A. J. R. Russell-Wood (Baltimore, 1975), p. 82.

2. "Projecto de Constituição," arts. 122-37, in Brazil, Assembléia Geral Constituinte e Legislativa, *Diário* (1823; facsim., Brasília, 1973), II, 694-95; Brazil, *Constituição política do Império do Brasil*, arts. 90-97; *LB*, Decreto, 7 Mar. 1821, Decreto 3 June 1822, Decisão 57 (Reino), 19 June 1822, Decreto 26 Mar. 1824, Decreto 157, 4 May 1842; José Honório Rodrigues, *Conciliação e reforma no Brasil. Um desafio histórico-político* (Rio de Janeiro, 1965), pp. 135-38. Before 1842 in the few parishes that had a resident royal judge, he served as the chairman of the electoral assembly instead of a county councilman.

3. "Lei, 1846." The legislative history of this law is summarized in BCCD, *Reforma eleitoral: Projectos offerecidos á consideração do corpo legislativo desde o ano de 1826 até o anno de 1875 ... colligidos na secretaria da Camara dos Deputados* (Rio de Janeiro, 1875), pp. 127-226. Many of the laws are reproduced in Francisco Belisário Soares de Souza, *O sistema eleitoral no império (com apêndice contendo a legislação eleitoral no período 1821-1889)* (Brasília, 1979), pp. 163-208.

4. "Lei, 1846," arts. 40, 92; Brazil, *Ato adicional [à Constituição política do Império do Brasil]*, art. 4; "Decreto, 1855," art. 1; "Decreto, 1860," art. 1; "Decreto, 1875," art. 1. When a Deputy entered the Cabinet, he had to stand for re-election: Brazil, *Constituição*, arts. 29, 30. Before 1860 substitutes for Deputies were simply those further down the list

in the order of votes received: "Lei, 1846," art. 89. Also see Paulino José Soares de Souza, visconde de Uruguay, *Estudos praticos sobre a administração das provincias do Brasil. . . . Primeira parte: Acto Addicional* (Rio de Janeiro, 1865), I, 76-85. The careful attention to the electoral schedule is reflected in Braz Carneiro Nogueira da Costa e Gama, visconde de Baependy to unidentified, Sta. Rosa, 27 Jan. 1857, AN, SAP, Cód. 112, Vol. 8, 2d part, fl. 28. To be sure, through negligence or with an ulterior motive, sometimes years passed without a new list being drawn up: MI to PP-PE, Rio, 22 Oct. 1860, copy, AN, SPE, IJJ 5-3, fl. 34. Beginning in 1875 the process of drawing up the electoral roll was required only every other year.

5. Brazil, *Constituição*, art. 90.

6. Ibid., art. 92, par. 5. The electoral law gratuitously added the phrase, "in silver" ("Lei, 1846," art. 18), and the government then declared this to be equivalent to 200 milreis in currency, a figure retained until the end of the Empire: *LB*, Decreto 484, 25 Nov. 1846.

7. According to José Antonio Pimenta Bueno, *Direito publico brazileiro e analyse da Constituição do Imperio* (Rio de Janeiro, 1857), p. 472, the income requirement would only exclude "idlers and vagabonds," but he slightly modifies this on p. 194 by saying one would "almost have to be a beggar not to have such an income, or at least a perfectly idle and useless man." José de Alencar, *Systema representativo* (Rio de Janeiro, 1868), p. 93, agrees that only the "vagabond" was thus excluded. As early as 1837 a conservative newspaper claimed suffrage had been extended to men "of the lowest social position aside from slaves and criminals": *O Constitucional Cachoeirano*, 21 Nov. 1837, p. 3, in AN, SPE, IJ 1-708.

8. Justiniano José da Rocha, quoted in Thomas Flory, *Judge and Jury in Imperial Brazil, 1808-1871: Social Control and Political Stability in the New State* (Austin, Tex., 1981), p. 118 (also see p. 141); speech of Martinho Campos, 24 Sept. 1875, BCCD, *Anais*, 1875, V, 208; speech of Saraiva, 4 June 1880, BCCD, *Anais*, 1880, II, 35. A later defender of the Empire also said the law of 1846 really implied "universal suffrage": [João Cardoso de Meneses e Sousa], barão de Paranapiacaba, "Elleições," in Affonso Celso de Assis Figueiredo, visconde de Ouro Preto, et al., *A decada republicana* (Rio de Janeiro, 1900), III, 252.

9. C. F. van Delden Laerne, *Brazil and Java: Report on Coffee-Culture in America, Asia and Africa to H.E. the Minister of the Colonies* (London, 1885), p. 304. Cooks could earn 300 milreis annually in 1877, and a wet nurse, if nursing, as much as 600 in early 1881: Sandra Lauderdale Graham, *House and Street: The Domestic World of Servants and Masters in Nineteenth-Century Rio de Janeiro* (Cambridge, Eng., 1988), p. 14; also see Ubaldo Soares, *O passado heróico da Casa dos Expostos* (Rio de Janeiro, 1959), p. 48. Pedro Carvalho de Mello shows that from 1852 onward the average cost of hiring slaves would have been more than 200 milreis annually: "The Economics of Labor in Brazilian Coffee Plantations, 1850-1888" (Ph.D. diss., Univ. of Chicago, 1977), p. 66, Table 19. A very different conclusion was drawn for workers in the interior by the intransigent reformer André Rebouças, as cited in *HGCB*, no. 7, p. 223.

10. Pedro Autran da Matta Albuquerque, in Antonio Herculano de Souza Bandeira, ed., *Reforma eleitoral, eleição directa: Collecção de diversos artigos sobre a eleição directa dos quaes são autores os seguintes senhores* . . . (Recife, 1862), p. 243; Alencar, *Systema representativo*, p. 92.

11. Brazil, *Constituição*, art. 92 (my italics); *LB*, Decisão, no. 57 (Reino), 19 June 1822, cap. I, par. 8; Projecto de Constituição, art. 124, par. 7, in Brazil, Assembléia Geral Constituinte e Legislativa, *Diário*, p. 694.

12. The definition was made explicit in "Decreto, 1881," art. 3, par. 3. On a similar view of public employment elsewhere, see Richard Hofstadter, *The Idea of a Party System: The Rise of Legitimate Opposition in the United States, 1780-1840* (Berkeley, Calif., 1969), p. 157.

13. José Antônio Saraiva, quoted in *HGCB*, no. 7, p. 242; Bueno, *Direito publico*, p. 194; F. B. S. Sousa, *Sistema eleitoral*, p. 26; Aureliano Cândido Tavares Bastos, *Os males do presente e as esperanças do futuro ([e outros] estudos brasileiros)*, 3d ed. (São Paulo, 1976), p. 143; Recurso de Qualificação, 1860, Francisco Antonio Feiteiro recorrente, Conselho Municipal de Recurso da Villa de Caçapava [RGS] recorrido, AN, SPJ, Apelação, no. 1242, Cx. 11.880 [old Cx. 32, Gal. C].

14. Luiz Peixoto de Lacerda Werneck, *Idéias sobre colonização, precedidas de uma sucinta exposição dos princípios que regem a população* (Rio de Janeiro, 1855), p. 38; Francisco Freire Alemão, diary entry for 19 Nov. 1859, in "Os manuscritos do botânico Freire Alemão," ed. Darcy Damasceno and Waldyr da Cunha, in *Rio de Janeiro, Biblioteca Nacional, Anais*, vol. 81 (1961), p. 293; José Pereira da Camara to Peregrino José de America Pinheiro, Ubá (RJ), 7 July 1863, AN, SAP, Cód. 112, Vol. 8, Doc. 4; statement of Antonio Borges Rodrigues and Antonio Lourenço Torres, speech of Manoel Furtado da Silva Leite, speech of Julio Cesar de Morais Carneiro, all in Congresso Agricola, *Congresso Agricola: Coleção de documentos* (Rio de Janeiro, 1878), pp. 32, 47, 147; also see Stanley J. Stein, *Vassouras, a Brazilian Coffee County, 1850-1900* (Cambridge, Mass., 1957), p. 57n.

15. "Lei, 1846," arts. 2, 8-14; "Decreto, 1855," art. 1; *LB*, Decreto 1812, 23 Aug. 1856, arts. 1-17; Affonso d'Albuquerque Mello, *A liberdade no Brasil: Seu nascimento, vida, morte, e sepultura* (Recife, 1864), p. 111.

16. [Braz Carneiro Nogueira da Costa e Gama], visconde de Baependy, to João Vieira Machado da Cunha, Sta. Rosa, 8 Jan. 1858, AN, SAP, Cód. 112, Vol. 8, Doc. 32.

17. "Lei, 1846," arts. 19, 25, 26; Recurso de Qualificação, 1860, Francisco Antonio Feiteiro recorrente, Conselho Municipal de Recurso da Villa de Caçapava [RGS] recorrido, AN, SPJ, Apelação, no. 1242, Cx. 11.880 [old Cx. 32, Gal. C]; F. B. S. Souza, *Sistema eleitoral*, p. 26. I have never found an instance where accusations of perjury on this matter led to a trial.

18. Speech of José Antonio Saraiva, 4 June 1880, BCCD, *Anais*, 1880, II, 39.

19. Brazil, Ministerio do Imperio, *Relatorio*, 1870, Anexo C; Brazil, Directoria Geral de Estatistica, *Recenseamento da população do imperio do Brazil a que se procedeu no dia 1º de agosto de 1872* (Rio de Janeiro, 1873-76).

20. The minutes of electoral boards I examined show that most registered voters were said to have voted. Since manuscript censuses often show a large number of female-headed households in Brazil, many entire households went unrepresented: Donald Ramos, "Marriage and the Family in Colonial Vila Rica," *Hispanic American Historical Review*, 55: 2 (May 1975), 218-23; Elizabeth Kuznesof, "The Role of the Female-Headed Household in Brazilian Modernization, 1765-1836," *Journal of Social History*, 13: 4 (Summer 1980), 589-613.

21. The total population of Brazil of all ages and both sexes, slave and free, was 9,930,478 in 1872, so more than 10% were registered. During the Republic, after 1889, we know voter participation remained below 6% of the population: Joseph L. Love, "Political Participation in Brazil, 1881-1969," *Luso-Brazilian Review*, 7: 2 (Dec. 1970), 3-24; Steven Topik, *The Political Economy of the Brazilian State, 1889-1930* (Austin, Tex., 1987), p. 8. These authors do not calculate figures for adult males only, an especially important step, given the youthfulness of that population. Even in 1945, when women could vote, the registration rate only reached 16% of the total population: Lawrence S. Graham, *Civil Service Reform in Brazil: Principles Versus Practice* (Austin, Tex., 1968), p. 117.

22. Nelson Werneck Sodré, *História da burguesia brasileira* (Rio de Janeiro, 1964), pp. 102-3. The confusion has continued, so that one historian simultaneously argues that the 1846 law allowed few to vote and a large number to vote: José Murilo de Carvalho, *Teatro de sombras: A política imperial* (São Paulo, 1988), pp. 140-43. When Carvalho turns to actual records of elections, he discovers (pp. 142-43) that indeed the propertyless voted.

23. See, for example, Recurso de Qualificação, 1860, Francisco Antonio Feiteiro recorrente, Conselho Municipal de Recurso da Villa de Caçapava [RGS] recorrido, AN, SPJ, Apelação, no. 1242, Cx. 11.880 [old Cx. 32, Gal. C]. The list of registered voters used by Luiz R. B. Mott, *Sergipe del Rey: População, economia e sociedade* (Maceió, 1986), p. 60, includes race, with the following breakdown:

White	136	35.05%
Black	41	10.57
Mulatto	211	54.38
Total	388	100.00%

24. Acta da Mesa Parochial, Freguezia de S. Sebastião dos Afflictos, Ubá, 7 Sept. 1860, copy encl. in PP-MG to MI, Ouro Preto, 19 Oct. 1860, AN, SPE, IJJ 9-482; Acta da Mesa Eleitoral da Villa Nova do Príncipe e Santa Anna de Caiteté, 10 Jan. 1858, ibid., 5-25. For an example involving the rural property of an electoral board chairman, see Depoimento, Pirassinunga, Feb. 2, 1873, encl. in PP-SP to MI, São Paulo, 15 Feb. 1873, ibid.,

5-30. Normally those who sat on the registration board also formed the electoral board, but the process of setting it up could easily occupy half a day.

25. Francisco de Paula Ferreira de Rezende, *Minhas recordações* (Rio de Janeiro, 1944), p. 124 (to be sure, Rezende is speaking specifically of the election of 1840, but he contrasts it with the sedate and closed affairs that began only in 1881, so by implication he is describing the intervening period); Acta de recolhimento, numeração das listas, apuração dos votos, e reunião de Eleitores desta freguezia, N.S. do Livramento das Minas do Rio das Contas, 26 Feb. 1823, AN, SPE, IJJ 5-26; "Lei, 1846," arts. 4, 8, 21, 42 (also see "Decreto, 1860," art. 6; and "Decreto, 1875," art. 2, par. 10); Mesa Parochial de Victoria to PP-BA, Victoria, 19 Sept. 1860, AN, SPE, IJJ 5-25; Acta da Mesa Parochial de Pirassinunga, 18 Aug. 1872, copy encl. in PP-SP to MI, São Paulo, Feb. 15, 1873, AN, SPE, IJJ 5-30; Acta da Mesa Parochial, Freguezia de S. Sebastião dos Afflictos, Ubá, 7 Sept. 1860, copy encl. in PP-MG to MI, Ouro Preto, 19 Oct. 1860, AN, SPE, IJJ 9-482. An *edital* summoning the voters, dated from Santa Thereza (Valença), 7 Aug. 1860, can be found in AN, SAP, Cód. 112, Vol. 8, Doc. 13.

26. Delegado to PP-PA, Breves, 27 July 1860, copy encl. in PP-PA to MJ, Belém, 1 Aug. 1860, AN, SPE, IJJ 5-43; PP-CE, circular, to delegados and subdelegados of the province, encl. in PP-CE to MI, 13 Aug. 1860, ibid., 5-43.

27. F. B. S. Souza, *Sistema eleitoral*, p. 34; Rezende, *Minhas recordações*, p. 126; Delegado to PP-CE, Sobral, 12 Dec. 1860, copy encl. in PP-CE to MJ, Fortaleza, 29 Dec. 1860, AN, SPE, IJJ 5-43.

28. Recurso de Qualificação, 1860, Francisco Antonio Feiteiro recorrente, Conselho Municipal de Recurso da Villa de Caçapava [RGS] recorrido, AN, SPJ, Apelação, no. 1242, Cx. 11.880 [old Cx. 32, Gal. C].

29. "Lei, 1846," art. 18; *LB*, Decreto 6097, 12 Jan. 1876, art. 27. It is worth comparing these purposes with those of 18th-century Virginia: Rhys Isaac, *The Transformation of Virginia, 1740-1790* (Chapel Hill, N.C., 1982), pp. 110-14. On elections in 19th-century Virginia, see Daniel P. Jordan, *Political Leadership in Jefferson's Virginia* (Charlottesville, Va., 1983), pp. 103-56.

30. JD-Muriahé to PP-MG, Ubá, 12 Oct. 1860, encl. in PP-MG to MI, Ouro Preto, 19 Oct. 1860, AN, SPE, IJJ 9-482; Acta da Mesa Parochial de Pirassinunga, 18 Aug. 1872, copy encl. in PP-SP to MI, São Paulo, 15 Feb. 1873, ibid. 5-30; "Lei, 1846," art. 46 (if the list drawn up by the registration board were missing, the chairman could use any authenticated copy: *LB*, Aviso 168, 28 June 1849); F. B. S. Souza, *Sistema eleitoral*, pp. 31-32.

31. Actas da Mesa Parochial de Pirassinunga, 7 Sept. 1872, copy encl. in PP-SP to MI, 25 Nov. 1872, AN, SPE, IJJ 5-30; JD-Muriahé to PP-MG, Ubá, 12 Oct. 1860, encl. in PP-MG to MI, Ouro Preto, 19 Oct. 1860, ibid., 9-482; MI to PP-SE, Rio, 4 Jan. 1858, copy, ibid., 5-8, fl. 1v; "Lei, 1846," arts. 48, 49; *LB*, Aviso 298 (Imperio), 11 Sept. 1856; Alencar, *Systema representativo*, p. 118.

32. "Lei, 1846," art. 51; Acta da Meza Eleitoral de São Braz do Pôrto de Moz, 1 Nov. 1824, AN, SPE, IJJ 5-18.

33. Actas da Mesa Parochial de Pirassinunga, 7 Sept. 1872, copy encl. in PP-SP to MI, 25 Nov. 1872, ibid., 5-30; Acta da Mesa Eleitoral de Nazareth da Vigia (Pará), 2 Nov. 1824, ibid., 5-18; [Acta da Mesa Eleitoral da Freguezia de Inhaúma, MN], 9 Nov. [1852], AGCRJ, 61-4-14, fl. 133; "Lei, 1846," arts. 54, 56, 115. On the drawing of lots, this one at an Electoral College, see Braz Carneiro Nogueira da Costa e Gama, conde de Baependy, to Jeronimo José Teixeira Júnior, Sta. Rosa [Valença], 26 Dec. 1860, AN, SAP, Col. Teixeira Júnior, AP23, Correspondência Passiva, Doc. 99.

34. A typical and routine set of minutes from such an Electoral College is the Acta da Reunião do Colegio Eleitoral da Comarca de Caravellas, 14 Feb. 1856, AN, SPE, IJJ 5-25. Also see Actas da Mesa Eleitoral do 2º Districto, Salvador, 11 Feb. 1858, ibid., 5-25; "Lei, 1846," arts. 69, 70, 71, 73; and *LB*, Decreto 565, 10 July 1850, art. 1.

35. "Lei, 1846," arts. 85-89. For examples of the Councils' work, see Atas de Apuração de Eleições, Arquivo Municipal de Salvador, 12.1. They played a similar role in the election of provincial assemblymen: Nancy Naro, "The 1848 Praieira Revolt in Brazil" (Ph.D. diss., Univ. of Chicago, 1981), p. 183.

36. Acta da Mesa Parochial na freguezia de S. Sebastião dos Afflictos, Ubá, 7 Sept. 1860, copy encl. in PP-MG to MI, Ouro Preto, 19 Oct. 1860, AN, SPE, IJJ 9-482; Acta da Mesa Eleitoral de Villa Nova do Príncipe e Santa Anna de Caeteté, 10 Jan. 1858, ibid., 5-25; Actas da Mesa Parochial de Pirassinunga, 7 Sept. 1872, copy encl. in PP-SP to MI, 25 Nov. 1872, ibid., 5-30; Mesa Parochial de Victoria to PP-BA, Victoria, 19 Sept. 1860, ibid., 5-25; [Braz Carneiro Nogueira da Costa e Gama], visconde de Baependy, to João Vieira Machado da Cunha, Rio, 6 June 1856, AN, SAP, Cód. 112, Vol. 8, Doc. 69; PP-BA to MI, 29 May 1867, AN, SPE, IJJ 9-343 and enclosures, especially fl. 63v. Also see the query about the legality of an election that had been held in a chapel because the parish church was not yet complete: Domingos Cardoso N. to Padre Manoel José Alvim, Paripe, 25 Sept. 1852, and reply, APEB, Presidência, Religião, Vigários, M.5215. On the use of a cathedral, see Acta da Mesa Eleitoral de Santa Maria do Belém do Grão Pará, 2 Nov. 1824, AN, SPE, IJJ 5-18.

37. Actas da Mesa Parochial de Pirassinunga, 7 Sept. 1872, copy encl. in PP-SP to MI, 25 Nov. 1872, AN, SPE, IJJ 5-30; Recibo, Rio, 3 July 1847, AGCRJ, 61-4-34, fl. 20; Procurador to Presidente da Camara, Rio, 30 Mar. 1869, AGCRJ, 62-1-21, fl. 2; Acta de recolhimento, numeração das listas, apurações dos votos e reunião de Eleitores desta Freguezia de N.S. do Livramento das Minas de Rio das Contas, 26 Feb. 1823, AN, SPE, IJJ 5-26; Acta da Mesa do Colegio Eleitoral do 2º Districto, Salvador, 11 Feb. 1858, AN, SPE, IJJ 5-25. These practices followed the law: "Lei, 1846," arts. 42, 58, 72, 90.

38. Parecer da 1ª Commissão de verificação de poderes, 17 Apr. 1861, BCCD, *Anais*, 1861, I, 14; also see *LB*, Aviso 168, 28 June 1849, art. 15.

39. "Lei, 1846," arts. 42-44. On the construction of the necessary railing, see Joaquim Pinheiro de Campos to President of Camara Municipal,
Rio, 14 Oct. 1847, AGCRJ, 61-4-34. The law indicated that everyone else
was to be seated in the church "without precedence," suggesting both the
attempt at democracy and the contrasting normal order of things: "Lei,
1846," art. 42.

40. PP-RN to MJ, Natal, 24 Sept. 1860, AN, SPE, IJJ 5-43; "Lei,
1846," arts. 15, 21, 24, 36, 43, 67; "Decreto, 1881," art. 29, par. 8. One
list of registered voters was returned by the provincial president because it
had not been initialed on every page: marginal comment on JP to PP-BA,
Sta. Anna do Catú, 8 June 1855, APEB, Presidência, Eleições, M.2794. The
21% literacy figure is calculated from Brazil, Directoria Geral de Estatistica, Recenseamento . . . 1872, and refers to the free population over six
years of age.

41. See, for example, Comandante do Quartel do Comando do Corpo
Policial em Pôrto Alegre to PP-RGS, 20 Dec. 1871, AN, Cx. 781, Pac. 2,
[Doc. 20]; and PP-RN to MJ, Natal, 24 Sept. 1860, AN, SPE, IJJ 5-43.
Delegados and subdelegados, for instance, could not be illiterate: Caetano
José de Andrade Pinto, Attribuições dos presidentes de provincia (Rio de
Janeiro, 1865), p. 182.

42. Actas da Mesa Parochial de Pirassinunga, 7 Sept. 1872, copy encl.
in PP-SP to MI, 25 Nov. 1872, AN, SPE, IJJ 5-30; Acta da Mesa Eleitoral
de Nazareth da Vigia, Pará, 2 Nov. 1824, ibid., 5-18; Votantes do 3° districto da Villa de Victoria to the Juiz de Paz, 12 Sept. 1860, encl. in Mesa
Parochial de Victoria to PP-BA, Victoria, 14 Sept. 1860, ibid., 5-25; "Lei,
1846," arts. 22, 43, 51, 54, 70, 73, 100. "Decreto, 1855," art. 1, removed
the requirement that electors sign their ballots; on the other hand, the 1875
law, which called for issuing election cards to the voters, required that they
be signed, and that this signature be repeated in the act of voting, but also
recognized the right of illiterates to rely on sworn statements by others:
"Decreto, 1875," art. 1, par. 20.

43. MI to VPP-ES, 14 June, 1858, copy, AN, SPE, IJJ 5-8, fl. 6. Also
see Manoel Caetano Ribeiro, Justificação, n.d, encl. in PP-MG to MI,
Ouro Preto, 19 Oct. 1860, ibid., 9-482; and JD-Muriahé to PP-MG, Ubá,
12 Oct. 1860, encl. in ibid.

44. [Braz Carneiro Nogueira da Costa e Gama], visconde de Baependy,
to João Vieira Machado da Cunha, Sta. Rosa, 28 Oct. 1856, AN, SAP,
Cód. 112, Vol. 8, Doc. 26; PP-SE to MI, Sergipe, 10 Dec. 1851, AN, SAP,
Cx. 783, Pac. 2; PP-RJ to MJ, n.p., 17 Sept. 1860, AN, SPE, IJJ, 5-43.

45. "Lei 1846," arts. 57-59, 79; JP-Freguezia de S. José to Presidente da
Camara Municipal, Rio, 23 Jan. 1849, AGCRJ, 61-4-14, fl. 108. In more
prosperous locations the minutes, rather than being copied, were printed
in script-like type: Copia Authentica da Acta da Apuração dos Votos para
os Doze Eleitores da Parochia de Sta. Thereza do Municipio da Cidade de
Valença, 19 Aug. 1862, AN, SAP, Cód. 112, Vol. 7.

46. LB, Decreto, 14 June 1831, art. 2; [Braz Carneiro Nogueira da

Costa e Gama], visconde de Baependy, to unidentified, Sta. Rosa, 27 Jan. 1857, AN, SAP, Cód. 112, Vol. 8, 2d part, fl. 28; Vigario to PP-BA, Canavieiras, 18 Jan. 1858, APEB, Presidência, Religião, Vigarios, M.5215. The minutes of at least one Electoral College were kept by "me, vicar ——, secretary": Actas da Meza do Colegio Eleitoral do 2º Districto, Salvador, 11 Feb. 1858, AN, SPE, IJJ 5-25. Before 1846 the parish priest was by definition a member of the electoral board.

47. Commandante Superior of [?] to PP-RJ, n.p., 1 Feb. 1845, quoted by Fernando Uricoechea, *O minotauro imperial: A burocratização do estado patrimonial brasileiro no século XIX* (São Paulo, 1978), p. 200 (also see p. 292); Uniformes dos officiaes aos commandos superiores da Guarda Nacional do Imperio, AN, SAP, Cód. 112, Vol. 7, fl. 1.

48. JP to MI, Rio, 31 Dec. 1860, encl. in Acta da Meza Parochial da Freguezia de Sant'Anna, 30 Dec. 1860-20 Jan. 1861, AGCRJ, 63-3-32; [Antonio Alves de Souza Carvalho], *O imperialismo e a reforma, anotado por um constitucional do Maranhão* (Maranhão [São Luiz?], 1866), p. 42; Rezende, *Minhas recordações*, p. 126. On shoes as "the mark of freedom," see Maria Dundas Graham (Lady Maria Calcott), *Journal of a Voyage to Brazil and Residence There during Part of the Years 1821, 1822, 1823* (1824; rpt., New York, 1969), p. 108.

49. Vigario to PP-BA, Canavieiras, 18 Jan. 1858, APEB, Presidência, Religião, Vigarios, M.5215; Acta da Mesa Parochial, Freguezia de S. Sebastião dos Afflictos, Ubá, 7 Sept. 1860, copy encl. in PP-MG to MI, Ouro Preto, 19 Oct. 1860, AN, SPE, IJJ 9-482.

50. Procurador da Camara Municipal to Presidente da Camara Municipal, Rio, 1 June 1847, AGCRJ, 61-4-34, fl. 15; Acta da Mesa Parochial de Pirassinunga, 18 Aug. 1872, copy encl. in PP-SP to MI, São Paulo, 15 Feb. 1873, AN, SPE, IJJ 5-30; Actas da Mesa Parochial de Pirassinunga, 7 Sept. 1872, copy encl. in PP-SP to MI, São Paulo, 25 Nov. 1872, AN, SPE, IJJ 5-30; JM quoted in Mesa Parochial de Victoria to PP-BA, Victoria, 14 Sept. 1860, AN, SPE, IJJ 5-25. On the size and construction of the strongbox, see Acta da Mesa Eleitoral de Villa Nova do Principe e Santa Anna de Caetete, 15 Jan. 1858, AN, SPE, IJJ 5-25; and marginal notes dated 19 Feb 1847 in Procurador da Camara to Presidente da Camara, Rio, 9 Feb. 1847, AGCRJ, 61-4-34, fl. 14.

51. "Lei, 1846," art. 126, par. 7; Actas da Mesa Parochial de Pirassinunga, 7 Sept. 1872, copy encl. in PP-SP to MI, São Paulo, 25 Nov. 1872, AN, SPE, IJJ 5-30. Electors who failed to turn up for the organization of the electoral board, however, could be fined as an act of political vengeance: Parish priest to PP-BA, Canavieiras, 18 Jan. 1858, APEB, Presidência, Religião, Vigarios, M.5215.

52. Acta da Mesa Eleitoral de Santa Maria de Belém do Grão Pará, 2 Nov. 1824, AN, SPE, IJJ 5-18; Acta da Mesa Parochial, Freguezia de S. Sebastião dos Afflictos, Ubá, Sept. 9, 1860, copy encl. in PP-MG to MI, Ouro Preto, 19 Oct. 1860, ibid., 9-482; Acta da Mesa do Colegio Eleitoral do 2º Districto, Salvador, 11 Feb 1858, ibid., 5-25; *LB*, Aviso 168, 28 June

1849, art. 22; "Lei 1846," arts. 59 and 78. Since the bulk of the Brazilian population lived outside large cities, I have concentrated my attention on rural elections. Of course, in the capital cities other dramas took place to reinforce hierarchy. When the County Council of Rio de Janeiro, as required by law, asked the city's best preacher to say mass at the meeting of the Electoral College, he brusquely replied that he could not because on that day he would be celebrating the Pontifical Mass of Ashes before the Emperor and the court: Msgr. Felix . . . de Freitas e [illegible] to Presidente da Camara Municipal da Corte, Rio, 18 Feb. 1867, AGCRJ, 61-4-12, fl. 68. Elections, however, were specifically to take place "in all the Empire" ("Lei 1846," art. 40)—and there was only one court.

Chapter 5

1. José Thomaz Nabuco de Araújo to Paes Barreto, 1855, quoted by Joaquim Nabuco, *Um estadista do império*, [3d ed.?] (Rio de Janeiro, 1975), p. 289.

2. Later commentators, in their desire to criticize the First Republic, tended to ignore this fact. Sylvio Romero, *A bancarrota do regime federativo no Brasil: Ação dissolvente das oligarchias, ação indispensavel do exército* (Porto, 1912), p. 14, goes so far as to claim that the Empire, by exercising centralized control through presidents and judges, "knocked caudillismo to the ground and prevented the formation of oligarchies." Francisco José de Oliveira Vianna, *Instituições políticas brasileiras* (Rio de Janeiro, 1949), I, 286, shows a better understanding of the 19th-century origins of *coronelismo*. On 20th-century practices that mimicked those I describe here, see Victor Nunes Leal, *Coronelismo: The Municipality and Representative Government in Brazil* (Cambridge, Eng., 1977), p. 19. The *política dos governadores* under the First Republic, that is, the tendency of the national Presidents to accept as legitimate whatever local or state faction proved strongest, was also prefigured in the Empire.

3. Congresso Agricola, *Congresso Agricola: Coleção de documentos* (Rio de Janeiro, 1878), p. 17.

4. Stanley J. Stein, *Vassouras, a Brazilian Coffee County, 1850-1900* (Cambridge, Mass., 1957), pp. 16-20, 120, 159; Joseph E. Sweigart, *Coffee Factorage and the Emergence of a Brazilian Capital Market, 1850-1988* (New York, 1987) p. 86.

5. Acta da Eleição de Eleitores, Freguezia de N.S. da Conceição do Paty do Alferes, 9 Sept. 1842, AN, SAP, Cód. 112, Vol. 4, Doc. 110. Lacerda Werneck became state assemblyman the next year: Actas da Camara de Nictheroy para a apuração de 36 deputados á Assembleia Provincial, 22 Dec. 1843, ibid.

6. *Almanak [Laemmert] administrativo, mercantil e industrial do Rio de Janeiro e indicador. . . . Obra estatistica e de consulta* (Rio de Janeiro, 1855), Suplemento, pp. 135-41. For an earlier example of these families' monopoly of official positions, see Thomas Flory, *Judge and Jury in Imperial Brazil, 1808-1871: Social Control and Political Stability in the New*

State (Austin, Tex., 1981), p. 95. Laureano Correia de Castro, barão de Campo Belo, owner of the Fazenda do Secretário with its imposing mansion, was the first commandant of the National Guard in Vassouras: Alberto Ribeiro Lamego, "A aristocracia rural do café na provincia fluminense," *Anuário do Museu Imperial*, 7 (1946), pp. 88, 90.

7. Luiz Ascendino Dantas, *Esboço biographico do dr. Joaquim José de Souza Breves. Origem das fazendas S. Joaquim da Gramma e St° Antonio da Olaria. Subsidios para a historia do municipio de S. João Marcos* (Rio de Janeiro, 1931), pp. 17-18; declaration of José [Joaquim] de Souza Breves, 27 Feb. 1856, APERJ, Livros Paroquiais de Registros de Terras, no. 66, Arrozal, unpaged, unbound, unnum. Still another Morais daughter married José Joaquim de Lima e Silva, conde de Tocantins, the brother of the duque de Caxias: Affonso d'Escragnolle Taunay, *História do café no Brasil* (Rio de Janeiro, 1939), VI, 265 (see pp. 259-83, for a general account of the Breves family).

8. Production figures compiled from data in Sebastião Ferreira Soares, *Historico da Companhia Industrial da Estrada de Mangaratiba e analyse critica e economica dos negocios desta companhia* (Rio de Janeiro, 1861), pp. 232-50.

9. Flory, *Judge*, p. 100; Stein, *Vassouras*, pp. 208-9; Henry John Temple, viscount Palmerston, to José Marques Lisboa, London, Sept. 30, 1851, AHI, 216/2/15; Affonso Taunay, *História do café*, VI, 259. Breves's biographer later denied that the planter had mistreated his slaves; on the contrary, he had "spared no effort through advice, sacrifice, and help" to turn the freedmen of his plantation into "honest workers": L. A. Dantas, *Esboço biographico*, pp. 19, 20.

10. ACMRJ, Visitas Pastorais, Livro 35, 1855, fl. 3; Ata de 1° de agosto de 1887, in Brazil, Conselho de Estado, *Atas* (Brasília, 1978), VI, 363-83; L. A. Dantas, *Esboço biographico*, pp. 6, 19. Also see Affonso Taunay, *História do café*, VI, 259, 272-73.

11. Flory, *Judge*, pp. 100, 125-26, 232 n.74; Leão, quoted in ibid., p. 189 (and see p. 243 n.24); Parocho, quoted in Camara Municipal to PP-RJ, Pirahy, 20 Oct. 1844, APERJ, Col. 37, PP 2/5.22; Protesto de Antonio Perier Barreto [illegible] to Camara Apuradora, n.p., n.d. [received 19 Dec. 1849], AGCRJ, 61-4-12, fls. 46-49v; Breves to José Thomaz Nabuco de Araújo, Fazenda São Joaquim da Gramma, 7 Feb. 1859, quoted in Roderick J. Barman, "Brazil at Mid-Empire: Political Accommodation and the Pursuit of Progress Under the *Conciliação* Ministry, 1853-1857" (Ph.D. diss., Univ. of California, Berkeley, 1970), p. 69; PP-RJ to MI, Niterói, 31 Dec. 1860, 2 Jan. 1861, AN, SPE, IJJ 5-43; JD of [?] to MJ, 9 July 1871, quoted in staff summary on JMs, in Magistratura, Registro dos Fatos Notaveis, AN, SPE, IJ4-32, fl. 26v.

12. Peter L. Eisenberg, *The Sugar Industry in Pernambuco: Modernization Without Change, 1840-1910* (Berkeley, Calif., 1974), pp. 131-34. On similar control by sugar families in Bahia, see Flory, *Judge*, pp. 78-80.

13. Nabuco de Araújo, quoted in Nabuco, *Estadista do império*, p. 67.

14. Billy Jaynes Chandler, *The Feitosas and the Sertão dos Inhamuns: The History of a Family and a Community in Northeast Brazil, 1700-1930* (Gainesville, Fla., 1972), p. 58 (and see p. 83). Maria Sylvia de Carvalho Franco, *Homens livres na ordem escravocrata*, 2d ed. (São Paulo, 1974), p. 154, cites various foreign observers to the same effect.

15. Camara Municipal to PP-BA, Urubú, undated [before 12 July 1888], APEB, Presidência, Agricultura, Abastecimento, M.4632; PP-BA to unidentified, 16 Aug. 1848, quoted by Fernando Uricoechea, *O minotauro imperial: A burocratização do estado patrimonial brasileiro no século XIX* (São Paulo, 1978), p. 273; PP-SP to MJ, São Paulo, 25 Sept. 1860, and enclosures, AN, SPE, IJJ 5-43; speech of Saraiva, 4 June 1880, BCCD, *Anais*, 1880, II, 37. For a different view on the relationship between central government and local faction, see Uricoechea, *Minotauro*, p. 156; and Flory, *Judge*, pp. 86, 103, 107.

16. PP-SE to MI, Sergipe, 10 Dec. 1851, AN, SAP, Cx. 783, Pac. 2; Manuel Pinto de Souza Dantas to Cotegipe, S. Amaro, 31 Mar. 1856, Salvador, 24 June 1856, AIHGB, CC, L19, D14, D17. On José Dantas's official positions, see J. C. Dantas Júnior, "O capitão-mór João d'Antas e sua descendência," *Revista Genealógica Brasileira*, 1: 2 (2d sem. 1940), 384. On his family's wealth and control of official positions, see Dossier sobre João Dantas dos Reis Portatil, APEB, Seção de Registros Documentais e Arquivos Privados, unnum. On the role of the Dantas clan in the war of independence (1822-23), see F. W. O. Morton, "The Conservative Revolution of Independence: Economy, Society and Politics in Bahia, 1790-1840" (Ph.D. diss., Univ. of Oxford, 1974), p. 266.

17. PP-RN to MGuerra, Natal, 11 May 1850, AN, SAP, Cx. 823, Pac. 2, fl. 273.

18. João Alfredo Correia de Oliveira to Cotegipe, Rio, 30 June 1872 (italics in the original; the reference is to Manuel Joaquim de Mendonça Castelo Branco, barão de Anadia), Belém, 9 Mar. 1870, AIHGB, CC, L50, D98, D89. See also João Alfredo Correia de Oliveira to Cotegipe, Belém, 8 Dec. 1869, ibid., D81.

19. José Antonio Saraiva [PP-PE] to José Thomaz Nabuco de Araújo [MJ], Recife, 4 Mar. 1859, AIHGB, L386, D14 (the *coronel* was José Pedro da Lage).

20. Ibid.

21. These charges were hurled back and forth by various authorities in one location: JP to JD, Caçapava, 26 Dec. 1860, JP to PP-SP, Caçapava, 1 Jan. 1861, and JM to PP-SP, Caçapava, 30 Dec. 1860, all copies encl. in PP-SP to MJ, São Paulo, 20 Jan. 1861, AN, SPE, IJJ 5-43. A particularly revealing example of a clash between a National Guard commandant and a *delegado* can be found in PP-SP to MI, São Paulo, 23 Jan. 1873, ibid., 5-30.

22. PP-SE to MI, Sergipe, 1 Aug., 3 Sept. 1851, AN, SAP, Cx. 783, Pac. 2; José Thomaz Nabuco de Araújo [MJ] to Francisco Xavier Paes Barreto, 1855, quoted in Nabuco, *Estadista do império*, p. 289.

23. MJ to CP-Corte, Rio, 28 Dec. 1860, draft, AN, SPE, IJJ 5-43 (italics mine); Francisco de Paula Ferreira de Rezende, *Minhas recordações* (Rio de Janeiro, 1944), p. 124; PP-RJ to MI, Niterói, 31 Dec. 1860, AN, SPE, IJJ 5-43.

24. "Lei, 1846," art. 2; PP-RS to MJ, Pôrto Alegre, 30 Aug. 1860, AN, SPE, IJJ 5-43; PP-CE to MJ, Fortaleza, 14 Dec. 1860, AN, SPE, IJJ 5-43. The 1846 law responded to such steps as reported in 2º JP to PP-BA, Cachoeira, 26 Nov. 1840, APEB, Presidência, Juizes, Cachoeira, M.2273.

25. Actas da Mesa Parochial de Pirassinunga, 7 Sept. 1872, copy encl. in PP-SP to MI, São Paulo, 25 Nov. 1872, AN, SPE, IJJ 5-30; Mesa Parochial de Victoria to PP-BA, Victoria, 19 Sept. 1860, ibid., 5-25; JM to PP-SP, Pirassinunga, n.d., encl. in PP-SP to MI, 25 Nov. 1872, ibid., 5-30; Acta da Meza Parochial da Freguezia de Sant'Anna, Rio de Janeiro, 30 Dec. 1860-22 Jan. 1861, AGCRJ, 63-3-32; Acta da Mesa Parochial da Freguezia de S. Sebastião dos Aflitos, Ubá, Sept. 9, 1860, copy encl. in PP-MG to MI, Ouro Preto, 19 Oct. 1860, AN, SPE, IJJ 9-482; Delegado to PP-PA, Macapá, 6 Jan. 1861, copy encl. in PP-PA to MJ, Belém, 26 Jan. 1861, AN, SPE, IJJ 5-43; PP-CE to JP-Crato, Fortaleza, 4 Dec. 1860, copy encl. in PP-CE to MJ, Fortaleza, 14 Dec. 1860, AN, SPE, IJJ 5-43.

26. [Antonio Alves de Souza Carvalho], *O imperialismo e a reforma, anotado por um constitucional do Maranhão* (Maranhão [São Luiz?], 1866), pp. 46-47.

27. BCCD, Secretaria, comp., *Falas do Trono desde o ano de 1823 até o ano de 1889, acompanhadas dos respectivos votos de graça da câmara temporária e de diferentes informações*, [2d ed.?] (São Paulo, [1977?]), p. 222.

28. Instruções, 27 Sept. 1856, appended to *LB*, Decreto 2621, 22 Aug. 1860; "Decreto, 1860," arts. 11, 13 (compare "Lei, 1846," art. 50).

29. JD to PP-RS, São Borja, 6 Jan. 1861, Acta da Mesa Parochial de São Francisco de São Borja, 30 Dec. 1860, copy, both encl. in PP-RS to MJ, Pôrto Alegre, 13 May 1861, AN, SPE, IJJ 5-43; "Decreto, 1881," art. 15, par. 19. The Republic's first electoral law required that the empty ballot box be shown to the voters before the first voter was summoned to vote, thus suggesting another common way of fraudulent victory: *LB*, Lei 35, 26 Jan. 1892, art. 43, par. 8.

30. Cotegipe to Junqueira, Rio, 4 Oct. 1884, copy of draft, AIHGB, CC, L31, D97; Acta da Meza Parochial da Freguezia de Sant'Anna, Rio de Janeiro, 30 Dec. 1860-22 Jan. 1861, AGCRJ, 63-3-32; PP-RN to MJ, Natal, 24 Sept. 1860, AN, SPE, IJJ 5-43; *LB*, Aviso 168, 28 June 1849; Auto de Exame, Freguezia da Conceição da Feira, Cachoeira, 2 Dec. 1856, copy in [Álvaro Tiberio de Moncorvo e Lima], *Eleição do 3º districto da provincia da Bahia* (Salvador, 1857), p. 40; Actas do Conselho de Estado Pleno, 14 Oct. 1858, AN, Cód. 307, Vol. 3, fl. 33; A. Carvalho, *Imperialismo*, p. 47; Francisco Belisário Soares de Souza, *O sistema eleitoral no império (com apêndice contendo a legislação eleitoral no período 1821-1889)* (Brasília, 1979), p. 33. Only in 1881 did the law call for poll watch-

ers: *LB*, Decreto 8213, 13 Aug. 1881, art. 131. In 1892 lawmakers specified that two members of the board should see each ballot before a third
one read the name "in a loud voice," and that still another board member
should write the name down while "adding the votes in a loud voice": *LB*,
Lei 35, 26 Jan. 1892.

31. Manoel de Freitas Bello to JD, 27 Aug. 1860, encl. in PP-MG to MI,
Ouro Preto, 19 Oct. 1860, AN, SPE, IJJ 9-482.

32. "Lei, 1846," art. 87; Antonio Moreira de Barros to Cotegipe, n.p.,
21 Dec. 1880, AIHGB, CC, L9, D42; João Francisco Lisboa, *Obras*, 2d
ed. (Lisbon, 1901), I, 158; speech of Viriato Bandeira Duarte, 15 Apr.
1861, BCCD, *Anais*, 1861, I, 4.

33. F. B. S. Souza, *Sistema eleitoral*, p. 40; Braz Carneiro Nogueira da
Gama, conde de Baependy, to Jeronimo José Teixeira Júnior, Sta. Rosa, 26
Dec. 1860, AN, SAP, Col. Teixeira Júnior, AP 23, Correspondência Pas-
siva, Doc. 99.

34. Actas do Conselho de Estado Pleno, 14 Oct. 1858, AN, Cód. 307,
Vol. 3, fl. 36; Junqueira to Cotegipe, Salvador, 26 Sept. 1884, AIHGB, CC,
L31, D97 (italics in original); Manuel Luiz Osorio, marquês do Herval,
Papeis relativos a eleições, AIHGB, L233, D7950, D7959.

35. Speech of Antonio Gonçalves Barbosa da Cunha, 10 June 1861,
BCCD, *Anais*, 1861, II, 93; Antonio de Moraes Silva, *Diccionario da lingua portugueza*, 8th ed. (Rio de Janeiro, 1889-91) (the word has African
origins); F. B. S. Souza, *Sistema eleitoral*, p. 31; JP to JD-Taubaté, Caçapava, 26 Dec. 1860, copy encl. in PP-SP to MJ, São Paulo, 20 Jan. 1861,
AN, SPE, IJJ 5-43.

36. Acta da Meza Parochial da Freguezia de Sant'Anna 30 Dec. 1860-
22 Jan. 1861, with encl. JP-Freguezia de Sant'Anna to MI, Rio, 31 Dec.
1860, copy, AGCRJ, 63-3-32; Junqueira to Cotegipe, Rio, 22 Aug. 1872,
AIHGB, CC, L31, D30; Delegado to PP-CE, Sobral, 12 Dec. 1860, copy
encl. in PP-CE to MJ, Fortaleza, 29 Dec. 1860, AN, SPE, IJJ, 5-43; MI to
PP-PE, 13 Aug. 1863, draft, AN, SPE, IJJ, 1-316; PP-CE to MJ, 28 Sept.
1860, CP-Corte to MJ, Rio, 30 Dec. 1860, both in ibid., 5-43.

37. PP-CE to MJ, 28 Sept. 1860, AN, SPE, IJJ 5-43; PP-BA to PM,
Salvador, 19 Jan. 1886, telegram, reproduced in editor's note in Pedro II,
Cartas do imperador D. Pedro II ao barão de Cotegipe (São Paulo, 1933),
p. 268.

38. Delegado and JM to PP-CE, Quixeramobim, 10 Dec. 1860, encl. in
PP-CE to MJ, Fortaleza, 20 Dec. 1860, AN, SPE, IJJ 5-43; Delegado to PP-
CE, Sobral, 12 Dec. 1860, copy encl. in PP-CE to MJ, Fortaleza, 29 Dec.
1860, ibid., 5-43; speech of Silveira Lobo, 18 Apr. 1861, BCCD, *Anais*,
1861, I, 21. Also see Antonio Alves de Souza Carvalho, *O Brasil em 1870,
estudo político* (Rio de Janeiro, 1870), p. 39.

39. JP-Freguezia de Sant'Anna to MI, Rio, 31 Dec. 1860, encl. in Acta
da Meza Parochial, 30 Dec. 1860-22 Jan. 1861, AGCRJ, 63-3-32; Manoel
Francisco Correia to Cotegipe, Rio, 22 Aug. 1872, AIHGB, CC, L17, D58;
JD-Muriahé to PP-MG, Ubá, 12 Oct. 1860, encl. in PP-MG to MI, Ouro

Preto, 19 Oct. 1860, AN, SPE, IJJ 9-482, fls. 147ff; PP-CE to MJ, Fortaleza, 28 Sept. 1860, AN, SPE, IJJ 5-43.
40. A. Carvalho, *Brasil em 1870*, p. 40. On the costs and benefits of electoral clientelism, compare N. A. O. Lyttleton, "El patronazgo en la Italia de Giolitti (1892-1924)," *Revista de Occidente*, 127 (Oct. 1973), 95, with John Duncan Powell, "Peasant Society and Clientist Politics," *American Political Science Review*, 64: 12 (June 1970), 416.
41. Actas do Conselho de Estado Pleno, 14 Oct. 1858, AN, Cód. 307, Vol. 3, fl. 36v; Delegado supplente to JD, Taperoa, 12 Dec. 1856, APEB, Presidência, Eleições, M.2794.
42. JD to PP-PB, Pombal, 26 Dec. 1860, copy encl. in PP-PB to MJ, 9 Mar. 1861, AN, SPE, IJJ 5-43; Affonso Celso de Assis Figueiredo [Sr.] to Cotegipe, Rio, 25 Jan. 1888, AIHGB, CC, L23, D93.
43. Enclosures in PP-CE to MJ, Fortaleza, 14 Dec. 1860, AN, SPE, IJJ 5-43.
44. PP-CE to MJ, Fortaleza, 29 Dec. 1860, ibid., 5-43. The same technique was used in Sergipe two years earlier: Actas do Conselho de Estado Pleno, 14 Oct. 1858, AN, Cód. 307, Vol. 3, fl. 33v. As early as 1655 the Governor General of São Paulo resolved interfamily struggles by arranging for equal numbers of officials from each group to serve in the County Council: Provisão que veiu do senhor governador geral da cidade da Bahia Dom Jeronymo de Athaide, conde de Athougia," [Salvador, 24 Nov. 1655], in São Paulo (city), Prefeitura, Arquivo Municipal, *Registo geral da câmara da cidade de São Paulo*, II: *1637-1660* (São Paulo, 1917), pp. 440-47.
45. JD to PP-BA, Caitité, 12 Dec. 1856, copy, APEB, Presidência, Eleições, M.2794. Encouraging the submission of duplicate minutes was not unusual. See also PP-BA to MI, Salvador, 16 Feb. 1867, AN, SPE, IJJ 9-343.
46. Rio de Janeiro (diocese), Bishop, *Representação dirigida ao illm. e exm. sr. ministro e secretario de estado dos negocios do Imperio pelo bispo de S. Sebastião do Rio de Janeiro pedindo para que as eleições politicas se fação fóra das igrejas* (Rio de Janeiro, 1872), pp. 3-4, 10-11, 12-13. Indeed, foreigners were scandalized: José Murilo de Carvalho, *Os bestializados: O Rio de Janeiro e a república que não foi* (São Paulo, 1987), p. 175 n.32.
47. JD-Taubaté to PP-SP, Caçapava, 3 Jan. 1861, copy encl. in PP-SP to MJ, 20 Jan. 1861, AN, SPE, IJJ 5-43; Parecer da commissão de poderes, 27 May 1861, BCCD, *Anais*, 1861, I, 414.

Chapter 6

1. Quoted in JM to PP-SP, Caçapava, 30 Dec. 1860, copy encl. in PP-SP to MJ, São Paulo, 20 Jan. 1861, AN, SPE, IJJ 5-43. Except where otherwise noted, the account of these events is drawn from this provincial president's report or from the following enclosures (all of which are copies): JP to JD-Taubaté, Caçapava, 26 Dec. 1860; JM to PP-SP, Caçapava, 30 Dec. 1860; Delegado-Caçapava to PP-SP, Taubaté, 30 Dec. 1860; PP-SP to JD-Taubaté, São Paulo, 31 Dec. 1860; JM-Caçapava to PP-SP, Taubaté, 30 Dec.

1860, 1 Jan. 1861; JP to PP-SP, Caçapava, 1 Jan. 1861; JD-Taubaté to PP-SP, Caçapava, 3 Jan. 1861 (two letters of this date); PP-SP to CP-SP, São Paulo, 5 Jan. 1861. I will refer to these letters and other enclosures in short form hereafter.

2. JD-Taubaté to JP-Caçapava, Pindamonhangaba, 27 Dec. 1860; Marcelino José de Carvalho quoted in ibid. On the lands owned by these four men and the names of their neighbors, see Registro de Terras, AESP, no. 51: Caçapava, Regs. 4, 92, 138, 236, fls. 2v, 28v, 43, 70v, respectively.

3. JP to PP-SP, Caçapava, 1 Jan. 1861; Delegado-Caçapava to PP-SP, Taubaté, 30 Dec. 1860.

4. BCCD, *Anais*, 1861, I, 415.

5. CP-SP to PP-SP, Itaquaquecituba, 3 Jan. 1861.

6. Maria Thereza Schorer Petrone, "Terras devolutas, posses, e sesmarias no Vale do Paraíba paulista em 1854," *Revista de História*, 52 (July-Sept. 1976), 388; Brazil, Directoria Geral de Estatistica, *Recenseamento da população do Imperio do Brazil a que se procedeu no dia 1º de agosto de 1872* (Rio de Janeiro, 1873-76); Brazil, MI, *Relatorio*, 1870, Anexo C, p. 48. Taubaté had a population of 18,933 in 1872, including 3,708 slaves.

7. Speech of Joaquim Otavio Nebias, 7 June 1861, BCCD, *Anais*, 1861, II, 65 (I have translated *parcialidade* as faction throughout this book); Delegado-Caçapava to PP-SP, Taubaté, 30 Dec. 1860, JD-Taubaté to PP-SP, Caçapava, 3 Jan. 1861; Lista dos cidadãos votantes e elegiveis da freguesia de Cassapava e seu termo, 19 Aug. 1842, Copia autentica da acta de qualificação, Cassapava, 18 Jan. 1847, 16 Jan. 1848, Acta da revisão qualificadora, Cassapava, 21 Jan. 1849, Lista dos cidadãos votantes, Cassapava, 16 Jan. 1853, Acta da apuração das listas, Caçapava, 8 Nov. 1856, Copia da lista geral dos cidadãos votantes, Cassapava, 17 Jan. 1860, all in AESP, L47, no. 5735. Also see Camara Municipal de Caçapava to PP-SP, 8 Apr. 1856, AESP, Cx. 52, no. 846.

8. JD-Taubaté to PP-SP, Caçapava, 3 Jan. 1861 (first letter of this date); PP-SP to MJ, São Paulo, 20 Jan. 1861.

9. JD-Taubaté to PP-SP, Pindamonhangaba, 27 Dec. 1860; PP-SP to JD-Taubaté, São Paulo, 31 Dec. 1860; JD to CP-SP, n.p., 5 Jan. 1861; JD-Taubaté to PP-SP, Caçapava, 3 Jan. 1861; PP-SP to JD-Taubaté, São Paulo, 31 Dec. 1860.

10. In addition, he held power-of-attorney for other landowners, including an illiterate who had purchased his land from Carvalho: Registro de Terras, AESP, no. 43: Parahybuna, Regs. 355, 380, 381, 382, 383, 385, 387, fls. 93v, 100-120v.

11. Delegado-Caçapava to PP-SP, Taubaté, 30 Dec. 1860; JP to PP-SP, Caçapava, 1 Jan. 1861.

12. JM to PP-SP, Caçapava, 30 Dec. 1860; JD-Taubaté to PP-SP, Caçapava, 1 Jan. 1861 (second letter of this date); JM-Caçapava to PP-SP, Taubaté, 30 Dec. 1860 (the public prosecutor, or *promotor*, was the son-in-law of Joaquim Francisco de Moura). On Moura's property, a large *fazenda*, see AESP, Registro de Terras, no. 51: Caçapava, Reg. 185, fl. 56,

14 Apr. 1856; and on Moura's position as delegado in Taubaté and the importance of his family there, Emília Viotti da Costa, *Da senzala à colônia* (São Paulo, 1966), p. 47.

13. Cotegipe to Junqueira, Rio, 23 Nov. 1882, AIHGB, CC, L31, D86; marginal comments by "Silva," 30 Jan. 1861, and João Lustosa da Cunha Paranaguá, Feb. 3, 1861, on PP-SP to MJ, 20 Jan. 1861, AN, SPE, IJJ 5-43. On Paranaguá, also see Robert Brent Toplin, *The Abolition of Slavery in Brazil* (New York, 1972), p. 81; and Robert Edgar Conrad, *The Destruction of Brazilian Slavery, 1850-1888* (Berkeley, Calif., 1972), p. 183.

14. BCCD, *Anais*, 1861, I, 418; Acta da installação da mesa para a nomeação de quinze eleitores, Cassapava, 25 Aug. 1861, AESP, L47, no. 5735. Caçapava was still considered a spot of likely disorder at election time 15 years later: JD-Taubaté to PP-SP, Caçapava, 20 Oct. 1876, telegram, ibid.

15. Venancio Felix da Rocha to JD-Taubaté, Caçapava, 10 Feb. 1859, AESP, Cx. 52, no. 846; John Armitage, *The History of Brazil from the Period of the Arrival of the Braganza Family in 1808 to the Abdication of Don Pedro the First in 1831* (London, 1836), II, 148; Herculano Ferreira Penna (PP-MG) to José Thomaz Nabuco de Araújo (MJ), Ouro Preto, 2 Nov., 6 Nov. 1856, AIHGB, L365, D11. On local personal connections in elections, also see PP-RS to PM, Pôrto Alegre, 9 Dec. 1871, draft, AN, SAP, Cx. 781, Pac. 2; and Affonso Celso de Assis Figueiredo Júnior, *Oito annos de parlamento. Poder pessoal de D. Pedro II. Reminiscencias e notas* (São Paulo: Melhoramentos, n.d.), pp. 15, 20-21. A comparable situation in Sardinia is described by Alex Weingrod, "Patrons, Patronage, and Political Parties," *Comparative Studies in Society and History*, 10: 4 (July 1968), 392; also note the relationship between formal and informal political structures described by Eric R. Wolf, "Kinship, Friendship, and Patron-Client Relations in Complex Societies," in *The Social Anthropology of Complex Societies*, ed. Michael Banton (London, 1966) pp. 1-2.

16. João Antonio de Vasconcellos to Zacharias de Góes e Vasconcellos, Salvador, 24 Nov. 1865, AMIP, I-ZGV, 24.11.865, Vasc.c.; Manuel Pinto de Souza Dantas to Cotegipe, Salvador, 18 July 1856, AIHGB, CC, L19, D19. Also see *HGCB*, no. 5, p. 52.

17. João Lins Vieira Cansansão de Sinimbú, quoted in Manoel Pinto de Souza Dantas to Cotegipe, Salvador, 26 Sept. 1856, AIHGB, CC, L19, D25; Francisco de Paula de Negreiros Sayão Lobato to João Vieira Machado da Cunha, Rio, 21 July 1863, AN, SAP, Cód. 112, Vol. 8, Doc. 13w; Paulino José Soares de Souza (2º), form letter, Rio, 26 Aug. 1872, AN, SAP, Cód. 112, Vol. 6, Doc. 38; Ruy Barbosa to Francisco Gomes de Oliveira, Salvador, 2 Aug. 1878, draft, CRB, unnum. See also Ruy Barbosa to Antonio Coutinho de Souza, Salvador, 19 Aug. 1878, copy, CRB, Col. F. Nery, unnum.

18. Paulino José Soares de Souza (2º) to Francisco Belisario Soares de Sousa, Cantagallo, 29 June 1863, AIHGB, L277, D71. Referring to the

campaign as a "pilgrimage" was not uncommon; see Francisco Primo de Sousa Paraíso to Ruy Barbosa, Cachoeira, 29 Nov. 1885, CRB. Given the hazards of travel, the term was apt: during the entire course of the Empire, only one candidate for Parliament ever visited the district of northern Minas Gerais: Figueiredo Jr., *Oito annos*, p. 16. On linkages between national deputies and local factions in Spain and Italy, see N. A. O. Lyttleton, "El patronazgo en la Italia de Giolitti (1892-1924)," *Revista de Occidente*, 127 (Oct. 1973), 98.

19. Guahy to Cotegipe, Salvador, 19 Dec. 1885, AIHGB, CC, L38, D32 (italics in original). On letters by women, see Manuel Pinto de Souza Dantas to Cotegipe, Salvador, 18 Jan. 1856, ibid., L19, D9; and Ana Benigna de Sá Barreto Nabuco de Araújo to João Lustosa da Cunha Paranaguá, visconde de Paranaguá, Santa Catarina, 19 Oct. 1884, AMIP, I-DPP, 19.10.884, Nab.c. Women penned 3% of the 577 letters of recommendation examined in Chap. 8; an additional 3% of the letters referred to the office seeker as an in-law.

20. Figueiredo Jr., *Oito annos*, pp. 121-26.

21. VPP-SE to MJ, Sergipe, [1851], AN, SAP, Cx. 783, Pac. 2; Guahy to Cotegipe, Salvador, 19 Dec. 1885, AIHGB, CC, L38, D32; PP-SE to MJ, Sergipe, n.d. [1851] and 3 Feb. 1851, AN, SAP, Cx. 783, Pac. 2 (also PP-SE to MJ, Sergipe, 3 Sept. 1851, ibid.). In these letters of 1851 I have translated Saquarema as Conservative and Luzia as Liberal, avoiding the nicknames that soon fell into disuse. On Maroim's place in Parliament, see Brazil, Arquivo Nacional [Jorge João Dodsworth, 2º barão de Javari], *Organizações e programas ministeriais. Regime parlamentar no império*, 2d ed. (Rio de Janeiro, 1962), pp. 315, 416.

22. Pedro II, "Conselhos à regente d. Isabel (1876)," in Hélio Viana, *D. Pedro I e D. Pedro II: Acréscimos às suas biografias* (São Paulo, 1966), p. 241.

23. Francisco Belisário Soares de Souza, *O sistema eleitoral no império (com apêndice contendo a legislação eleitoral no período 1821-1889)* (Brasília, 1979), p. 6.

24. Junqueira to Cotegipe, Salvador, 6 Sept. 1881, AIHGB, CC, L31, D84; Brazil, Arquivo Nacional, *Organizações e programas*, pp. 262, 375, 394. Cicero Dantas Martins, barão de Geremoabo, did present a complaint to parliament: Relação da 2ª Commissão, sessão preparatoria, 5 Jan. 1882, BCCD, *Anais*, 1881 [i.e., 1881-82], I, 60.

25. Cotegipe to Junqueira, Rio, 23 Aug., 15 Sept. 1881, typescript copies of drafts, AIHGB, CC, L31, D82, D84.

26. VPP-SE to MJ, Sergipe, [1851], AN, SAP, Cx. 783, Pac. 2.

27. João Francisco Lisboa, *Obras*, 2d ed. (Lisbon, 1901), I, 110, 158. The tendency continues today: Daniel R. Gross, "Factionalism and Local Level Politics in Rural Brazil," *Journal of Anthropological Research*, 29: 2 (Summer 1973), 123-44.

28. F. B. S. Souza, *Sistema eleitoral*, p. 80; Relatorio da commissão do Senado, 5 June 1846, in BCCD, *Reforma eleitoral: Projectos offerecidos á consideração do corpo legislativo desde o ano de 1826 até o anno de 1875*

... *colligidos na secretaria da Camara dos Deputados* (Rio de Janeiro, 1875), p. 208; Joaquim Pinto de Campos [Um Pernambucano], *Os anarquistas e a civilização: Ensaio politico sobre a situação* (Rio de Janeiro, 1860), p. 25; Antonio Ferreira Vianna, quoted by Raimundo Magalhães Júnior, *Três panfletários do segundo reinado: Francisco de Sales Torres Homem e o "Líbelo do povo"; Justiniano José da Rocha e "Ação; reação; transação"; Antônio Ferreira Vianna e "A conferência dos divinos"* (São Paulo, 1956), p. 223. Compare Richard Hofstadter, *The Idea of a Party System: The Rise of Legitimate Opposition in the United States, 1780-1840* (Berkeley, Calif., 1969), pp. 2-65, 224, 258-60. Hofstadter points out that it is the development of a mass electorate that leads to the creation of parties in the modern sense, for they are needed to mediate between parliamentary "parties" and the voters. This need did not arise in the U.S. until the 1820s and in England until the 1860s: pp. 41-42, 45. Some later historians followed contemporaries in bewailing the gap between Brazilian politics and the imagined situation in Europe: compare Figueiredo Jr., *Oito annos*, pp. 216-20, with Francisco José de Oliveira Vianna, *Instituições políticas brasileiras* (Rio de Janeiro, 1949), I, 203.

29. E.g., PP-SE to MI, Aracajú, [22 July 1851], AN, SAP, Cx. 783, Pac. 2; Cotegipe to Junqueira, Rio, Aug. 7, 1881, typescript copy of draft, AIHGB, CC, L31, D81.

30. See, on this point, William Nisbet Chambers, *Political Parties in a New Nation: The American Experience, 1776-1809* (New York, 1963), p. 82; and John Duncan Powell, "Peasant Society and Clientist Politics," *American Political Science Review*, 64: 2 (June 1970), 416.

31. Cotegipe to Junqueira, Salvador, 7 June 1872, draft, AIHGB, CC, L31, D19; Lisboa, *Obras*, I, 158; speech of Martin Francisco, 18 Apr. 1861, BCCD, *Anais*, 1861, I, 18.

32. Cotegipe to Junqueira, Rio, 8 Apr. [1856?], draft, AIHGB, CC, L30, D166.

33. Cotegipe to Junqueira, Salvador, 7 June 1872, typescript copy of draft, Junqueira to Cotegipe, Rio, 6 July 1872, Junqueira to Cotegipe, Salvador, 2 July 1881, Cotegipe to Junqueira, Rio, Aug. 7, 1881, typescript copy of draft, all in AIHGB, CC, L31, D19, D21, D80, D81.

34. Junqueira to Cotegipe, Salvador, 2 July 1881, ibid., L31, D80 (on his *compadrio*, see Guahy to Cotegipe, Salvador, 24 Jan. 1884, ibid., L37, D178); Junqueira to Cotegipe, Salvador, 26 July 1881, Cotegipe to Junqueira, Rio, Aug. 7, 1881, typescript copy of draft, both in ibid., L31, D81.

35. João Alfredo Correia de Oliveira to Cotegipe, Recife, 28 Sept. 1876, Belém, 8 Feb., 20 Jan., 8 Apr. 1870, all in AIHGB, L50, D109, D81, D83, D91; PP-RS to PM, Pôrto Alegre, 9 Dec. 1871, draft, AN, SAP, Cx. 781, Pac. 2; Cotegipe (PM) to Henrique Pereira de Lucena (PP-RS), Rio, 20 Nov. 1885, APEP, Col. Lucena, 562. Party directorates were endlessly formed and reformed; see, for example, Domingos de Sousa Leão, barão de Villa Bella, to Pedro de Araújo Lima, marquês de Olinda, Recife, 28 Oct. 1869, BN/SM, Col. Tobias Monteiro, Pasta 7.

36. Acta da Meza Parochial da Freguezia de Sant'Anna, 30 Dec. 1860-

22 Jan. 1861, AGCRJ, 63-3-32; PP-RS to PM, Pôrto Alegre, 9 Dec. 1871, draft, AN, SAP, Cx. 781, Pac. 2; Atas do Centro Liberal, 29 Dec. 1875, AIHGB, L495, D6, fl. 18v (also see 13 Dec., 23 Dec. 1874, fls. 7v, 10v); Manuel Pinto de Souza Dantas to Luiz Felipe de Souza Leão, Rio, 6 June 1880, telegram, AIHGB, L457, D46; José Antonio Saraiva (PM) to André Augusto de Pádua Fleury (PP-CE), Rio, [end of 1880], draft, AIHGB, L275, P40; Affonso Celso de Assis Figueiredo, visconde de Ouro Preto, to Joaquim José de Sant'Anna, Rio, 8 July 1889, draft, AIHGB, L427, D17; Campos Sales, Caderno de Apontamentos sobre sua vida politica, ms, Museu Republicano da Convenção de Itú, unnum.

37. Affonso Pena to the following, all in AN, Affonso Pena Papers, uncatalogued at time of use: José Rodrigues, Santa Barbara (MG), 27 June 1875; Inácio Antonio de Assis Martins, Santa Barbara, 1 July 1875; and Candido de Luis Maria de Oliveira, Santa Barbara, 27 Mar., 15 Nov. 1876; José Bento da Cunha Figueiredo to Cotegipe, Recife, 16 Dec. 1858, AIHGB, CC, L23, D143.

38. Guahy to Cotegipe, Salvador, 25 Sept. 1884, AIHGB, CC, L38, D9; Junqueira to Cotegipe, Salvador, 11 Oct. 1884, ibid., L31, D99; Brazil, Arquivo Nacional, *Organizações e programas*, p. 375. See the frank acknowledgment of nepotism in constructing Liberal Party tickets in Figueiredo Jr., *Oito annos*, pp. 13-15.

39. Guahy to Cotegipe, Salvador, 25 Sept. 1884, AIHGB, CC, L38, D9. On Cotegipe's view of Dantas's support for Guahy, see Cotegipe to Junqueira, Rio, 9 Sept. 1881, typescript copy of draft, ibid., L31, D83.

40. Innocencio de Almeida to Ruy Barbosa, Macahubas, 6 Sept. 1878, CRB, unnum.; Lourenço Albuquerque to Luiz Felipe de Souza Leão, Engenho Velho (PE), 11 June 1885, AIHGB, L456, D47 (italics in original).

41. Manuel Pinto de Souza Dantas to Ruy Barbosa, Petrópolis, 12 Jan. 1879, in Manuel Pinto de Souza Dantas, *Correspondência* (Rio de Janeiro, 1962), p. 34.

42. Manuel Pinto de Souza Dantas to Cotegipe, S. Amaro, 31 Mar. 1856, Salvador, 24 June 1856, Rio, 7 June 1884, all in AIHGB, CC, L19, D14, D19, D55; Rufino Eneas Gustavo Galvão, visconde de Maracajú (PP-PA), to Cotegipe, 20 May 1883, ibid., L25, D82.

43. Guahy to Cotegipe, Salvador, 31 Oct. 1883, ibid., L37, D173; Barbara Weinstein, *The Amazon Rubber Boom, 1850-1920* (Stanford, Calif., 1983), pp. 102, 298 n.8.

44. Junqueira to Cotegipe, Rio, 14 Sept., 30 Sept. 1872, AIHGB, CC, L31, D33, D35.

45. Guahy to Cotegipe, Salvador, 5 Apr., 14 Sept., 25 Sept. 1884, AIHGB, CC, L38, D5, D8, D9.

46. João Alfredo Correia de Oliveira (PP-PA) to Cotegipe, Belém, 8 Feb. 1870, ibid., L50, D85.

47. References to "party" permeated contemporary political discourse, but what that term meant to those who used it has not been properly examined; unless the focus remains exclusively on members or would-be

members of Parliament, the term can be seriously misleading as, for instance, in Afonso Arinos de Melo Franco, *História e teoria dos partidos políticos no Brasil,* 2d ed. (São Paulo, 1974), pp. 29-53; José Murilo de Carvalho, "A composição social dos partidos políticos imperiais," in Minas Gerais, Universidade Federal, Departamento de Ciências Políticas, *Cadernos,* no. 2 (Dec. 1974), p. 14; and J. M. Carvalho, *Teatro de sombras: A política imperial* (São Paulo, 1988), pp. 150-57. For an analysis of the historiography of party history before 1850, see Ilmar Rohloff de Mattos, *O tempo saquarema* (São Paulo, 1987), pp. 129n-132n.

48. José de Alencar, "Cartas de Erasmo," in *Obra completa* (Rio de Janeiro, 1960), IV, 1074 (Mary Goodwin showed me this reference). On the parliamentary tendency to avoid real issues, see F. B. S. Souza, *Sistema eleitoral,* p. 46; and speech of Leopoldo Bulhões, 10 Aug. 1882, BCCD, *Anais,* 1882, III, 431.

49. The material on the political events of the Empire in these pages, unless otherwise noted, is drawn from Joaquim Nabuco, *Um estadista do império,* [3d ed.?] (Rio de Janeiro, 1975); Euclides da Cunha, *À margem da história,* in *Obra completa* (Rio de Janeiro, 1966), I, 326-76; José Maria dos Santos, *A política geral do Brasil* (São Paulo, 1930), pp. 11-185; Basílio de Magalhães, *Estudos de história do Brasil* (São Paulo, 1940), pp. 40-68; Paula Beiguelman, *Formação política do Brasil,* Vol. I: *Teoria e ação no pensamento abolicionista* (São Paulo, 1967); HGCB, nos. 5-7; Heitor Lyra, *História de Dom Pedro II, 1825-1891,* 2d rev. ed. (Belo Horizonte, 1977), II, 295-98; and Pedro Calmon, *História de D. Pedro II* (Rio de Janeiro, 1975), Vol. II.

50. Nancy Naro, "The 1848 Praieira Revolt in Brazil" (Ph.D. diss., Univ. of Chicago, 1981), pp. 105-9, 116-17, 129-36. The Conservatives in Pernambuco were also divided: ibid., pp. 98-99.

51. The process of ending the slave trade is explored by Leslie Bethell, *The Abolition of the Brazilian Slave Trade: Britain, Brazil, and the Slave Trade Question, 1807-1869* (Cambridge, Eng., 1970); and Robert Edgar Conrad, *World of Sorrow: The African Slave Trade to Brazil* (Baton Rouge, La., 1986).

52. Americo Brasiliense [de Almeida Mello], *Os programas dos partidos e o 2º imperio. Primeira parte: Exposição de principios* (São Paulo, 1878), pp. 33-57.

53. LB, Lei 2033, 20 Sept. 1871, Decreto 4824, 22 Nov. 1871, Lei 2395, 10 Sept. 1873; F. B. S. Souza, *Sistema eleitoral,* p. 15n; Conrad, *Destruction of Brazilian Slavery,* pp. 90-117; José Maria da Silva Paranhos (2º), barão do Rio Branco, *O visconde do Rio Branco,* [2d ed.?] (Rio de Janeiro, [1943?]); Lidia Besouchet, *José Mª Paranhos, Vizconde do Río Branco* (Buenos Aires, [1944]).

54. It is significant that João Camillo de Oliveira Tôrres is forced to include even heads of Liberal Cabinets in his pantheon of great Conservatives in *Os construtores do império: Ideais e lutas do Partido Conservador brasileiro* (São Paulo, 1968).

55. Conrad, *Destruction of Brazilian Slavery*, pp. 217, 221, 302. The second vote occurred before all the Deputies had arrived in Rio and been credentialed.

56. Cristiano Benedito Ottoni, *O advento da república no Brasil* (Rio de Janeiro, 1890), pp. 44-45.

57. Conrad, *Destruction of Brazilian Slavery*, pp. 121-277. The source of emancipationist strength is much debated; see Richard Graham, "Causes for the Abolition of Negro Slavery in Brazil: An Interpretive Essay," *Hispanic American Historical Review*, 46: 2 (May 1966), 123-38; R. Graham, "Brazilian Slavery Re-Examined: A Review Article," *Journal of Social History*, 3: 4 (Summer 1970), 431-53; and Costa, *Da senzala*, pp. 428-55.

58. Some contemporaries attributed the Conservative Party's greater frequency in power to the Emperor's preference for it: speech of Martinho Campos, 24 Sept. 1875, BCCD, *Anais*, 1875, V, 212; Joaquim Nabuco, *Eleições liberaes e eleições conservadoras* (Rio de Janeiro, 1886), p. 54; Luiz Peixoto de Lacerda Werneck, *Le Brésil. Dangers de sa situation politique et économique; moyens de les conjurer. Lettre à son fils. . . . Ouvrage posthume revu par F. P. de Lacerda Werneck* (Rio de Janeiro, 1889), p. 54.

59. Speech of João Alfredo, 5 Oct. 1888, BCCD, *Anais*, 1888, VI, 122; L. P. L. Werneck, *Brésil*, p. 62. On Souza's motivation, see João Manuel de Carvalho, *Reminiscencias sobre vultos e factos do imperio e da republica* (Amparo, 1894), p. xi.

60. A most conspicuous example of this argument is found in Nelson Werneck Sodré, *História da burguesia brasileira* (Rio de Janeiro, 1964), pp. 102, 172, 196-203.

61. [Antonio Coelho Rodrigues], *Manual do Subdito Fiel* [pseud.] *ou, Cartas de um lavrador a sua magestade o Imperador sobre a questão do elemento servil* (Rio de Janeiro, 1884), p. 12; JP to PP-CE, Crato, 19 Nov. 1860, copy encl. in PP-CE to MJ, Fortaleza, 14 Dec. 1860, AN, SPE, IJJ 5-423. Thomas Flory, *Judge and Jury in Imperial Brazil, 1808-1871: Social Control and Political Stability in the New State* (Austin, Tex., 1981), pp. 182-83, explores some of these issues for the first half of the 19th century; José M. Carvalho, "Composição social dos partidos," pp. 18, 21, does so for the second.

62. On ties between merchants and landowners, see Joseph E. Sweigart, *Coffee Factorage and the Emergence of a Brazilian Capital Market, 1850-1888* (New York, 1987), pp. 66-108; Pierre Monbeig, *Pionniers et planteurs de São Paulo* (Paris, 1952), p. 84; Alcir Lenharo, *As tropas da moderação (O abastecimento da Corte na formação política do Brasil, 1808-1842)* (São Paulo, 1979), pp. 47, 76; and Eugene W. Ridings, "Class Sector Unity in an Export Economy: The Case of Nineteenth-Century Brazil," *Hispanic American Historical Review*, 58: 3 (Aug. 1978), 432-50. Drawing their inspiration from other lands or from Brazil at other times, some authors have seen more opposition there than I have; see, for example, Lidia Besouchet, *Mauá y su época* (Buenos Aires, 1940), p. 74; and Raymundo Faoro, *Os donos do poder: Formação do patronato político brasileiro*, 2d ed. (Pôrto Alegre, 1975), II, 418-20.

63. Miguel Lemos, *A incorporação do proletariado escravo. Protesto da Sociedade Positivista do Rio de Janeiro contra o recente projecto do governo* (Recife, 1883), p. 10.

64. Luiz Ascendino Dantas, *Esboço biographico do dr. Joaquim José de Souza Breves. Origem das fazendas S. Joaquim da Gramma e St° Antonio da Olaria. Subsidios para a historia do municipio de S. João Marcos* (Rio de Janeiro, 1931), p. 12; Eduardo Silva, *Barões e escravidão: Três gerações de fazendeiros e a crise da estrutura escravista* (Rio de Janeiro, 1984), p. 99; Weinstein, *Amazon*, pp. 106-7; João Vieira Machado da Cunha (2°) to Braz Carneiro Nogueira da Gama, [Valença], 6 May [1890], draft, AN, SAP, Cód. 112, Vol. 9, Doc. 57. Also see Nícia Villela Luz, "O papel das classes médias brasileiras no movimento republicano," *Revista de História*, 28: 57 (Jan.-Mar. 1964), 13-27, and Richard Graham, "Landowners and the Overthrow of the Empire," *Luso-Brazilian Review*, 7: 2 (Dec. 1970), 44-56.

65. José Murilo de Carvalho, in his "Elite and State Building in Imperial Brazil" (Ph.D. diss., Stanford Univ., 1974), p. 99, shows that 75% of Senators held law degrees, with the rest being almost evenly divided among those who had studied medicine, religion, science, and military affairs. Joseph L. Love, *São Paulo in the Brazilian Federation, 1889-1937* (Stanford, Calif., 1980), p. 285, makes much the same point for a later period. Compare Eugene D. Genovese's comment, in "Yeoman Farmers in a Slaveholders' Democracy," *Agricultural History*, 49: 2 (Apr. 1975), 339, that politicians in the U.S. South were usually lawyers, "as every fool always knew." On Ruy Barbosa, see Richard Graham, *Britain and the Onset of Modernization in Brazil, 1850-1914* (Cambridge, Eng., 1968), pp. 267-76, and the sources cited therein. On Inhomerim, see Magalhães Jr., *Três panfletários*, pp. 126-59; and Floriano Torres Homem, "Francisco de Salles Torres Homem, visconde de Inhomerim," in 3° Congresso de História Nacional (1938), *Anais* (Rio de Janeiro, 1942), VI, 85-165.

66. Some analysts would call the Deputies brokers on the grounds that they did not themselves control resources but could put those who did (local bosses and Cabinet members, whether clients or patrons) in touch with one another. See Richard P. Saller, *Personal Patronage Under the Early Empire* (Cambridge, Eng., 1982), p. 74; Sharon Kettering, *Patrons, Brokers, and Clients in Seventeenth-Century France* (New York, 1986), pp. 4-11, 40-67; and Arturo Valenzuela, *Political Brokers in Chile: Local Government in a Centralized Polity* (Durham, N.C., 1977), pp. 158-61, 166-68. I myself do not find the terminology particularly helpful.

67. In analyzing the property of those Deputies who became Senators or Cabinet members, José M. Carvalho, "Composição social dos partidos," pp. 14, 26, finds that both parties drew members from the landowning class, but also notes that the Conservatives counted more heavily on judges (whom he calls bureaucrats) than the Liberals did, and that the Liberals attracted Senators and Ministers from other liberal professions. Since most liberal professionals differed from judges not in their education but in their success in gaining advantageous placement, one could conclude from their success, cor-

rectly I think, that one difference between the parties consisted in the degree of their members' satisfaction. Also see José M. Carvalho, "Elite and State Building," p. 145. On judges in Parliament, see Flory, *Judge*, p. 195.

68. Cotegipe to João Alfredo Correia de Oliveira, Rio, 3 July [1875?], typescript copy of draft, AIHGB, CC, L50, D108; Junqueira to Cotegipe, Rio, 20 Feb. 1873, ibid., L31, D45; Guahy to Cotegipe, [Salvador], 2 Oct. 1883, ibid., L37, D170; Adolpho Hasselman to Ruy Barbosa, Salvador, 23 Mar. 1875, CRB, unnum. On the home as venue for political discussion, see also Paulino José Soares de Souza, visconde de Uruguay, to José Maria da Silva Paranhos (Sr.), Rio, 1 Nov. 1858, AHI, Visc. R. B., L321, M2, P1.

69. *O Brasil*, 24 Nov. 1840, quoted by Flory, *Judge*, p. 153.

70. Affonso d'Albuquerque Mello, *A liberdade no Brasil: Seu nascimento, vida, morte, e sepultura* (Recife, 1864), p. 8; Lisboa, *Obras*, I, 107.

Chapter 7

1. J. Palhano de Jesus, "Rapida noticia da viação ferrea do Brasil," in Instituto Historico e Geographico Brasileiro, *Diccionario historico, geographico e ethnographico do Brasil (Commemorativo do primeiro centenario da independencia)* (Rio de Janeiro, 1922), I, 736-37; Brazil, Instituto Brasileiro de Geografia e Estatística, *Anuário estatístico do Brasil*, 1939-40, p. 1381; Stanley J. Stein, *The Brazilian Cotton Manufacture: Textile Enterprise in an Underdeveloped Area, 1850-1950* (Cambridge, Mass., 1957), pp. 21, 191; Robert Edgar Conrad, *The Destruction of Brazilian Slavery, 1850-1888* (Berkeley, Calif., 1972), p. 135. See also, more generally, Nathaniel H. Leff, *Underdevelopment and Development in Brazil*, Vol. I: *Economic Structure and Change, 1822-1947* (London, 1982); Caio Prado Júnior, *História econômica do Brasil*, 5th ed. (São Paulo, 1959); Nelson Werneck Sodré, *História da burguesia brasileira* (Rio de Janeiro, 1964); and Paul Singer, *Desenvolvimento econômico e evolução urbana (análise da evolução econômica de São Paulo, Blumenau, Pôrto Alegre, Belo Horizonte, e Recife)* (São Paulo, 1968).

2. See, for example, João Alfredo Correia de Oliveira to Cotegipe, Belém, 8 Apr. 1870, AIHGB, L50, D91.

3. Henrique Augusto Milet, *Os quebra-kilos e a crise da lavoura* (Recife, 1876), p. 3; Affonso Celso de Assis Figueiredo, *Reforma administrativa e municipal: Parecer e projectos* (Rio de Janeiro, 1883), pp. 73-74. The parallel fears in the city are explored by Sandra Lauderdale Graham, *House and Street: The Domestic World of Servants and Masters in Nineteenth-Century Rio de Janeiro* (Cambridge, Eng., 1988), pp. 108-16.

4. José Antonio de Figueiredo, in Antonio Herculano de Souza Bandeira, ed., *Reforma eleitoral, eleição directa: Collecção de diversos artigos sobre a eleição directa dos quaes são autores os seguintes senhores . . .* (Recife, 1862), p. 146; Ruy Barbosa, *Liberdade commercial. O partido liberal bahiano. Discurso proferido . . . na Assembléa Provincial da Bahia, na sessão de 27 de junho de 1878* (Bahia, 1878), p. 8; R. Barbosa and Francisco de Paula Belfort Duarte, quoted in *HGCB*, no. 7, pp. 219, 210,

respectively; Joaquim Pinto de Campos [Um Pernambucano], *Os anarquistas e a civilização: Ensaio politico sobre a situação* (Rio de Janeiro, 1860), pp. 58-59.

5. Figueiredo, in Bandeira, ed., *Reforma eleitoral*, pp. 164-65; Campos, *Anarquistas*, p. 58; José de Alencar, *Systema representativo* (Rio de Janeiro, 1868), pp. 96, 103; [Antonio Alves de Souza Carvalho], *O imperialismo e a reforma, anotado por um constitucional do Maranhão* (Maranhão [São Luiz?], 1866), p. 57. Far from being a new idea, direct elections had been advocated by many writers long before: Augusto Tavares de Lyra, *Esboço historico do regimen eleitoral do Brasil (1821-1921)* (Rio de Janeiro, 1922), p. 21.

6. Figueiredo, in Bandeira, ed., *Reforma eleitoral*, pp. 143, 145, 147, 152, 159, 183; Abreu e Lima, in ibid., p. 276.

7. Figueiredo, in ibid., pp. 143, 158-59, 169-70.

8. Joaquim Rodrigues de Souza, *Systema eleitoral da Constituição do Imperio do Brazil* (São Luiz, 1863), pp. 19, 21, 30, 43; Alencar, *Systema representativo*, p. 103; Americo Brasiliense [de Almeida Mello], *Os programas dos partidos e o 2° imperio. Primeira parte: Exposição de principios* (São Paulo, 1878), p. 16.

9. "Annexo no. 1," arts. 1-2, in Brasiliense, *Programas dos partidos*, p. 45; José Thomaz Nabuco de Araújo to Domingos de Sousa Leão, barão de Villa Bella, [Rio], 6 May 1869, quoted in Joaquim Nabuco, *Um estadista do império*, [3d ed.?] (Rio de Janeiro, 1975), pp. 677-78n. A. Lyra, *Esboço historico*, p. 22, correctly understands Nabuco de Araújo's thought to be that under direct elections the "serfs" would vote as told, whereas with indirect elections the rural potentates would "depend on an intermediary class," that is, on judges, lawyers, and civil servants who joined them in the Electoral Colleges, a point that Victor Nunes Leal, *Coronelismo: The Municipality and Representative Government in Brazil* (Cambridge, Eng., 1977), p. 144 n.7, does not correctly understand.

10. BCCD, *Reforma eleitoral: Projectos offerecidos á consideração do corpo legislativo desde o anno de 1826 até o anno de 1875 ... colligidos na secretaria da Camara dos Deputados* (Rio de Janeiro, 1875), pp. 416-20; Brazil, Ministerio do Imperio [Paulino José Soares de Souza (2°)], *Relatorio*, 1870, p. 19.

11. Francisco Belisário Soares de Souza, *O sistema eleitoral no império (com apêndice contendo a legislação eleitoral no período 1821-1889)* (Brasília, 1979). On the articles that led to the book, see pp. 1-2. On the author's background and earlier voting record, see *HGCB*, no. 7, pp. 141, 148-49, 151.

12. F. B. S. Souza, *Sistema eleitoral*, pp. 21, 31-34, 36, 86, 116-17, 131. For his negative view of the French Revolution, see p. 127.

13. Aureliano Cândido Tavares Bastos, *Os males do presente e as esperanças do futuro ([e outros] estudos brasileiros)*, 3d ed. (São Paulo, 1976), pp. 143-44. On his background, see Richard Graham, *Britain and the Onset of Modernization in Brazil, 1850-1914* (Cambridge, Eng.,

1968), pp. 108-9. Tavares Bastos believed that giving the urban voters greater electoral weight would aid the abolitionist cause: Aureliano Candido Tavares Bastos, manuscript scrapbook and diary, [after 1873], BN/ SM, 11, 1, 29.

14. Pedro II, *Conselhos à regente* (Rio de Janeiro, 1958), pp. 29-30, 57; Pedro II to José Antonio Pimenta Bueno, visconde de São Vicente, 29 Sept. 1870, in Nabuco, *Estadista do império*, pp. 1003-1004. For one skeptical response to proportional representation, see F. B. S. Souza, *Sistema eleitoral*, p. 15.

15. "Decreto, 1875," art. 1, pars. 2, 21; art. 2, par. 16. See model *título* attached to *LB*, Decreto 6097, 12 Jan. 1876. On the legislative history of this law from the introduction of the bill in April 1873, see BCCD, *Reforma eleitoral*, pp. 565-90, 603-5.

16. "Decreto, 1875," art. 1, par. 4; AGCRJ, 62-1-28.

17. Pedro II, "Conselhos de D. Pedro II à Regente D. Isabel (1876)," in Hélio Viana, *D. Pedro I e D. Pedro II: Acréscimos às suas biografias* (São Paulo, 1966), pp. 241-42; Pedro II, quoted in Nabuco, *Estadista do império*, p. 674. See also João Camilo de Oliveira Tôrres, *A democracia coroada (Teoria política do império do Brasil)* (Rio de Janeiro, 1957), pp. 257-58.

18. Pedro II to Luis Alves de Lima e Silva, duque de Caxias, [[Jan. 1878], quoted in Viana, *D. Pedro I e D. Pedro II*, pp. 184-85. Also see Heitor Lyra, *História de Dom Pedro II, 1825-1891*, 2d rev. ed. (Belo Horizonte, 1977), II, 277-78; and HGCB, no. 7, pp. 185-88.

19. Congresso Agricola, *Congresso Agricola: Coleção de documentos* (Rio de Janeiro, 1878), pp. 43, 48, 49, 156, 196, 207. Also see pp. 32, 47, 52, 147, 222. On the impending end of slavery, see the extended statement by one of the participants in the Congress: Henrique de Beaurepaire Rohan, *O futuro da grande lavoura e da grande propriedade no Brazil: Memoria apresentada ao Ministerio de Agricultura, Commercio e Obras Publicas* (Rio de Janeiro, 1878).

20. For the remainder of this chapter I rely heavily on HGCB, no. 7, pp. 176-243. Also see José Honório Rodrigues, *Conciliação e reforma no Brasil: Um desafio histórico-político* (Rio de Janeiro, 1965), pp. 138-63.

21. Joseph L. Love, *Rio Grande do Sul and Brazilian Regionalism, 1882-1930* (Stanford, Calif., 1971), pp. 21-23.

22. Ata da Conferencia de 7 Nov. 1878, in Brazil, Conselho de Estado, *Atas* (Brasília, 1973), X, 137-67; quotation at p. 162.

23. "Projecto de reforma da Constituição," 13 Feb. 1879, BCCD, *Anais*, 1878 [*sic*], II, 492.

24. José Bonifácio de Andrade e Silva (the Younger) and Joaquim Nabuco, quoted in HGCB, no. 7, pp. 205, 207, 209.

25. Ruy Barbosa and Lafayete Rodrigues Pereira, quoted in ibid., pp. 215, 219. Also see pp. 211, 216.

26. [Cotegipe, Parecer sobre a eleição directa], 1879[?], ms, AIHGB, CC, L88, D28; speech of João da Silva Carrão, 28 Dec. 1880, BCS, *Anais*, 1880, Sessão Extraordinaria, III, 293.

27. H. Lyra, *História de Dom Pedro II*, II, 277; Sandra Lauderdale Graham, "The Vintem Riot and Political Culture: Rio de Janeiro, 1880," *Hispanic American Historical Review*, 60: 3 (Aug. 1980), 431-49.

28. José Wanderley de Araújo Pinho, *Política e políticos no império* (Rio de Janeiro, 1930), pp. 7-11; Eul-Soo Pang, *O Engenho Central do Bom Jardim na economia baiana. Alguns aspectos de sua história, 1875-1891* (Rio de Janeiro, 1979), p. 45.

29. Ata da Conferencia de 7 Nov. 1878, in Brazil, Conselho de Estado, *Atas*, X, 142, 144, 149-51, 159-60, 163.

30. Speech of Saraiva, 7 June 1880, BCCD, *Anais*, 1880, II, 92. The basic idea here was not new. Francisco Gê Acaiaba de Montezuma, visconde de Jequitinhonha, had years before made the argument that if net income were properly defined, direct elections could be safely conducted without constitutional amendment; cited by Figueiredo, in Bandeira, ed., *Reforma eleitoral*, p. 226. Francisco Belisário Soares de Souza had made the same point in his *Sistema eleitoral*, p. 26; and, as we have seen, that was the idea of the 1875 law, although it allowed many loopholes.

31. José Antonio Saraiva, "Bases para o projecto da reforma eleitoral," [Mar. or Apr. 1880], facsim., in Rui Barbosa, *Discursos parlamentares, Camara dos Deputados*, in *Obras completas*, 7 (1880), Tomo 1 (Rio de Janeiro, 1945), pp. 259-79. On the history of this bill, see ibid., pp. 283-313, 321-58; and Americo Jacobina Lacombe, ibid., pp. 4-5. Barbosa's own views were certainly consistent with the thrust of the law, even though he sometimes imagined himself on the side of the workers: Barbosa to Manuel Pinto de Souza Dantas, Rio, 17 May 1880, in Manuel Pinto de Souza Dantas, *Correspondência* (Rio de Janeiro, 1962), pp. 39-43; "Estatutos . . . 1876," encl. in Sociedade Liga Operaria Bahiana to PP-BA, Salvador, 18 Aug. 1876, APEB, M.1575, caderno 35.

32. "Decreto, 1881," arts. 2-4; speech of Saraiva, 7 June 1880, BCCD, *Anais*, 1880, II, 92.

33. Joaquim Nabuco, quoted in J. H. Rodrigues, *Conciliação e reforma*, p. 150.

34. "Decreto, 1881," art. 6. In the 20th century this trend was completed with the creation of a separate court system to deal exclusively with electoral matters: V. Leal, *Coronelismo*, p. 66; Francisco José de Oliveira Vianna, *Instituições políticas brasileiras* (Rio de Janeiro, 1949), pp. 200-201.

35. Speeches of Saraiva, 4 June, 7 June 1880, BCCD, *Anais*, 1880, II, 34-44, 91.

36. "Projecto," art. 4, par. 9, 2 July 1880, BCS, *Anais*, 1880, III, 30; "Decreto, 1881," art. 8. See also *LB*, Decreto 8213, 13 Aug. 1881, art. 60; and "Consultas sobre of projecto de regulamento para execução da Lei no. 3029 de 9 de janeiro de 1881, 11 de agosto de 1881," ms in Consultas do Conselho de Estado, Seção do Imperio, AN, SPE, Cx. 558, Pac. 3, D47. Although it is often said that the Republic, declared in 1889, instituted a literacy test for voting, this is not entirely true. Those who had been electors in 1881, even if not literate, continued to be qualified to vote under

the Republic, but new voters, as had been true since 1882, had to prove their literacy: *LB*, Decreto 200-A, 8 Feb. 1890, arts. 58, 69, Lei 35 de 26 Jan. 1892, art. 22.

37. "Proposta," arts. 2, 8, BCCD, *Anais*, 1880, Extraordinaria, I, 30-31.

38. Brazil, *Constituição política do Império do Brasil*, art. 5. Art. 95 had excluded from Parliament those who did not profess the religion of the state, and proof of eligibility had heretofore depended on sworn oral statements; now the law required written sworn statements covering various matters (e.g., income, age), but religion was not among them.

39. Alencar, *Systema representativo*, p. 145; Rio de Janeiro (diocese), Bishop, *Representação dirigida ao illm. e exm. sr. ministro e secretario de estado dos negocios do Imperio pelo bispo de S. Sebastião do Rio de Janeiro pedindo para que as eleições politicas se fação fóra das igrejas* (Rio de Janeiro, 1872), p. 13; "Decreto, 1881," art. 15, par. 6. The original bill had still placed elections in the churches: "Proposta," art. 14, BCCD, *Anais*, 1880, Extraordinaria, I, 32.

40. "Decreto, 1881," art. 15, pars. 1, 2, 4 (elections no longer took place on Sundays, but were held on the first weekday of the month); Francisco de Paula Ferreira de Rezende, *Minhas recordações* (Rio de Janeiro, 1944), p. 124. An example of the new businesslike proceedings can be found in Acta . . . da mesa eleitoral . . . parochia do Espirito Santo . . . Municipio Neutro, 31 Aug. 1889, AGCRJ, 65-2-51, fls. 1-3; also see the bids received for the iron railings "1.5 meters (7 hands) high": AGCRJ, 61-4-34, fls. 58-59.

41. On the number of registered electors, compare João Manuel Pereira da Silva, *Memorias do meu tempo* (Paris, [1896?]), II, 225, from which I have taken this estimate for 1881, with Brazil, Ministerio do Imperio, *Relatorio*, 1870, p. 20, which shows 1,039,659 registered voters in 1870. The number of electors who actually voted in 1881 (as distinct from those registered to vote) was 96,411: Brazil, Arquivo Nacional [Jorge João Dodsworth, 2° barão de Javari], *Organizações e programas ministeriais. Regime parlamentar no império*, 2d ed. (Rio de Janeiro, 1962), p. 379. Admittedly, there had been only 20,006 electors in 1870, so the number directly choosing Deputies had certainly increased. On reaction to the new law, see H. Lyra, *História de Dom Pedro II*, II, 289.

42. Consultas do Conselho de Estado, Secção de Justiça, 10 May 1881, AN, SPE, Cx. 558, Pac. 3. One Councillor noted attempts to evade the law by sales contracts providing for land to revert automatically to the original owner after a certain period: Luiz Pedreira do Couto Ferraz, visconde do Bom Retiro, Parecer, 11 Aug. 1881, in ibid. Other issues concerning the application of the law can be found in Consultas for 9 Aug. 1882, ibid., Cx. 559, Pac. 4, D49.

43. Recurso eleitoral, 30 Dec. 1882, Antonio Alves da Rocha, recorrente, Juizado do Direito de Pirahy, recorrido, AN, SPJ, Appellação, no. 664, Cx. 11.917 [old Cx. 69, Gal. C]; *LB*, Decreto 3133, 7 Oct. 1882. The

lessor in question was a close relative of Joaquim José de Souza Breves in Piraí.

44. Martinho Alvares da Silva Campos to José Antonio Saraiva, Rio, 1 May 1880, Niterói, 19 Nov. 1881, AIHGB, L270, D8; José Luiz de Almeida Nogueira to Martim Francisco Ribeiro de Andrade (on district boundaries), Bananal, 11 Oct. 1880, AIHGB, L325, D15; F. Sodré to Cupertino do Amaral, Santo Amaro (BA), Mar. 29, 1881, AN, SAP, Amaro Cavalcanti Papers (being renumbered at time of use); Affonso Pena to José Antonio da Silva Drummond, Santa Barbara, 23 Apr. 1881, AN, SAP, Affonso Pena Papers (uncatalogued at time of use); [Manoel Peixoto de Lacerda Werneck], *O visconde de Ipiabas, Peregrino José de America Pinheiro: Perfil biographico, acompanhado do retracto do finado e seguido de algumas allocuções pronunciadas por ocasião de seus funeraes* (Rio de Janeiro, 1882), p. 20.

45. Henrique Augusto Milet, *Miscellanea economica e politica* (Recife, 1882), p. 73.

46. Guahy to Cotegipe, Salvador, 16 Oct. 1885, AIHGB, CC, L38, D19; PP-BA to PM, Salvador, 18 Feb. 1886, quoted in editor's note in Pedro II, *Cartas do imperador D. Pedro II ao barão de Cotegipe* (São Paulo, 1933), p. 273.

47. Brazil, Arquivo Nacional, *Organizações e programas*, pp. 379, 388, 398; H. Lyra, *História de Dom Pedro II*, II, 290-91. Joaquim Nabuco, *Eleições liberaes e eleições conservadoras* (Rio de Janeiro, 1886), pp. 51-52, could still charge the Conservatives with the major responsibility for thwarting the will of the people by controlling elections.

48. C. F. van Delden Laerne, *Brazil and Java: Report on Coffee-Culture in America, Asia and Africa to H.E. the Minister of the Colonies* (London, 1885), p. 309n. On gathering necessary documents, see, for example, Zacharias Vieira Machado da Cunha to JD-Valença, Sta. Thereza de Valença, 17 Jan. 1883, AN, SAP, Cód. 112, Vol. 9, D130.

49. Joseph L. Love, *São Paulo in the Brazilian Federation, 1889-1937* (Stanford, Calif., 1980), pp. 105-6; Luiz Peixoto de Lacerda Werneck, *Le Brésil. Dangers de sa situation politique et économique; moyens de les conjurer. Lettre à son fils. . . . Ouvrage posthume revu par F. P. de Lacerda Werneck* (Rio de Janeiro, 1889), p. 47 (quoted). Raymundo Faoro is mistaken, however, in arguing that the landed classes *desired* direct elections in order to increase their influence: *Os donos do poder: Formação do patronato político brasileiro*, 2d ed. (Pôrto Alegre, 1975), I, 374.

50. Lourenço de Albuquerque (Min. Foreign Affairs) interrupting speech of Felicio dos Santos, 23 Aug. 1882, BCCD, *Anais*, 1882, IV, 133; speech of Carvalho Rezende, 15 Sept. 1882, ibid., p. 555.

51. Speech of Affonso Celso Júnior, 17 Aug. 1887, ibid. 1887, IV, 261.

52. Affonso Celso de Assis Figueiredo, visconde de Ouro Preto, Parecer, Rio, 13 April 1880, AIHGB, L222, D20; A. C. A. Figueiredo, ["Programa"], June 7, 1889, quoted in Basílio de Magalhães, *Estudos de história do Brasil* (São Paulo, 1940), p. 71.

53. *LB*, Lei 35, 26 Jan. 1892.
54. Cesar Zama to Ruy Barbosa, Salvador, 6 Jan. 1890, CRB, unnum.; João Cardoso de Meneses e Sousa, barão de Paranapiacaba, "Elleições," in Affonso Celso de Assis Figueiredo, visconde de Ouro Preto, et al., *A decada republicana* (Rio de Janeiro, 1900), III, 256, 254; Euclides da Cunha, *À margem da história*, in *Obra completa* (Rio de Janeiro, 1966), I, 375. For complaints about the election of 1890, see Eduardo Silva, *Barões e escravidão: Três gerações de fazendeiros e a crise da estrutura escravista* (Rio de Janeiro, 1984), p. 105 (and on 1897, see pp. 116-17); also see Love, *São Paulo*, p. 132. As I have noted, those who had been electors in 1881, even if illiterate, were allowed to vote in the Republic, so Paranapiacaba was wrong on both counts.

Chapter 8

1. Leonardo Arroyo, *A carta de Pero Vaz de Caminha. Ensaio de informação a procura de constantes válidas de método*, 2d ed. (São Paulo, 1976), p. 118; Luiz Gonçalves dos Santos (Padre Perereca), *Memórias para servir à história do reino do Brasil*, 3d ed. (1st, 1825) (Belo Horizonte, 1981), I, 185; Pedro I, quoted in *HGCB*, no. 7, p. 87; Thomas Flory, *Judge and Jury in Imperial Brazil, 1808-1871: Social Control and Political Stability in the New State* (Austin, Tex., 1981), pp. 163-67; Paula Beiguelman, *Formação política do Brasil*, Vol. I: *Teoria e ação no pensamento abolicionista* (São Paulo, 1967), p. 60. For sample charters granted proprietary governors, see "Carta de poder para o capitão-mór criar tabeliães e mais officiaes de justiça [20 Nov. 1530]" and "Carta de doação da capitania de Pernambuco a Duarte Coelho (5 Sept. 1534)," in Carlos Malheiro Dias, ed., *História da colonização portuguesa do Brasil. Edição monumental comemorativa do primeiro centenário da independência do Brasil* (Porto, 1924), III, 160, 309-12. On the royal factories, see Rômulo Garcia de Andrade, "Burocracia e economia na primeira metade do século xix (A Junta do Comércio e as atividades artesanais e manufatureiras na cidade do Rio de Janeiro, 1808-1850)" (M.A. thesis, Univ. Federal Fluminense, 1980). On the early bureaucracy, see Alan K. Manchester, "The Transfer of the Portuguese Court to Rio de Janeiro," in *Conflict and Continuity in Brazilian Society*, ed. Henry Keith and S. F. Edwards (Columbia, S.C., 1969), pp. 148-83; A. K. Manchester, "The Growth of Bureaucracy in Brazil, 1808-1821," *Journal of Latin American Studies*, 4: 1 (May 1972), 77-83; and José Murilo de Carvalho, *A construção da ordem: A elite política imperial* (Rio de Janeiro, 1980), pp. 111-31. Also see Petitions to Conselho Interino, 1822, APEB, Cx. 322 [old M.637], pasta 6, the bulk of which, even as the provisional government in Bahia still struggled for independence from Portugal, already centered on acquiring or holding onto positions.

2. Fernando Uricoechea, *O minotauro imperial: A burocratização do estado patrimonial brasileiro no século XIX* (São Paulo, 1978), pp. 98-101, demonstrates the steady growth in the bureaucracy by using figures on government budgets, but he does not adjust the data for inflation. Ex-

penditures for administrative purposes accounted for about one-fifth of the central government's budget in the last decade of the Empire: Richard Graham, "Government Expenditures and Political Change in Brazil, 1880-1899," *Journal of Inter-American Studies*, 19: 3 (Aug. 1977), 368.

3. Conde da Ponte to Fernando José de Portugal, Salvador, 17 May 1808 (quoted), 5 Sept. 1808, AN, SPE, IJJ 9-317; Leonardo José Duarte Gameleiro to visconde de Camamú (PP-BA), Salvador, 19 Mar. 1829, APEB, M.1609; PP-SP to MJ, São Paulo, 25 Mar. 1861, AN, SPE, IJJ 5-43; Francisco de Paula da Silveira Lobo to Paranaguá, Recife, 28 Feb. 1867, AMIP, I-DPP, 9.2.867, LOB-C.; Antonio de Moraes Silva, *Diccionario da lingua portugueza*, 8th ed. (Rio de Janeiro, 1889-91). In colonial Brazil, as elsewhere at that time, some positions could be inherited; one was even passed on to a son-in-law: Muriel Smith Nazzari, "Women, the Family and Property: The Decline of the Dowry in São Paulo, Brazil (1600-1870)" (Ph.D. diss., Yale Univ., 1986), p. 119. Well into the 20th century, a public post in Spain was understood as a man's property: Julian Alfred Pitt-Rivers, *The People of the Sierra* (London, 1954), p. 126 n.1.

4. Joaquim Nabuco, *Um estadista do império*, [3d ed.?] (Rio de Janeiro, 1975), p. 938; Anfriso Fialho, *Processo da monarchia brazileira: Necessidade da convocação de uma constituinte* (Rio de Janeiro, 1885), pp. 5-27.

5. José Marcellino Pereira de Vasconcellos, *Roteiro dos delegados e subdelegados de polícia; ou, Colleção dos actos, atribuições e deveres destas autoridades* (Rio de Janeiro, 1862), pp. 9, 18, 21; speeches of Nebias and Lessa, 8 June 1861, BCCD, *Anais*, 1861, II, 76; CP-BA to Delegado-Santa Rita do Rio Preto, Salvador, 11 Dec. 1868; CP-BA to Delegado-Pombal, Salvador, 9 Mar. 1869, both copies in APEB, Presidência, Polícia, Delegados, Registro, M.5802; Manuel Pinto de Souza Dantas to Franklin Americo de Menezes Doria, Rio, 4 Sept. 1880, AIHGB, L173, D1, Vol. I, fl. 56; Pedro II, *Conselhos à regente* (Rio de Janeiro, 1958), pp. 33, 60; *LB*, Lei 40, 3 Oct. 1834, art. 5, par. 6; PP-RS to MJ, Pôrto Alegre, 30 Aug. 1860, AN, SPE, IJJ 5-43; *LB*, Decreto 817, 30 Aug. 1851, art. 13. The pattern is familiar to historians in the case of Church appointments: bishops appointed as parish priests only those whose names had been presented to them by civil authorities.

6. J. M. P. Vasconcellos, *Roteiro dos delegados*, p. 20; CP-BA to Delegado-Lençois, Salvador, 9 Mar. 1869, copy, APEB, Presidência, Polícia, Delegados, Registro, M.5802; *LB*, Regulamento 120, 31 Jan. 1842, arts. 46, 48.

7. Manuel Pinto de Souza Dantas to Cotegipe, Salvador, 16 Dec. 1865, 11 Oct. 1856, AIHGB, CC, L19, D51, D27, respectively; Congresso Agricola, *Congresso Agricola: Coleção de documentos* (Rio de Janeiro, 1878), p. 191.

8. Affonso Celso de Assis Figueiredo, *As finanças da regeneração: Estudo politico offerecido aos mineiros* (Rio de Janeiro, 1876), p. 23. The barão de Guahy used the same word, *empregomania*, in Guahy to Cotegipe, Salvador, 16 Nov. 1885, AIHGB, CC, L38, D24, yet he himself was one of the most frequent solicitors of positions for his clients.

9. Cotegipe, "Confidencial: Parahyba do Norte," [1886] notes, AIHGB, CC, L90, D29.

10. Junqueira to Cotegipe, Salvador, 9 July 1856, ibid., L30, D178; Cotegipe, unlabeled notes, ibid., L19, D20. See the similar analysis for Spain in Joaquim Romero-Maura, "Caciquismo as a Political System," in *Patrons and Clients in Mediterranean Societies*, ed. Ernest Gellner and John Waterbury (London, 1977), pp. 53-62.

11. Luiz Alves dos Santos, "Discurso pronunciado no dia 22 de julho de 1882 pelo vigario . . . ," in [Manoel Peixoto de Lacerda Werneck], *O visconde de Ipiabas, Peregrino José de America Pinheiro: Perfil biographico, acompanhado do retracto do finado e seguido de algumas allocuções pronunciadas por ocasião de seus funeraes* (Rio de Janeiro, 1882), p. 34.

12. The letters are in the following archives: Arquivo do Instituto Histórico e Geográfico Brasileiro, Arquivo do Museu Imperial de Petrópolis, and Arquivo Nacional, Rio de Janeiro. Olinda received 82 of them, Paranaguá 308, Dória 86, and Pena 101. As is usually true for historical sources, these letters were not selected as a statistically significant sample—I have simply counted them as well as quoted them. I owe special thanks to Fernanda Maria Montel de Batissaco, who helped me do the counting.

13. Afonso Pena to Olegario Herculano de Quino e Castro, Sta. Barbara, 28 Nov. 1884, copy, AN, SAP, Affonso Pena Papers, uncat.; Affonso d'Albuquerque Mello, *A liberdade no Brasil: Seu nascimento, vida, morte, e sepultura* (Recife, 1864), p. 106. The letter of recommendation was also a common practice in Spain and Italy: Michael Kenny, "Patterns of Patronage in Spain," *Anthropological Quarterly*, 33: 1 (Jan. 1960), 20; Sydel F. Silverman, "Patronage and Community-Nation Relationships in Central Italy," *Ethnology*, 4: 2 (Apr. 1965), 187, 189 n.6; A. L. Maraspini, *The Study of an Italian Village* (Paris, 1968), pp. 110-12.

14. Prime Ministers, to be sure, also held portfolios of their own: Olinda preferred to be Minister of Empire, Paranaguá Treasury Minister. But when the recipients held the Empire or Treasury posts without being Prime Minister, they received few letters. Of course, Prime Ministers often passed letters on to other Cabinet members for action: see, for example, Diogo Velho Cavalcanti de Albuquerque, visconde de Cavalcanti (MJ) to Cotegipe (PM), Rio, 5 May 1876, AIHGB, CC, L1, D118.

15. A. Mello, *Liberdade*, p. 104.

16. Ibid., p. 106; João Alfredo (PP-PA) to Cotegipe, Salvador (where he was vacationing), 8 Apr. 1870, AIHGB, CC, L50, D91.

17. José Bento da Cunha Figueiredo to Cotegipe, Recife, 16 Dec. 1858, AIHGB, CC, L23, D143; PP-RN to MGuerra, Natal, 11 May 1850, AN, SAP, Cx. 823, Pac. 2, fl. 272; Manuel Buarque de Macedo to Luis Felipe de Souza Leão, [Jan.-March 1880], n.p., AIHGB, L456, D76. Also see Manoel Pinto de Souza Dantas (PP-BA) to Cotegipe, Salvador, 13 Dec. 1865, AIHGB, CC, L19, D50.

18. Quadro dos Suplentes de Juizes Municipaes nomeados de conformidade com a nova lei de reforma judiciaria, [Pôrto Alegre, 1872?], AN, SAP, Cx. 781, Pac. 2, Doc. 12. A conservative historian, however, has claimed that during the Empire "candidates for [judicial] promotions . . . had to meet the most rigorous test of professional honesty and public virtue": Pedro Calmon, "Organização judiciária: (a) na Colônia; (b) no Império; (c) na República," in *Livro do centenário dos cursos jurídicos*, (Rio de Janeiro, 1928), I, 95.

19. Candido Mendes de Almeida, ed., *Codigo Philippino; ou, Ordenações e leis do reino de Portugal* (Rio de Janeiro, 1870), Liv. 1, Tit. 78-85, and notes; *LB*, Decreto of 30 Jan. 1834; Bahia, *Colleção das leis e resoluções da Assembléa Legislativa e regulamentos do governo da Bahia, sanccionadas e publicadas* . . . , Lei 723, 17 Dec. 1858, Lei 801, 4 June 1860; JM to PP-SP, Taubaté, 1 Jan. 1861, copy encl. in PP-SP to MJ, São Paulo, 20 Jan 1861, AN, SPE, IJJ 5-43; PP-AL to MJ, Alagoas, 13 Oct. 1868, quoted in Magistratura, Registro de Fatos Notaveis, AN, SPE, IJ 4-32.

20. Speech of Silveira da Mota, BCS, *Anais*, 1880, Extraordinaria, III, 291.

21. And perhaps some subtle influence on policy: the annual report of the Ministry of War, for instance, was written by the head of the Ministry's staff; see [José Maria Lopes da Costa], barão de Piraquara, to Franklin Américo de Menezes Dória (MW), Rio, 31 Oct. 1881, AIHGB, L172, D2, fl. 157.

22. Leoncio de Carvalho to Cupertino do Amaral, São Paulo, 6 July 1882, AN, SAP, Amaro Cavalcanti Papers, being recatalogued at time of use (was Cx. 998); Antonio Nicolau Tolentino, quoted in *HGCB*, no. 7, p. 89n.; Luiz Tarquinio to Serzedelo Correia, Salvador, [1890?], quoted in Péricles Madureira do Pinho, *Luís Tarquínio, pioneiro da justiça social no Brasil* (Salvador, 1944), pp. 71, 72.

23. Brazil, Ministerio do Imperio, *Relatorio*, 1857, p. 104; Luiz Pedreira do Couto Ferraz to Cotegipe, Rio, 26 Nov. [1853], AIHGB, CC, L22, D101; Firmino de Sousa Martins to João Lustosa da Cunha Paranaguá, Buritisinho, 28 Mar. 1876, AMIP, I-Dpp, 28.3.876, MAR-C.

24. Affonso Pena to Lima Duarte, Rio, [Oct. 1883], AIHGB, CC, L21, D85; PP-BA to MI, Salvador, 4 Sept. 1867, AN, SPE, IJJ 9-343, fl. 149ff; Cotegipe to Junqueira, Salvador, 26 Nov. 1874, copy of draft, AIHGB, CC, L31, D60; Cincinatto Pinto da Silva to Pedro de Araújo Lima, marquês de Olinda, Salvador, 15 Dec. 1862, AIHGB, L213, D114; Domingos Soares Ferreira Penna, *A região occidental da provincia do Pará: Resenhas estatisticas das comarcas de Obidos e Santarem* (Pará [Belém], 1869), p. 230. Also see Manuel Pinto de Souza Dantas to Pedro de Araújo Lima, marquês de Olinda, n.p., 13 Oct. 1862, AIHGB, L213, D113. On the Recife law school as a source of patronage, see Robert M. Levine, *Pernambuco in the Brazilian Federation, 1889-1937* (Stanford, Calif., 1978), p. 79.

25. José Gomes de Sousa Portugal, barão do Turvo, to Jeronimo José

338 Notes to Pages 222-26

Teixeira Jr., Dores do Pirahy, 27 Aug. 1863, AN, SAP, Col. Teixeira Jr., AP 23, Correspondencia, Doc. 104; Junqueira (MW) to Cotegipe, Rio, 5 Oct. 1872, AIHGB, CC, L31, D36; Ambrosio Leitão da Cunha, barão de Mamoré, to Cotegipe, Rio, [Mar. 1887], AIHGB, CC, L18, D133; Henrique Francisco de Ávila to Cotegipe, Rio, 3 May 1886, AIHGB, CC, L7, D39; PP-BA to MI, Salvador, 20 Nov. 1867, AN, SPE, IJJ 9-343, 1867, fl. 176; Guahy to Cotegipe, Salvador, 28 Mar., 5 Apr. 1884, AIHGB, CC, L38, D4, D5.

26. See, for example, Joaquim Raimundo de Lamare to Franklin Americo de Menezes Doria, Rio, 19 Aug. 1881, AIHGB, L172, D2, Vol. II, fl. 110, where he asks for a sergeant's position for one of his protégés [*protegido seu*].

27. João José de Oliveira Junqueira (father) to Cotegipe, Salvador, 6 Aug. 1855, AIHGB, CC, L30, D147; Junqueira to Cotegipe, Salvador, 4 July 1855, ibid., L30, D169; José Mariano Carneiro da Cunha to Afonso Pena, n.p, n.d., AN, Affonso Pena Papers, Lata 5, 1.2.338 L:C. On the concentration of troops in Rio Grande do Sul, see Joseph L. Love, *Rio Grande do Sul and Brazilian Regionalism, 1882-1930* (Stanford, Calif., 1971), pp. 15-16.

28. Manuel Antonio Duarte de Azevedo to Cotegipe, Rio, 14 July 1872, AIHGB, CC, L7, D80.

29. Luiz Pedreira do Couto Ferraz to Cotegipe, [Rio], 15 May [1854 or 1855], ibid., L22, D108; Guahy to Cotegipe, Salvador, 26 May, 6 Aug. 1874, ibid., L37, D108, D113. See also Guahy to Cotegipe, Salvador, 26 Oct. 1872, ibid., L37, D148.

30. José Rodrigues de Lima Duarte to Afonso Pena, Rio, 5 Nov. 1883, AN, Affonso Pena Papers, Lata 5, 1.2.371, L:D; Guahy to Cotegipe, [Salvador], n.d., AIHGB, CC, L37, D107; Guahy to Cotegipe, Salvador, 17 Mar. 1884, AIHGB, CC, L38, D2. On the responsibilities of *porteiros*, see Regulamento da Secretaria Provincial, APEB, Secretaria, 1837-71, M.1513.

31. Guahy to Cotegipe, Salvador, 19 Dec. 1882, AIHGB, CC, L37, D165; Guahy to Cotegipe, Salvador, 19 Apr. 1884, ibid., L38, D5.

32. Antonio Augusto da Costa Aguiar, "A continuação da confissão dos meus intimos pensamentos," 28 Sept. 1862, ms, AMIP, CXXI, 6422, fl. 2; Bernardo Avelino Gavião Peixoto to João Lustosa da Cunha Paranaguá, São Paulo, 18 Jan. 1860, AMIP, I-DPP, 18.1.860, Pei-C1.2; Mello, *Liberdade*, p. 105. Compare Kenny, "Patterns of Patronage," p. 21.

33. Junqueira to Cotegipe, Salvador, 11 Mar. 1856, AIHGB, CC, L30, D175; Manuel Pinto de Souza Dantas to Cotegipe, Salvador, 18 Feb. [1857], ibid., L19, D37; Junqueira to Cotegipe, Rio, 21 May 1886, ibid., L31, D140; Junqueira (MGuerra) to Cotegipe, Rio, 13 Nov. 1872, ibid., L31, D43.

34. Compare the view of João Lins Vieira Cansansão de Sinimbú in Congresso Agricola, *Coleção*, p. 127. Also see Roderick J. Barman and Jean Barman, "The Role of the Law Graduate in the Political Elite of Im-

perial Brazil," *Journal of Inter-American Studies*, 18: 4 (Nov. 1976), 423-50.

35. Helio Jaguaribe, *Political Development: A General Theory and a Latin American Case Study* (New York, 1973), p. 480. The arrival of impoverished aristocrats was perhaps first alleged in 1883 by Joaquim Nabuco, *O abolicionismo*, [2d ed.?] (Rio de Janeiro, 1938), p. 179, and repeated by him in his speech of 10 July 1888, BCCD, *Anais*, 1888, III, 86. N. A. O. Lyttleton, "El patronazgo en la Italia de Giolitti (1892-1924)," *Revista de Occidente*, 127 (Oct. 1973), 105, also argues that the decline of a class drives its members to seek public employment.

36. [João Cardoso de Meneses e Souza], barão de Paranapiacaba, "Elleições," in Affonso Celso de Assis Figueiredo, visconde de Ouro Preto, et al., *A decada republicana* (Rio de Janeiro, 1900), III, 244 (citing Auguste van der Straten-Ponthoz, *Le Budget du Brésil ou, Recherches sur les ressources de cet empire dans leurs rapports avec les intérêts européens du commerce e de l'émigration* [Brussels, 1854]); Sérgio Buarque de Hollanda, in *HGCB*, no. 7, p. 86. This point is also made by Frances Rothstein, "The Class Basis of Patron-Client Relations," *Latin American Perspectives*, 6: 2 (Spring 1979), 28.

37. Charles R. Boxer, *Portuguese Society in the Tropics: The Municipal Councils of Goa, Macao, Bahia, and Luanda* (Madison, Wis., 1965), p. 149; Levine, *Pernambuco*, pp. 115-16. Some historians have expressed surprise that the search for positions attracted the attention even of men of substance; see, for example, Maria Odila Silva Dias, "The Establishment of the Royal Court in Brazil," in *From Colony to Nation: Essays on the Independence of Brazil*, ed. A. J. R. Russell-Wood (Baltimore, 1975), p. 102n.

38. Eul-Soo Pang and Ron L. Seckinger, "The Mandarins of Imperial Brazil," *Comparative Studies in Society and History*, 14: 2 (March 1972), 217, 223-26; José M. Carvalho, *A construção da ordem*, pp. 93-96. Compare Barman and Barman, "Role of the Law Graduate," p. 446 n.13.

39. Manuel Pinto de Souza Dantas to Cotegipe, Salvador, 6 July 1855, AIHGB, CC, L19, D6; Antônio Paulino Limpo de Abreu, visconde de Abaeté, to Cotegipe, Rio, 29 Mar. 1859, ibid., L1, D20. Abaeté explained to the *baiano* Cotegipe that he need not worry about appointments there: Bahia's "favorite son," Minister of Justice Manuel Vieira Tosta, barão de Muritiba, would "attend with all care to the interests of the land where he was born."

40. Speech of Araujo Góes, 5 Nov. 1888, BCCD, *Anais*, 1888, VII, 21; Ambrósio Leitão da Cunha, barão de Mamoré, to Cotegipe, Rio, 9 Mar. 1887, AIHGB, CC, L18, D134.

41. Cesar Zama to Ruy Barbosa, Salvador, 6 Jan. 1890, CRB, unnum. On Zama's response, see João Dunshee de Abranches [Moura], ed. *Actas e actos do governo provisorio*, 3d ed. (Rio de Janeiro, 1953), p. 374.

42. José Antonio Saraiva to Affonso Celso de Assis Figueiredo, [Salvador], 11 Mar. 1880, AIHGB, L427, D23; Manuel Buarque de Macedo to

Luis Felipe de Souza Leão, [Rio], 9 Mar. 1880, AIHGB, L456, D74; speech of Affonso Celso de Assis Figueiredo Jr., 19 July 1888, BCCD, *Anais*, 1888, III, 214.

43. Junqueira to Cotegipe, Rio, 25 Oct., 8 Nov. 1873, AIHGB, CC, L41, D51, D52; JD to PP-BA, Caetité, 12 Dec. 1856, copy, APEB, Presidência, Eleições, M.2794; Pedro Leão Veloso to João Lustosa da Cunha Paranaguá, Salvador, 28 Sept. 1865, AMIP, I-DPP, 30.5.865, Vel. cl-2.

44. Junqueira to Cotegipe, Salvador, 2 Nov. 1855, AIHGB, CC, L30, D174.

45. Mesa Parochial to PP-BA, Victoria, 19 Sept. 1860, AN, SPE, IJJ 5-25; speech of D. Manuel [de Assis Mascarenhas], 21 Mar. 1850, BCCD, *Anais*, 1850 (1st session), II, 193. See also Antonio Alves de Souza Carvalho, *O Brasil em 1870, estudo político* (Rio de Janeiro, 1870), pp. 34-35.

Chapter 9

1. José Antonio Saraiva to Henrique Garcez Pinto de Madureira, Rio, 2 Apr., 10 Apr. 1848, quoted in José Wanderley de Araújo Pinho, *Política e políticos no império* (Rio de Janeiro, 1930), pp. 35-37; Roderick J. Barman and Jean Barman, "The Role of the Law Graduate in the Political Elite of Imperial Brazil," *Journal of Inter-American Studies*, 18: 4 (Nov. 1976), 441, 447 n.16. João de Souza Werneck and his two sons Paulino de Souza Werneck (justice of the peace) and Saturnino de Souza Werneck (4th substitute subdelegado), along with Ignacio Barbosa dos Santos Werneck (1st substitute subdelegado) and José Luiz de Azevedo [Santos?] Werneck, signed a petition for the priest's removal: Moradores da Freguezia de São José do Rio Preto *v*. Pe. Manoel Florentino Cassiano de Campos, Município de Paraíba do Sul, 7 July 1863, ACMRJ, Queixas contra padres, 1863.

2. Miguel Calmon du Pin e Almeida to Condessa de Itapagipe, Salvador, 25 Nov. 1833, as quoted by Pedro Calmon, *História de D. Pedro II* (Rio de Janeiro, 1975), I, 328; VPP-Sergipe to MJ, Aracajú, [1851], AN, SAP, Cx. 783, Pac. 2. One example of a woman's participation in the process of securing appointment for family members will do: João Vicente Torres Homem, later barão de Torres Homem, asked Joaquim Henrique de Araújo, barão de Pirassinunga, for his help in getting a position; Pirassinunga then wrote to his wife, asking her to speak to her father, the marquês de Olinda: Pirassinunga to Bambina (his wife), 27 Nov. 1865, AIHGB, L210, D77.

3. Domingos de Souza Leão to Pedro de Araújo Lima, marquês de Olinda, 21 Aug. 1865, AIHGB, L207, D72; PP-CE to MJ, Fortaleza, 8 Nov. 1849, quoted by Fernando Uricoechea, *O minotauro imperial: A burocratização do estado patrimonial brasileiro no século XIX* (São Paulo, 1978), p. 114; Herculano Ferreira Penna (PP-MG) to José Thomaz Nabuco de Araújo (MJ), Ouro Preto, 6 Nov. 1856, AIHGB, L365, D11.

4. José Manoel de Freitas (PP-PE) to João Lustosa da Cunha Paranaguá, visconde de Paranaguá, [Recife], 15 Apr. 1884, AMIP, I-Dpp, 3.1.884, Fre-

cl.18; *LB*, Lei de 1 Oct. 1828, art. 23; "Lei, 1846," art. 125; Guahy to Cotegipe, Salvador, 16 Oct., 31 Oct. 1885, AIHGB, CC, L38, D19, D21; Antonio Alves Guimarães de Azambuja to PP-RGS, Rio Pardo, 1872, AN, SAP, Cx. 781, Pac. 2, Doc. 15. Exclusions from County Council positions were extended in 1861 to fathers- and sons-in-law: *LB*, Aviso 386 (Imperio), 6 Sept. 1861. Also see Candido Mendes de Almeida, ed. *Codigo Philippino; ou, Ordenações e leis do reino de Portugal* (Rio de Janeiro, 1870), pp. 372n, 373n. In colonial times a County Council urged that Brazilians not be appointed to positions of public authority within Brazil because "family ties and friendships pervert that integrity which they should have"; quoted in Charles R. Boxer, *Portuguese Society in the Tropics: The Municipal Councils of Goa, Macao, Bahia, and Luanda* (Madison, Wis., 1965), p. 88n. The King of Portugal took elaborate—although useless—steps to prevent family connections between High Court judges and local potentates in Brazil: Stuart B. Schwartz, *Sovereignty and Society in Colonial Brazil: The High Court of Bahia and Its Judges, 1609-1751* (Berkeley, Calif., 1973), pp. 177-81. Families were also associated in business and for the same reasons; because that kind of association persists into our own day, it seems to require little comment.

5. In this regard Brazilians followed Roman precedent: Richard P. Saller, *Personal Patronage Under the Early Empire* (Cambridge, Eng., 1982), pp. 11, 13.

6. Antonio de Moraes Silva, *Diccionario da lingua portugueza*, 8th ed. (Rio de Janeiro, 1889-91); Julian Alfred Pitt-Rivers, *The People of the Sierra* (London, 1954), p. 140; Luiz Tarquinio to Serzedelo Correia, Salvador, n.d., quoted in Pericles Madureira do Pinho, *Luís Tarquínio, pioneiro da justiça social no Brasil* (Salvador, 1944), p. 72; Manuel Pinto de Souza Dantas to Cotegipe (MM), Santo Amaro, 31 Mar. 1856, AIHGB, CC, L19, D14. One letter writer said an office seeker was *um amigo de serviços*: Domingos de Souza Leão to Pedro de Araújo Lima, marquês de Olinda, Caraúna, 9 Oct. 1865, AIHGB, L207, D72. Recall in an earlier chapter (p. 24) the father who wished his children to merit his "friendship," that is, his patronal care.

7. Speech of Pedro de Calazans, 20 Apr. 1861, BCCD, *Anais*, 1861, I, 39; Manuel Buarque de Macedo to Luís Felipe de Souza Leão, [Rio], 9 Mar. 1880, AIHGB, L456, D74; A. M. Silva, *Diccionario*; Miguel Arcanjo Galvão, *Relação dos cidadãos que tomaram parte no govêrno do Brasil no período de março de 1808 a 15 de novembro de 1889*, 2d ed. (Rio de Janeiro, 1969), p. 61; Cotegipe to João Alfredo Correia de Oliveira, Salvador, 21 July 1872, typescript copy, AIHGB, CC, L50, D99.

8. Uricoechea, *Minotauro*, p. 116, makes this assertion; it is then repeated by Décio Saes, *A formação do estado burguês no Brasil (1888-1891)* (Rio de Janeiro, 1985), p. 125.

9. Compare Joseph L. Love, *Rio Grande do Sul and Brazilian Regionalism, 1882-1930* (Stanford, Calif., 1971), p. 73, who says "family and station, which counted for so much in other parts of the country, meant relatively less in Rio Grande [do Sul]."

342 *Notes to Pages 243-47*

10. João Lins Vieira Cansansão de Sinimbú to Pedro de Araújo Lima, marquês de Olinda, Rio, 13 Apr. 1863, AIHGB, L213, D38; Olinda to Luiz Carlos (his cousin), Ouro Preto, 2 Feb. 1867, AIHGB, L211, D54. What most troubled Olinda was the appointment of one Joaquim, "the most despicable creature here because of his immorality; an incorrigible drunkard; [although] married, he does not hesitate, when taken by drink, to give himself to men who have him play the role of the other sex."

11. Junqueira to Cotegipe, Salvador, 9 July, 5 Aug., 23 Aug., 2 Oct. 1856, 9 Jan., 3 Feb., 24 Mar. 1857, and, from Teresina, 30 Jan. 1858, AIHGB, CC, L30, D178-80, D182, D185, D187, D190, D195.

12. Manuel Pinto de Souza Dantas to Cotegipe, Salvador, 31 May 1855, S. Amaro, 31 Mar. 1856, Salvador, [early 1857], ibid., L19, D3, D14, D2.

13. Junqueira to Cotegipe, Rio, 30 July 1872, ibid., L31, D25; Affonso Augusto Moreira Pena to Francisco de Paula da Silveira Lobo and Affonso Celso de Assis Figueiredo (Sr.), Santa Barbara, 19 Mar. 1876, separate letters, both in AN, SAP, Affonso Pena Papers, uncatalogued at time of use.

14. José Bento da Cunha Figueiredo to Cotegipe, Recife, 16 Oct. 1855, AIHGB, CC, L23, D138. A similar tone of pique characterizes some letters of Luiz Pedreira do Couto Ferraz, visconde do Bom Retiro, to Cotegipe: for example, from Gastain (Austria) 11 Aug. 1876 and from Tijuca, 17 May 1881, ibid., L22, D165, D174. On salaries of presidents, see Caetano José de Andrade Pinto, *Attribuições dos presidentes de provincia* (Rio de Janeiro, 1865), pp. 18-22; and Joaquim Nabuco, *Um estadista do império*, [3d ed.?] (Rio de Janeiro, 1975), p. 582; even the wealthy coffee planter Brás Carneiro Nogueira da Costa e Gama, conde de Baependy, had to borrow money to cover his expenses as president of Pernambuco: Manuel Jacintho Carneiro Nogueira da Gama, barão de Juparanã, *Testamento* (Freguezia de Santa Thereza [Valença], 1883), p. 8n. (The place of publication may be fictitious.)

15. José Antonio Saraiva to Henrique Garcez Pinto de Madureira, Jacobina, 18 June 1849, quoted in J. W. A. Pinho, *Política e políticos*, pp. 45-46. He finally chose to side with the Cabinet: "I came out well in the election, and the government should be pleased by the complete exclusion of the opposition": 10 Dec. 1849, ibid., p. 47.

16. [João Vieira Machado da Cunha (2º)] to Luiz Alves Santos, n.p., [after 1882], draft, AN, SAP, Cód. 112, Vol. 9, Doc. 50.

17. Junqueira to Cotegipe, Rio, 5 Aug. 1872, AIHGB, CC, L31, D27; Affonso Celso de Assis Figueiredo Júnior, *Oito annos de parlamento. Poder pessoal de D. Pedro II. Reminiscencias e notas* (São Paulo: Melhoramentos, n.d.), p. 21; Francisco Belisário Soares de Souza, *O sistema eleitoral no império (com apêndice contendo a legislação eleitoral no período 1821-1889)* (Brasília, 1979), p. 44.

18. F. B. S. Souza, *Sistema eleitoral*, p. 20; Luís Martins, *O patriarca e o bacharel* (São Paulo, [1953]).

19. Speech of João Lustosa da Cunha Paranaguá, 16 Apr. 1850, BCCD,

Anais, 1850, I, 336; JD to PP-CE, Icó, 19 Sept. 1860, encl. in PP-CE to MJ, Fortaleza, 4 Oct. 1860, AN, SPE, IJJ 5-43.

20. PP-RN to MJ, Natal, 11 May 1850, quoted in Uricoechea, *Minotauro*, p. 271; PP-SE to MJ, Sergipe, 3 Feb. 1851, AN, SAP, Cx. 783, Pac. 2.

21. Antonio Alves de Souza Carvalho, *O Brasil em 1870, estudo político* (Rio de Janeiro, 1870), p. 62; Manuel Buarque de Macedo to Luís Felipe de Souza Leão, [Rio], 9 Mar. 1880, AIHGB, L456, D74.

22. Luiz Pedreira do Couto Ferraz, visconde do Bom Retiro, to Cotegipe, Rio, 13 Sept., 2 Oct. [1856], AIHGB, CC, L22, D135, D136. On barão de Nova Friburgo's wealth, see Joseph E. Sweigart, *Coffee Factorage and the Emergence of a Brazilian Capital Market, 1850-1888* (New York, 1987), pp. 78-80.

23. Affonso d'Albuquerque Mello, *A liberdade no Brasil: Seu nascimento, vida, morte, e sepultura* (Recife, 1864), p. 107.

24. Cotegipe, "Circumstancias que Precederam a Retirada do Ministerio de 16 de julho," in J. W. A. Pinho, *Política e políticos*, pp. 166-70; quotations at pp. 166, 167. The Minister of War was Manuel Vieira Tosta (1°), the Minister of Empire Paulino José Soares de Souza (2°).

25. Affonso Celso de Assis Figueiredo, visconde de Ouro Preto, to José Antonio Saraiva, 17 Sept. 1889, Rio, AIHGB, L274, P16.

26. Junqueira to Cotegipe, Salvador, 2 Oct., 23 Aug. 1856, AIHGB, CC, L30, D182, D180, respectively (the reference is to Sen. Francisco Gonçalves Martins, 1831-72). On Martins, see Thomas Flory, *Judge and Jury in Imperial Brazil, 1808-1871: Social Control and Political Stability in the New State* (Austin, Tex., 1981), pp. 72-73; Roderick J. Barman, "Brazil at Mid-Empire: Political Accommodation and the Pursuit of Progress Under the *Conciliação* Ministry, 1853-1857" (Ph.D. diss., Univ. of California, Berkeley, 1970), pp. 143, 238; José Wanderley [de Araújo] Pinho, *Cotegipe e seu tempo, primeira phase, 1815-1867* (São Paulo, 1937), pp. 494-98. Junqueira's rival for nomination was Zacharias de Góes e Vasconcellos.

27. Joaquim Henrique de Araújo, barão de Pirassinunga, to Bambina (his wife), Barbacena, 27 Nov. 1865, AIHGB, L210, D77; Cotegipe to Junqueira, Salvador, 25 Oct. 1872, copy of draft, AIHGB, CC, L31, D40. On the contrasting effectiveness of patrons in 18th-century England, see Douglas Hay, "Property, Authority and the Criminal Law," in *Albion's Fatal Tree: Crime and Society in Eighteenth-Century England*, ed. Douglas Hay et al. (New York, 1975), p. 46.

28. Guahy to Cotegipe, Salvador, 19 Dec. 1882, AIHGB, CC, L37, D165; Cotegipe to João Alfredo Correia de Oliveira, Rio, 14 Feb. 1870, typescript copy of draft, ibid., L50, D86.

29. A. A. Mello, *Liberdade*, p. 114; Junqueira to Cotegipe, Rio, July 6, 1872, AIHGB, CC, L31, D21; Guahy to Cotegipe, Salvador, 8 Oct. 1884, 10 Oct. 1887, AIHGB, CC, L38, D13, D72. A student of Brazil in the early 20th century similarly concluded that "the political leader, while seeming to be the owner of everything, finally came to be himself owned by every-

body": Rubens do Amaral, quoted by Victor Nunes Leal, *Coronelismo: The Municipality and Representative Government in Brazil* (Cambridge, Eng., 1977), p. 150 n.41. Also see Maria Sylvia de Carvalho Franco, *Homens livres na ordem escravocrata*, 2d ed. (São Paulo, 1974), pp. 86-88; and Michael Kenny, "Patterns of Patronage in Spain," *Anthropological Quarterly*, 33: 1 (Jan. 1960), 23.

30. Guahy to Cotegipe, Salvador, 23 Nov. 1885, AIHGB, CC, L38, D26.

31. Junqueira (MGuerra) to Cotegipe, Rio, 31 Aug. 1872, 24 Nov. 1873, ibid., L31, D32, D53.

32. Luiz Pedreira do Couto Ferraz, visconde do Bom Retiro, to Cotegipe, Rio, 10 Jan [1854], ibid., L22, D104; Manuel Francisco Correia to Cotegipe, Rio, 13 Aug. 1872, ibid., L17, D57; Affonso Celso de Assis Figueiredo to José Antonio Saraiva, Rio, 2 Feb. 1880, AIHGB, L274, P16.

33. Ildefonso P. Correia to Manoel Francisco Correia, Curitiba, 11 Nov. 1885, AIHGB, CC, L17, D60; [João Vieira Machado da Cunha (2°)] to Dr. Braz [Carneiro Nogueira da Gama (3°), Valença], 6 May [1890], draft, AN, SAP, Cód. 112, Vol. 9, Doc. 57; speech of Antonio Cesario de Faria Alvim, in Congresso Agricola, *Congresso Agricola: Coleção de documentos* (Rio de Janeiro, 1878), p. 132.

34. Compare Sydel F. Silverman, "Patronage and Community-Nation Relationships in Central Italy," *Ethnology*, 4: 2 (Apr. 1965), 189 n.6.

35. PP-CE to MI, Fortaleza, 29 Apr. 1860, AN, SPE, IJJ 5-43; Figueiredo Jr., *Oito annos*, p. 21; Guahy to Cotegipe, Salvador, 6 Feb. 1888, AIHGB, CC, L38, D94; Luiz Pedreira do Couto Ferraz, visconde do Bom Retiro, to Cotegipe, Salvador, 3 Mar. 1856, AIHGB, CC, L22, D95; Cotegipe (PM) to Henrique Pereira de Lucena (PP-RS), Rio, 20 Nov. 1885, APEP, Col. Lucena, 562. See for similar patterns later and elsewhere, V. Leal, *Coronelismo*, p. 15; and N. A. O. Lyttleton, "El patronazgo en la Italia de Giolitti (1892-1924)," *Revista de Occidente*, 127 (Oct. 1973), 110. The set of values that informed the system of patronage are insightfully discussed by Emília Viotti da Costa, "Brazil: The Age of Reform, 1870-1889," in *The Cambridge History of Latin America*, ed. Leslie Bethell (Cambridge, Eng., 1987), V, 735-50.

36. Guahy to Cotegipe, Salvador, 6 Sept. 1877, AIHGB, CC, L37, D144.

37. Pedro II, "Conselhos de D. Pedro II à regente D. Isabel (1876)," in Hélio Viana, *D. Pedro I e D. Pedro II: Acréscimos às suas biografias* (São Paulo, 1966), p. 245.

38. João Mendes de Almeida to Franklin Americo de Menezes Dória, barão de Loreto, Olinda, 8 June 1889, AIHGB, L174, D2, Vol. II, fl. 15.

39. APEB, Presidência, Tesouraria, Exames, M.4588; *LB*, Decreto 817, 30 Aug. 1851, art. 13, Decreto 1294, 16 Dec. 1853, art. 9; Cotegipe to Junqueira, Salvador, 26 Nov. 1874, copy of draft, AIHGB, L31, D60. On the beginnings of *concursos*, see Tomas de Vilanova Monteiro Lopes, "A seleção de pessoal para o serviço público brasileiro," *Revista do Serviço Público*, 4: 1 (Oct. 1952), 19.

40. Franklin Americo de Menezes Doria to João Lustosa da Cunha Paranaguá, Salvador, 20 Mar. 1868, AMIP, I-DPP, 20.3.868, Lat-c.; Francisco do Rego Barros, visconde de Boa Vista, to Pedro de Araújo Lima, marquês de Olinda, Recife, 6 July 1863, AIHGB, L213, D122; Manuel Buarque de Macedo to Paranaguá, n.p., 6 Dec. 1879, AMIP, I-DPP, 10.10.879, Mac-c.

41. A. M. Silva, *Diccionario*.

42. Ibid.

43. The *homem ilustrado* is vividly contrasted with the country bumpkin in speech of Ottoni, 7 Mar. 1861, BCCD, *Anais*, 1861, I, 243.

44. Guahy to Cotegipe, Salvador, 16 Oct. 1885, AIHGB, CC, L38, D18.

45. Guahy to Cotegipe, Salvador, 19 Dec. 1885, ibid., L38, D32.

46. Carlos Luis de Amour to João Lustosa da Cunha Paranaguá, visconde de Paranaguá, 7 Nov. 1882, AMIP, I-DPP, 7.11.882, Amo-cl.; Cotegipe to Junqueira, Salvador, 6 Mar. 1875, copy of draft, AIHGB, CC, L31, D64.

47. PP-PA to MI, Belém, 31 Jan. 1870, copy encl. in João Alfredo Correia de Oliveira to Cotegipe, Belém, 31 Jan. 1870, AIHGB, CC, L50, D84.

Epilogue

1. William S. Dudley, "Institutional Sources of Officer Discontent in the Brazilian Army, 1870-1889," *Hispanic American Historical Review*, 55: 1 (Feb. 1975), 44-65. In June 1889 Gen. Floriano Peixoto wrote the civilian Minister of Empire on behalf of a friend, only to have his request denied: Floriano Peixoto to Franklin Americo de Menezes Doria, barão de Loreto, Rio, 13 June 1889, AIHGB, L174, D2. On such questions may have hung the future of Brazil: Peixoto supported the Republican coup five months later and became the first Vice-President of the new government, succeeding to the top post in 1891. One supposes that when he was President, his letters proved more efficacious: Peixoto to unidentified, Rio, 17 Mar. 1892, BN/SM, Col. Tobias Monteiro, no. 55. Also see June E. Hahner, *Civilian-Military Relations in Brazil, 1889-1898* (Columbia, S.C., 1969), p. 134 n.23. In the period 1853-71, 20% of Cabinet members had been military officers, compared with a mere 6% in 1871-1889: José Murilo de Carvalho, *A construção da ordem: A elite política imperial* (Rio de Janeiro, 1980), p. 79.

2. Roderick J. Barman and Jean Barman, "The Role of the Law Graduate in the Political Elite of Imperial Brazil," *Journal of Inter-American Studies*, 18: 4 (Nov. 1976), p. 436.

3. Americo Brasiliense [de Almeida Mello], *Os programas dos partidos e o 2º imperio. Primeira parte: Exposição de principios* (São Paulo, 1878), p. 30; Manuel Pinto de Souza Dantas to Ruy Barbosa, n.p., [between 1875 and 1877], in Manuel Pinto de Souza Dantas, *Correspondência* (Rio de Janeiro, 1962), p. 14; Francisco Octaviano de Almeida Rosa to Affonso Celso de Assis Figueiredo, Rio, 22 Dec. 1882, AIHGB, L427, D24.

4. Affonso Celso de Assis Figueiredo, *Reforma administrativa e municipal: Parecer e projectos* (Rio de Janeiro, 1883), pp. xxxvii, xl, 66, 78-81. The action of several provincial legislatures is reported in Brazil, Commissão Encarregada de Rever e Classificar as Rendas Geraes, Provinciaes, e Municipaes do Imperio, *Relatorio e projecto de lei* (Rio de Janeiro, 1883), p. 89.

5. *LB*, Decreto 7 of 20 Nov. 1889, art 2, par. 6.

6. Richard Graham, "Government Expenditures and Political Change in Brazil, 1880-1899," *Journal of Inter-American Studies*, 19: 3 (Aug. 1977), 368; Joseph L. Love, *São Paulo in the Brazilian Federation, 1889-1937* (Stanford, Calif., 1980), pp. 302-3; João Manuel de Carvalho, *Reminiscencias sobre vultos e factos do imperio e da republica* (Amparo, 1894), pp. xxiv-xxv; James Fenner Lee to [U.S. Secretary of State James G.] Blaine, 12 Dec. 1890, quoted in Hahner, *Civilian-Military Relations*, p. 35. Also see Cesar Zama to Ruy Barbosa, Salvador, 6 Jan. 1890, CRB, unnum.; [João Francisco?] Barcellos to Ernesto Vieira, Niterói, 30 Aug. 1892, AN, SAP, Cód. 112, D70; Barbara Weinstein, *The Amazon Rubber Boom, 1850-1920* (Stanford, Calif., 1983), p. 247; John D. Wirth, *Minas Gerais in the Brazilian Federation, 1889-1937* (Stanford, Calif., 1977), pp. 178-80; and Shepard Forman and Joyce F. Riegelhaupt, "The Political Economy of Patron-Clientship: Brazil and Portugal Compared," in *Brazil, Anthropological Perspectives: Essays in Honor of Charles Wagley*, ed. Maxine L. Margolis and William E. Carter (New York, 1979), pp. 379-400.

7. Many of the issues addressed in this book regarding the relationships between local leaders and national ones are also hotly debated for the 20th century. For an introduction to the debate, see Amilcar Martins Filho, "Clientelismo e representação em Minas Gerais durante a Primeira República: Uma crítica a Paul Cammack," *Dados—Revista de Ciências Sociais*, 27: 2 (1984), 175-97. Also useful is Edgard Carone, "Coronelismo: Definição, história, e bibliografia," *Revista de Administração de Empresas*, 11: 3 (July-Sept. 1971), 85-92. How present-day practices of patronage in Europe are affected by earlier governmental structures is explored by Martin Shefter, "Party and Patronage: Germany, England, and Italy," *Politics and Society*, 7: 4 (1977), 403-51.

8. Florestan Fernandes, *A Revolução burguesa no Brasil: Ensaio de interpretação sociológica* (Rio de Janeiro, 1975), pp. 31-146; Wilson Cano, *Raízes da concentração industrial em São Paulo* (São Paulo, 1977), pp. 20-87; Décio Saes, *A formação do estado burguês no Brasil (1888-1891)* (Rio de Janeiro, 1985). This general view of the contrast also undergirds the basic argument of Emília Viotti da Costa, *Da senzala à colônia* (São Paulo, 1966), especially p. 467.

SOURCES CITED

Sources Cited

Archives and Special Collections

Arquivo da Cúria Metropolitana do Rio de Janeiro, Rio de Janeiro
Arquivo da Santa Casa de Misericórdia, Salvador
Arquivo do Estado de São Paulo, São Paulo
Arquivo do Instituto Histórico e Geográfico Brasileiro, Rio de Janeiro
    Coleção Cotegipe
Arquivo do Museu Imperial, Petrópolis
Arquivo Geral da Cidade do Rio de Janeiro, Rio de Janeiro
Arquivo Histórico do Itamaraty, Rio de Janeiro
Arquivo Municipal de Salvador, Salvador
Arquivo Nacional, Rio de Janeiro
    Affonso Pena Papers
    Seção de Arquivos Particulares
    Seção do Poder Executivo
    Seção do Poder Judiciário
Arquivo Público do Estado da Bahia, Salvador
Arquivo Público do Estado de Pernambuco, Recife
Arquivo Público do Estado do Rio de Janeiro, Niterói
Biblioteca Nacional, Rio de Janeiro
    Seção de Manuscritos
Casa Rui Barbosa, Rio de Janeiro
Museu Republicano da Convenção de Itú, Itú

Other Sources

O abolicionismo perante a historia ou, O dialogo das tres provincias. Rio de Janeiro, 1888.
Abranches [Moura], João Dunshee de, ed. *Actas e actos do governo provisorio. Copias authenticas dos protocollos das sessões secretas do Conselho de Ministros desde a proclamação da Republica até a organisação*

do gabinete Lucena, acompanhados de importantes revelações e docu-mentos. Obras Completas no. 4. 3d ed. Rio de Janeiro, 1953.

Alencar, José de. *Obra completa.* Série Brasileira no. 11. 4 vols. Rio de Janeiro, 1960.

———. *Systema representativo.* Rio de Janeiro, 1868.

———. *O tronco do ipê, romance brasileiro.* Obras de ficção de José de Alencar no. 10. [2d? ed.] Rio de Janeiro, 1953.

Alencastro, Luiz Felipe de. "Le Traite négrière et l'unité nationale brésili-enne," *Revue Française d'Histoire d'Outre-Mer,* 66:244/245 (3ème/ 4ème trimestres, 1979), 395-419.

Almanak [Laemmert] administrativo, mercantil e industrial do Rio de Ja-neiro e indicador. . . . Obra estatistica e de consulta. Rio de Janeiro, various years.

Almeida, Aluísio de [Luís Castanho de Almeida]. *A revolução liberal de 1842.* Documentos Brasileiros no. 46. Rio de Janeiro, 1944.

Almeida, Candido Mendes de. *Atlas do Imperio do Brasil comprehen-dendo as respectivas divisões administrativas, ecclesiasticas, eleitoraes e judiciarias.* Rio de Janeiro, 1868.

———, ed. *Codigo Philippino; ou, Ordenações e leis do reino de Portugal, recopiladas por mandado d'el rey D. Philippe I. Decima-quarta edição segundo a primeira de 1603 e a nona de Coimbra de 1824. Addicionada com diversas notas.* . . . Rio de Janeiro, 1870.

———, comp. and ed. *Direito civil ecclesiastico brazileiro antigo e mo-derno em suas relações com o direito canonico ou, Colleção completa . . . a que se addicionão notas historicas e explicativas, indicando a legis-lação actualmente em vigor e que hoje constitue a jurisprudencia civil ecclesiastica do Brasil.* Tomo I in 2 vols. Rio de Janeiro, 1866.

Almeida, Luis C. *Vida e morte do tropeiro.* São Paulo, 1971.

Almeida, Tito Franco de. *O Conselheiro Francisco José Furtado. Biografia e estudo de história política contemporânea.* 2d ed. Brasiliana no. 245. São Paulo, 1944.

Andrade, Manuel Correia de. *A terra e o homen no Nordeste.* São Paulo, 1963.

Andrade, Rômulo Garcia de. "Burocracia e economia na primeira metade do século xix (A Junta do Comércio e as atividades artesanais e manu-fatureiras na cidade do Rio de Janeiro, 1808-1850)." M.A. thesis, Univ. Federal Fluminense, 1980.

Armitage, John. *The History of Brazil from the Period of the Arrival of the Braganza Family in 1808 to the Abdication of Don* [sic] *Pedro the First in 1831.* 2 vols. London, 1836.

Arroyo, Leonardo. *A carta de Pero Vaz de Caminha. Ensaio de informação a procura de constantes válidas de método.* 2d ed. São Paulo, 1976.

Associação Industrial, Rio de Janeiro. *O trabalho nacional e seus adver-sarios.* Rio de Janeiro, 1881.

Bahia. *Colleção das leis e resoluções da Assembléa Legislativa e regula-*

mentos do governo da Bahia, sanccionadas e publicadas. . . . Various years.

Bandeira, Antonio Herculano de Souza, ed. *Reforma eleitoral, eleição directa: Collecção de diversos artigos sobre a eleição directa dos quaes são autores os seguintes senhores*: . . . Recife, 1862.

Barbosa, Rui. *Discursos parlamentares, Camara dos Deputados*. In *Obras completas*, Vol. VII, 1880, Tomo 1. Rio de Janeiro, 1945.

————. *Liberdade commercial. O partido liberal bahiano. Discurso proferido* . . . *na Assembléa Provincial da Bahia, na sessão de 27 de junho de 1878*. Bahia, 1878.

Barman, Roderick J. "Brazil at Mid-Empire: Political Accommodation and the Pursuit of Progress Under the *Conciliação* Ministry, 1853-1857." Ph.D. diss., Univ. of California, Berkeley, 1970.

————. *Brazil: The Forging of a Nation, 1798-1852*. Stanford, Calif., 1988.

————. "The Brazilian Peasantry Reexamined: The Implications of the Quebra-Quilos Revolt, 1874-1875," *Hispanic American Historical Review*, 57:3 (Aug. 1977), 401-24.

Barman, Roderick J., and Jean Barman. "The Role of the Law Graduate in the Political Elite of Imperial Brazil," *Journal of Inter-American Studies*, 18:4 (Nov. 1976), 423-50.

Barreto, [Afonso Henrique de] Lima. *Triste fim de Policarpo Quaresma*. Obras de Lima Barreto no. 2. 7th ed. São Paulo, 1969.

[Barros, José Antonio Nogueira de]. *Tributo de gratidão á memoria do capitão João Pinheiro de Sousa*. Rio de Janeiro, 1860.

Barros, Roque Spencer Maciel de. *A ilustração brasileira e a idéia de universidade*. Universidade de São Paulo, Cadeira de História e Filosofia da Educação Boletim no. 241-2. São Paulo, 1959.

Barroso, Gustavo. *História militar do Brasil*. 2d ed. São Paulo, 1938.

Bastos, Aureliano Cândido Tavares. *Os males do presente e as esperanças do futuro ([e outros] estudos brasileiros)*. Brasiliana no. 151. 3d ed. São Paulo, 1976.

Beiguelman, Paula. *Formação política do Brasil*. Vol. I: *Teoria e ação no pensamento abolicionista*. Vol. II: *Contribuição à teoria da organização política brasileira*. São Paulo, 1967.

Beik, William. *Absolutism and Society in Seventeenth-Century France: State Power and Provincial Aristocracy in Languedoc*. Cambridge, Eng., 1985.

Besouchet, Lidia. *José Mª Paranhos, Vizconde do Río Branco*. Buenos Aires, [1944].

————. *Mauá y su época*. Buenos Aires, 1940.

Bethell, Leslie. *The Abolition of the Brazilian Slave Trade: Britain, Brazil, and the Slave Trade Question, 1807-1869*. Cambridge Latin American Studies no. 6. Cambridge, Eng., 1970.

————. "The Independence of Brazil." In *The Cambridge History of Latin*

America, ed. Leslie Bethell. Cambridge, Eng., 1985. Vol. III, pp. 157-96.

Bethell, Leslie, and José Murilo de Carvalho. "Brazil from Independence to the Middle of the Nineteenth Century." In *The Cambridge History of Latin America,* ed. Leslie Bethell. Cambridge, Eng., 1985. Vol. III, pp. 679-746.

Blassingame, John W. *The Slave Community: Plantation Life in the Ante-Bellum South.* New York, 1971.

Boxer, Charles R. *Portuguese Society in the Tropics: The Municipal Councils of Goa, Macao, Bahia, and Luanda.* Madison, Wis., 1965.

Brandão, Berenice Cavalcante, Ilmar Rohloff de Mattos, and Maria Alice Rezende de Carvalho. *Estudo das características histórico-sociais das instituições policiais brasileiras, militares e paramilitares, de suas origens até 1930: A polícia e a força policial no Rio de Janeiro.* Série Estudos-PUC/RJ no. 4. Rio de Janeiro, 1981.

Brasiliense [de Almeida Mello], Americo. *Os programas dos partidos e o 2° imperio. Primeira parte: Exposição de principios.* São Paulo, 1878.

Brazil. *Ato adicional [à Constituição política do Império do Brasil].*

———. *Colleção das leis do Imperio do Brasil (LB).*

———. *Constituição política do Império do Brasil.*

———, Arquivo Nacional [Jorge João Dodsworth, 2° barão de Javari]. *Organizações e programas ministeriais. Regime parlamentar no império.* 2d ed. Rio de Janeiro, 1962.

———, Assembléia Geral Constituinte e Legislativa. *Diário.* 1823; facsim. Brasília, 1973.

———, Commissão Encarregada da Revisão da Tarifa em Vigor. *Relatorio . . . que acompanhou o projecto de tarifa apresentado pela mesma commissão ao governo imperial.* Rio de Janeiro, 1853.

———, Commissão Encarregada de Rever e Classificar as Rendas Geraes, Provinciaes, e Municipaes do Imperio. *Relatorio e projecto de lei.* Rio de Janeiro, 1883.

———, Congresso, Câmara dos Deputados (BCCD). *Anais.*

———, ———, ———. *Livro do centenário da Camara dos Deputados.* 2 vols. Rio de Janeiro, 1926.

———, ———, ———. *Manual parlamentar. Regimento interno da Camara dos Deputados . . . .* Rio de Janeiro, 1887.

[———, ———, ———]. *Reforma eleitoral: Projectos offerecidos á consideração do corpo legislativo desde o ano de 1826 até o anno de 1875 . . . colligidos na secretaria da Camara dos Deputados.* Rio de Janeiro, 1875.

———, ———, ———, Secretaria, comp. *Falas do Trono desde o ano de 1823 até o ano de 1889, acompanhadas dos respectivos votos de graça da câmara temporária e de diferentes informações. . . .* [2d? ed.] São Paulo, [1977?].

———, ———. Senado (BCS). *Anais.*

———, Conselho de Estado. *Atas.* 13 vols. Brasília, 1973-78.

———, Directoria Geral de Estatistica. *Recenseamento da população do*

Imperio do Brazil a que se procedeu no dia 1º de agosto de 1872. Rio de Janeiro, 1873-76.

————, ————. *Synopse do recenseamento de 31 de dezembro de 1890.* Rio de Janeiro, 1898.

————, Instituto Brasileiro de Geografia e Estatística. *Anuário estatístico do Brasil.* 1908-.

————, Ministerio da Agricultura. *Relatorio.*

————, Ministerio da Fazenda (MF). *Relatorio.*

————, Ministerio da Justiça (MJ). *Relatorio.*

————, Ministerio da Justiça e Negocios Interiores. *Noticia historica dos serviços, instituições e estabelecimentos pertencentes a esta repartição, elaborada por ordem do respectivo ministro, Dr. Amaro Cavalcanti.* Rio de Janeiro, 1898.

————, ————. *Relatorio.*

————, Ministerio do Imperio. *Relatorio.*

Bueno, José Antonio Pimenta. *Direito publico brazileiro e analyse da Constituição do Imperio.* Rio de Janeiro, 1857.

Calmon, Pedro. *História de D. Pedro II.* Documentos Brasileiros nos. 165A-165D. 5 vols. Rio de Janeiro, 1975.

————. "Organização judiciária: (a) na Colônia; (b) no Império; (c) na República." In *Livro do centenário dos cursos jurídicos.* 2 vols. Rio de Janeiro, 1928. Vol. I, pp. 79-98.

Campos, Joaquim Pinto de [Um Pernambucano]. *Os anarquistas e a civilização: Ensaio politico sobre a situação.* Rio de Janeiro, 1860.

Cannabrava, Alice P. *Desenvolvimento da cultura do algodão na província de São Paulo (1861-1875).* São Paulo, 1951.

Cano, Wilson. *Raízes da concentração industrial em São Paulo.* Corpo e Alma do Brasil no. 53. São Paulo, 1977.

Cardoso, Fernando Henrique, and Enzo Faletto. *Dependency and Development in Latin America,* tr. Marjory Mattingly Urquidi. Berkeley, Calif., 1979.

Carone, Edgard. "Coronelismo: Definição, história, e bibliografia," *Revista de Administração de Empresas,* 11:3 (July-Sept. 1971), 85-92.

Carvalho, Antonio Alves de Souza. *O Brasil em 1870, estudo politico.* Rio de Janeiro, 1870.

[————]. *O imperialismo e a reforma, anotado por um constitucional do Maranhão.* Maranhão [São Luiz?], 1866.

Carvalho, João Manuel de. *Reminiscencias sobre vultos e factos do imperio e da republica.* Amparo, 1894.

Carvalho, José Murilo de. *Os bestializados: O Rio de Janeiro e a república que não foi.* São Paulo, 1987.

————. "A composição social dos partidos políticos imperiais." In Minas Gerais, Universidade Federal, Departamento de Ciências Políticas, *Cadernos,* no. 2 (Dec. 1974), 1-34.

————. *A construção da ordem: A elite política imperial.* Contribuições em Ciências Sociais no. 8. Rio de Janeiro, 1980.

————. "Elite and State Building in Imperial Brazil." Ph.D. diss., Stanford Univ., 1974.

————. "Political Elites and State Building: The Case of Nineteenth-Century Brazil," *Comparative Studies in Society and History*, 24:3 (July 1982), 378-99.

————. *Teatro de sombras: A política imperial*. Formação do Brasil no. 4. São Paulo, 1988.

Castro, Jeanne Berrance de. *A milícia cidadã: A Guarda Nacional de 1831 a 1850*. Brasiliana no. 359. São Paulo, 1977.

Castro, José Antonio de Magalhães. *Refutação da exposição circumstanciada que fez o doutor Justiano Baptista de Madureira . . . ao Presidente da Provincia da Bahia, sobre as elleições do Collegio de Villa Nova da Rainha*. Rio de Janeiro, 1857.

Chagas, Paulo Pinheiro. *Teófilo Ottoni, ministro do povo*. 2d rev. ed. Rio de Janeiro, 1956.

Chambers, William Nisbet. *Political Parties in a New Nation: The American Experience, 1776-1809*. New York, 1963.

Chandler, Billy Jaynes. *The Feitosas and the Sertão dos Inhamuns: The History of a Family and a Community in Northeast Brazil, 1700-1930*. Gainesville, Fla., 1972.

Congresso Agricola. *Congresso Agricola: Coleção de documentos*. Rio de Janeiro, 1878.

Conrad, Robert Edgar. *Brazilian Slavery: An Annotated Research Bibliography*. Boston, 1977.

————. *Children of God's Fire: A Documentary History of Black Slavery in Brazil*. Princeton, N.J., 1983.

————. *The Destruction of Brazilian Slavery, 1850-1888*. Berkeley, Calif., 1972.

————. *World of Sorrow: The African Slave Trade to Brazil*. Baton Rouge, La., 1986.

Contier, Arnaldo Daraya. *Imprensa e ideologia em São Paulo (1822-1842). (Matizes do vocabulário político e social)*. Coleção História Brasileira no. 4. Petrópolis, 1979.

Costa, Emília Viotti da. "Brazil: The Age of Reform, 1870-1889." In *The Cambridge History of Latin America*, ed. Leslie Bethell. Cambridge, Eng., 1987. Vol. V, pp. 725-77.

————. *The Brazilian Empire: Myths and Realities*. Chicago, 1985.

————. *Da senzala à colônia*. Corpo e Alma do Brasil no. 19. São Paulo, 1966.

————. "The Political Emancipation of Brazil." In *From Colony to Nation: Essays on the Independence of Brazil*, ed. A. J. R. Russell-Wood. Baltimore, 1975. Pp. 43-88.

Cunha, Euclides da. *À margem da história*. In *Obra completa*, ed. Afrânio Coutinho. Rio de Janeiro, 1966. Vol. I, pp. 221-384.

————. *Rebellion in the Backlands*, tr. Samuel Putnam. Chicago, 1944.

[Dacanal, José Hildebrando, and Sergius Gonzaga, eds.]. *RS: Economia & política*. Série Documenta no. 2. Pôrto Alegre, 1979.

Damasceno, Darcy, and Waldyr da Cunha, eds. "Os manuscritos do botânico Freire Alemão." In Rio de Janeiro, Biblioteca Nacional, *Anais*. Vol. 81 (1961).

Dantas, Luiz Ascendino. *Esboço biographico do dr. Joaquim José de Souza Breves. Origem das fazendas S. Joaquim da Gramma e Sᵗᵒ Antonio da Olaria. Subsidios para a historia do municipio de S. João Marcos*. Rio de Janeiro, 1931.

Dantas, Manuel Pinto de Souza. *Correspondência*, ed. Américo Jacobina Lacombe. Rio de Janeiro, 1962.

Dantas Júnior, J. C. "O capitão-mór João d'Antas e sua descendência," *Revista Genealógica Brasileira*, 1:2 (2d sem. 1940), 379-419.

Dealy, Glen C. *The Public Man: An Interpretation of Latin American and Other Catholic Countries*. Amherst, Mass., 1977.

Dean, Warren. "Latifundia and Land Policy in Nineteenth-Century Brazil," *Hispanic American Historical Review*, 51:4 (Nov. 1971), 606-25.

———. *Rio Claro: A Brazilian Plantation System, 1820-1920*. Stanford, Calif., 1976.

Degler, Carl N. *Neither Black nor White: Slavery and Race Relations in Brazil and the United States*. New York, 1971.

Dent, Hastings Charles. *A Year in Brazil, with Notes on the Abolition of Slavery, the Finances of the Empire, Religion, Meteorology, Natural History, Etc.* London, 1886.

Dias, Carlos Malheiro, ed. *História da colonização portuguesa do Brasil. Edição monumental comemorativa do primeiro centenário da independência do Brasil*. 3 vols. Porto, 1921-24.

Dias, Maria Odila Silva. "The Establishment of the Royal Court in Brazil." In *From Colony to Nation: Essays on the Independence of Brazil*, ed. A. J. R. Russell-Wood. Baltimore, 1975. Pp. 89-108.

———. "Ideologia liberal e a construção do estado do Brasil," *Anais do Museu Paulista*, 30 (1980-81), 211-25.

Duarte, Nestor. *A ordem privada e a organização politica nacional (Contribuição á sociologia politica brasileira*. Brasiliana no. 172. São Paulo, 1939.

Dudley, William S. "Institutional Sources of Officer Discontent in the Brazilian Army, 1870-1889," *Hispanic American Historical Review*, 55:1 (Feb. 1975), 44-65.

Dumont, Louis. *Homo Hierarchicus: The Caste System and Its Implications*, tr. Mark Sainsbury, Louis Dumont, and Basia Gulati. Rev. ed. Chicago, 1980.

Eisenberg, Peter L. *The Sugar Industry in Pernambuco: Modernization Without Change, 1840-1910*. Berkeley, Calif., 1974.

Eisenstadt, S. N. *The Political Systems of Empires*. New York, 1963.

Faoro, Raymundo. *Os donos do poder: Formação do patronato político brasileiro*. 2d ed. 2 vols. Pôrto Alegre, 1975.

Fél, Edit, and Tamás Hofer. "Tanyakert-s, Patron-Client Relations and Political Factions in Átány," *American Anthropologist*, 75:3 (June 1973), 787-801.

Fernandes, Florestan. *A Revolução burguesa no Brasil: Ensaio de interpretação sociológica.* Rio de Janeiro, 1975.

Fernandes, Heloisa Rodrigues. *Política e segurança: Força pública do Estado de São Paulo. Fundamentos histórico-sociais.* São Paulo, 1974.

Fialho, Anpriso [Anfriso]. "Biographical Sketch of Dom Pedro II, Emperor of Brazil." In Smithsonian Institution, *Annual Report of the Board of Regents.* Washington, D.C., 1877. Pp. 173-204.

———. *Processo da monarchia brazileira: Necessidade da convocação de uma constituinte.* Rio de Janeiro, 1885.

Figueiredo, Affonso Celso de Assis. *As finanças da regeneração: Estudo politico offerecido aos mineiros.* Rio de Janeiro, 1876.

———. *Reforma administrativa e municipal: Parecer e projectos.* Rio de Janeiro, 1883.

Figueiredo, Affonso Celso de Assis, visconde de Ouro Preto, et al. *A decada republicana.* 8 vols. Rio de Janeiro, 1899-1901.

Figueiredo Júnior, Affonso Celso de Assis, conde de Affonso Celso. *Oito annos de parlamento. Poder pessoal de D. Pedro II. Reminiscencias e notas.* São Paulo: Melhoramentos, n.d.

Filler, Victor M. "Liberalism in Imperial Brazil: The Regional Rebellions of 1842." Ph.D. diss., Stanford Univ., 1976.

Flory, Thomas. *Judge and Jury in Imperial Brazil, 1808-1871: Social Control and Political Stability in the New State.* Latin American Monographs no. 53. Austin, Tex., 1981.

———. "Race and Social Control in Independent Brazil," *Journal of Latin American Studies,* 9:2 (Nov. 1977), 199-224.

Flynn, Peter. "Class, Clientelism, and Coercion: Some Mechanisms of Internal Dependency and Control," *Journal of Commonwealth and Comparative Politics,* 12:2 (July 1974), 133-56.

Forman, Shepard, and Joyce F. Riegelhaupt. "The Political Economy of Patron-Clientship, Brazil and Portugal Compared." In *Brazil, Anthropological Perspectives: Essays in Honor of Charles Wagley,* ed. Maxine L. Margolis and William E. Carter. New York, 1979. Pp. 379-400.

Franco, Afonso Arinos de Melo. *História e teoria dos partidos políticos no Brasil.* Biblioteca Alfa-Omega de Ciências Sociais série 1, no. 3. 2d ed. São Paulo, 1974.

Franco, Maria Sylvia de Carvalho. *Homens livres na ordem escravocrata.* Ensaios no. 3. 2d ed. São Paulo, 1974.

Freyre, Gilberto. *The Masters and the Slaves (Casa-Grande & Senzala): A Study in the Development of Brazilian Civilization,* tr. Samuel Putnam. New York, 1956.

Galvão, Miguel Arcanjo. *Relação dos cidadãos que tomaram parte no govêrno do Brasil no período de março de 1808 a 15 de novembro de 1889.* 2d ed. Rio de Janeiro, 1969.

Gama, Manuel Jacintho Carneiro Nogueira da. *Testamento.* Freguezia de Santa Thereza [Valença], 1883. [Place of publication and publisher (Typ. de Santa Rosa) may be fictitious].

Genovese, Eugene D. "Yeomen Farmers in a Slaveholders' Democracy," *Agricultural History*, 49:2 (Apr. 1975), 331-42.

Gilsenan, Michael. "Against Patron-Client Relations." In *Patrons and Clients in Mediterranean Societies*, ed. Ernest Gellner and John Waterbury. London, 1977. Pp. 167-82.

Goulart, José Alípio. *Da fuga ao suicídio (aspectos da rebeldia dos escravos no Brasil)*. Rio de Janeiro, 1972.

———. *Tropas e tropeiros na formação do Brasil*. Coleção Temas Brasileiros no. 4. Rio de Janeiro, 1961.

Graham, Lawrence S. *Civil Service Reform in Brazil: Principles Versus Practice*. Latin American Monographs no. 13. Austin, Tex., 1968.

Graham, Maria Dundas (Lady Maria Calcott). *Journal of a Voyage to Brazil and Residence There During Part of the Years 1821, 1822, 1823.* 1824 rpt. New York, 1969.

Graham, Richard. "Brazilian Slavery Re-Examined: A Review Article," *Journal of Social History*, 3:4 (Summer 1970), 431-53.

———. *Britain and the Onset of Modernization in Brazil, 1850-1914.* Cambridge Latin American Studies no. 4. Cambridge, Eng., 1968.

———. "Causes for the Abolition of Negro Slavery in Brazil: An Interpretive Essay," *Hispanic American Historical Review*, 46:2 (May 1966), 123-38.

———. *Escravidão, reforma e imperialismo*. Coleção Debates no. 146. São Paulo, 1979.

———. "Government Expenditures and Political Change in Brazil, 1880-1899," *Journal of Inter-American Studies*, 19:3 (Aug. 1977), 339-67.

———. "Landowners and the Overthrow of the Empire," *Luso-Brazilian Review*, 7:2 (Dec. 1970), 44-56.

———. "Slavery and Economic Development: Brazil and the United States South in the Nineteenth Century," *Comparative Studies in Society and History*, 23:4 (Oct. 1981), 620-55.

Graham, Sandra Lauderdale. *House and Street: The Domestic World of Servants and Masters in Nineteenth-Century Rio de Janeiro*. Cambridge Latin American Studies no. 68. Cambridge, Eng., 1988.

———. "Slave Prostitutes and Small-Time Mistresses: The Campaign of 1871 in Rio de Janeiro." Unpublished ms.

———. "The Vintem Riot and Political Culture: Rio de Janeiro, 1880," *Hispanic American Historical Review*, 60:3 (Aug. 1980), 431-49.

Gross, Daniel R. "Factionalism and Local Level Politics in Rural Brazil," *Journal of Anthropological Research*, 29:2 (Summer 1973), 123-44.

Hahner, June E. *Civilian-Military Relations in Brazil, 1889-1898*. Columbia, S.C., 1969.

Hauk, João Fagundes, et al. *História da igreja no Brasil: Ensaio de interpretação a partir do povo. Segunda época: A igreja no Brasil no século XIX.* História Geral da Igreja na América Latina no. II/2. Petrópolis, 1980.

Hay, Douglas. "Property, Authority and the Criminal Law." In *Albion's*

Fatal Tree: Crime and Society in Eighteenth-Century England, ed. Douglas Hay et al. New York, 1975. Pp. 17-63.

Hofstadter, Richard. *The Idea of a Party System: The Rise of Legitimate Opposition in the United States, 1780-1840*. Berkeley, Calif., 1969.

Holanda, Sérgio Buarque de, ed. *História geral da civilização brasileira (HGCB)*, Tomo II: *O Brasil monárquico*: Vol. II [no. 4]: *Dispersão e unidade*; Vol. III [no. 5]: *Reações e transações*; Vol. IV [no. 6]: *Declínio e queda do Império*; Vol. V [no. 7]: *Do império a república*. São Paulo, 1964-72. Cited by the numbers shown in brackets.

Holloway, Thomas H. "The Brazilian 'Judicial Police' in Florianópolis, Santa Catarina, 1841-1871," *Journal of Social History*, 20:4 (Summer 1987), 733-56.

———. *Immigrants on the Land: Coffee and Society in São Paulo, 1886-1934*. Chapel Hill, N.C., 1980.

Homem, Floriano Torres. "Francisco de Salles Torres Homem, visconde de Inhomerin." In 3° *Congresso de Historia Nacional, 1938, Anais*. 10 vols. Rio de Janeiro, 1939-44. Vol. VI, pp. 85-165.

Honras funebres em memoria do ... visconde de Inhaúma, Grand-Mest. ... do Gr.°. Or.°. e Sup.°. Cons.°. do Brasil. Rio de Janeiro, 1869.

Iglesias, Francisco. *Política econômica do govêrno provincial mineiro (1835-1889)*. Rio de Janeiro, 1958.

Isaac, Rhys. *The Transformation of Virginia, 1740-1790*. Chapel Hill, N.C., 1982.

Jaguaribe, Helio. *Political Development: A General Theory and a Latin American Case Study*. New York, 1973.

Jesus, J. Palhano de. "Rapida noticia da viação ferrea do Brasil." In Instituto Historico e Geographico Brasileiro, *Diccionario historico, geographico e ethnographico do Brasil (Commemorativo do primeiro centenario da independencia)*. 2 vols. Rio de Janeiro, 1922. Vol. I, pp. 723-56.

Jordan, Daniel P. *Political Leadership in Jefferson's Virginia*. Charlottesville, Va., 1983.

Karasch, Mary C. *Slave Life in Rio de Janeiro, 1808-1850*. Princeton, N.J., 1987.

Kennedy, John N. "Bahian Elites," *Hispanic American Historical Review*, 53:3 (Aug. 1973), 415-39.

Kenny, Michael. "Patterns of Patronage in Spain," *Anthropological Quarterly*, 33:1 (Jan. 1960), 14-23.

Kettering, Sharon. *Patrons, Brokers, and Clients in Seventeenth-Century France*. New York, 1986.

Kidder, Daniel Parish, and James Cooley Fletcher. *Brazil and the Brazilians Portrayed in Historical and Descriptive Sketches*. Philadelphia, 1857.

Klein, Herbert S. "Nineteenth-Century Brazil." In *Neither Slave nor Free: The Freedman of African Descent in the Slave Societies of the New World*, ed. David W. Cohen and Jack P. Greene. Baltimore, 1972. Pp. 309-34.

Sources Cited   359

Koster, Henry. *Travels in Brazil in the Years from 1809 to 1815.* 2 vols. Philadelphia, 1817.
Kuznesof, Elizabeth. "Clans, the Militia, and Territorial Government: The Articulation of Kinship with Polity in Eighteenth-Century São Paulo." In *Social Fabric and Spatial Structure in Colonial Latin America,* ed. David J. Robinson. Syracuse, N.Y., 1979. Pp. 181-226.
———. "The Role of the Female-Headed Household in Brazilian Modernization, 1765-1836," *Journal of Social History,* 13:4 (Summer 1980), 589-613.
Laerne, C. F. van Delden. *Brazil and Java: Report on Coffee-Culture in America, Asia and Africa to H.E. the Minister of the Colonies.* London, 1885.
Lamego, Alberto Ribeiro. "A aristocracia rural do café na provincia fluminense," *Anuário do Museu Imperial,* 7 (1946), 53-123.
Laxe, João Batista Cortines. *Regimento das camaras municipais ou, Lei de 1º de outubro de 1828, annotada com leis, decretos . . . ; precedida de uma introdução historica e seguida de sete appensos,* ed. Antonio Joaquim de Macedo Soares. 2d ed. Rio de Janeiro, 1885.
Leal, Aurelino. "História judiciária do Brasil." In Instituto Historico e Geographico Brasileiro, *Diccionario historico, geographico e ethnographico do Brasil.* Rio de Janeiro, 1922. Vol. I, pp. 1107-1187.
Leal, Victor Nunes. *Coronelismo: The Municipality and Representative Government in Brazil,* tr. June Henfrey. Cambridge Latin American Studies no. 28. Cambridge, Eng., 1977.
Le Roy Ladurie, Emmanuel. *Montaillou, the Promised Land of Error,* tr. Barbara Bray. New York, 1978.
Leff, Nathaniel H. *Underdevelopment and Development in Brazil.* Vol. I: *Economic Structure and Change, 1822-1947.* London, 1982.
Leitman, Spencer L. *Raízes socio-econômicas da Guerra dos Farrapos: Um capítulo de história do Brasil no século xix.* Rio de Janeiro, 1979.
Lemos, Miguel. *A incorporação do proletariado escravo. Protesto da Sociedade Positivista do Rio de Janeiro contra o recente projecto do governo.* Recife, 1883.
Lenharo, Alcir. *As tropas da moderação (O abastecimento da Corte na formação política do Brasil, 1808-1842.* Coleção Ensaio e Memória no. 21. São Paulo, 1979.
Leonzo, Nanci, and Rita Maria Cardoso Barbosa. "As 'virtudes' do bacharelismo." In Sociedade Brasileira de Pesquisa Histórica, IIª Reunião (1983), *Anais.* São Paulo, 1983. Pp. 125-28.
Levi, Darrell E. *The Prados of São Paulo Brazil: An Elite Family and Social Change, 1840-1930.* Athens, Ga., 1987.
Levine, Robert M. *Pernambuco in the Brazilian Federation, 1889-1937.* Stanford, Calif., 1978.
Lewin, Linda. *Politics and Parentela in Paraíba: A Case Study of Family-Based Oligarchy in Brazil.* Princeton, N.J. 1987.
[Lima, Álvaro Tiberio de Moncorvo e]. *Eleição do 3º districto da provincia da Bahia.* Salvador, 1857.

Lima, Manuel de Oliveira. *Dom João VI no Brasil, 1808-1821.* Documentos Brasileiros nos. 49-49B. 2d ed. 3 vols. Rio de Janeiro, 1945.

Lisboa, João Francisco. *Obras.* 2d ed. 2 vols. Lisbon, 1901.

Lopes, Tomas de Vilanova Monteiro. "A seleção de pessoal para o serviço público brasileiro," *Revista do Serviço Público,* 4:1 (Oct. 1952), 19-23.

Love, Joseph L. "Political Participation in Brazil, 1881-1969," *Luso-Brazilian Review,* 7:2 (Dec. 1970), 3-24.

——. *Rio Grande do Sul and Brazilian Regionalism, 1882-1930.* Stanford, Calif., 1971.

——. *São Paulo in the Brazilian Federation, 1889-1937.* Stanford, Calif., 1980.

Luz, Nícia Villela. "O papel das classes médias brasileiras no movimento republicano," *Revista de História,* 28:57 (Jan.-Mar. 1964), 13-27.

Lyra, Augusto Tavares de. *Esboço historico do regimen eleitoral do Brasil (1821-1921).* Rio de Janeiro, 1922.

Lyra, Heitor. *História de Dom Pedro II, 1825-1891.* Reconquista do Brasil nos. 39-41. 2d rev. ed. 3 vols. Belo Horizonte, 1977.

Lyttleton, N. A. O. "El patronazgo en la Italia de Giolitti (1892-1924)," *Revista de Occidente,* 127 (Oct. 1973), 94-117.

Macedo, Ubiratan Borges de. *A liberdade no Império.* São Paulo, 1977.

Magalhães, Basílio de. *Estudos de história do Brasil.* Brasiliana no. 171. São Paulo, 1940.

Magalhães Júnior, Raimundo. *José de Alencar e sua época.* 2d ed. Rio de Janeiro, 1977.

——. *Três panfletários do segundo reinado: Francisco de Sales Torres Homem e o "Líbelo do povo"; Justiniano José da Rocha e "Ação; reação; transação"; Antônio Ferreira Vianna e "A conferência dos divinos."* Brasiliana no. 286. São Paulo, 1956.

Malheiro, Agostinho Marques Perdigão. *A escravidão no Brasil. Ensaio histórico, jurídico, social.* Coleção Dimensões do Brasil nos. 3-3a. 3d ed. 2 vols. Petrópolis, 1976.

Manchester, Alan K. "The Growth of Bureaucracy in Brazil, 1808-1821," *Journal of Latin American Studies,* 4:1 (May 1972), 77-83.

——. "The Transfer of the Portuguese Court to Rio de Janeiro." In *Conflict and Continuity in Brazilian Society,* ed. Henry Keith and S. F. Edwards. Columbia, S.C., 1969. Pp. 148-83.

Maraspini, A. L. *The Study of an Italian Village.* Publications of the Social Science Centre (Athens) no. 5. Paris, 1968.

Marcílio, Maria Luiza. "Crescimento demográfico e evolução agrária paulista, 1700-1836." Tese de Livre-Docência, Univ. de São Paulo, 1974.

Marinho, José Antônio. *História do movimento político de 1842.* Reconquista do Brasil no. 42. 3d ed. Belo Horizonte, 1977.

——. *Sermão que recitou na capella imperial . . . por occasião do baptisado da serenissima princeza a sra. D. Leopoldina Thereza.* Rio de Janeiro, 1847.

Martins, Luís. *O patriarca e o bacharel.* São Paulo, [1953].

Martins, Roberto Borges. "Growing in Silence: The Slave Economy of Nineteenth-Century Minas Gerais, Brazil." Ph.D. diss., Vanderbilt Univ., 1980.

Martins Filho, Amilcar. "Clientelismo e representação em Minas Gerais durante a Primeira República: Uma crítica a Paul Cammack," *Dados— Revista de Ciências Sociais,* 27:2 (1984), 175-97.

Mascarenhas, Nelson Lage. *Um jornalista do império (Firmino Rodrigues Silva).* Brasiliana no. 309. São Paulo, 1961.

Mattos, Ilmar Rohloff de. *O tempo saquarema.* São Paulo, 1987.

Mattoso, Kátia M. de Queirós. *A presença francesa no movimento democrático baiano de 1798.* Salvador, 1969.

Maxwell, Kenneth R. *Conflicts and Conspiracies: Brazil and Portugal, 1750-1808.* Cambridge Latin American Studies no. 16. Cambridge, Eng., 1973.

———. "The Generation of the 1790s and the Idea of a Luso-Brazilian Empire." In *Colonial Roots of Modern Brazil. Papers of the Newberry Library Conference,* ed. Dauril Alden. Berkeley, Calif., 1973. Pp. 107-44.

Mello, Affonso d'Albuquerque. *A liberdade no Brasil: Seu nascimento, vida, morte, e sepultura.* Recife, 1864.

Mello, Pedro Carvalho de. "The Economics of Labor in Brazilian Coffee Plantations, 1850-1888." Ph.D. diss., Univ. of Chicago, 1977.

Mesquita, Eni de. "O papel do agregado na região de Itú—1780 a 1830," *Coleção Museu Paulista,* 6 (1977), 13-121.

Metcalf, Alida C. "Families of Planters, Peasants, and Slaves: Strategies for Survival in Santana de Parnaíba, Brazil, 1720-1820." Ph.D. diss., Univ. of Texas at Austin, 1983.

Meznar, Joan E. "Deference and Dependence: The World of Small Farmers in a Northeastern Brazilian Community, 1850-1900." Ph.D. diss., Univ. of Texas at Austin, 1986.

Milet, Henrique Augusto. *Auxilio a lavoura e credito real.* Recife, 1876.

———. *Miscellanea economica e politica.* Recife, 1882.

———. *Os quebra-kilos e a crise da lavoura.* Recife, 1876.

Monbeig, Pierre. *Pionniers et planteurs de São Paulo.* Collection des Cahiers de la Fondation Nationale des Sciences Politiques no. 28. Paris, 1952.

Monteiro, Tobias [do Rego]. *Historia do Império: A elaboração da independencia.* Rio de Janeiro, 1927.

———. *Historia do Império: O primeiro reinado.* 2 vols. Rio de Janeiro, 1939-46.

Morse, Richard M. "Brazil's Urban Development: Colony and Empire." In *From Colony to Nation: Essays on the Independence of Brazil,* ed. A. J. R. Russell-Wood. Baltimore, 1975. Pp. 155-81.

———. "Some Themes of Brazilian History," *South Atlantic Quarterly,* 61 (Spring 1962), 159-82.

Morton, F. W. O. "The Conservative Revolution of Independence:

Economy, Society and Politics in Bahia, 1790-1840." Ph.D. diss., Univ. of Oxford, 1974.

Mota, Carlos Guilherme, and Fernando A. Novais. *A independência política do Brasil.* São Paulo, 1986.

Mott, Luiz R. B. *Sergipe del Rey: População, economia e sociedade.* Maceió, 1986.

Moura, Clovis. *Rebeliões da senzala (quilombos, insurreições, guerrilhas).* São Paulo, 1959.

Mourão, João Martins de Carvalho. "Os municipios, sua importancia politica no Brasil-colônia e no Brasil-reino. Situação em que ficaram no Brasil imperial pela Constituição de 1824 e pelo Ato Adicional." In Primeiro Congresso de Historia Nacional, *Anais.* 5 vols. Rio de Janeiro, 1916. Vol. III, pp. 299-318.

Nabuco, Joaquim. *O abolicionismo.* [2d ed.?] Rio de Janeiro, 1938.

———. *Eleições liberaes e eleições conservadoras.* Rio de Janeiro, 1886.

———. *Um estadista do império.* [3d ed.?] Rio de Janeiro, 1975.

Naro, Nancy. "The 1848 Praieira Revolt in Brazil." Ph.D. diss., Univ. of Chicago, 1981.

Nazzari, Muriel Smith. "Women, the Family and Property: The Decline of the Dowry in São Paulo, Brazil (1600-1870)." Ph.D. diss., Yale Univ., 1986.

Neder, Gizlene, Nancy Naro, and José Luiz Werneck da Silva. *Estudo das características histórico-sociais das instituições policiais brasileiras, militares e paramilitares, de suas origens até 1930: A polícia na Corte e no Distrito Federal, 1831-1930.* Série Estudos-PUC/RJ no. 3. Rio de Janeiro, 1981.

Nequete, Lenine. *O poder judiciário no Brasil a partir da Independência.* 2 vols. Pôrto Alegre, 1973.

Nishida, Mieko. "Negro Slavery in Brazil: Master-Slave Relations on the Sugar Plantations in the Northeast." Unpublished ms.

Normano, J. F. *Brazil, a Study of Economic Types.* Chapel Hill, N.C., 1935.

Novais, Fernando A. *Portugal e Brasil na crise do Antigo Sistema Colonial (1777-1808).* São Paulo, 1979.

Oakes, James. *The Ruling Race: A History of American Slaveholders.* New York, 1982.

Oliveira, Candido de. "A justiça." In Affonso Celso de Assis Figueiredo, visconde de Ouro Preto, et al., *A decada republicana.* 8 vols. Rio de Janeiro, 1899-1901. Vol. III, pp. 7-148.

Ottoni, Cristiano Benedito. *O advento da república no Brasil.* Rio de Janeiro, 1890.

Pang, Eul-Soo. *Bahia in the First Brazilian Republic: Coronelismo and Oligarchies, 1889-1934.* Latin American Monographs, 2d ser., no. 23. Gainesville, Fla., 1979.

———. *O Engenho Central do Bom Jardim na economia baiana. Alguns aspectos de sua história, 1875-1891.* Rio de Janeiro, 1979.

Pang, Eul-Soo, and Ron L. Seckinger. "The Mandarins of Imperial Brazil," *Comparative Studies in Society and History*, 14:2 (Mar. 1972), 215-44.

Paraíba, Presidente. *Relatorio.*

Paranhos, José Maria da Silva, 2º barão do Rio Branco. *O visconde do Rio Branco* [2d ed.?], ed. Renato de Mendonça. Rio de Janeiro, [1943?].

Pedro II. *Cartas do imperador D. Pedro II ao barão de Cotegipe*, ed. José Wanderley de Araújo Pinho. Brasiliana no. 12. São Paulo, 1933.

———. *Conselhos à regente.* Rio de Janeiro, 1958.

Penna, Domingos Soares Ferreira. *A região occidental da provincia do Pará: Resenhas estatisticas das comarcas de Obidos e Santarem.* Pará [Belém], 1869.

Petrone, Maria Thereza Schorer. *A lavoura canavieira em São Paulo. Expansão e declínio (1765-1851).* Corpo e Alma do Brasil no. 21. São Paulo, 1968.

———. "Terras devolutas, posses, e sesmarias no Vale do Paraíba paulista em 1854," *Revista de História*, 52 (July-Sept. 1976), 375-400.

Pinho, José Wanderley de Araújo. *Cotegipe e seu tempo, primeira phase, 1815-1867.* Brasiliana no. 85. São Paulo, 1937.

———. *Política e políticos no império.* Rio de Janeiro, 1930.

Pinho, Péricles Madureira do. *Luís Tarquínio, pioneiro da justiça social no Brasil.* Salvador, 1944.

Pinto, Caetano José de Andrade. *Attribuições dos presidentes de provincia.* Rio de Janeiro, 1865.

Pinto, L. A. Costa. *Lutas de famílias no Brasil (Introdução ao seu estudo).* Brasiliana no. 263. São Paulo, 1949.

Pitt-Rivers, Julian Alfred. *The People of the Sierra.* London, 1954.

Pontes, Carlos. *Tavares Bastos (Aureliano Cândido), 1839-1875.* Brasiliana no. 136. São Paulo, 1939.

Powell, John Duncan. "Peasant Society and Clientist Politics," *American Political Science Review*, 64:2 (June 1970), 411-25.

Prado, F. Silveira do. *A polícia militar fluminense no tempo do império (1835-1889).* Rio de Janeiro, 1969.

Prado Júnior, Caio. *The Colonial Background of Modern Brazil*, tr. Suzette Macedo. Berkeley, Calif., 1967.

———. *Evolução política do Brasil e outros estudos.* [? ed.] São Paulo, 1957.

———. *História econômica do Brasil.* 5th ed. São Paulo, 1959.

Queiroz, Maria Isaura Pereira de. *O mandonismo local na vida política brasileira (da Colônia à Primeira República): Ensaio de sociologia política.* Publicações do IEB no. 14. São Paulo, 1969.

Ramos, Donald. "Marriage and the Family in Colonial Vila Rica," *Hispanic American Historical Review*, 55:2 (May 1975), 200-225.

Reis, João José. *Rebelião escrava no Brasil: A história do levante dos malês, 1835.* São Paulo, 1986.

Rezende, Francisco de Paula Ferreira de. *Minhas recordações.* Documentos Brasileiros no. 45. Rio de Janeiro, 1944.

Ridings, Eugene W. "Class Sector Unity in an Export Economy: The Case of Nineteenth-Century Brazil," *Hispanic American Historical Review*, 58:3 (Aug. 1978), 432-50.

Rio de Janeiro (city), Prefeitura. *Codigo de posturas da Illma. Camara municipal do Rio de Janeiro e editaes da mesma Camara.* Nova ed. Rio de Janeiro, 1870.

———, ———. *Consolidação das leis e posturas municipais.* Rio de Janeiro, 1905.

Rio de Janeiro (diocese), Bishop. *Representação dirigida ao illm. e exm. sr. ministro e secretario de estado dos negocios do Imperio pelo bispo de S. Sebastião do Rio de Janeiro pedindo para que as eleições politicas se fação fóra das igrejas.* Rio de Janeiro, 1872.

[Rodrigues, Antonio Coelho]. *Manual do Subdito Fiel* [pseud.] *ou, Cartas de um lavrador a sua magestade o Imperador sobre a questão do elemento servil.* Rio de Janeiro, 1884.

Rodrigues, Antonio Edmilson Martins, Francisco José Calazans Falcon, and Margarida de Souza Neves. *Estudo das características histórico-sociais das instituições policiais brasileiras, militares e paramilitares, de suas origens até 1930: A Guarda Nacional no Rio de Janeiro, 1831-1918.* Série Estudos-PUC/RJ no. 5. Rio de Janeiro, 1981.

Rodrigues, José Honório. *Conciliação e reforma no Brasil. Um desafio histórico-político.* Retratos do Brasil no. 32. Rio de Janeiro, 1965.

———. *O Conselho de Estado: O quinto poder?* Brasília, 1978.

———. *Independência: Revolução e contra-revolução.* 5 vols. Rio de Janeiro, 1975.

Rodrigues, José W. de. "Fardas do Reino Unido e do Império," *Anuário do Museu Imperial*, 11 (1950), 5-52.

Rohan, Henrique de Beaurepaire. *O futuro da grande lavoura e da grande propriedade no Brazil: Memoria apresentada ao Ministerio de Agricultura, Commercio e Obras Publicas.* Rio de Janeiro, 1878.

Romero, Sylvio. *A bancarrota do regime federativo no Brasil: Ação dissolvente das oligarchias, ação indispensavel do exército.* Porto, 1912.

Romero-Maura, Joaquim. "Caciquismo as a Political System." In *Patrons and Clients in Mediterranean Societies*, ed. Ernest Gellner and John Waterbury. London, 1977. Pp. 53-62.

Roniger, Luis. "Clientelism and Patron-Client Relations: A Bibliography." In *Political Clientelism, Patronage and Development*, ed. S. N. Eisenstadt and René Lemarchand. Sage Studies in Contemporary Political Sociology no. 3. Beverly Hills, Calif., 1981. Pp. 297-330.

Rothstein, Frances. "The Class Basis of Patron-Client Relations," *Latin American Perspectives*, 6:2 (Spring 1979), 25-35.

Russell-Wood, A. J. R. "Local Government in Portuguese America: A Study in Cultural Divergence," *Comparative Studies in Society and History*, 16:2 (Mar. 1974), 187-231.

Saes, Décio. *A formação do estado burguês no Brasil (1888-1891).* Estudos Brasileiros no. 86. Rio de Janeiro, 1985.

Saller, Richard P. *Personal Patronage Under the Early Empire.* Cambridge, Eng., 1982.

Sánchez-Albornoz, Nicolás. *The Population of Latin America: A History,* tr. W. A. R. Richardson. Berkeley, Calif., 1974.

Sant'Ana, Moacir Medeiros de. *Contribuição à história do açucar em Alagoas.* Recife, 1970.

Santos, Ana Maria dos. "Agricultural Reform and the Idea of 'Decadence' in the State of Rio de Janeiro, 1870-1910." Ph.D. diss., Univ. of Texas at Austin, 1984.

Santos, José Maria dos. *A politica geral do Brasil.* São Paulo, 1930.

Santos, Luiz Gonçalves dos (Padre Perereca). *Memórias para servir à história do reino do Brasil.* Reconquista do Brasil n.s. nos. 36-37. 3d ed. 2 vols. Belo Horizonte, 1981.

São Paulo (city), Prefeitura, Arquivo Municipal. *Registo geral da câmara da cidade de São Paulo.* São Paulo, 1917- .

Schmidt, Carlos Borges. *Tropas e tropeiros.* São Paulo, 1932.

Schwartz, Stuart B. "Elite Politics and the Growth of a Peasantry in Late Colonial Brazil." In *From Colony to Nation: Essays on the Independence of Brazil,* ed. A. J. R. Russell-Wood. Baltimore, 1975. Pp. 133-54.

———. *Sovereignty and Society in Colonial Brazil: The High Court of Bahia and Its Judges, 1609-1751.* Berkeley, Calif., 1973.

Schwarz, Roberto. *Ao vencedor as batatas: Forma literária e processo social nos inícios do romance brasileiro.* São Paulo, 1977.

Scott, James C. "Political Clientelism: A Bibliographical Essay." In *Friends, Followers, and Factions: A Reader in Political Clientelism,* ed. Steffen W. Schmidt, Laura Guasti, Carl H. Landé, and James C. Scott. Berkeley, Calif., 1977. Pp. 483-505.

Scullard, H. H. *Roman Politics, 220-150 BC.* Oxford, Eng., 1951.

Semana illustrada. 1858-78.

Shefter, Martin. "Party and Patronage: Germany, England, and Italy," *Politics and Society,* 7:4 (1977), 403-51.

Silva, Antonio de Moraes. *Diccionario da lingua portugueza.* 8th ed. 2 vols. Rio de Janeiro, 1889-91.

Silva, Eduardo. *Barões e escravidão: Três gerações de fazendeiros e a crise da estrutura escravista.* Rio de Janeiro, 1984.

Silva, João Manuel Pereira da. *Memorias do meu tempo.* 2 vols. Paris, [1896?].

Silva, Joaquim Norberto de Souza. *Investigações sobre os recenseamentos da população geral do Imperio e de cada provincia de per si tentados desde os tempos coloniaes até hoje.* . . . Rio de Janeiro, 1870.

Silva, Moacir Fecury Ferreira da. "O desenvolvimento comercial do Pará no período da borracha (1870-1914)." M.A. thesis, Univ. Federal Fluminense, 1978.

Silverman, Sydel F. "Patronage and Community-Nation Relationships in Central Italy," *Ethnology,* 4:2 (Apr. 1965), 172-89.

Singer, Paul. *Desenvolvimento econômico e evolução urbana (análise da evolução econômica de São Paulo, Blumenau, Pôrto Alegre, Belo Horizonte e Recife).* Biblioteca Universitária, ser. 2: Ciências Sociais no. 22. São Paulo, 1968.

Sisson, S. A. *Galeria dos representantes da nação (1861).* Rio de Janeiro, 1862.

Slenes, Robert Wayne. "The Demography and Economics of Brazilian Slavery, 1850-1888." Ph.D. diss., Stanford Univ., 1975.

Smith, Herbert H. *Brazil—The Amazons and the Coast.* New York, 1879.

Soares, Luiz Carlos. "A manufatura na formação econômica e social escravista no Sudeste. Um estudo das atividades manufatureiras na região fluminense: 1840-1880." M.A. thesis, Univ. Federal Fluminense, 1980.

Soares, Sebastião Ferreira. *Elementos de estatistica comprehendendo a theoria da sciencia e a sua applicação á estatistica commercial do Brasil.* 2 vols. Rio de Janeiro, 1865.

―――. *Historico da Companhia Industrial da Estrada de Mangaratiba e analyse critica e economica dos negocios desta companhia.* Rio de Janeiro, 1861.

―――. *Notas estatísticas sobre a produção agricola e a carestia dos generos alimenticios no Império do Brasil.* Rio de Janeiro, 1860.

Soares, Ubaldo. *O passado heróico da Casa dos Expostos.* Rio de Janeiro, 1959.

Sociedade Auxiliadora da Agricultura de Pernambuco. *Trabalhos do Congresso Agricola do Recife em 1878 comprehendendo os documentos relativos aos factos que o precederam.* 1879, facsim. Recife, 1978.

Sodré, Nelson Werneck. *História da burguesia brasileira.* Retratos do Brasil no. 22. Rio de Janeiro, 1964.

Souza, Braz Florentino Henriques de. *Do Poder Moderador: Ensaio de direito constitucional contendo a análise do título V, capítulo I, da Constituição Política do Brasil.* Coleção Bernardo Pereira de Vasconcelos no. 7. 2d ed. Brasília, 1978.

Souza, Francisco Belisário Soares de. *O sistema eleitoral no império (com apêndice contendo a legislação eleitoral no período 1821-1889),* ed. Octaciano Nogueira. Coleção Bernardo Pereira de Vasconcelos no. 18. Brasília, 1979.

[Souza, João Cardoso de Meneses e], barão de Paranapiacaba. "Elleições." In Affonso Celso de Assis Figueiredo, visconde de Ouro Preto, et al., *A decada republicana.* 8 vols. Rio de Janeiro, 1899-1901. Vol. III, pp. 151-279.

Souza, Joaquim Rodrigues de. *Systema eleitoral da Constituição do Imperio do Brazil.* São Luiz, 1863.

Souza, José Antônio Soares de. *A vida do visconde do Uruguai (1807-1866) (Paulino José Soares de Souza).* Brasiliana no. 243. São Paulo, 1944.

Sousa, Octávio Tarquínio de. *História dos fundadores do império do Brasil.* Vol. V: *Bernardo Pereira de Vasconcelos.* 2d ed. Rio de Janeiro, 1957.

Souza, Paulino José Soares de, visconde de Uruguay. *Estudos praticos sobre a administração das provincias do Brasil. . . . Primeira parte: Acto Addicional.* 2 vols. Rio de Janeiro, 1865.

Souza (2°), Paulino José Soares de [Um Conservador]. *Carta aos fazendeiros e commerciantes fluminenses sobre o elemento servil ou, Refutação do parecer do Sr. Conselheiro Christiano Benedicto Ottoni acerca do mesmo assumpto.* Rio de Janeiro, 1871.

Stein, Stanley J. *The Brazilian Cotton Manufacture: Textile Enterprise in an Underdeveloped Area, 1850-1950.* Cambridge, Mass., 1957.

———. *Vassouras, a Brazilian Coffee County, 1850-1900.* Harvard Historical Studies no. 69. Cambridge, Mass., 1957.

Stepan, Alfred. *The State and Society: Peru in Comparative Perspective.* Princeton, N.J., 1978.

Straten-Ponthoz, Auguste van der. *Le Budget du Brésil ou, Recherches sur les ressources de cet empire dans leurs rapports avec les intérêts européens du commerce e de l'émigration.* 3 vols. Brussels, 1854.

Strickon, Arnold, and Sidney M. Greenfield, eds. *Structure and Process in Latin America: Patronage, Clientage, and Power Systems.* Albuquerque, N.M., 1972.

Sweigart, Joseph E. *Coffee Factorage and the Emergence of a Brazilian Capital Market, 1850-1888.* New York, 1987.

Tannenbaum, Frank. *Slave and Citizen: The Negro in the Americas.* New York, 1947.

Taunay, Affonso d'Escragnolle. *História do café no Brasil.* 15 vols. Rio de Janeiro, 1939-43.

———. *Pequena história do café no Brasil (1727-1937).* Rio de Janeiro, 1945.

Taunay, Alfredo d'Escragnolle. *Homens e cousas do Imperio,* ed. Affonso d'Escragnolle Taunay. São Paulo, 1924.

Thompson, E. P. "Patrician Society, Plebeian Culture," *Journal of Social History,* 7:4 (Summer 1974), 382-405.

Topik, Steven. *The Political Economy of the Brazilian State, 1889-1930.* Latin American Monographs no. 71. Austin, Tex., 1987.

Toplin, Robert Brent. *The Abolition of Slavery in Brazil.* New York, 1972.

Tôrres, João Camilo de Oliveira. *O Conselho de Estado.* Rio de Janeiro, 1956.

———. *Os construtores do império: Ideais e lutas do Partido Conservador brasileiro.* Brasiliana no. 340. São Paulo, 1968.

———. *A democracia coroada (Teoria política do império do Brasil).* Documentos Brasileiros no. 93. Rio de Janeiro, 1957.

Uricoechea, Fernando. *O minotauro imperial: A burocratização do estado patrimonial brasileiro no século XIX.* Corpo e Alma do Brasil no. 55. São Paulo, 1978.

Valenzuela, Arturo. *Political Brokers in Chile: Local Government in a Centralized Polity.* Durham, N.C., 1977.

Vangelista, Chiara. *Le braccia per la fazenda: Immigrati e 'caipiras' nella formazione del mercato del lavoro paulista (1850-1930).* Milan, 1982.

Vasconcellos, José Marcellino Pereira de. *Roteiro dos delegados e subde-*

legados de polícia; ou, Colleção dos actos, atribuições e deveres destas autoridades. . . . Rio de Janeiro, 1862.

Vasconcellos, Zacharias de Góes e. *Da natureza e limites do poder moderador.* 2d ed. Rio de Janeiro, 1862.

Viana, Hélio. *D. Pedro I e D. Pedro II: Acréscimos às suas biografias.* Brasiliana no. 330. São Paulo, 1966.

Vianna, Francisco José de Oliveira. *Instituições políticas brasileiras.* 2 vols. Rio de Janeiro, 1949.

Walsh, Robert. *Notices of Brazil in 1828 and 1829.* 2 vols. London, 1830.

Weingrod, Alex. "Patrons, Patronage, and Political Parties," *Comparative Studies in Society and History,* 10: 4 (July 1968), 377-400.

Weinstein, Barbara. *The Amazon Rubber Boom, 1850-1920.* Stanford, Calif., 1983.

Wells, James W. *Exploring and Travelling Three Thousand Miles Through Brazil from Rio de Janeiro to Maranhão. With an Appendix Containing Statistics and Observations on Climate, Railways, Central Sugar Factories, Mining, Commerce, and Finance; the Past, Present, and Future, and Physical Geography of Brazil.* London, 1886.

Werneck, André Peixoto de Lacerda. *A lavoura e o governo. II° apelo aos fazendeiros. Artigos publicados no "Jornal do Commercio" de 15 a 21 de junho de 1890.* Rio de Janeiro, 1890.

[Werneck or] Verneck, Francisco Peixoto de Lacerda. *Memoria sobre a fundação de huma fazenda na provincia do Rio de Janeiro, sua administração, e épocas em que se devem fazer as plantações, suas colheitas, etc., etc.* Rio de Janeiro, 1847.

Werneck, Luiz Peixoto de Lacerda. *Le Brésil. Dangers de sa situation politique et économique; moyens de les conjurer. Lettre à son fils.* . . . *Ouvrage posthume revu par F. P. de Lacerda Werneck [Neto].* Rio de Janeiro, 1889.

——. *Idéias sobre colonização, precedidas de uma sucinta exposição dos princípios que regem a população.* Rio de Janeiro, 1855.

[Werneck, Manoel Peixoto de Lacerda]. *O visconde de Ipiabas, Peregrino José de America Pinheiro: Perfil biographico, acompanhado do retracto do finado e seguido de algumas allocuções pronunciadas por ocasião de seus funeraes.* Rio de Janeiro, 1882.

Williams, Lesley Ann. "Prostitutes, Policemen and Judges in Rio de Janeiro, Brazil, 1889-1910." M.A. thesis, Univ. of Texas at Austin, 1983.

Williams, Mary Wilhelmine. "The Treatment of Negro Slaves in the Brazilian Empire: A Comparison with the United States of America," *Journal of Negro History,* 15: 3 (July 1930), 315-36.

Wirth, John D. *Minas Gerais in the Brazilian Federation, 1889-1937.* Stanford, Calif., 1977.

Wolf, Eric R. "Kinship, Friendship and Patron-Client Relations in Complex Societies." In *The Social Anthropology of Complex Societies,* ed. Michael Banton. Association of Social Anthropologists Monographs no. 4. London, 1966.

Zenha, Edmundo. *O município no Brasil (1532-1700).* São Paulo, 1948.

Index

Library of Congress Cataloging-in-Publication Data

Graham, Richard, 1934-
    Patronage and politics in nineteenth-century Brazil / Richard
Graham.
    p. cm.
Includes bibliographical references.
ISBN 0-8047-1593-9 (alk. paper):
    1. Patronage, Political—Brazil—History—19th century.
2. Political leadership—Brazil—History—19th century. 3. Elite
(Social sciences)—Brazil—History—19th century 4. Elections—
Brazil—History—19th century. 5. Brazil—Politics and
government—1822-   I. Title.
JL2481.G73 1990   89-21598
306.2'0981—dc20   CIP

∞